# THE WORLD ALMANAC® FOR KIDS

## 1999

WORLD ALMANAC BOOKS
A PRIMEDIA Company

# THE WORLD ALMANAC FOR KIDS
# 1999

**EDITOR:**
Elaine Israel

**CURRICULUM CONSULTANT:**
Jean Craven
Director of Instructional Support
Albuquerque, NM, Public Schools

**CONTRIBUTORS:**
Michael Cusack, Joan Gampert, Bill Gutman, Judith S. Levey, Randi Metsch-Ampel, Heather Miller,
Marguerite Renz, Richard Steins, Jerilyn Famighetti, Robert Gampert, Irene Gunther,
Robin Greene Hagey, Bonny R. Hart, Judith Leale, Alan D. Levy, Susan R. Norton, Terry Simon
**Consultants:** Lee T. Shapiro, Ph.D. (Astronomy); Helen Schirmer (Health);
Anthony T. Padovano, S.T.D., Ph.D., and Abdulaziz Sachedina, Ph.D. (Religion)

**DESIGN:**
Todd Cooper, Brad Holroyd—Bill Smith Studio
**Cover Design:** Todd Cooper—Bill Smith Studio

**WORLD ALMANAC BOOKS**
**Vice President and Publisher:** Richard W. Eiger

**Vice President–**
**Sales and Marketing:**
James R. Keenley

**Deputy Editor:**
William McGeveran, Jr.

**Marketing &**
**Licensing Administrator:**
Jacqueline J. Sloan

**Editorial Staff:** Lori P. Wiesenfeld, Senior Editor;
Beth R. Ellis, Mark S. O'Malley, Associate Editors;
Melissa Janssens, Desktop Publishing Associate

**PRIMEDIA REFERENCE INC.**
**Vice President and Editorial Director:** Robert Famighetti
**Director of Editorial Production:** Andrea J. Pitluk
**Director–Purchasing and Production:** Edward Thomas
**Director of Indexing Services:** Marjorie B. Bank
**Index Editor:** Walter Kronenberg
**Desktop Publishing Assistant:** Hana Shaki

THE WORLD ALMANAC FOR KIDS 1999
Copyright © 1998 by PRIMEDIA Reference Inc.
A PRIMEDIA Company

The World Almanac and The World Almanac For Kids are registered trademarks of PRIMEDIA Reference Inc.

ISBN (softcover) 0-88687-826-8
ISBN (hardcover) 0-88687-827-6

Printed in the United States of America

The softcover and hardcover editions are distributed to the
trade in the United States by St. Martin's Press.

WORLD ALMANAC® BOOKS
An Imprint of PRIMEDIA Reference Inc.
One International Boulevard
Mahwah, New Jersey 07495-0017
E-Mail: Walmanac@aol.com

The addresses and content of Web sites referred to in this book
are subject to change. Although The World Almanac For Kids carefully
reviews these sites, we cannot take responsibility for their content.

# CONTENTS

**E-Mail** ▼ ⬍

Send    Compose    Send Later    Delete

## HEALTH 105-112

## HOLIDAYS 113-114

## INVENTIONS 115-117

## LANGUAGE 118-123

## LAW 124-125

## MONEY AND BUSINESS 126-134

## UNITED STATES · 214-280

## WEATHER · 281-283

## WEIGHTS AND MEASURES · 284-287

## WORLD HISTORY · 288-301

## PUZZLES AND ANSWERS

## INDEX · 306-319

# Meet Facto the Factosaurus

Facto is here. Facto is there. Facto is everywhere. Facto is the mascot of *The World Almanac for Kids*. He's big and strong—and friendly. He looks like a dinosaur. Sometimes he even acts like one (or what he thinks a dinosaur ought to act like).

Facto is always hungry, but he doesn't eat meat or plants. He's hungry for facts, for figures, for information! He has a magic pendant that looks like a little globe to mere humans. Facto can just rub the magic globe and zoom through space and time.

The pages that follow are filled with facts, pictures, and puzzles about everything from U.S. states (see page 257) to faraway planets (page 152), from science (page 181) to sports (page 192), from peoples long ago (page 288) to people in today's headlines (page 12) or your favorite stars (pages 11 and 138).

You'll find Facto himself wherever there are Did You Know entries. (Those are extra fascinating facts.) See him in the Animals section (pages 21 and 24) joining beasts from the past and the present. Who's that at the White House? It's Facto (page 218)! And isn't that Facto chilling out with Thomas Edison (page 116)? Where will he turn up next? Computing (page 40)? Listening to music (page 142)? Catching a football (page 198)? The fantastic thing is that, whatever Facto is doing, he takes you along!

*So hang on and watch for Facto! With him, every page will be an adventure.*

# COUNTDOWN to the MILLENNIUM

For people everywhere, the year 2000 marks the start of the next millennium, or period of 1,000 years. So huge parties, concerts, fireworks, and other events have been planned for December 31, 1999.

One of the biggest free celebrations will be at Times Square in New York City. There, a 24-hour party is planned, with huge video screens showing millennium events around the world. In Paris, crowds will gather at the Eiffel Tower. In London, a 500-foot-high Ferris wheel and enormous dome are being built for the occasion.

To be exact about it, the new millennium actually begins on January 1, 2001. That's because there was no year zero. So the first year of every millennium ends in a 1. But no one wants to wait until 2001 to celebrate.

# IN THE NEWS

## ANNIVERSARIES IN 1998

### 100 YEARS AGO — 1898

- ☑ The first table tennis sets were made in England. The game was then called Gossima. It became popular after the sets were sold under a new name, as Ping Pong.
- ☑ Marie and Pierre Curie first measured and named radioactivity.
- ☑ Pepsi-Cola was introduced.
- ☑ Spain and the United States fought each other in the Spanish-American War.

### 50 YEARS AGO — 1948

- ☑ President Truman issued an order ending segregation in the U.S. armed services.
- ☑ The Jewish state of Palestine was established as Israel, May 14, 1948.
- ☑ The first Emmy Awards for television were presented.
- ☑ General Mills and Pillsbury introduced the first cake mixes.

## ANNIVERSARIES IN 1999

### 100 YEARS AGO — 1899

- ☑ Aspirin was invented.
- ☑ The first children's museum was opened, in New York City.
- ☑ William McKinley became the first U.S. president to ride in an automobile.

### 50 YEARS AGO — 1949

- ☑ The first round-the-world nonstop airplane flight was made.
- ☑ The New York Yankees beat the Brooklyn Dodgers to win the first of five World Series in a row.
- ☑ The first long-distance telephone call by dialing, instead of by going through an operator, was made on October 17 between Oakland, California, and New York City.

## FASCINATING FIRSTS

- ☑ The **first jeans** were made in 1850 by Levi Strauss, a German immigrant in California. During the Gold Rush, Strauss took bales of cloth to San Francisco hoping to sell them as coverings for tents and wagons. But then he heard a miner complain that his pants did not stand up to the wear they got while he was digging. Rivets were added in 1874. At that time, you could get a dozen pairs of jeans for $13.50.
- ☑ The **first known zoos** were established in China during the 12th century B.C., when animals were kept near the emperor's palace for his entertainment.
- ☑ The **first comic book**, *Famous Funnies*, was published in 1934. The most popular comic-book hero of all times was Superman. The first Superman comic book was called *Action Comics*. It came out in 1938.

# BIRTHDAYS of CELEBRITIES

Here are the birthdays of some of your favorite stars, sports heroes, and public figures.

**January**
| | |
|---|---|
| Rowan Atkinson | Jan. 6, 1955 |
| Jim Carrey | Jan. 17, 1962 |
| Tiffani-Amber Thiessen | Jan. 23, 1974 |
| Wayne Gretzky | Jan. 26, 1961 |
| Elijah Wood | Jan. 28, 1981 |
| Andrew Keegan | Jan. 29, 1979 |

**February**
| | |
|---|---|
| Sheryl Crow | Feb. 11, 1963 |
| Jennifer Aniston | Feb. 11, 1969 |
| Brandy | Feb. 11, 1979 |
| Judy Blume | Feb. 12, 1938 |
| Michael Jordan | Feb. 17, 1963 |
| Jennifer Love Hewitt | Feb. 21, 1979 |
| Drew Barrymore | Feb. 22, 1975 |
| Chelsea Clinton | Feb. 27, 1980 |

**March**
| | |
|---|---|
| Shaquille O'Neal | March 6, 1972 |
| Rosie O'Donnell | March 21, 1962 |
| Mariah Carey | March 27, 1970 |
| Celine Dion | March 30, 1968 |
| Al Gore | March 31, 1948 |

**April**
| | |
|---|---|
| Eddie Murphy | April 3, 1961 |
| Beverly Cleary | April 12, 1916 |
| Claire Danes | April 12, 1979 |
| Sarah Michelle Gellar | April 14, 1977 |
| Melissa Joan Hart | April 18, 1976 |
| Jerry Seinfeld | April 29, 1955 |

**May**
| | |
|---|---|
| Jewel | May 3, 1974 |
| George Clooney | May 6, 1961 |
| Drew Carey | May 23, 1961 |

**June**
| | |
|---|---|
| Alanis Morissette | June 1, 1974 |
| Tara Lipinski | June 10, 1982 |
| Tim Allen | June 13, 1953 |
| Ashley Olsen | June 13, 1986 |
| Mary-Kate Olsen | June 13, 1986 |
| Courteney Cox | June 15, 1964 |

**July**
| | |
|---|---|
| Bill Cosby | July 12, 1937 |
| Harrison Ford | July 13, 1942 |
| Barry Sanders | July 16, 1968 |
| Robin Williams | July 21, 1952 |
| Matt LeBlanc | July 25, 1968 |
| Brad Renfro | July 25, 1982 |
| Arnold Schwarzenegger | July 30, 1947 |
| Lisa Kudrow | July 30, 1963 |

**August**
| | |
|---|---|
| Whitney Houston | August 9, 1963 |
| Ann Martin | August 12, 1955 |
| Magic Johnson | August 14, 1959 |
| Bill Clinton | August 19, 1946 |
| Matthew Perry | August 19, 1969 |
| Cal Ripken Jr. | August 24, 1960 |
| Michael Jackson | August 29, 1958 |

**September**
| | |
|---|---|
| Gloria Estefan | Sept. 1, 1957 |
| Devon Sawa | Sept. 7, 1978 |
| Jonathan Taylor Thomas | Sept. 8, 1981 |
| Will Smith | Sept. 25, 1968 |

**October**
| | |
|---|---|
| Neve Campbell | Oct. 3, 1973 |
| Alicia Silverstone | Oct. 4, 1976 |
| Kate Winslet | Oct. 5, 1975 |
| Matt Damon | Oct. 8, 1970 |
| R. L. Stine | Oct. 8, 1943 |
| Brett Favre | Oct. 10, 1969 |
| Luke Perry | Oct. 11, 1966 |
| Hillary Rodham Clinton | Oct. 26, 1947 |

**November**
| | |
|---|---|
| Sinbad | Nov. 10, 1956 |
| Leonardo DiCaprio | Nov. 11, 1974 |
| David Schwimmer | Nov. 12, 1966 |
| Ken Griffey Jr. | Nov. 21, 1969 |

**December**
| | |
|---|---|
| Steven Spielberg | Dec. 18, 1947 |
| Brad Pitt | Dec. 18, 1964 |
| Tiger Woods | Dec. 30, 1975 |

# IN THE HEADLINES

## CAN KIDS STOP SMOKING?

Most adults who smoke cigarettes began before they were 18 years old. Every day more than 3,000 kids in the United States start smoking. Once kids start this habit, it is hard to give it up. When they get older, many of them will die from diseases that come from smoking.

For this reason, health experts and many other people want tobacco companies to help prevent kids from smoking. In 1997, one company agreed to stop using its Joe Camel ads. Many people thought these ads were aimed at getting kids to try cigarettes. Most of the states have also sued the tobacco companies to get them to help pay for the health costs of smoking and help prevent kids from starting to smoke. During early 1998, the U.S. Congress was considering laws that would help do these things.

## EL NIÑO TURNS DEADLY

El Niño is a current of warm water in the Pacific Ocean that comes every few years. One result can be strange weather in parts of the United States. The 1997–1998 El Niño was very strong. As a result, the western states, especially California, were soaked with heavy rains that led to floods and mudslides. Much of the northeast, on the other hand, had nice weather, with an unusually mild winter. One big exception was a disastrous ice storm—also a result of El Niño—that knocked out electricity over New England, New York, and parts of Canada for days.

In the south, El Niño was blamed for powerful tornadoes that touched down in Florida, Georgia, Alabama, Tennessee, and North Carolina, killing dozens of people and causing heavy damage. One tornado appeared in a place not used to such horrifying weather—downtown Nashville, Tennessee. Some people also blamed El Niño for a twister that destroyed a South Dakota town.

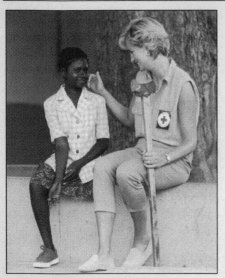

▲ *Princess Diana with land mine victim*

## NATIONS AID IN BATTLE AGAINST LAND MINES

Land mines are small bombs hidden in the ground during a war. They are meant to kill or injure people—especially, enemy soldiers—who step on them. But, more often, land mines kill people who are not soldiers. About 110 million land mines remain today in some 68 countries. They kill or badly hurt 26,000 people a year, many of them children.

Before her death in August 1997, Princess Diana of Great Britain brought world attention to the problem. She visited kids in Bosnia and Africa who suffered land-mine injuries. In 1997, officials from more than 100 countries met in Oslo, Norway, to sign a treaty to rid the world of these weapons. And the 1997 Nobel Peace Prize was awarded to an American group, the International Campaign to Ban Landmines, and its coordinator, Jody Williams, for their efforts against land mines. The United States, however, did not sign the Oslo treaty, because it would then have to remove mines along the border between North and South Korea.

## PEACE IN NORTHERN IRELAND?

Some people call it a miracle. In 1998, after years of violence between Catholic and Protestant groups in Northern Ireland, leaders agreed to a peace plan. Conflict between these groups goes back a long time. In 1920, the British government, which ruled the whole island, tried to solve the conflict by dividing the island in two. Northern Ireland, which is mostly Protestant, remained part of Britain, while the rest of Ireland, which is mostly Catholic, became independent. But the violence continued.

In 1968, Catholics in the North started a movement to protest what they said was bad treatment by Protestants. After many terrorist attacks and killings on both sides, British troops were sent in, but this did not help. Under the new peace plan, Catholics and Protestants would join in a new government in Northern Ireland, and the independent country of Ireland would give up claiming the territory of Northern Ireland. In May 1998 the people of Ireland voted by a large majority to accept this plan.

## A TITANIC SUCCESS

The movie *Titanic* was supposed to open in the summer of 1997. Instead, its producers moved the premiere to December. Gossips in Hollywood predicted that the $200 million film would be an embarrassing flop. Instead, *Titanic* turned out to be the most successful movie the world has ever seen.

*Titanic* is the story of a British ocean liner that was supposed to be unsinkable. But on its first voyage—from England to New York in April 1912—the ship sank after hitting an iceberg. More than 1,500 people died. The movie had earned more than $1 billion by early 1998 and was number one at the box office for a record 15 weeks. Young fans, especially teenage girls, returned again and again to see the movie and its star-hero, 23-year-old Leonardo DiCaprio.

At the Oscar ceremonies in April 1998, *Titanic* won 11 awards, tying the record set by *Ben-Hur* in 1959.

## FIRSTS IN SPACE

The U.S. space program celebrated some firsts in 1997 and 1998. Air Force Lieutenant Colonel Eileen Collins of Elmira, New York, was appointed the first woman space shuttle commander. She was picked to command the shuttle *Columbia* on a mission scheduled for December 1998. Another woman—Barbara Morgan, a 46-year-old teacher from Idaho—was expected to take up astronaut training in the summer of 1998. And the age barrier in space seemed likely to be broken soon. In 1962, John Glenn became the first American to orbit the Earth. Now in his late 70s and a U.S. senator from Ohio, he was scheduled to join the crew on a future shuttle flight. NASA hopes that Glenn's mission will tell us more about the effects of space travel on older people.

▲ *Eileen M. Collins*

## SEPTUPLETS DEFY THE ODDS

On November 19, 1997, Bobbi McCaughey, 29, from Carlisle, Iowa, became the mother of the world's first-ever thriving set of septuplets. In six minutes she gave birth to Kenneth Robert, Alexis May, Natalie Sue, Kelsey Ann, Brandon James, Nathan Roy, and Joel Steven. The chances that all would survive were not very big. But after several weeks in the hospital, the septuplets went home to their parents and older sister. The city chipped in with a new house. Neighbors promised to help in caring for the seven tiny infants—and changing over 350 diapers a week!

# SPORTS HIGHLIGHTS

▲ John Elway

## ELWAY WINS THE BIG ONE

When his team faced the Green Bay Packers in Super Bowl XXXII in January 1998, no quarterback had ever been more of a sentimental favorite than the Denver Broncos' John Elway. After all, Elway had been one of the National Football League's greatest passers since 1983. He had done everything but win a Super Bowl. Three times Elway led his Broncos to the title game and three times he came up empty. But the fourth time, the Broncos upset the Packers, 31-14, to take the Super Bowl at last!

## THE MIGHTY MARLINS

By winning the 1997 World Series in just their fifth year of existence, the Florida Marlins made baseball history. When the Marlins defeated the Cleveland Indians in seven games, they became champions faster than any other new team in baseball. They also became the first "wild card" team to win the Series. The Series MVP was rookie righthanded pitcher Livan Hernandez, from Cuba. Just two years earlier, Hernandez had left Cuba by sneaking onto a flight from Mexico (where his Cuban team was playing) to Venezuela and freedom. Despite their triumph, the owners of the Marlins broke the team up after the Series by cutting loose a dozen key players.

## THE FABULOUS TENNIS TEENS

A group of young stars is taking over women's tennis. Martina Hingis of Switzerland became the number-one-ranked women's player in 1997, at the age of 16. By early 1998, while still only 17, she had won four of the last five grand slam tournaments. Venus Williams of the United States, who turned 18 in June 1998, came in second in the 1997 U.S. Open and won the Lipton Championships early the next year. Anna Kournikova of Russia, who turned 17 in June 1998, was runner-up to Williams in the Lipton finals. And Williams's little sister, Serena, at the age of 16, has already upset some highly ranked players.

These fabulous tennis teens should give fans plenty of excitement for years to come.

## OLYMPIC SURPRISES ON ICE

When ice hockey in the Winter Olympics was strictly for amateurs, the 1980 U.S. men's team pulled off the upset of the century. They won a gold medal by beating the highly favored Soviet Union in what people called the "Miracle on Ice." Now professionals can play, and both U.S. and Canadian teams at the 1998 Winter Games in Nagano, Japan, were filled with stars from the National Hockey League. The Czech Republic, with a smaller number—about half its roster—made up of NHL players, came away with the gold medal. The Czech team was led by star goalie Dominik Hasek of the NHL Buffalo Sabres.

Meanwhile, in another surprise, the U.S. women roared through the competition unbeaten, then upset the highly-favored Canadian team, 3-1, to win the gold. Unlike the U.S. men, the women were all amateurs. As coach Ben Smith said, "They gave up careers, relationships, and jobs just to take a shot at this." Their hard work paid off!

# CLASSIFYING ANIMALS

**T**here are so many types of animals that scientists had to find a way to organize them into groups. Carolus Linnaeus (1707-1778) worked out a system for classifying both animals and plants. We still use it today.

## ANIMAL KINGDOM

The animal kingdom is separated into two large groups—animals with backbones, called **vertebrates**, and animals without backbones, called **invertebrates**. These large groups are divided into smaller groups called *phyla*. And phyla are divided into even smaller groups called *classes*. The animals in each group are classified together when their bodies are similar in certain ways. Below are examples of some of the animals in these groups.

### VERTEBRATES:
### Animals With Backbones

**FISH:** Swordfish, tuna, salmon, trout, halibut

**AMPHIBIANS:** Frogs, toads, mud puppies

**REPTILES:** Turtles, alligators, crocodiles, lizards

**BIRDS:** Sparrows, owls, turkeys, hawks

**MAMMALS:** Kangaroos, opossums, dogs, cats, bears, seals, rats, squirrels, rabbits, chipmunks, porcupines, horses, pigs, cows, deer, bats, whales, dolphins, monkeys, apes, humans

### INVERTEBRATES:
### Animals Without Backbones

**PROTOZOA**
The simplest form of animals

**COELENTERATES**
Jellyfish, sea anemones, coral, hydra

**MOLLUSKS**
Clams, snails, squid, oysters

**ANNELIDS**
Earthworms

**ARTHROPODS**
**Crustaceans:**
Lobsters, crayfish
**Centipedes and Millipedes**
**Arachnids:** Spiders, scorpions
**Insects:** Butterflies, grasshoppers, bees, termites, cockroaches

**ECHINODERMS**
Starfish, sea urchins, sea cucumbers

# What's the DIFFERENCE?

## Between a crocodile and an alligator?

**Crocodile**
Pointed snout
More fierce
Fourth tooth on each
   side on the bottom sticks
   out over the upper lip

**Alligator**
Broad, flat snout
Less fierce

## Between a leopard, a jaguar, and a cheetah?

**Leopard**
Lives in Africa and Asia

Spots are broken circles,
   no dot in the center
Black markings on the
   backs of the ears

**Jaguar**
Lives in Central and South
   America
Spots are circles, with a dot
   in the center
Belly is white

**Cheetah**
Lives in Africa and Arabian
   Peninsula
Spots are solid circles

Black mark from the nose
   to the eye

## Between an African elephant and an Indian elephant?

**African elephant**
Larger than the Indian elephant
Huge ears
Two lobes at the end of the trunk
Both the males (bulls) and females (cows)
   have long tusks
Usually lives in the wild

**Indian elephant**
Smaller than the African elephant
Small ears
One lobe at the end of the trunk
Only the males (bulls) have
   long tusks
More easily trained
   to do work
   for humans

## Between a frog and a toad?

**Frog**
Slim
Lighter skin, often green
Long back legs for jumping
Smooth skin
Spends most of its time in water

**Toad**
Stout
Darker skin
Shorter back legs
Warty skin
Spends most of its time on land

## Between a mountain lion, a puma, and a cougar?

Nothing! These are all local names for the same large cats, *Felis concolor*, whose original range extended through North and South America. In some areas these animals are also called **panthers**; the name panther is also used for a leopard with a black coat.

# The LARGEST and the FASTEST

## THE LARGEST ANIMALS
**World's Largest Animal:** blue whale (110 feet long, 209 tons)

▲ blue whale

**Largest Land Animal:** African bush elephant (13 feet high, 8 tons)
**Tallest Animal:** giraffe (19 feet tall)
**Largest Reptile:** saltwater crocodile (16 feet long, 1,150 pounds)
**Largest Snake: Heaviest:** anaconda (27 feet, 9 inches long, 500 pounds)
 **Longest:** reticulated python (26-32 feet long)
**Longest Fish:** whale shark (41 ½ feet long)

▲ anaconda snake

**Largest Bird:** ostrich (9 feet tall, 345 pounds)

▼ ostrich

**Largest Insect:** stick insect (15 inches long)

## THE FASTEST ANIMALS
**World's Fastest Animal:** swift, a bird (100–200 miles per hour)
**Fastest Marine Animal:** blue whale (30 miles per hour)
**Fastest Land Animal:** cheetah (70 miles per hour)
**Fastest Fish:** sailfish (68 miles per hour)
**Fastest Bird:** swift (100–200 miles per hour)
**Fastest Insect:** dragonfly (36 miles per hour)

▲ dragonfly

## How Fast Do Animals Run?

**D**id you know that some animals can run as fast as a car can move or that a snail would need more than 30 hours just to go one mile? If you look at this table, you will see how fast some common land animals can move.

MILES PER HOUR

| Animal | Miles per hour |
|---|---|
| Cheetah | 70 |
| Lion | 50 |
| Cape hunting dog | 45 |
| Zebra | 40 |
| Rabbit | 35 |
| Grizzly bear | 30 |
| Cat (domestic) | 30 |
| Human | 28 |
| Elephant | 25 |
| Squirrel | 12 |
| Pig (domestic) | 11 |
| Chicken | 9 |
| Snail | 0.03 |

▲ cheetah

▲ rabbit

◄ snail

 **DID YOU KNOW?** The blue whale may be the largest animal that ever lived. But it is no match for humans. Tens of thousands of blue whales were killed in the early 1900s. They are now protected, and there are about 5,000 of them in the world. These fussy eaters feed mainly on tiny shrimp-like creatures called krill, which they find in their summer homes near the North and South Poles. They eat about 4 tons of food a day. When winter sets in, the whales head for warmer water, and go on a diet. That is also the time when they mate.

# HABITATS: Where Animals Live

**T**he area in nature where an animal lives is called its **habitat**. The table below lists some large habitats and some of the animals that live in them.

| HABITAT | SOME ANIMALS THAT LIVE THERE |
|---|---|
| Deserts (hot, dry regions) | camels, bobcats, coyotes, kangaroos, mice, gila monsters, scorpions, rattlesnakes |
| Tropical Forests (warm, humid climate) | orangutans, gibbons, leopards, tamandua anteaters, tapirs, iguanas, parrots, tarantulas |
| Grasslands (flat, open lands) | African elephants, kangaroos, Indian rhinoceroses, giraffes, zebras, prairie dogs, ostriches |
| Mountains (highlands) | yaks, snow leopards, vicunas, bighorn sheep, chinchillas, pikas, eagles, mountain goats |
| Polar Regions (cold climate) | polar bears, musk oxen, caribous, ermines, arctic foxes, walruses, penguins, Siberian huskies |
| Oceans (sea water) | whales, dolphins, seals, manatees, octopuses, stingrays, coral, starfish, lobsters, many kinds of fish |

# FOSSILS: Clues to Ancient Animals

**A** fossil is the remains of an animal or plant that lived long ago. Most fossils are formed from the hard parts of an animal's body, such as bones, shells, or teeth. Some are large, like dinosaur footprints. Some are so tiny that you need a microscope to see them. Most fossils are found in rocks formed from the mud or sand that collects at the bottom of oceans, rivers, and lakes. Fossils offer scientists clues to ancient animals.

### WHAT DO FOSSILS TELL US?
Scientists study fossils to help them understand plant and animal life in ancient periods of the world's history. The age and structure of the rocks in which fossils are found can help scientists tell how long ago certain kinds of animals or plants lived. For example, dinosaurs lived millions of years ago, but people have known about dinosaurs only since the first dinosaur fossils were uncovered, less than 200 years ago.

### WHERE ARE FOSSILS FOUND?
Fossils, including dinosaur fossils, are found on every continent on the earth. In eastern and southern Africa, people have found fossils that are ancestors of early humans. Insects that lived millions of years ago are sometimes found preserved in amber. Amber is hardened tree sap. Fossils have also been found in ice and tar. In 1991 a frozen corpse of a man believed to have lived over 5,000 years ago was found in the Austrian Alps.

| | |
|---|---|
| Box turtle | 100 years |
| Asian elephant | 40 years |
| Grizzly bear | 25 years |
| Horse | 20 years |
| Gorilla | 20 years |
| Polar bear | 20 years |
| Rhinoceros (white) | 20 years |
| Black bear | 18 years |
| Lion | 15 years |
| Lobster | 15 years |
| Rhesus monkey | 15 years |
| Rhinoceros (black) | 15 years |
| Camel (Bactrian) | 12 years |
| Cat (domestic) | 12 years |
| Dog (domestic) | 12 years |
| Leopard | 12 years |
| Giraffe | 10 years |
| Pig | 10 years |
| Squirrel | 10 years |
| Red fox | 7 years |
| Kangaroo | 7 years |
| Chipmunk | 6 years |
| Rabbit | 5 years |
| Guinea pig | 4 years |
| Mouse | 3 years |
| Opossum | 1 year |

# How Long Do Animals Live?

**M**ost animals do not live as long as human beings. A monkey that is 14 years old is thought to be old. A person who is 14 is considered young. In 1998, the average life span of a human being is 70 to 80 years. The average life spans of some animals are shown here. Only one lives longer than human beings.

## What to Call ANIMALS and THEIR YOUNG

| ANIMAL | MALE | FEMALE | YOUNG |
|---|---|---|---|
| bear | boar | sow | cub |
| pig | boar | sow | piglet |
| horse | stallion | mare | foal, filly (female), colt (male) |
| lion | lion | lioness | cub |
| cattle, elephant, giraffe, whale | bull | cow | calf |
| deer | buck | doe | fawn |
| goat | buck, billy goat | doe, nanny goat | kid |
| rabbit | buck | doe | bunny, kit |
| duck | drake | duck | duckling |
| goose | gander | goose | gosling |
| sheep | ram | ewe | lamb |
| tiger | tiger | tigress | cub |

# ENDANGERED SPECIES

When an animal becomes less and less plentiful on one part of the Earth or in the entire world, the animal is said to be **endangered** or **threatened**. The U.S. Department of the Interior keeps track of endangered and threatened animals. Throughout the world today, 1,015 species of animals are endangered or threatened. These include:

☑ 331 species of mammals    ☑ 114 species of reptiles    ☑ 72 other
☑ 274 species of birds    ☑ 64 species of clams       species
☑ 119 species of fish    ☑ 41 species of insects

### A FEW ENDANGERED SPECIES
**Mammals:** *Giant panda* in China; *Gray whale* in North Pacific Ocean
**Fish:** *Sockeye (red) salmon* in North Pacific from the United States to Russia
**Bird:** *American peregrine falcon* from Canada to Mexico
**Reptile:** *American crocodile* from the southeastern United States to South America

### HOW DO ANIMALS BECOME ENDANGERED?
Over very long periods of time, many kinds of animals and plants have disappeared from the earth (become extinct). This happens for several reasons:

☑ **Changes in Climate.** Animals are threatened when the climate of their habitat (where they live) changes in a major way. For example, if an area becomes very hot and dry and a river dries up, the fish and other plant and animal life in the river will die.

☑ **Habitat Destruction.** Sometimes animal habitats are destroyed when people need the land. Wetlands, for example, where many types of waterfowl, fish, and insects live, might be drained for new houses or a mall. The animals that lived there would either have to find a new home or else die out.

☑ **Over-hunting.** Bison or buffalo once ranged over the entire Great Plains of the United States, but they were hunted almost to extinction in the 19th century. Since then, they have been protected by laws, and their numbers are increasing. Sometimes, when an animal population is too large, controlled hunting may reduce the number of animals enough so that the surviving animals can live comfortably with the food available to them.

# What Are GROUPS of ANIMALS Called?

The next time you see a group of these animals, rather than saying that you saw a bunch of fish, sheep, or ants, use the expressions below.

**ants:** *colony* of ants
**bees:** *swarm* of bees
**chicks:** *clutch* of chicks
**clams:** *bed* of clams
**ducks:** *brace* of ducks
**elks:** *gang* of elks
**fish:** *school* of fish
**geese:** *flock* or *gaggle*
**gorillas:** *band* of gorillas
**hares:** *down* of hares

**hens:** *brood* of hens
**kangaroos:** *troop* of kangaroos
**leopards:** *leap* of leopards
**lions:** *pride* of lions
**monkeys:** *troop* of monkeys
**oxen:** *yoke* of oxen
**seals:** *pod* of seals
**sheep:** *flock* of sheep
**swans:** *bevy* of swans
**whales:** *pod* of whales

▲ *gaggle of geese*

# Do You Want a PET?

**P**ets can be lots of fun. If you already have one, you also know that a pet may need a lot of care. And proper care takes time, effort, and money. If you are thinking of getting a pet, the questions below will help you choose one that will be a good match for you and your family. Look for information on pets and their care at a public library, a local pet shelter, or a veterinarian's office.

**QUESTIONS TO ASK BEFORE YOU GET A PET**

☑ Why do you want a pet? Do you want an animal to cuddle or keep you company? Do you want to teach a bird to talk? Or watch fish swim?
☑ How much space does the animal need? Do you have enough space?
☑ What kind of shelter should it live in?
☑ Does the animal you want like to be held or left alone?
☑ What kind of food is best for the animal? How often and how much food does it eat? How much does the food cost?
☑ What kind of exercise should the pet get? How often?
☑ What kind of grooming does the animal need?
☑ Is there a veterinarian nearby to meet your pet's health needs?
☑ Does the animal need regular care from a veterinarian? How much does this cost?
☑ Are you or anyone in your family allergic to any animals?

**DID YOU KNOW?** Some animals seem to make better pets than others. In the United States the most popular pets are cats, dogs, fish, birds, rabbits, hamsters, snakes, ferrets, turtles, and guinea pigs.

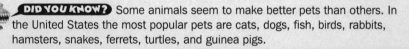

**PET DOCTOR PUZZLE**

**S**ee how many other words you can find using the letters in the word "veterinarian." Your words have to be at least three letters long. (Answers are on page 302.)

# AMAZING ANIMAL FACTS

**F**acts about animals are often surprising. Here are a few.

- Whales, dolphins, and porpoises are the only mammals to spend their whole lives in water. (But they still have to come to the surface to breathe.)

- The albatross is a big bird that can sleep while it flies. It can stay in the air for months without landing.

- Sharks can have as many as 24,000 teeth in a lifetime. When one falls out, another grows in its place.

- Sloths, which live in the tropical forests of Central and South America, spend most of their lives hanging upside down from the branches of trees. These mammals are so adapted to tree life that they find it hard to walk.

- Many hedgehogs in England have been hit by cars and killed as they try to cross busy roads. To protect them, people have built tunnels under the roads for the hedgehogs to use.

- Moles can move backward just as well as they can move forward. Hairs on their tails warn them of danger when they are traveling in reverse.

- Red howler monkeys, which live in South America, have that name for a reason. The males can make incredibly loud sounds. They shout to defend their territory and can be heard more than one mile away.

- Gila monsters hardly ever have to worry about going hungry. They have large tails in which they store body fat. If food is hard to find, the lizard can live on the stored fat.

- Camels' humps serve the same purpose. The humps carry stores of fat, so there's always a good meal available no matter what the desert conditions. Their humps and fur also help protect camels from cold and heat.

- What color is a white polar bear? Polar bears have white fur, but most have black skin! Their black noses are a clue.

- Porcupines have sharp spikes that rattle when the porcupine is disturbed. The rattling sound is meant as a warning that says, "keep away." If this doesn't work, the porcupine may ram an attacking animal, sticking some of its spikes into it.

- In the wild, flocks of monk parakeets build big houses—you could call them bird apartment houses. Each of the 20 or so apartments is a home for one pair of birds and has its own entrance.

# ANIMAL LIFE on Earth

This time line shows how animal life developed on Earth and when land plants developed. The earliest animals are at the top of the chart. The most recent are at the bottom of the chart.

| | YEARS AGO | | ANIMAL LIFE ON EARTH |
|---|---|---|---|
| PRECAMBRIAN | 4.5 billion | | Formation of the Earth. No signs of life. |
| PRECAMBRIAN | 2.5 billion | | First evidence of life in the form of bacteria and algae. All life is in water. |
| PALEOZOIC | 570-500 million | | Animals with shells (called trilobites) and some mollusks. Some fossils begin to form. |
| PALEOZOIC | 500-430 million | | Jawless fish appear, oldest known animals with backbones (vertebrates). |
| PALEOZOIC | 430-395 million | | Many coral reefs, jawed fishes, and scorpion-like animals. First land plants. |
| PALEOZOIC | 395-345 million | | Many fishes. Earliest known insect. Amphibians (animals living in water and on land) appear. |
| PALEOZOIC | 345-280 million | | Large insects appear. Amphibians increase in numbers. First trees appear. |
| PALEOZOIC | 280-225 million | | Reptiles and modern insects appear. Trilobites, many corals, and fishes become extinct. |
| MESOZOIC | 225-195 million | | Dinosaurs and turtles appear. Many reptiles and insects develop further. Mammals appear. |
| MESOZOIC | 195-135 million | | Many giant dinosaurs. Reptiles increase in number. First birds and crablike animals appear. |
| MESOZOIC | 135-65 million | | Dinosaurs develop further and then become extinct. Flowering plants begin to appear. |
| CENOZOIC | 65-2.5 million | | Modern-day land and sea animals begin to develop, including such mammals as rhinoceroses, whales, cats, dogs, apes, seals. |
| CENOZOIC | 2.5 million-10,000 | | Earliest humans appear. Mastodon, mammoths, and other huge animals become extinct. |
| CENOZOIC | 10,000-present | | Modern human beings and animals. |

# Dinosaur FACTS and FIGURES

From dinosaur fossils found throughout the world, scientists have gained evidence about when dinosaurs lived, what they ate, and how large they grew. Dinosaurs lived during the Mesozoic era, from 225 to 65 million years ago. The Mesozoic era is divided into the three periods shown below.

---

### TRIASSIC PERIOD, from 225 to 195 million years ago

☑ **First dinosaurs** appeared during the **Triassic period.**
Most early dinosaurs were small, rarely longer than 15 feet.

☑ **Early meat-eating dinosaurs** were called **Theropods.**

☑ **Earliest-known dinosaurs** were meat-eaters, found in Argentina: **Eoraptor** (the most primitive dinosaur, only about 40 inches long) and **Herrerasaurus.**

☑ **Early plant-eating dinosaurs** were called **Prosauropods. Plateosaurus** and **Anchisaurus** were two early plant-eating dinosaurs.

---

### JURASSIC PERIOD, from 195 to 135 million years ago

☑ Dinosaurs that lived during the **Jurassic period** were gigantic.

☑ Jurassic dinosaurs included the **Sauropods,** giant long-necked plant-eaters, the **largest land animals** ever. **Apatosaurus** and **Brachiosaurus** (70-80 feet) and **Diplodocus** (over 80 feet) were Sauropods.

☑ **Stegosaurus** (30 feet), a large plant-eater, had sharp, bony plates along its back.

☑ **Allosaurus** and **Megalosaurus,** two giant meat-eaters, fed on large plant-eating dinosaurs like the Apatosaurus and Stegosaurus. Megalosaurus grew to 30 feet in length; Allosaurus, 30-36 feet.

---

### CRETACEOUS PERIOD, from 135 to 65 million years ago

☑ New dinosaurs appeared during the **Cretaceous period,** but by the end of the Cretaceous period, all dinosaurs had died out.

☑ New plant-eaters: **Triceratops** and other horned dinosaurs, **Anatosaurus** and other duckbilled dinosaurs, **Ankylosaurus** and other armored dinosaurs.

☑ New meat-eater: **Tyrannosaurus Rex**, the largest and one of the fiercest meat-eaters, growing to 20 feet high and 40 feet long.

---

**DID YOU KNOW?**

☑ Tyrannosaurus Rex had teeth that were 7 inches long! Sauropods had teeth that were not good for chewing, so they ate stones, which ground up the food in their stomachs.

☑ The Stegosaurus had the smallest brain of any dinosaur. Its brain weighed only 2.5 ounces.

☑ Scientists studying dinosaur bones believe that birds are probably descended from small dinosaurs.

☑ Although we do not know for sure why dinosaurs became extinct, one theory is that an asteroid from space hit the Earth 65 million years ago and blocked out the sunlight. This possibly caused drastic climate changes that made the dinosaurs starve to death.

# Which U.S. ZOOS Have the LARGEST NUMBERS of Species?

**San Diego Zoo**
2920 Zoo Drive
San Diego, California 92101
Phone:
  (619) 231-1515
Number of
  Species: 800
*Popular Exhibits:*
  Tiger River,
  Komodo dragons,
  koalas,
  Hippo Beach

**Cincinnati Zoo**
3400 Vine Street
Cincinnati, Ohio 45220
Phone: (800) 94HIPPO
Number of Species: 750
*Popular Exhibits:* Gorilla World, white
  Bengal tigers, Jungle Trails

**St. Louis Zoological Park**
Forest Park
St. Louis, Missouri 63110
Phone: (314) 781-0900
Number of Species: 740
*Popular Exhibits:* Living World, Bear Pits,
  Jungle of the Apes

**Houston Zoological Gardens**
Hermann Park
1513 North MacGregor
Houston, Texas 77030
Phone: (713) 525-3300
Number of Species: 730
*Popular Exhibits:* Wortham World
  of Primates, Mexican wolves, cheetahs

**Columbus Zoo**
9990 Riverside Drive
Powell, Ohio 43065-0400
Phone: (614) 645-3400
Number of Species: 700
*Popular Exhibits:* Discovery Reef, Ohio
  Wetlands, Tidepool Touch Tank

**Bronx Zoo/Wildlife Conservation Park**
Fordham Road and Bronx River Pkwy.
Bronx, New York 10460
Phone: (718) 367-1010
Number of Species: 657
*Popular Exhibits:* Himalayan Highlands,
  Jungle World, endangered species

**Omaha/Henry Doorly Zoo**
3701 South 10th Street
Omaha, Nebraska 68107
Phone: (402) 733-8401
Number of Species: 629
*Popular Exhibits:* Indoor rain forest,
  aquarium, cat complex

**Denver Zoological Gardens**
City Park
Denver, Colorado 80205
Phone: (303) 331-4100
Number of Species: 600
*Popular Exhibits:*
  Tropical Discovery,
  Northern Shores,
  Primate
  Panorama

**San Antonio
Zoological Gardens
and Aquarium**
3903 North
  St. Mary's Street
San Antonio, Texas 78212
Phone: (210) 734-7184
Number of Species: 600
*Popular Exhibits:* Australian Walkabout,
  Amazonia, children's zoo

**Cleveland Metroparks Zoo**
3900 Brookside Drive
Cleveland, Ohio 44109
Phone: (216) 661-6500 x233
Number of Species: 599
*Popular Exhibits:* Rain Forest with 600
  animals and 7,000 plants

# PAINTING:
# Landscape, Portrait, and Still Life

**A**rt can be real or imaginary, funny or sad, beautiful or disturbing. Before photography was invented, most artists tried to show things as they saw them or as they imagined them to look. Throughout history, artists have painted pictures of nature (called **landscapes**); or pictures of people (called **portraits**); or pictures of flowers in vases, food, and other objects (known as **still lifes**). When artists paint people and things to look as they do in real life, their art is called **realistic**, or **representational**.

## SOME FAMOUS PAINTERS AND LANDSCAPES

A drawing or painting of nature is called a **landscape**. A picture of the sea is called a **seascape**. A picture of city buildings is called a **cityscape**. Below are a few famous painters, when they lived, their nationality, and the name of one of their landscapes.

▲ *A landscape*

**El Greco** (1541-1614), Spanish painter: "View of Toledo" (cityscape)
**Jan Vermeer** (1632-1675), Dutch painter: "View of Delft" (cityscape)
**Katsushika Hokusai** (1760-1849), Japanese painter: "Views of Mount Fuji" (landscape)
**John Constable** (1776-1837), English painter: "The Cornfield" (landscape)
**Winslow Homer** (1836-1910), American painter: "Northeaster" (seascape)
**Georgia O'Keeffe** (1887-1986), American painter: "Grey Hills" (landscape)

## SOME FAMOUS PAINTERS AND PORTRAITS

A painting of a person (or more than one person) is called a **portrait**. When a person paints a picture of himself or herself, it is called a **self-portrait**. Below are a few famous painters, when they lived, their nationality, and the name of one of their portraits.

▲ *A portrait*

**Leonardo da Vinci** (1452-1519), Italian painter:
  "Mona Lisa"
**Rembrandt** (1606-1669), Dutch painter: "Self Portrait"
**John Singleton Copley** (1737-1815), American painter:
  "Paul Revere"
**Edouard Manet** (1832-1883), French painter: "The Fifer"
**Pierre Auguste Renoir** (1841-1919), French painter:
  "Madame Charpentier and Her Children"
**Mary Cassatt** (1844-1926), American painter: "The Bath"

## SOME FAMOUS PAINTERS AND STILL LIFES

A picture of small objects—like flowers, bottles, books, food, and other things—is called a **still life**. Below are a few famous painters, when they lived, their nationality, and the name of one of their still-life paintings.

**Henri Fantin-Latour** (1836-1904), French painter: "Still Life With Flowers and Fruit"

**Paul Cézanne** (1839-1906), French painter: "Apples and Pears"

**William Michael Harnett** (1848-1892), American painter: "Still Life—Violin and Music"

**Vincent van Gogh** (1853-1890), Dutch painter: "Sunflowers"

▲ *A still life*

 **DID YOU KNOW?** Thousands of years ago, people painted pictures on the walls of caves. Many of these paintings—of bison, horses, deer, and other wild animals—can be found in caves in Altamira, Spain, and Lascaux, France. These caves were discovered by accident (Lascaux in 1940 and Altamira in 1879). Some of the cave art in France is believed to be as much as 30,000 years old.

# Modern Art

**M**any artists still paint pictures that can be recognized as landscapes and portraits. But some artists today create pictures using shapes or colors or textures in interesting ways that do not look like anything in the real world. These paintings are called **abstract**, or **nonrepresentational**. Abstract art is also called **modern art**.

## SOME FAMOUS MODERN ARTISTS AND ABSTRACT PAINTINGS

Below are a few famous painters known for their abstract paintings, along with the years they lived, their nationality, and the name of one of their paintings. Sometimes an abstract painting has a name that sounds realistic—like Picasso's "Three Musicians"—even though the painting is abstract.

**Pablo Picasso** (1881-1973), Spanish painter: "Three Musicians"

**Joan Miró** (1893-1983), Spanish painter: "Composition"

**Helen Frankenthaler** (born 1928), American painter: "Blue Territory"

**Wassily Kandinsky** (1866-1944), Russian painter: "Impression No. 30"

**Piet Mondrian** (1872-1944), Dutch painter: "Composition"

**Jackson Pollock** (1912-1956), American painter: "Number 1"

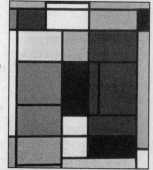

▲ *Modern art*

# SCULPTURE

Sculpture is a three-dimensional form made from clay, stone, metal, or other material. Many sculptures stand freely so that you can walk around them. Some are mobiles that hang from the ceiling. Sculptures can be large, like the Statue of Liberty or the statue of Abraham Lincoln in the Lincoln Memorial, or they can be small. Some sculpture is representational (looks like the person or animal it represents). Some modern sculpture is abstract and has no form that can be recognized.

## SOME FAMOUS SCULPTORS AND SCULPTURE

Below is a list of a few sculptors, when they lived, their nationality, and the name of one of their sculptures.

**Michelangelo Buonarroti** (1475-1564), Italian sculptor and painter: "Pietà" (representational)

**Edgar Degas** (1834-1917), French painter and sculptor: "Little Fourteen-Year-Old Dancer" (representational)

**Auguste Rodin** (1840-1917), French sculptor: "The Thinker" (representational)

**Henry Moore** (1898-1986), English sculptor: "Family Group" (abstract)

**Louise Nevelson** (1899-1988), American sculptor: "Royal Tide II" (abstract)

**Isamu Noguchi** (1904-1988), American sculptor, "Unidentified Object" (abstract)

▲ A sculpture

# WHERE TO LOOK AT ART

There are art museums in many cities in the United States. Some of them are general art museums, where you can see art from many different countries and from many different time periods—sometimes from early Egyptian art to modern art. Many cities also have museums of American art, museums of modern art, and other special collections. For museums that focus on ethnic art, culture, and history, such as African or Asian culture, see the section called ETHNIC MUSEUMS, page 140. A few general art museums are listed below.

Art Institute of Chicago
Baltimore Museum of Art
Boston Museum of Fine Arts
Cleveland Museum of Art
Dallas Museum of Art
Denver Art Museum
Detroit Institute of Arts
Houston Museum of Fine Arts
Kansas City Art Institute
Los Angeles County Museum of Art

Metropolitan Museum of Art
 (New York City)
Minneapolis Institute of Arts
National Gallery of Art
 (Washington, D.C.)
North Carolina Museum of Art (Raleigh, NC)
Philadelphia Museum of Art
San Antonio Museum of Art
San Francisco Museum of Art
Seattle Art Museum

# BOOK AWARDS, 1997-1998

**E**very year, librarians from across the United States choose the new year's best children's books. Below are some of the awards given out in 1997 or 1998, with an explanation of what each award means. Are you in the mood for unforgettable characters? For exciting stories? For an experience that will make you think about life in a fresh way? Then read one of the following award-winning books.

**Boston Globe-Horn Book Award**—These are given every year.
**1997 winners:**
Fiction: *The Friends*, by Kazumi Yumoto
Nonfiction: *Lily's Crossing*, by Patricia Reilly Giff
Picture Book: *Harlem*, by Walter Dean Myers,
Illustrated by Christopher Myers

**Caldecott Medal**—This is the highest honor a picture book can receive. It is given to the best American illustrated book of the year.
**1998 winner:** *Rapunzel,* by Paul O. Zelinsky

**Coretta Scott King Awards**—These are given to artists and authors whose works promote the cause of peace and world brotherhood.
**1998 winners:**
Author Award: *Forged by Fire*, by Sharon M. Draper
Illustrator Award: *In Daddy's Arms I AM TALL: African Americans Celebrating Fathers*, by Javaka Steptoe

**Golden Kite Awards**—A group of children's book writers and illustrators gives these awards every year.
**1997 winners:**
Fiction: *Stones in Water*,
by Donna Jo Napoli
Picture Illustration: *The Paper Dragon*,
Robert Sabuda

Nonfiction: *Carmine's Story: A Book About a Boy Living With AIDS,* by Arlene Schulman
Picture Book Writing: *The Paper Dragon*,
by Marguerite W. Davol

**Newbery Medal**—This is an award for writing. It is the highest honor for a children's fiction book that is not a picture book.
**1998 winner:** *Out of the Dust*, by Karen Hesse

**Hans Christian Andersen Awards**—These are given every two years to an author and an illustrator whose works have made an important contribution to children's literature.
Author: Uri Orlev (Israel), author of *The Lady With the Hat* and other books
Illustrator: Klaus Ensikat (Germany)

# BEST NEW BOOKS of the Year

(Some of those chosen in 1998 by the American Library Association)

*Charles A. Lindbergh: A Human Hero*,
  by James Cross Giblin

*Echoes of the Elders: The Stories and
  Paintings of Chief Lelooska*, edited by
  Christine Normandin

*Ella Enchanted*, by Gail Carson Levine

*Habibi*, by Naomi Shihab Nye

*Hoops*, by Robert Burleigh

*The Hunterman and the Crocodile*,
  by Baba Wague Diakite

*The Iron Ring*, by Lloyd Alexander

*Lou Gehrig: The Luckiest Man*,
  by David A. Adler

*Marven of the Great North Woods*,
  by Kathryn Lasky

*Mr. Semolina-Semolinus: A Greek
  Folktale*, by Anthony L. Manna and
  Christodoula Mitakidou

*Noah's Ark*, adapted by Heinz Janisch

*Passage to Freedom: The Sugihara Story*,
  by Ken Mochizuki

*Red Scarf Girl: A Memoir of the Cultural
  Revolution*, by Ji-Li Jiang

*The Robber and Me*, by Josef Holub

*Sun & Spoon*, by Kevin Henkes

*Wringer*, by Jerry Spinelli

## Ten ALL-TIME BEST-SELLING Paperbacks

*Charlotte's Web*, by E. B. White, illustrated by Garth Williams

*The Outsiders*, by S. E. Hinton

*Tales of a Fourth Grade Nothing*, by Judy Blume

*Shane*, by Jack Schaefer

*Are You There, God? It's Me, Margaret*, by Judy Blume

*Where the Red Fern Grows*, by Wilson Rawls

*A Wrinkle in Time*, by Madeleine L'Engle

*Island of the Blue Dolphins*, by Scott O'Dell

*Little House on the Prairie*, by Laura Ingalls Wilder

*Little House in the Big Woods*, by Laura Ingalls Wilder

## Three Children's Book Authors

These three authors work hard at writing excellent books for children.

**E.L. Konigsburg** won the 1968 Newbery Medal for the first novel she ever wrote, *From the Mixed-Up Files of Mrs. Basil E. Frankweiler*. Amazingly, in the very same year, she also won a Newbery Honor award for her second novel. And she is still going strong. In 1997, she won her second Newbery Medal, for *The View From Saturday*. She often thinks about her plots and characters while walking on the beach near her home in Florida.

**Gail Carson Levine** won a Newbery Honor Award in 1998 for her very first book, *Ella Enchanted*. It is based on the fairy tale *Cinderella*, but with lots of changes. Gail worked in an office every day and took writing classes at night for several years. But she had great faith in her talent and found a publisher for her story. She has more books on the way.

**Walter Dean Myers** developed a great love of reading as a child growing up in Harlem. He explains, "Books took me to a place inside myself that I have been exploring ever since." In 1997, Walter wrote a picture book about his childhood neighborhood and called it *Harlem*. His son, Christopher, illustrated it. Together, the poetry and pictures brought the Harlem of Walter's memories to life. *Harlem* won a Caldecott Honor Award in 1998.

# Some BOOKS YOU MAY ENJOY Reading

**T**he books listed on this page and the next one have been praised by many people.

 **WEB SITE** For more on children's books, go to: http://www.ucalgary.ca/ dkbrown/index.html

## FICTION

Fiction books are stories that come out of the writer's imagination. They are not true. Some fiction books are set in a world of fantasy. Others seem incredibly real.

**Daring to Be Abigail,** by Rachel Vail
Abby goes to summer camp hoping to change her personality. She also makes some funny and moving discoveries.

**A Girl Named Disaster,** by Nancy Farmer
Eleven-year old Nhamo's struggle to escape drowning and starvation while traveling to Zimbabwe brings her close to the world of African spirits.

**Ghost Canoe,** by Will Hobbs
When a ship crashes near the lighthouse where Nathan lives, and the captain's murdered body washes ashore, Nathan becomes an amateur sleuth.

**I Thought My Soul Would Rise and Fly: The Diary of Patsy, A Freed Girl,** by Joyce Hansen
Twelve-year old Patsy writes in her journal of the time following the Civil War, when slaves were granted their freedom.

**Johnny Tremain,** by Esther Forbes
Experience the American Revolution through the eyes of a teenager working as a silversmith's apprentice.

**Nero Corleone: A Cat's Story,** by Elke Hendenreich
Nero Corleone, a cat, is the big boss of a farm in Italy, his home. Life seems fine to him—until he climbs through a window and discovers new luxuries he's never imagined before.

**Parrot in the Oven: Mi Vida,** by Victor Martinez
The story of Manny and his childhood in a poor Mexican-American family.

**Poppy,** by Avi
Poppy, a deer mouse, has a plan that will ensure food for her family forever. But Mr. Ocax, a scary owl, has other ideas.

**Slam!,** by Walter Dean Myers
A teen learns to bring his winning spirit in basketball to other parts of his life.

**The Subtle Knife,** by Philip Pullman
Lyra helps Will search for his father and a powerful, magical knife in this well-liked book, a follow-up to *The Golden Compass*.

**The View From Saturday,** by E. L. Konigsburg
As four students and their teacher prepare for an academic contest, they learn as much from one another as they do from books.

**Thank You, Jackie Robinson,** by Barbara Cohen
Sam and Davy come from different races, religions, and generations. But their interest in baseball brings them together, and they find they have more in common than they ever imagined.

## POETRY

Poems use language in creative and imaginative ways, sometimes in rhyme.

**Love Letters**, by Arnold Adoff, illustrated by Lisa Desimini
Twenty poems written by kids, secret admirers, friends, and enemies.

**The Beauty of the Beast: Poems From the Animal Kingdom**, selected by
Jack Prelutsky, illustrated by Mielo So.
An illustrated multicultural collection of poems about animals, insects, and birds.

**Navajo: Visions and Voices Across the Mesa**, by Shonto Begay
Beautifully illustrated poems reflect the ancient spirits and stories of the Navajo.

## NONFICTION

Nonfiction includes true stories, provides information, and can be used as reference.
The books below prove that fact can be just as interesting as fiction.

**Amazing African-American History: A Book of Answers for Kids**, by Diane Patrick
This compelling book covers the most important events in African-American
history and the people who shaped them.

**Children Just Like Me**, by Barnabas and Anabel Kindersley
The author and photographer traveled the world to create this book about children
and their lives in countries around the globe.

**The Chinese-American Family Album**, by Dorothy and Thomas Hoobler
The history of the Chinese in the United States is told with rich detail and charm.

**A Drop of Water**, by Walter Wick, with photographs by the author
Extraordinary photos draw readers into trying 15 easy science experiments, all to
do with water.

**Eleanor Roosevelt: A Life of Discovery**, by Russell Freedman
A photobiography of the first first lady to have her own career.

**Hostage to War: A True Story**, by Tatjana Wassiljewa
When the Germans invaded Russia during World War II, a young girl relied on her
own courage and strength to survive.

**The Most Beautiful Roof in the World: Exploring the Rain Forest Canopy**,
by Kathryn Lasky, illustrations by Christopher G. Knight
Two young boys and their mother, a scientist, explore a rain forest.

**Orphan Train Rider: One Boy's True Story**, by Andrea Warren
One of the 200,000 orphans who rode the Orphan Train to the Midwest in search
of a new family tells his exciting story.

**Winning Ways: A Photohistory of American Women in Sports**, by Sue Macy
About women's struggle to be taken seriously as athletes.

## REFERENCE BOOKS: WHERE THE ANSWERS ARE

Many reference materials like these are stored on CD-ROMs,
and some may also be available on the Internet.

**Almanac**: A one-volume book of facts and statistics.

**Atlas**: A collection of maps.

**Dictionary**: A book of words in alphabetical order. A dictionary
gives the meanings and spelling of words and shows how they
are pronounced.

**Encyclopedia**: The place to go first for information on almost any
subject. Encyclopedias cover the past and the present, the arts
and sciences, and the countries of the world, either in one volume
or in several.

# The 7 WONDERS of the Ancient World

These were considered the most remarkable structures of ancient times. Only one of them—the pyramids in Egypt—has survived and can be visited today.

**Pyramids of Egypt**
At Giza, Egypt, built as royal tombs from 3000 to 1800 B.C. The largest is the **Great Pyramid of Khufu** (or Cheops).

**Hanging Gardens of Babylon**
Terraced gardens built by King Nebuchadnezzar II around 600 B.C. for his wife.

**Temple of Artemis**
At Ephesus (now part of Turkey), built mostly of marble around 550 B.C. in honor of the Greek goddess Artemis.

**Statue of Zeus**
At Olympia, Greece. The statue, made about 462 B.C. by the ancient Greek sculptor Phidias from ivory and gold, showed the king of the gods sitting on a throne.

**Mausoleum of Halicarnassus**
(Now part of Turkey), built about 353 B.C. in honor of King Mausolus, a ruler of ancient Caria.

**Colossus of Rhodes**
Overlooking the harbor on the island of Rhodes (Greece), a bronze statue of the sun god Helios, built about 280 B.C. Probably 120 feet high.

**Lighthouse of Alexandria, Egypt**
Built about 270 B.C. during the reign of King Ptolemy II. It may have been around 500 feet tall.

# TALLEST BUILDINGS in the World

**H**ere are some of the world's tallest buildings.

**Petronas Towers 1 & 2**, Kuala Lumpur, Malaysia (completed 1997)
   **Height**: each building 88 stories, 1,483 feet
**Sears Tower**, Chicago, Illinois (completed 1974). **Height**: 110 stories, 1,450 feet
**Jin Mao Building**, Shanghai, China (under construction in early 1998)
   **Height**: 88 stories, 1,380 feet
**World Trade Center 1 & 2**, New York, New York (completed 1972 and 1973)
   **Height**: each building 110 stories, over 1,360 feet
**Empire State Building**, New York, New York (completed 1931). **Height**: 102 stories,
   1,250 feet
**Central Plaza**, Hong Kong, China (completed 1992). **Height**: 78 stories, 1,227 feet
**Bank of China Tower**, Hong Kong (completed 1989). **Height**: 70 stories, 1,209 feet
**T & C Tower**, Kaohsiung, Taiwan  (completed 1997). **Height**: 85 stories, 1,140 feet
**Amoco**, Chicago, Illinois (completed 1973). **Height**: 80 stories, 1,136 feet
**John Hancock Center**, Chicago, Illinois (completed 1969). **Height**: 100 stories, 1,127 feet

# LONGEST BRIDGES in the World

**T**he **span** of a bridge is the distance between its supports. The bridges below, as measured by main spans, are the world's longest suspension bridges (those that hang from cables). The longest in the U.S. is the Verrazano-Narrows Bridge in New York (4,260 feet).

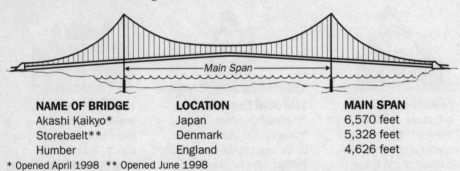

| NAME OF BRIDGE | LOCATION | MAIN SPAN |
|---|---|---|
| Akashi Kaikyo* | Japan | 6,570 feet |
| Storebaelt** | Denmark | 5,328 feet |
| Humber | England | 4,626 feet |

* Opened April 1998  ** Opened June 1998

# LONGEST TUNNELS in the World

**A** **tunnel** is a long underground passageway, dug through rock or earth or built underwater. Vehicular tunnels (on land and under water) are for automobiles, trucks, and the like. Railroad tunnels are for trains and subway traffic. Water tunnels are for water mains, drainage, sewage, mining, and storage. Here are the longest tunnels of each type:

| TYPE OF TUNNEL | NAME | LOCATION | LENGTH |
|---|---|---|---|
| Land Vehicular | St. Gotthard | Switzerland | 10.1 miles |
| Underwater Vehicular | Brooklyn-Battery | New York, USA | 1.7 miles |
| Railroad | Seikan | Japan | 33.5 miles |
| Water | Delaware Aqueduct | New York, USA | 85.0 miles |

# WHAT Do COMPUTERS Do?

**A**t first, computers were used to add, subtract, multiply, and divide big numbers. Today they can do many things with information of all kinds. A pizza shop owner can use a computer to keep track of what pizzas people buy every day and what toppings need to be ordered. This information is organized and stored in a **database**. A student can use a computer to get information from the Internet (see page 41), play a game, or do homework.

### COMPUTERS HELP PEOPLE COMMUNICATE.

☑ Computers can be used to write letters or stories or reports for school.
☑ Computers help create newspapers, magazines, and books.
☑ People use computers to send electronic mail (e-mail), sometimes across the continent or to other countries.
☑ People who cannot speak can type in messages that the computer translates into speech. People who cannot type can speak into a computer that translates their speech into text.

### COMPUTERS HELP PEOPLE CREATE.

☑ People use computers to create artwork and music or to design buildings.
☑ Computers help create special effects for movies and television.

### COMPUTERS HELP PEOPLE LEARN.

☑ Programs on computers help teach school subjects.
☑ The computer can keep track of students' progress.
☑ Pilots and astronauts use computer flight simulators.

### COMPUTERS KEEP INFORMATION ORGANIZED.

☑ Many companies and organizations keep a database with information. The FBI has a database that police departments can use to find information about criminals or stolen goods from all around the United States.

### COMPUTERS HELP PREDICT THE FUTURE.

☑ Companies use computer programs to help them make decisions for the future.
☑ Computer programs use data from satellites to help forecast weather.

### COMPUTERS ARE USED TO MANUFACTURE PRODUCTS.

☑ Engineers use special software to create detailed drawings of an object and then test it to see how to make it stronger or cheaper.
☑ Computers can then be used to control machinery used to make the new product.

### COMPUTERS AREN'T JUST FOUND ON DESKS.

☑ Computers are used in automatic teller machines at the bank and with the price scanner at the supermarket checkout.
☑ Cars, microwave ovens, VCRs, and digital watches all have built-in computers.

# HOW COMPUTERS WORK

**C**omputers perform tasks by using programs called **software**. These programs tell the computer what to do when the user enters certain information or commands. This is called **input**.

The computer then processes the information and gives the user the results (**output**). The computer can also **store** the information so that it can be used again and again.

There are many different types of computers. The largest and most powerful computers are called **mainframes**. Scientists use them to perform calculations that would take years to do by hand. The computers most people are familiar with are personal computers (PCs). These can be used at a desk (**desktops**) or even carried around (**laptops**).

## INPUT:
### Selecting the Right Software.

To write a story (or letter or school report) you need to use a type of software called a word-processing program. This program can be selected by using the **keyboard** or a **mouse**.

### Entering Data.

Once you are in the right program, you can begin to input the story by typing on the **keyboard**. The backspace and delete keys are like electronic erasers. You can also press special keys (called **function keys**) or sometimes click on certain symbols (**icons**), to center or underline words, move words and sentences around, check your spelling, print out a page, and do other tasks. When you input a command, the word-processing program tells the computer what to do.

## PROCESSING:
### Inside the Computer.

The instructions from the word-processing program are carried out inside the computer by the **central processing unit**, or **CPU**. The CPU is the computer's brain.

## OUTPUT:
### Getting the Results.

The **monitor** and **printer** are the most commonly used output devices. As you type your story, the words appear on a **monitor**, which is similar to a television screen. Your story can then be printed on paper by using a **printer**.

If you print out your story, you can mail it to a friend. But if you and your friend both have **modems**, the story can be sent from your computer directly to your friend's computer. A **modem** allows information from a computer to travel over telephone lines.

## STORAGE:
### Keeping Data To Use It Later.

A computer also stores information that you may want to use later. Suppose you want to stop working and eat lunch. You can save the work you've done and then go back to it later.

## Floppy Disk.

Information can be saved on a "floppy" plastic disk that goes into a slot in the computer called a **disk drive**. If you use a disk to save your story, you can use the disk on another computer and your story will be there to work on. Disks today are usually $3\frac{1}{2}"$ and are stiff. Older computers used larger disks that were light and easy to bend, so people began calling them floppy disks.

## Zip Disk.

Zip disks hold much more information than a floppy disk. They are used in special zip drives.

## Hard Disk.

Most computers have a **hard drive**. The hard drive contains a **hard disk** made of metal that is not removed. This disk holds much more information than zip or floppy disks. It stores your software and information you have entered into the computer.

## SOFTWARE

Besides word-processing programs, there are many other types of software. Common types of software include programs for doing mathematics, keeping records, playing games, and creating pictures.

## CD-ROMS

Many computers have a CD-ROM drive. This allows you to play special disks called **CD-ROMs**, which are similar to music CDs. A CD-ROM can hold a huge amount of information, including pictures and sound. Almanacs, games, encyclopedias, and many other types of information and entertainment are on CD-ROMs.

## DVDS

**Digital Versatile Disks** look like CD-ROMs, but hold about 8 times more information on a single side. DVDs are currently used to store full-length movies, encyclopedias, and other products with lots of data.

### A COMPUTER SYSTEM

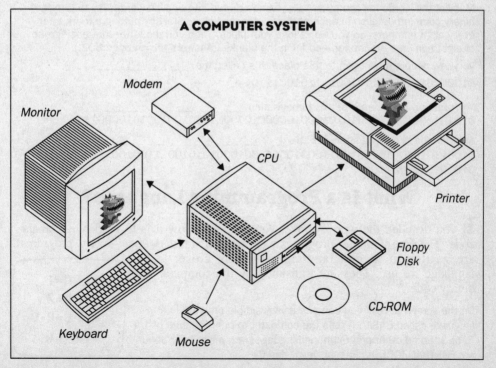

Monitor, Modem, CPU, Printer, Floppy Disk, CD-ROM, Keyboard, Mouse

# The BINARY SYSTEM

**A** computer can do many impressive things, but one thing it cannot do is understand English. For a computer to do its work, every piece of information given to it must be translated into binary code. You are probably used to using ten digits, 0 through 9, when you do arithmetic. When the computer uses the **binary code**, it uses only two digits, 0 and 1. Think of it as sending messages to the computer by switching a light on and off.

Each 0 or 1 digit is called a **bit**, and most computers use a sequence of 8 bits (called a **byte**) for each piece of data. Almost all computers use the same code, called ASCII (pronounced "askey"), to stand for letters of the alphabet, number digits, punctuation, and other special characters that control the computer's operation. Below is a list of ASCII bytes for the alphabet.

| | | | | | |
|---|---|---|---|---|---|
| A | 01000001 | J | 01001010 | S | 01010011 |
| B | 01000010 | K | 01001011 | T | 01010100 |
| C | 01000011 | L | 01001100 | U | 01010101 |
| D | 01000100 | M | 01001101 | V | 01010110 |
| E | 01000101 | N | 01001110 | W | 01010111 |
| F | 01000110 | O | 01001111 | X | 01011000 |
| G | 01000111 | P | 01010000 | Y | 01011001 |
| H | 01001000 | Q | 01010001 | Z | 01011010 |
| I | 01001001 | R | 01010010 | | |

Many of the words in "computer talk" can be turned into English words. Try to turn the binary code into English in each of the sentences below. Start by putting a mark after every eight numbers, so you won't lose your place. Then find the letter that each group of eight numbers stands for, and fill in the blanks. (Answers are on page 302.)

Very few people have been to this place. It's called the ___ ___ ___ ___ .
01001101010011110100111101001110

You probably have heard of this famous ship ___ ___ ___ ___ ___ ___ ___.
0101010001001001010101000100000101001110010010010101000011

Another one is coming soon. It's the ___ ___ ___ ___ ___ ___ ___ ___ ___ ___ .
0100110101001001010011000100110001000100010101001110010011100100100101010101010101001101

# What Is a Programming Language?

**I**f you decoded the words above, you saw how slow it is to work with binary code. The first computer programs were written in binary code. Today, programs are written in special languages that are closer to the language we use. They are translated by the computer into binary code.

On the screen at right you can see a very simple program in a language called BASIC. It tells the computer to print the sum of 1 + 2, or 3. Some other programming languages you might hear about are FORTRAN, COBOL, Pascal, Java, and C++.

```
LET A=1
LET B=2
LET C=A+B
PRINT C
```

# COMPUTER TALK

**artificial intelligence or AI**

The ability of computers and robots to imitate human intelligence by learning and making decisions.

**boot**

To turn on a computer.

**browser**

A program to help get around the Internet.

**bug or glitch**

An error in a program or in the computer.

**database**

A large collection of information organized so that it can be retrieved and used in different ways. A list of names and addresses is an example of a database.

**desktop publishing**

The use of computers for combining text and pictures to design and produce magazines, newspapers, and books.

**download**

To transfer information from a host computer to a personal computer, often through a modem.

**e-mail or electronic mail**

Messages sent from one computer to another over a network.

**gig or gigabyte (GB)**

An amount of information equal to 1,000 (or 1,024) megabytes.

**hard copy**

Computer output printed on paper or similar material.

**Internet**

A worldwide system of linked computer networks.

**Internet Service Provider or ISP**

An organization that connects a modem to the Internet.

**laptop or notebook**

A portable personal computer that can run on batteries.

**megabyte (MB)**

An amount of information equal to 1 million (or 1,048,516) bytes.

**multimedia**

Software that includes pictures, video, and sound. In multimedia software, you can see pictures move and hear music and other sounds.

**network**

A group of computers linked together so that they can share information.

**password**

A secret code that keeps people who do not know it from using a computer or software.

**program**

Instructions for a computer to follow.

**RAM or random access memory**

This is the memory your computer uses to open programs and store your work until you save it to the hard drive or a disk. The information in RAM disappears when the computer is turned off.

**ROM or read only memory**

ROM contains permanent instructions for the computer and cannot be changed. The information in ROM remains after the computer is turned off.

**scanner**

A device that can read and transfer words and pictures from a printed page into the computer.

**upload**

To send information from a personal computer to a host computer, often through a modem.

**virtual reality**

Three-dimensional images on a screen that are viewed using special equipment (like gloves and goggles). The user feels as if he or she is part of the image and can interact with everything around.

**virus**

A program that damages other programs and data. It gets into a computer through telephone lines or shared disks.

**Web site**

A place on the Internet's World Wide Web where text and pictures are stored. The contents are sent to computers when the correct World Wide Web address (which begins with http://) is entered.

# SUPER SOFTWARE

You can learn and have a lot of fun with software programs. The American Library Association thinks these programs are super. But you may have other favorites.

**The Magic School Bus**, Microsoft. Windows. Mrs. Frizzle takes her students on incredible field trips.

**What's the Secret?** Imation. Mac, Windows. Interactive science experiments that the user can do.

**Somebody Catch My Homework**, Discis. Mac, Windows. Join in the fun with 20 poems by David Harrison that are funny and fun to read. There's also an interview with the poet.

**With Open Eyes**: Images from the Art Institute of Chicago, Voyager. Mac, Windows. Discover more than 200 images that you can save to a scrapbook. Enjoy the puzzles and games, too.

**Chicka Chicka Boom Boom**, Davidson. Mac, Windows. Everyone will be singing with you. You can also record your own songs and "play" instruments.

**DID YOU KNOW?**

☑ In ancient times people did computing with numbers using an *abacus*, which is made up of rods and beads. A modern version of the abacus is still used today in Japan. A person who is skilled with an abacus can *add more than 15 numbers in one minute*.

☑ The high-powered computers of today can do in a few seconds calculations that would take a person working by hand days, or even years, to do. A modern personal computer can *perform more than one trillion mathematical operations in one second*.

☑ Many computers have a big problem. They cannot make use of dates past 1999, because they use only the last 2 digits for a year (99 for 1999, for example). This is called Y2K, the Year 2000 Problem. It could cost $600 billion to be fixed for all computers.

# COMPUTER MUSEUMS

Some museums have sections where you can learn about computers and use them to do many fascinating things. A few museums are devoted entirely to the computer. Here are three:

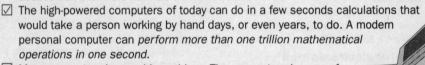

| THE COMPUTER MUSEUM, INC. | AMERICAN COMPUTER MUSEUM | TECH MUSEUM OF INNOVATION |
|---|---|---|
| 300 Congress Street | 234 East Babcock Street | 145 West San Carlos Street |
| Boston, MA 02210 | Bozeman, MT 59715 | San Jose, CA 95113 |
| **Phone:** (617) 426-2800 | **Phone:** (406) 587-7545 | **Phone:** (408) 279-7150 |
| **WEB SITE** http://www. net.org | **WEB SITE** http://www. compu-story.com | **WEB SITE** http:// www.thetech.org |
| | **E-MAIL** bitenbyte @aol.com | **E-MAIL** info @thetech.org |

# The INTERNET

**P**eople all around the world can communicate with one another through the world's largest computer network, called the **Internet**. The Internet connects government agencies and offices, colleges, science laboratories, businesses, individuals, and schools. When computers are connected to the Internet, people can send and receive e-mail, enjoy games and activities, and look at and download many kinds of information. The Internet has news about world events, sports, and movies and TV shows, information to help with homework or reports, and recipes and cooking tips. The **World Wide Web**—called "the Web" for short—is a part of the Internet that sends pictures and sound as well as words.

- No one should ask you for personal information such as your computer password, address, school, or telephone number.
- No one on the Internet should ask for your picture, or ask to meet you in person.
- If you get a message that is mean or upsetting, don't respond.

When you enter an address on the Internet, you must type it *exactly* the way it is written. Every letter, symbol, and space must be correct.

### SAFETY ON THE INTERNET
Many sites on the Internet are filled with great information for children and adults. But before you use the Internet, it is important to know how to use it safely. Never give people private information about yourself.

# SMILEYS

**W**hen you send e-mail to a friend, do you ever use smileys? Smileys are typed letters and symbols that look like faces when you turn them sideways. They are used to express feelings or tell other things about yourself in messages you send by computer. Here are a few smileys:

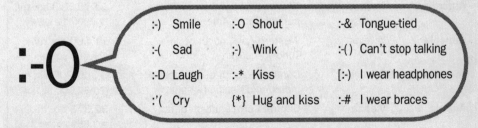

| :-) Smile | :-O Shout | :-& Tongue-tied |
| :-( Sad | ;-) Wink | :-() Can't stop talking |
| :-D Laugh | :-* Kiss | [:-) I wear headphones |
| :'( Cry | {*} Hug and kiss | :-# I wear braces |

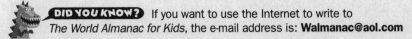
**DID YOU KNOW?** If you want to use the Internet to write to *The World Almanac for Kids*, the e-mail address is: **Walmanac@aol.com**

# COUNTRIES of the WORLD

**T**here are 192 countries in the world. The information for each country goes across two pages. The left-hand page gives the **name** and **capital** of each country, where the country is **located**, and its **area** in both square miles (sq. mi.) and square kilometers (sq. km.). On the right-hand page, the **population** column tells approximately how many people lived in each country (as of 1997). The **currency** column shows what the money is called in each country and how much one United States dollar was worth there at the start of 1998. The language column shows official languages or other languages that are commonly spoken. All of these countries belong to the United Nations except Kiribati, Nauru, Switzerland, Taiwan, Tonga, Tuvalu, and Vatican City.

| COUNTRY | CAPITAL | LOCATION OF COUNTRY | AREA |
|---------|---------|---------------------|------|
| Afghanistan | Kabul | Southern Asia, between Iran and Pakistan | 251,825 sq. mi. (652,227 sq. km.) |
| Albania | Tiranë | Eastern Europe, north of Greece | 11,100 sq. mi. (28,750 sq. km.) |
| Algeria | Algiers | North Africa on the Mediterranean Sea, between Libya and Morocco | 919,595 sq. mi. (2,381,751 sq. km.) |
| Andorra | Andorra la Vella | Europe, in the mountains between France and Spain | 181 sq. mi. (469 sq. km.) |
| Angola | Luanda | Southern Africa on the Atlantic Ocean, north of Namibia | 481,354 sq. mi. (1,246,707 sq. km.) |
| Antigua and Barbuda | St. John's | Islands on eastern edge of the Caribbean Sea | 171 sq. mi. (443 sq. km.) |
| Argentina | Buenos Aires | Fills up most of the southern part of South America | 1,073,518 sq. mi. (2,780,412 sq. km.) |
| Armenia | Yerevan | Western Asia, north of Turkey and Iran | 11,500 sq. mi. (29,800 sq. km.) |
| Australia | Canberra | Continent south of Asia, between Indian and Pacific Oceans | 2,966,200 sq. mi. (7,682,500 sq. km.) |
| Austria | Vienna | Central Europe, north of Italy | 32,378 sq. mi. (83,859 sq. km.) |
| Azerbaijan | Baku | Western Asia, north of Iran | 33,400 sq. mi. (86,500 sq. km.) |

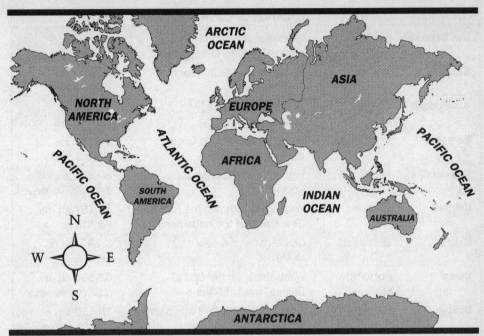

| POPULATION | CURRENCY | LANGUAGE | COUNTRY |
|---:|---|---|---|
| 23,738,085 | Afghani<br>$1 = 4,800 afghanis | Afghan Persian (Dari), Pashtu | **Afghanistan** |
| 3,293,252 | Lek<br>$1 = 150 leks | Albanian | **Albania** |
| 29,830,370 | Dinar<br>$1 = 60 dinars | Arabic, French | **Algeria** |
| 74,839 | French franc or Spanish peseta | Catalan, French | **Andorra** |
| 10,623,994 | New kwanza<br>$1 = 257,000 new kwanzas | Portuguese | **Angola** |
| 66,175 | East Caribbean dollar<br>$1 = $2\frac{2}{3}$ EC dollars | English | **Antigua and Barbuda** |
| 35,797,536 | Peso<br>$1 = 1 peso | Spanish | **Argentina** |
| 3,465,611 | Dram<br>$1 = 500 drams | Armenian | **Armenia** |
| 18,438,824 | Australian dollar<br>$1 = $1\frac{1}{2}$ Australian dollars | English | **Australia** |
| 8,054,078 | Schilling<br>$1 = $12\frac{1}{2}$ schillings | German | **Austria** |
| 7,735,918 | Manat<br>$1 = 4,000 manats | Azeri | **Azerbaijan** |

| COUNTRY | CAPITAL | LOCATION OF COUNTRY | AREA |
|---|---|---|---|
| The Bahamas | Nassau | Islands in the Atlantic Ocean, east of Florida | 5,382 sq. mi. (13,939 sq. km.) |
| Bahrain | Manama | In the Persian Gulf, near the coast of Qatar | 268 sq. mi. (694 sq. km.) |
| Bangladesh | Dhaka | Southern Asia, nearly surrounded by India | 56,977 sq. mi. (147,570 sq. km.) |
| Barbados | Bridgetown | Island in the Atlantic Ocean, north of Trinidad | 166 sq. mi. (430 sq. km.) |
| Belarus | Minsk | Eastern Europe, east of Poland | 80,153 sq. mi. (207,596 sq. km.) |
| Belgium | Brussels | Western Europe, on the North Sea, south of the Netherlands | 11,787 sq. mi. (30,528 sq. km.) |
| Belize | Belmopan | Central America, next to Mexico | 8,867 sq. mi. (22,966 sq. km.) |
| Benin | Porto-Novo | West Africa, on the Gulf of Guinea, west of Nigeria | 43,500 sq. mi. (112,700 sq. km.) |
| Bhutan | Thimphu | Asia, in the Himalaya Mountains, between China and India | 18,150 sq. mi. (47,009 sq. km.) |
| Bolivia | La Paz | South America, in the Andes Mountains, next to Brazil | 424,164 sq. mi. (1,098,585 sq. km.) |
| Bosnia and Herzegovina | Sarajevo | Southern Europe, on the Balkan Peninsula, west of Yugoslavia | 19,741 sq. mi. (51,129 sq. km.) |
| Botswana | Gaborone | Southern Africa, between South Africa and Zambia | 224,607 sq. mi. (581,732 sq. km.) |
| Brazil | Brasília | Occupies most of the eastern part of South America | 3,300,171 sq. mi. (8,547,443 sq. km.) |
| Brunei | Bandar Seri Begawan | On the island of Borneo, northwest of Australia in the Pacific Ocean | 2,226 sq. mi. (5,765 sq. km.) |
| Bulgaria | Sofia | Eastern Europe, on the Balkan Peninsula, bordering the Black Sea | 42,855 sq. mi. (110,994 sq. km.) |
| Burkina Faso | Ouagadougou | West Africa, between Mali and Ghana | 105,946 sq. mi. (274,400 sq. km.) |
| Burundi | Bujumbura | Central Africa, northwest of Tanzania | 10,740 sq. mi. (27,817 sq. km.) |
| Cambodia | Phnom Penh | Southeast Asia, between Vietnam and Thailand | 70,238 sq. mi. (181,916 sq. km.) |
| Cameroon | Yaoundé | Central Africa, between Nigeria and Central African Republic | 183,569 sq. mi. (475,444 sq. km.) |
| Canada | Ottawa | Occupies the northern part of North America, north of the United States | 3,849,674 sq. mi. (9,970,656 sq. km.) |
| Cape Verde | Praia | Islands off the western tip of Africa | 1,557 sq. mi. (4,033 sq. km.) |

| POPULATION | CURRENCY | LANGUAGE | COUNTRY |
|---|---|---|---|
| 262,034 | Bahamas dollar<br>Same value as U.S. dollar | English | **The Bahamas** |
| 603,318 | Dinar<br>$1 = \frac{2}{5}$ dinars | Arabic | **Bahrain** |
| 125,340,261 | Taka<br>$1 = 45 takas | Bangla | **Bangladesh** |
| 257,731 | Barbados dollar<br>$1 = 2 Barbados dollars | English | **Barbados** |
| 10,439,916 | Ruble<br>$1 = 27,200 rubles | Belarussian | **Belarus** |
| 10,203,683 | Franc<br>$1 = 35 francs | Flemish (Dutch),<br>French | **Belgium** |
| 224,663 | Belize dollar<br>$1 = 2 Belize dollars | English | **Belize** |
| 5,902,178 | CFA franc<br>$1 = 600 CFA francs | French | **Benin** |
| 1,865,191 | Ngultrum<br>$1 = 40 ngultrums | Dzongkha | **Bhutan** |
| 7,669,868 | Boliviano<br>$1 = 5\frac{2}{5}$ Bolivianos | Spanish,<br>Quechua, Aymara | **Bolivia** |
| 2,607,734 | New dinar<br>$1 = 6 new dinars | Serbo-Croatian | **Bosnia and Herzegovina** |
| 1,500,765 | Pula<br>$1 = 3\frac{3}{4}$ pula | English | **Botswana** |
| 164,511,366 | Real<br>$1 = 1\frac{1}{2}$ real | Portuguese | **Brazil** |
| 307,616 | Brunei dollar<br>$1 = 1\frac{2}{3}$ Brunei dollars | Malay | **Brunei** |
| 8,652,745 | Lev<br>$1 = 1,800 leva | Bulgarian | **Bulgaria** |
| 10,891,159 | CFA franc<br>$1 = 600 CFA francs | French | **Burkina Faso** |
| 6,052,614 | Franc<br>$1 = 400 francs | Kirundi,<br>French | **Burundi** |
| 11,163,861 | Riel<br>$1 = 3,000 riels | Khmer | **Cambodia** |
| 14,677,510 | CFA franc<br>$1 = 600 CFA francs | English,<br>French | **Cameroon** |
| 29,123,194 | Canadian dollar<br>$1 = 1\frac{2}{5}$ Canadian dollars | English,<br>French | **Canada** |
| 393,843 | Escudo<br>$1 = 95 escudos | Portuguese | **Cape Verde** |

| COUNTRY | CAPITAL | LOCATION OF COUNTRY | AREA |
|---------|---------|---------------------|------|
| Central African Republic | Bangui | Central Africa, south of Chad | 240,324 sq. mi. (622,439 sq. km.) |
| Chad | N'Djamena | North Africa, south of Libya | 495,755 sq. mi. (1,284,000 sq. km.) |
| Chile | Santiago | Along the western coast of South America | 292,135 sq. mi. (756,630 sq. km.) |
| China | Beijing | Occupies most of the mainland of eastern Asia | 3,696,100 sq. mi. (9,572,900 sq. km.) |
| Colombia | Bogotá | Northwestern South America, southeast of Panama | 440,762 sq. mi. (1,141,574 sq. km.) |
| Comoros | Moroni | Islands between Madagascar and the east coast of Africa | 719 sq. mi. (1,862 sq. km.) |
| Congo, Democratic Republic of the (*formerly* Zaire) | Kinshasa | Central Africa, north of Angola and Zambia | 905,354 sq. mi. (2,344,867 sq. km.) |
| Congo, Republic of the | Brazzaville | Central Africa, east of Gabon | 132,047 sq. mi. (342,000 sq. km.) |
| Costa Rica | San José | Central America, south of Nicaragua | 19,730 sq. mi (51,100 sq. km.) |
| Côte d'Ivoire (Ivory Coast) | Yamoussoukro | West Africa, on the Gulf of Guinea, west of Ghana | 124,504 sq. mi. (322,465 sq. km.) |
| Croatia | Zagreb | Southern Europe, south of Hungary | 21,889 sq. mi. (56,693 sq. km.) |
| Cuba | Havana | In the Caribbean Sea, south of Florida | 42,804 sq. mi. (110,862 sq. km.) |
| Cyprus | Nicosia | Island in the Mediterranean Sea, off the coast of Turkey | 3,572 sq. mi. (9,251 sq. km.) |
| Czech Republic | Prague | Central Europe, south of Poland, east of Germany | 30,450 sq. mi. (78,866 sq. km.) |
| Denmark | Copenhagen | Northern Europe, between the Baltic Sea and North Sea | 16,639 sq. mi. (43,095 sq. km.) |
| Djibouti | Djibouti | North Africa, on the Gulf of Aden, across from Saudi Arabia | 8,950 sq. mi. (23,200 sq. km.) |
| Dominica | Roseau | Island in the Caribbean Sea | 290 sq. mi. (750 sq. km.) |
| Dominican Republic | Santo Domingo | On an island, along with Haiti, in the Caribbean Sea | 18,704 sq. mi. (48,443 sq. km.) |
| Ecuador | Quito | South America, on the equator, bordering the Pacific Ocean | 105,037 sq. mi. (272,046 sq. km.) |
| Egypt | Cairo | Northeastern Africa, on the Red Sea and Mediterranean Sea | 385,229 sq. mi. (997,743 sq. km.) |

| POPULATION | CURRENCY | LANGUAGE | COUNTRY |
|---|---|---|---|
| 3,342,051 | CFA franc $1 = 600 CFA francs | French, Sangho | Central African Republic |
| 7,166,023 | CFA franc $1 = 600 CFA francs | French, Arabic | Chad |
| 14,508,168 | Peso $1 = 440 pesos | Spanish | Chile |
| 1,221,591,778 | Renminbi (yuan) $1 = 8$\frac{1}{4}$ renminbis | Mandarin | China |
| 37,418,290 | Peso $1 = 1,300 pesos | Spanish | Colombia |
| 589,797 | Franc $1 = 450 francs | Arabic, French, Comoran | Comoros |
| 47,440,362 | New zaire $1 = 108,000 new zaires | French | Congo, Democratic Republic of the (formerly Zaire) |
| 2,583,198 | CFA franc $1 = 600 CFA francs | French | Congo, Republic of the |
| 3,534,174 | Colon $1 = 240 colones | Spanish | Costa Rica |
| 14,986,218 | CFA franc $1 = 600 CFA francs | French | Côte d'Ivoire (Ivory Coast) |
| 5,026,995 | Kuna $1 = 6$\frac{1}{3}$ kunas | Croatian | Croatia |
| 10,999,041 | Peso $1 = 25 pesos | Spanish | Cuba |
| 752,808 | Pound $1 = 1$\frac{4}{5}$ pound | Greek, Turkish | Cyprus |
| 10,318,958 | Koruna $1 = 35 koruny | Czech | Czech Republic |
| 5,268,775 | Krone $1 = 6$\frac{4}{5}$ kroner | Danish | Denmark |
| 434,116 | Franc $1 = 175 francs | French, Arabic | Djibouti |
| 83,226 | East Caribbean dollar $1 = 2 EC dollars | English | Dominica |
| 8,228,151 | Peso $1 = 15 pesos | Spanish | Dominican Republic |
| 11,690,535 | Sucre $1 = 4,400 sucres | Spanish | Ecuador |
| 64,791,891 | Pound $1 = 3$\frac{2}{5}$ pounds | Arabic | Egypt |

| COUNTRY | CAPITAL | LOCATION OF COUNTRY | AREA |
|---|---|---|---|
| El Salvador | San Salvador | Central America, southwest of Honduras | 8,124 sq. mi. (21,041 sq. km.) |
| Equatorial Guinea | Malabo | West Africa, on the Gulf of Guinea, off the west coast of Cameroon | 10,831 sq. mi. (28,052 sq. km.) |
| Eritrea | Asmara | Northeast Africa, north of Ethiopia | 45,300 sq. mi. (117,400 sq. km.) |
| Estonia | Tallinn | Northern Europe, on the Baltic Sea, north of Latvia | 17,462 sq. mi. (45,227 sq. km.) |
| Ethiopia | Addis Ababa | East Africa, east of Sudan | 437,794 sq. mi. (1,133,886 sq. km.) |
| Fiji | Suva | Islands in the South Pacific Ocean, east of Australia | 7,055 sq. mi. (18,272 sq. km.) |
| Finland | Helsinki | Northern Europe, between Sweden and Russia | 130,559 sq. mi. (338,148 sq. km.) |
| France | Paris | Western Europe, between Germany and Spain | 210,026 sq. mi. (543,967 sq. km.) |
| Gabon | Libreville | Central Africa, on the Atlantic coast, south of Cameroon | 103,347 sq. mi. (267,669 sq. km.) |
| The Gambia | Banjul | West Africa, on the Atlantic Ocean, surrounded by Senegal | 4,127 sq. mi. (10,689 sq. km.) |
| Georgia | Tbilisi | Western Asia, south of Russia, on the Black Sea | 26,831 sq. mi. (69,492 sq. km.) |
| Germany | Berlin | Central Europe, northeast of France | 137,828 sq. mi. (356,975 sq. km.) |
| Ghana | Accra | West Africa, on the southern coast | 92,098 sq. mi. (238,534 sq. km.) |
| Great Britain (United Kingdom) | London | Off the northwest coast of Europe | 94,251 sq. mi. (244,110 sq. km.) |
| Greece | Athens | Southern Europe, in the southern part of the Balkan Peninsula | 50,949 sq. mi. (131,958 sq. km.) |
| Grenada | Saint George's | Island on the eastern edge of the Caribbean Sea | 133 sq. mi. (344 sq. km.) |
| Guatemala | Guatemala City | Central America, southeast of Mexico | 42,042 sq. mi. (108,889 sq. km.) |
| Guinea | Conakry | West Africa, on the Atlantic Ocean, north of Sierra Leone | 94,926 sq. mi. (245,858 sq. km.) |
| Guinea-Bissau | Bissau | West Africa, on the Atlantic Ocean, south of Senegal | 13,948 sq. mi. (36,125 sq. km.) |
| Guyana | Georgetown | South America, on the northern coast, east of Venezuela | 83,044 sq. mi. (215,084 sq. km.) |
| Haiti | Port-au-Prince | On an island, along with Dominican Republic, in the Caribbean Sea | 10,695 sq. mi. (27,700 sq. km.) |

| POPULATION | CURRENCY | LANGUAGE | COUNTRY |
|---:|---|---|---|
| 5,661,827 | Colon<br>$1 = 8\frac{3}{4}$ colones | Spanish | El Salvador |
| 442,516 | CFA franc<br>$1 = 600$ CFA francs | Spanish | Equatorial Guinea |
| 3,589,687 | Ethiopian Birr<br>$1 = 6\frac{3}{4}$ Ethiopian birr | Tigrinya | Eritrea |
| 1,444,721 | Kroon<br>$1 = 14$ kroons | Estonian | Estonia |
| 58,732,577 | Birr<br>$1 = 6\frac{2}{3}$ birr | Amharic | Ethiopia |
| 792,441 | Fiji dollar<br>$1 = 1\frac{1}{2}$ Fiji dollars | English | Fiji |
| 5,109,148 | Markka<br>$1 = 5\frac{1}{2}$ markkaa | Finnish, Swedish | Finland |
| 58,470,421 | Franc<br>$1 = 6$ francs | French | France |
| 1,190,159 | CFA franc<br>$1 = 600$ CFA francs | French | Gabon |
| 1,248,085 | Dalasi<br>$1 = 10$ dalasi | English | The Gambia |
| 5,174,642 | Lari<br>$1 = 1.2$ million laris | Georgian | Georgia |
| 84,068,216 | Mark<br>$1 = 1\frac{4}{5}$ marks | German | Germany |
| 18,100,703 | Cedi<br>$1 = 2,300$ cedis | English | Ghana |
| 58,610,182 | Pound<br>$1 = \frac{3}{5}$ pound | English | Great Britain (United Kingdom) |
| 10,583,126 | Drachma<br>$1 = 280$ drachmas | Greek | Greece |
| 95,537 | East Caribbean dollar<br>$1 = 2\frac{2}{3}$ EC dollars | English | Grenada |
| 11,558,407 | Quetzal<br>$1 = 6$ quetzals | Spanish | Guatemala |
| 7,405,375 | Franc<br>$1 = 1,100$ francs | French | Guinea |
| 1,178,584 | CFA franc<br>$1 = 600$ CFA franco | Portuguese | Guinea-Bissau |
| 706,116 | Guyana dollar<br>$1 = 140$ Guyana dollars | English | Guyana |
| 6,611,407 | Gourde<br>$1 = 17$ gourdes | Haitian Creole, French | Haiti |

# COUNTRIES

| COUNTRY | CAPITAL | LOCATION OF COUNTRY | AREA |
|---|---|---|---|
| Honduras | Tegucigalpa | Central America, between Guatemala and Nicaragua | 43,433 sq. mi. (112,491 sq. km.) |
| Hungary | Budapest | Central Europe, north of Yugoslavia | 35,919 sq. mi. (93,030 sq. km.) |
| Iceland | Reykjavik | Island off the coast of Europe, in the North Atlantic Ocean, near Greenland | 39,699 sq. mi. (102,819 sq. km.) |
| India | New Delhi | Southern Asia, on a large peninsula on the Indian Ocean | 1,222,243 sq. mi. (3,165,609 sq. km.) |
| Indonesia | Jakarta | Islands south of Southeast Asia, along the equator | 741,052 sq. mi. (1,919,325 sq. km.) |
| Iran | Tehran | Southern Asia, between Iraq and Pakistan | 632,457 sq. mi. (1,638,064 sq. km.) |
| Iraq | Baghdad | In the Middle East, between Syria and Iran | 167,975 sq. mi. (435,055 sq. km.) |
| Ireland | Dublin | Off the coast of Europe, in the Atlantic Ocean, west of Great Britain | 27,137 sq. mi. (70,285 sq. km.) |
| Israel | Jerusalem | In the Middle East, between Jordan and the Mediterranean Sea | 7,876 sq. mi. (20,399 sq. km.) |
| Italy | Rome | Southern Europe, jutting out into the Mediterranean Sea | 116,336 sq. mi. (301,310 sq. km.) |
| Jamaica | Kingston | Island in the Caribbean Sea, south of Cuba | 4,244 sq. mi. (10,992 sq. km.) |
| Japan | Tokyo | Four big islands and many small ones, off the east coast of Asia | 145,850 sq. mi. (377,752 sq. km.) |
| Jordan | Amman | In the Middle East, south of Syria, east of Israel | 34,342 sq. mi. (88,946 sq. km.) |
| Kazakhstan | Astana | Central Asia, south of Russia | 1,049,200 sq. mi. (2,717,428 sq. km.) |
| Kenya | Nairobi | East Africa, on the Indian Ocean, south of Ethiopia | 224,961 sq. mi. (582,649 sq. km.) |
| Kiribati | Tarawa | Islands in the middle of the Pacific Ocean, near the equator | 313 sq. mi. (811 sq. km.) |
| Korea, North | Pyongyang | Eastern Asia, in the northern part of the Korean Peninsula; China is to the north | 47,399 sq. mi. (122,763 sq. km.) |
| Korea, South | Seoul | Eastern Asia, south of North Korea, on the Korean Peninsula | 38,375 sq. mi. (99,391 sq. km.) |
| Kuwait | Kuwait City | In the Middle East, on the northern end of the Persian Gulf | 6,880 sq. mi. (17,818 sq. km.) |
| Kyrgyzstan | Bishkek | Western Asia, between Kazakhstan and Tajikistan | 76,600 sq. mi. (198,500 sq. km.) |

| POPULATION | CURRENCY | LANGUAGE | COUNTRY |
|---|---|---|---|
| 5,751,384 | Lempira<br>$1 = 13 lempiras | Spanish | **Honduras** |
| 9,935,774 | Forint<br>$1 = 200 forints | Hungarian<br>(Magyar) | **Hungary** |
| 272,550 | Krona<br>$1 = 70 kronor | Icelandic | **Iceland** |
| 967,612,804 | Rupee<br>$1 = 40 rupees | Hindi,<br>English | **India** |
| 209,774,138 | Rupiah<br>$1 = 6,100 rupiah | Bahasa<br>Indonesian | **Indonesia** |
| 67,540,002 | Rial<br>$1 = 3,000 rials | Persian<br>(Farsi) | **Iran** |
| 22,219,289 | Dinar<br>$1 = 1,200 dinars | Arabic | **Iraq** |
| 3,555,500 | Pound<br>$1 = $\frac{2}{5}$ pound | English,<br>Gaelic | **Ireland** |
| 5,534,672 | New shekel<br>$1 = $3\frac{1}{2}$ new shekels | Hebrew,<br>Arabic | **Israel** |
| 57,534,088 | Lira<br>$1 = 1,800 lire | Italian | **Italy** |
| 2,615,582 | Jamaican dollar<br>$1 = 35 Jamaican dollars | English | **Jamaica** |
| 125,716,637 | Yen<br>$1 = 130 yen | Japanese | **Japan** |
| 4,324,638 | Dinar<br>$1 = $\frac{2}{3}$ dinar | Arabic | **Jordan** |
| 16,898,572 | Tenge<br>$1 = 75 tenges | Kazakh | **Kazakhstan** |
| 28,803,085 | Shilling<br>$1 = 60 shillings | Swahili,<br>English | **Kenya** |
| 82,449 | Australian dollar<br>$1 = $1\frac{1}{2}$ Australian dollars | English | **Kiribati** |
| 24,317,004 | Won<br>$1 = $2\frac{1}{5}$ won | Korean | **Korea, North** |
| 45,948,811 | Won<br>$1 = 1,700 won | Korean | **Korea, South** |
| 2,076,805 | Dinar<br>$1 = $\frac{1}{3}$ dinar | Arabic | **Kuwait** |
| 4,540,185 | Som<br>$1 = 17 soms | Kyrgyz,<br>Russian | **Kyrgyzstan** |

| COUNTRY | CAPITAL | LOCATION OF COUNTRY | AREA |
|---|---|---|---|
| Laos | Vientiane | Southeast Asia, between Vietnam and Thailand | 91,429 sq. mi. (236,800 sq. km.) |
| Latvia | Riga | On the Baltic Sea, between Lithuania and Estonia | 24,946 sq. mi. (64,610 sq. km.) |
| Lebanon | Beirut | In the Middle East, between the Mediterranean Sea and Syria | 3,950 sq. mi. (10,230 sq. km.) |
| Lesotho | Maseru | Southern Africa, surrounded by the nation of South Africa | 11,720 sq. mi. (30,355 sq. km.) |
| Liberia | Monrovia | Western Africa, on the Atlantic Ocean, southeast of Sierra Leone | 38,250 sq. mi. (99,068 sq. km.) |
| Libya | Tripoli | North Africa, on the Mediterranean Sea, to the west of Egypt | 678,400 sq. mi. (1,757,056 sq. km.) |
| Liechtenstein | Vaduz | Southern Europe, in the Alps between Austria and Switzerland | 62 sq. mi. (161 sq. km.) |
| Lithuania | Vilnius | Northern Europe, on the Baltic Sea, north of Poland | 25,213 sq. mi. (65,302 sq. km.) |
| Luxembourg | Luxembourg | Western Europe, between France and Germany | 999 sq. mi. (2,587 sq. km.) |
| Macedonia | Skopje | Southern Europe, north of Greece | 9,928 sq. mi. (25,714 sq. km.) |
| Madagascar | Antananarivo | Island in the Indian Ocean, off the east coast of Africa | 226,658 sq. mi. (587,044 sq. km.) |
| Malawi | Lilongwe | Southern Africa, south of Tanzania and east of Zambia | 45,747 sq. mi. (118,485 sq. km.) |
| Malaysia | Kuala Lumpur | Southeast Asia, on the island of Borneo | 127,584 sq. mi. (330,443 sq. km.) |
| Maldives | Male | Islands in the Indian Ocean, south of India | 115 sq. mi. (298 sq. km.) |
| Mali | Bamako | West Africa, between Algeria and Mauritania | 482,077 sq. mi. (1,248,579 sq. km.) |
| Malta | Valletta | Island in the Mediterranean Sea, south of Italy | 122 sq. mi. (316 sq. km.) |
| Marshall Islands | Majuro | Chain of small islands in the middle of the Pacific Ocean | 70 sq. mi. (181 sq. km.) |
| Mauritania | Nouakchott | West Africa, on the Atlantic Ocean, north of Senegal | 398,000 sq. mi. (1,030,700 sq. km.) |
| Mauritius | Port Louis | Islands in the Indian Ocean, east of Madagascar | 788 sq. mi. (2,040 sq. km.) |
| Mexico | Mexico City | North America, south of the United States | 756,066 sq. mi. (1,958,211 sq. km.) |
| Micronesia | Palikir | Islands in the Western Pacific Ocean | 271 sq. mi. (702 sq. km.) |

| POPULATION | CURRENCY | LANGUAGE | COUNTRY |
|---:|---|---|---|
| 5,116,959 | Kip<br>$1 = 1,300$ kip | Lao | **Laos** |
| 2,437,649 | Lat<br>$1 = \frac{3}{5}$ lat | Latvian | **Latvia** |
| 3,858,736 | Pound<br>$1 = 1,500$ pounds | Arabic,<br>French | **Lebanon** |
| 2,007,814 | Maloti<br>$1 = 4\frac{5}{6}$ maloti | English,<br>Sesotho | **Lesotho** |
| 2,602,068 | Liberian dollar<br>Same as U.S. dollar | English | **Liberia** |
| 5,648,359 | Dinar<br>$1 = \frac{2}{5}$ dinar | Arabic | **Libya** |
| 31,461 | Swiss franc<br>$1 = 1\frac{1}{2}$ Swiss francs | German | **Liechtenstein** |
| 3,635,932 | Litas<br>$1 = 4$ litas | Lithuanian | **Lithuania** |
| 422,474 | Franc<br>$1 = 35$ francs | French,<br>German | **Luxembourg** |
| 2,113,866 | Denar<br>$1 = 55$ denar | Macedonian | **Macedonia** |
| 14,061,627 | Franc<br>$1 = 5,000$ francs | Malagasy,<br>French | **Madagascar** |
| 9,609,081 | Kwacha<br>$1 = 20$ kwacha | English,<br>Chichewa | **Malawi** |
| 20,376,235 | Ringgit<br>$1 = 4$ ringgits | Malay | **Malaysia** |
| 280,391 | Rufiyaa<br>$1 = 12$ rufiyaas | Divehi | **Maldives** |
| 9,945,383 | CFA franc<br>$1 = 600$ CFA francs | French | **Mali** |
| 379,365 | Maltese lira<br>$1 = 2\frac{1}{2}$ Maltese lira | Maltese,<br>English | **Malta** |
| 60,652 | U.S. dollar | English | **Marshall Islands** |
| 2,411,317 | Ouguiya<br>$1 = 170$ ouguiya | Wolof,<br>Hasaniya Arabic | **Mauritania** |
| 1,154,272 | Mauritian rupee<br>$1 = 20$ Mauritian rupees | English | **Mauritius** |
| 97,563,374 | New peso<br>$1 = 8$ new pesos | Spanish | **Mexico** |
| 127,616 | U.S. dollar | English | **Micronesia** |

| COUNTRY | CAPITAL | LOCATION OF COUNTRY | AREA |
|---|---|---|---|
| Moldova | Chisinau | Eastern Europe, between Ukraine and Romania | 13,000 sq. mi. (33,700 sq. km.) |
| Monaco | Monaco | Europe, on the Mediterranean Sea, surrounded by France | 3/4 of a sq. mi. (2 sq. km.) |
| Mongolia | Ulaanbaatar | Central Asia between Russia and China | 604,800 sq. mi. (1,566,500 sq. km.) |
| Morocco | Rabat | Northwest Africa, on the Atlantic Ocean and Mediterranean Sea | 177,117 sq. mi. (458,733 sq. km.) |
| Mozambique | Maputo | Southeastern Africa, on the Indian Ocean | 313,661 sq. mi. (812,382 sq. km.) |
| Myanmar (formerly Burma) | Yangôn (Rangoon) | Southern Asia, to the east of India and Bangladesh | 261,228 sq. mi. (676,581 sq. km.) |
| Namibia | Windhoek | Southwestern Africa, on the Atlantic Ocean, west of Botswana | 318,580 sq. mi. (825,122 sq. km.) |
| Nauru | Yaren | Island in the western Pacific Ocean, just below the equator | 8 sq. mi. (21 sq. km.) |
| Nepal | Kathmandu | Asia, in the Himalaya Mountains, between China and India | 56,827 sq. mi. (147,182 sq. km.) |
| Netherlands | Amsterdam | Northern Europe, on the North Sea, to the west of Germany | 16,033 sq. mi. (41,525 sq. km.) |
| New Zealand | Wellington | Islands in the Pacific Ocean east of Australia | 104,454 sq. mi. (270,536 sq. km.) |
| Nicaragua | Managua | Central America, between Honduras and Costa Rica | 50,838 sq. mi. (131,670 sq. km.) |
| Niger | Niamey | North Africa, south of Algeria and Libya | 496,900 sq. mi. (1,286,971 sq. km.) |
| Nigeria | Abuja | West Africa, on the southern coast between Benin and Cameroon | 356,669 sq. mi. (923,773 sq. km.) |
| Norway | Oslo | Northern Europe, on the Scandinavian Peninsula, west of Sweden | 125,050 sq. mi. (323,880 sq. km.) |
| Oman | Muscat | On the Arabian Peninsula, southeast of Saudi Arabia | 118,150 sq. mi. (306,000 sq. km.) |
| Pakistan | Islamabad | South Asia, between Iran and India | 339,697 sq. mi. (879,815 sq. km.) |
| Palau | Koror | Islands in North Pacific Ocean, southeast of Philippines | 188 sq. mi. (487 sq. km.) |
| Panama | Panama City | Central America, between Costa Rica and Colombia | 29,157 sq. mi. (75,517 sq. km.) |
| Papua New Guinea | Port Moresby | Part of the island of New Guinea, north of Australia | 178,704 sq. mi. (462,843 sq. km.) |

| POPULATION | CURRENCY | LANGUAGE | COUNTRY |
|---|---|---|---|
| 4,475,232 | Leu<br>$1 = 4\frac{1}{2}$ lei | Moldovan | **Moldova** |
| 31,892 | French franc<br>$1 = 6$ francs | French | **Monaco** |
| 2,538,211 | Tugrik<br>$1 = 800$ tugriks | Khalkha<br>Mongolian | **Mongolia** |
| 30,391,423 | Dirham<br>$1 = 9\frac{3}{4}$ dirhams | Arabic | **Morocco** |
| 18,165,476 | Metical<br>$1 = 11,500$ meticals | Portuguese | **Mozambique** |
| 46,821,943 | Kyat<br>$1 = 6\frac{1}{2}$ kyats | Burmese | **Myanmar**<br>(*formerly* **Burma**) |
| 1,727,183 | Rand<br>$1 = 4\frac{4}{5}$ rand | Afrikaans,<br>English | **Namibia** |
| 10,390 | Australian dollar<br>$1 = 1\frac{1}{2}$ Australian dollars | Nauruan | **Nauru** |
| 22,641,061 | Rupee<br>$1 = 60$ rupees | Nepali | **Nepal** |
| 15,653,091 | Guilder<br>$1 = 2$ guilders | Dutch | **Netherlands** |
| 3,587,275 | New Zealand dollar<br>$1 = 1\frac{3}{4}$ NZ dollars | English,<br>Maori | **New Zealand** |
| 4,386,399 | Gold cordoba<br>$1 = 10$ gold cordobas | Spanish | **Nicaragua** |
| 9,388,859 | CFA franc<br>$1 = 600$ CFA francs | French | **Niger** |
| 107,129,469 | Naira<br>$1 = 75$ nairas | English | **Nigeria** |
| 4,404,456 | Krone<br>$1 = 7\frac{2}{5}$ kroner | Norwegian | **Norway** |
| 2,264,590 | Rial Omani<br>$1 = \frac{2}{5}$ rial Omani | Arabic | **Oman** |
| 132,185,299 | Rupee<br>$1 = 45$ rupees | Urdu,<br>English | **Pakistan** |
| 17,240 | U.S. dollar | English,<br>Palauan | **Palau** |
| 2,693,417 | Balboa<br>Same value as U.S. dollar | Spanish | **Panama** |
| 4,496,221 | Kina<br>$1 = 1\frac{3}{4}$ kinas | English | **Papua New Guinea** |

| COUNTRY | CAPITAL | LOCATION OF COUNTRY | AREA |
|---------|---------|---------------------|------|
| Paraguay | Asunción | South America, between Argentina and Brazil | 157,048 sq. mi. (406,754 sq. km.) |
| Peru | Lima | South America, along the Pacific coast, north of Chile | 496,225 sq. mi. (1,285,223 sq. km.) |
| Philippines | Manila | Islands in the Pacific Ocean, off the coast of Southeast Asia | 115,860 sq. mi. (300,077 sq. km.) |
| Poland | Warsaw | Central Europe, on the Baltic Sea, east of Germany | 120,728 sq. mi. (312,686 sq. km.) |
| Portugal | Lisbon | Southern Europe, on the Iberian Peninsula, west of Spain | 35,574 sq. mi. (92,137 sq. km.) |
| Qatar | Doha | Arabian Peninsula, on the Persian Gulf | 4,412 sq. mi. (11,427 sq. km.) |
| Romania | Bucharest | Southern Europe, on the Black Sea, north of Bulgaria | 91,699 sq. mi. (237,500 sq. km.) |
| Russia | Moscow | Stretches from Eastern Europe across northern Asia to the Pacific Ocean | 6,592,800 sq. mi. (17,075,352 sq. km.) |
| Rwanda | Kigali | Central Africa, northwest of Tanzania | 10,169 sq. mi. (26,338 sq. km.) |
| Saint Kitts and Nevis | Basseterre | Islands in the Caribbean Sea, near Puerto Rico | 104 sq. mi. (269 sq. km.) |
| Saint Lucia | Castries | Island on eastern edge of the Caribbean Sea | 238 sq. mi. (616 sq. km.) |
| Saint Vincent and the Grenadines | Kingstown | Islands on eastern edge of the Caribbean Sea, north of Grenada | 150 sq. mi. (388 sq. km.) |
| Samoa (formerly Western Samoa) | Apia | Islands in the South Pacific Ocean | 1,093 sq. mi. (2,831 sq. km.) |
| San Marino | San Marino | Southern Europe, surrounded by Italy | 24 sq. mi. (62 sq. km.) |
| São Tomé and Príncipe | São Tomé | In the Gulf of Guinea, off the coast of West Africa | 386 sq. mi. (1,001 sq. km.) |
| Saudi Arabia | Riyadh | Western Asia, occupying most of the Arabian Peninsula | 865,000 sq. mi. (2,240,350 sq. km.) |
| Senegal | Dakar | West Africa, on the Atlantic Ocean, south of Mauritania | 75,951 sq. mi. (196,713 sq. km.) |
| Seychelles | Victoria | Islands off the coast of Africa, in the Indian Ocean, north of Madagascar | 176 sq. mi. (456 sq. km.) |
| Sierra Leone | Freetown | West Africa, on the Atlantic Ocean, south of Guinea | 27,699 sq. mi. (71,740 sq. km.) |

| POPULATION | CURRENCY | LANGUAGE | COUNTRY |
|---|---|---|---|
| 5,651,634 | Guarani<br>$1 = 2,300 guarani | Spanish | **Paraguay** |
| 24,949,512 | New sol<br>$1 = 2\frac{3}{4}$ new soles | Spanish,<br>Quechua | **Peru** |
| 76,103,564 | Peso<br>$1 = 40 pesos | Pilipino,<br>English | **Philippines** |
| 38,700,291 | Zloty<br>$1 = 3\frac{1}{2}$ zlotys | Polish | **Poland** |
| 9,867,654 | Escudo<br>$1 = 180 escudos | Portuguese | **Portugal** |
| 665,485 | Riyal<br>$1 = 3\frac{2}{3}$ riyals | Arabic | **Qatar** |
| 21,399,114 | Leu<br>$1 = 8,000 lei | Romanian | **Romania** |
| 147,987,101 | Ruble<br>$1 = 6 rubles | Russian | **Russia** |
| 7,737,537 | Franc<br>$1 = 350 francs | French,<br>Kinyarwanda | **Rwanda** |
| 41,803 | East Caribbean dollar<br>$1 = 2\frac{2}{3}$ EC dollars | English | **Saint Kitts<br>and Nevis** |
| 159,639 | East Caribbean dollar<br>$1 = 2\frac{2}{3}$ EC dollars | English | **Saint Lucia** |
| 119,092 | East Caribbean dollar<br>$1 = 2\frac{2}{3}$ EC dollars | English | **Saint Vincent<br>and the<br>Grenadines** |
| 219,509 | Tala<br>$1 = 2\frac{3}{4}$ tala | English,<br>Samoan | **Samoa (*formerly*<br>Western Samoa)** |
| 24,714 | Italian lira<br>$1 = 1,800 lire | Italian | **San Marino** |
| 147,865 | Dobra<br>$1 = 2,400 dobras | Portuguese | **São Tomé<br>and Príncipe** |
| 20,087,965 | Riyal<br>$1 = 3\frac{3}{4}$ riyals | Arabic | **Saudi Arabia** |
| 9,403,546 | CFA franc<br>$1 = 600 CFA francs | French | **Senegal** |
| 78,142 | Rupee<br>$1 = 5 rupees | English,<br>French | **Seychelles** |
| 4,891,546 | Leone<br>$1 = 900 leones | English | **Sierra Leone** |

| COUNTRY | CAPITAL | LOCATION OF COUNTRY | AREA |
|---|---|---|---|
| Singapore | Singapore | Mostly on one island, off the tip of Southeast Asia | 247 sq. mi. (640 sq. km.) |
| Slovakia | Bratislava | Eastern Europe, between Poland and Hungary | 18,933 sq. mi. (49,036 sq. km.) |
| Slovenia | Ljubljana | Eastern Europe, between Austria and Croatia | 7,821 sq. mi. (20,256 sq. km.) |
| Solomon Islands | Honiara | Western Pacific Ocean | 10,954 sq. mi. (28,371 sq. km.) |
| Somalia | Mogadishu | East Africa, east of Ethiopia | 246,000 sq. mi. (637,000 sq. km.) |
| South Africa | Pretoria | At the southern tip of Africa | 470,689 sq. mi. (1,219,085 sq. km.) |
| Spain | Madrid | Europe, south of France, on the Iberian Peninsula | 194,898 sq. mi. (504,786 sq. km.) |
| Sri Lanka | Colombo | Island in the Indian Ocean, southeast of India | 25,332 sq. mi. (65,610 sq. km.) |
| Sudan | Khartoum | North Africa, south of Egypt, on the Red Sea | 966,757 sq. mi. (2,503,901 sq. km.) |
| Suriname | Paramaribo | South America, on the northern shore, east of Guyana | 63,251 sq. mi. (163,820 sq. km.) |
| Swaziland | Mbabane | Southern Africa, almost surrounded by South Africa | 6,704 sq. mi. (17,363 sq. km.) |
| Sweden | Stockholm | Northern Europe, on the Scandinavian Peninsula, east of Norway | 173,732 sq. mi. (449,966 sq. km.) |
| Switzerland | Bern | Central Europe, in the Alps, north of Italy | 15,940 sq. mi. (41,285 sq. km.) |
| Syria | Damascus | In the Middle East, on the Mediterranean Sea, north of Jordan and Iraq | 71,498 sq. mi. (185,180 sq. km.) |
| Taiwan | Taipei | Island off southeast coast of China | 13,969 sq. mi. (36,180 sq. km.) |
| Tajikistan | Dushanbe | Asia, west of China, south of Kyrgyzstan | 55,300 sq. mi. (143,100 sq. km.) |
| Tanzania | Dar-es-Salaam | East Africa, on the Indian Ocean, south of Kenya | 364,017 sq. mi. (942,804 sq. km.) |
| Thailand | Bangkok | Southeast Asia, west of Laos | 198,115 sq. mi. (513,118 sq. km.) |
| Togo | Lomé | West Africa, between Ghana and Benin | 21,925 sq. mi. (56,786 sq. km.) |
| Tonga | Nuku'alofa | Islands in the South Pacific Ocean | 290 sq. mi. (751 sq. km.) |

| POPULATION | CURRENCY | LANGUAGE | COUNTRY |
|---|---|---|---|
| 3,461,929 | Singapore dollar<br>$1 = $1\frac{2}{3}$ Singapore dollars | Chinese, Malay,<br>Tamil, English | Singapore |
| 5,393,016 | Koruna<br>$1 = 35 koruny | Slovak | Slovakia |
| 1,945,998 | Tolar<br>$1 = 170 tolars | Slovenian | Slovenia |
| 426,855 | Solomon Islands dollar<br>$1 = $4\frac{3}{4}$ Solomon dollars | English | Solomon Islands |
| 9,940,232 | Shilling<br>$1 = 2,600 shillings | Somali | Somalia |
| 42,327,458 | Rand<br>$1 = $4\frac{4}{5}$ rand | Afrikaans, English,<br>Ndebele, Sotho | South Africa |
| 39,244,195 | Peseta<br>$1 = 150 pesetas | Castilian<br>Spanish | Spain |
| 18,762,075 | Rupee<br>$1 = 60 rupees | Sinhala,<br>Tamil | Sri Lanka |
| 32,594,128 | Pound<br>$1 = 1,400 pounds | Arabic | Sudan |
| 443,446 | Guilder<br>$1 = 400 guilders | Dutch | Suriname |
| 1,031,600 | Lilangeni<br>$1 = $4\frac{5}{6}$ emalangeni | English,<br>siSwati | Swaziland |
| 8,946,193 | Krona<br>$1 = 8 kronur | Swedish | Sweden |
| 7,248,984 | Franc<br>$1 = $1\frac{1}{2}$ francs | German,<br>French, Italian | Switzerland |
| 16,137,899 | Pound<br>$1 = 40 pounds | Arabic | Syria |
| 21,655,515 | New Taiwan dollar<br>$1 = 30 new Taiwan dollars | Mandarin<br>Chinese | Taiwan |
| 6,013,855 | Tajik ruble<br>$1 = 800 Tajik rubles | Tajik | Tajikistan |
| 29,460,753 | Shilling<br>$1 = 600 shillings | Swahili,<br>English | Tanzania |
| 59,450,818 | Baht<br>$1 = 50 bahts | Thai | Thailand |
| 4,735,610 | CFA franc<br>$1 = 600 CFA francs | French | Togo |
| 107,335 | Pa'anga<br>$1 = $1\frac{2}{5}$ pa'angas | Tongan,<br>English | Tonga |

| COUNTRY | CAPITAL | LOCATION OF COUNTRY | AREA |
|---|---|---|---|
| Trinidad and Tobago | Port-of-Spain | Islands off the north coast of South America | 1,980 sq. mi. (5,128 sq. km.) |
| Tunisia | Tunis | North Africa, on the Mediterranean, between Algeria and Libya | 63,378 sq. mi. (164,149 sq. km.) |
| Turkey | Ankara | On the southern shore of the Black Sea, partly in Europe and partly in Asia | 300,948 sq. mi. (779,455 sq. km.) |
| Turkmenistan | Ashgabat | Western Asia, north of Afghanistan and Iran | 188,500 sq. mi. (488,100 sq. km.) |
| Tuvalu | Funafuti | Chain of islands in the South Pacific Ocean | 9 sq. mi. (24 sq. km.) |
| Uganda | Kampala | East Africa, south of Sudan | 93,070 sq. mi. (241,040 sq. km.) |
| Ukraine | Kiev | Eastern Europe, south of Belarus and Russia | 233,100 sq. mi. (603,700 sq. km.) |
| United Arab Emirates | Abu Dhabi | Arabian Peninsula, on the Persian Gulf | 32,280 sq. mi. (83,605 sq. km.) |
| United States | Washington, D.C. | 48 (of 50) states in North America, between Canada and Mexico | 3,536,278 sq. mi. (9,158,160 sq. km.) |
| Uruguay | Montevideo | South America, on the Atlantic Ocean, south of Brazil | 68,037 sq. mi. (176,215 sq. km.) |
| Uzbekistan | Tashkent | Central Asia, south of Kazakhstan | 172,700 sq. mi. (447,293 sq. km.) |
| Vanuatu | Port-Vila | Islands in the South Pacific Ocean | 4,707 sq. mi. (12,191 sq. km.) |
| Vatican City | | Surrounded by the city of Rome, Italy | 1/5 sq. mi. (1/2 sq. km.) |
| Venezuela | Caracas | On the northern coast of South America, east of Colombia | 352,144 sq. mi. (912,053 sq. km.) |
| Vietnam | Hanoi | Southeast Asia, south of China, on the eastern coast | 127,816 sq. mi. (331,043 sq. km.) |
| Yemen | Sanaa | Asia, on the southern coast of the Arabian Peninsula | 205,356 sq. mi. (531,872 sq. km.) |
| Yugoslavia | Belgrade | Southern Europe, on the Balkan Peninsula, west of Romania and Bulgaria | 39,449 sq. mi. (102,173 sq. km.) |
| Zambia | Lusaka | Southern Africa, east of Angola | 290,586 sq. mi. (752,618 sq. km.) |
| Zimbabwe | Harare | Southern Africa, south of Zambia | 150,872 sq. mi. (390,758 sq. km.) |

| POPULATION | CURRENCY | LANGUAGE | COUNTRY |
|---|---|---|---|
| 1,273,141 | Trinidad and Tobago dollar $1 = 6\frac{1}{5}$ Trinidad dollars | English | Trinidad and Tobago |
| 9,183,097 | Dinar $1 = 1\frac{1}{10}$ dinar | Arabic | Tunisia |
| 63,528,225 | Turkish lira $1 = 200,000$ Turkish liras | Turkish | Turkey |
| 4,225,351 | Manat $1 = 5,200$ manats | Turkmen | Turkmenistan |
| 10,297 | Tuvaluan dollar $1= 1\frac{1}{2}$ Tuvaluan dollars | Tuvaluan, English | Tuvalu |
| 20,604,874 | Shilling $1 = 1,100$ shillings | English | Uganda |
| 50,684,635 | Hryvna $1 = 2$ hryvna | Ukranian | Ukraine |
| 2,262,309 | Dirham $1 = 3\frac{2}{3}$ dirhams | Arabic | United Arab Emirates |
| 267,636,061 | U.S. dollar | English | United States |
| 3,261,707 | Peso $1 = 10$ pesos | Spanish | Uruguay |
| 23,860,452 | Sum $1 = 70$ sums | Uzbek | Uzbekistan |
| 181,358 | Vatu $1 = 120$ vatus | French, English, Bislama | Vanuatu |
| 840 | Vatican lira, Italian lira $1 = 1,800$ lire | Italian, Latin | Vatican City |
| 22,396,407 | Bolivar $1 = 500$ bolivares | Spanish | Venezuela |
| 75,123,880 | Dong $1 = 12,300$ dong | Vietnamese | Vietnam |
| 13,972,477 | Rial $1 = 120$ rials | Arabic | Yemen |
| 10,655,317 | New dinar $1 = 6$ new dinars | Serbo-Croatian | Yugoslavia |
| 9,349,975 | Kwacha $1 = 1,400$ kwacha | English | Zambia |
| 11,423,175 | Zimbabwe dollar $1 = 19$ Zimbabwe dollars | English | Zimbabwe |

# A QUICK VISIT to Some COUNTRIES of the WORLD

Suppose you got a free round-trip ticket to visit any spot in the whole world. Where would you like to go? Here are a few sights you might want to see.

## AUSTRALIA

In Australia is **Ayers Rock**, the biggest exposed rock in the world. Located in a remote desert, it is about $1\frac{1}{2}$ miles long and shines bright red when the sun sets. Australia's first people, the Aborigines, thought it was sacred.

## CANADA

Want to feel like you're in France without leaving North America? Visit **Quebec City**. You'll see a high, walled fortress (the Citadel), a hotel that looks like a French castle (Château Frontenac), and people who speak French. In **Toronto**, however, English is the main language. You can get a view of that fast-growing city by going to the top of the **CN Tower**, the tallest free-standing structure in the world.

## CANADA—UNITED STATES

On the border between Canada and the United States is the famous waterfall **Niagara Falls**. About 20,000 bathtubs of water pour over the falls every second. You can put on a slicker and look at the falls from an observation deck—or ride by in a boat.

## CHINA

Some 2,400 years ago, workers started putting up the **Great Wall**. It became the world's longest structure, with a main section 2,150 miles long. It was built to keep out invaders, but it didn't stop Genghis Khan from conquering much of China in the 1200s.

*Eiffel Tower* ▶

## DENMARK

One of the world's oldest and most charming amusement parks is Denmark's **Tivoli Gardens**. There you will find everything from a mouse circus to the world's oldest roller coaster.

## ECUADOR

The **Galapagos Islands**, which belong to Ecuador, are remote islands in the Pacific Ocean, about 600 miles off South America. They are filled with wildlife (such as cormorants and penguins, giant tortoises and lizards) and odd plants.

## EGYPT

In Egypt you can see the **Great Sphinx**, a stone figure with a man's head and a lion's body. Carved in the desert 4,500 years ago, it's still there, despite wear and tear. Nearby, at Giza, are the great **pyramids** of ancient Egyptian pharaohs.

## FRANCE

A high point of a trip to France would be the **Eiffel Tower**. You get to the top of this open, cast-iron tower in four elevators, one after another. Then you can look down 1,000 feet on the beautiful city of Paris below.

## GERMANY

Though it was built in the 1800s, the mad King Ludwig II planned **Neuschwanstein Castle** to look just like a fairy-tale castle from the Middle Ages, complete with turrets and drawbridges.

## GREAT BRITAIN

The regular London home of the queen of England is **Buckingham Palace**. When she's there a royal flag is flying. Outside you can see the Changing of the Guard. Another attraction is the **Tower of London**, where many famous people were jailed, tortured, and killed. The crown jewels are shown there.

## GREECE

On the **Acropolis**, you will find the ruins of the Parthenon and other public buildings from ancient Athens. The remains of the buildings, some partly rebuilt, stand high on a hill overlooking the city.

## INDIA

One of the world's biggest and richest tombs is the **Taj Mahal**, which took about 20,000 workers to build. A ruler of India had the Taj Mahal built for his wife after her death in 1631.

## IRELAND

If you kiss the **Blarney Stone**, which is in the tower of Blarney Castle, legends say you'll be able to throw words around and get people to agree with you—even if what you say is nonsense.

## ISRAEL

In Israel you can visit **Jerusalem**—a Holy City for three faiths. You can see the **Dome of the Rock**, built over the rock where Muhammad, founder of Islam, is said to have risen to heaven. You can stop at the **Western Wall**, where Jews pray; it is said to contain stones from Solomon's Temple. And you can see the **Church of the Holy Sepulcher**, built where it is said that Jesus was crucified and buried.

## ITALY

The **Leaning Tower of Pisa** is proof that kids aren't the only ones who make mistakes. Long before it was finished, the bell tower began sinking into the soft ground and leaning to one side. Every year, it leans $\frac{1}{20}$ of an inch more.

▲ *The Taj Mahal in India*

## KENYA

Here and in other countries of East Africa, you can visit **National Parks**. You can go on safaris to see lions, zebras, giraffes, elephants, and other animals in their natural home.

## MEXICO

On the Yucatán peninsula, you can visit remains of the city of **Chichén Itzá**, where the Mayan people settled in the sixth century. Abandoned before the Spanish came, it's now partly rebuilt. You can see stone pyramids and temples and a Mayan ballfield.

## RUSSIA

A famous place to visit here is the **Kremlin**, a walled fortress in Moscow, with old churches, palaces, and towers with onion-shaped gold domes, dating back to the Middle Ages. Today the Kremlin is the headquarters for the Russian government.

## UNITED STATES

**Yellowstone National Park** was the world's first national park and is one of the best. (See page 280 for more details.) There are many other places to visit in Washington, D.C., and the 50 states (see FACTS ABOUT THE STATES in the UNITED STATES section for information).

# COUNTRY PUZZLE

## FIND THE HIDDEN COUNTRIES

The names of the countries listed below are hidden in this puzzle and can be found on pages 42 to 61. The words go up, down, across, backwards, and diagonally. Some letters are used in more than one word. The leftover letters are in **heavy black type**. Can you use these leftover letters to spell another country? (Answers are on page 302.)

The leftover letters spell the name of the Asian home of the Great Wall.

— — — — —

| | | | | | | | | | |
|---|---|---|---|---|---|---|---|---|---|
| N | O | R | T | H | K | O | R | E | A |
| I | **C** | **H** | A | F | G | E | L | I | I |
| A | A | L | I | R | E | L | A | N | D |
| P | D | I | W | R | R | I | O | D | O |
| S | A | B | A | N | M | H | S | I | B |
| O | N | E | N | C | A | C | L | A | M |
| M | A | R | G | E | N | T | I | N | A |
| A | C | I | **I** | Y | Y | **N** | Z | N | C |
| L | U | A | L | A | P | **A** | A | A | U |
| I | U | L | A | V | U | T | R | R | B |
| A | T | H | E | G | A | M | B | I | A |

| | | | |
|---|---|---|---|
| ARGENTINA | EGYPT | IRELAND | SPAIN |
| BRAZIL | FRANCE | LAOS | SOMALIA |
| CAMBODIA | GERMANY | LIBERIA | TAIWAN |
| CANADA | INDIA | NORTH KOREA | THE GAMBIA |
| CHILE | IRAN | PALAU | TUVALU |
| CUBA | | | |

## MATCH THE SIGHT WITH ITS SITE

If you have trouble, visit pages 62-63. (Answers are on page 302.)

| | |
|---|---|
| 1. TIVOLI GARDENS | a. Egypt |
| 2. CN TOWER | b. Ireland |
| 3. YELLOWSTONE NATIONAL PARK | c. Germany |
| 4. GREAT SPHINX | d. Australia |
| 5. WESTERN WALL | e. United States |
| 6. GALAPAGOS ISLANDS | f. Greece |
| 7. NEUSCHWANSTEIN CASTLE | g. Canada |
| 8. ACROPOLIS | h. Israel |
| 9. BLARNEY STONE | i. Ecuador |
| 10. AYERS ROCK | j. Denmark |

# MAPS and FLAGS of the COUNTRIES of the WORLD

Maps showing the continents and countries of the world appear on pages 65 through 76. Flags of the countries appear on pages 77 through 80.

Maps of the United States appear on pages 241-256

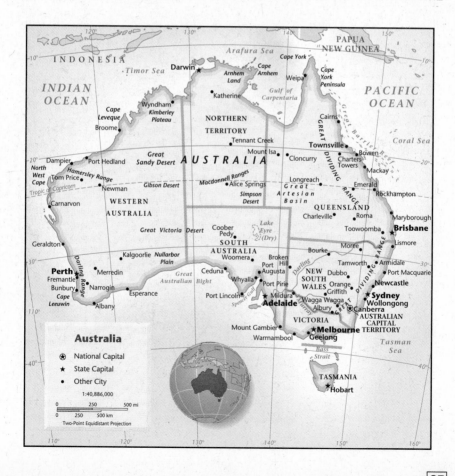

SWEDEN

NORWAY

GREAT BRITAIN

ICELAND

*Greenland Sea*

*Dennmark Strait*

Ammassalik

Cape Farewell

*Labrador Sea*

St. Anthony

NEWFOUNDLAND

Island of Newfoundland

St. John's

Corner Brook

St. Pierre & Miquelon Is. (Fr.)

Happy Valley Goose Bay

Anticosti

NFW P.E.I.

Nuuk (Godthaab)

GREENLAND (KALAALLIT NUNAAT) (Den.)

Hebron

Schefferville

Labrador City

QUÉBEC

Sept-Îles

CANADIAN SHIELD

Nord

Cape Morris Jessup

Knud Rasmussen Land

Qaanaaq (Thule)

*Baffin Bay*

Pangnirtung

Iqaluit

*Davis Strait*

Pond Inlet

*Hudson Strait*

Ungava Peninsula

Povungnituk

Chihougamau

Mooseonee

*James Bay*

North Pole

*Arctic Ocean*

Alert

Ellesmere I.

Grise Fiord

Arctic Bay

Baffin Island

Repulse Bay

Southampton I.

*Hudson Bay*

Belcher Is.

Churchill

York Factory

MANITOBA

Thompson

Flin Flon

L. Winnipeg

Spitsbergen

Queen Elizabeth Islands

Resolute

Victoria I.

Cambridge Bay

NORTHWEST TERRITORIES

CANADA

Yellowknife

Fort Smith

Uranium City

Lake Athabasca

SASK.

La Ronge

Prince Albert

Saskatoon

Winnipeg

Banks I.

Holman

Sachs Harbour

*Great Bear L.*

Déline

Ft. Simpson

*Great Slave L.*

Hay River

ALBERTA

Peace River

La Loche

Fort McMurray

Edmonton

*Beaufort Sea*

Kuglukuk

Fort McPherson

Inuvik

*Mackenzie*

Fort George

ROCKY

GREAT

Calgary

Point Barrow

Barrow

BROOKS RANGE

Fort Yukon

*Yukon*

Dawson

Mayo

YUKON

Carmacks

Watson Lake

BRITISH COLUMBIA

Prince George

Jasper

*Columbia*

*Fraser*

RUSSIA

Kotzebue

Fairbanks

ALASKA

ALASKA RANGE

Mt. McKinley (6,194 m) (20,320 ft.)

Valdez

Whitehorse

COAST MOUNTAINS

Williams Lake

Vancouver I.

Vancouver

Point Hope

Nome

Bethel

Kenai

Anchorage

Seward

Kodiak

Mt. Logan 5,951 m (19,524 ft.)

Yakutat

Skagway

Juneau

Sitka

Ketchikan

Prince Rupert

Queen Charlotte Is.

Kitimat

*Bering Strait*

*Gulf of Alaska*

*Bering Sea*

Arctic Circle

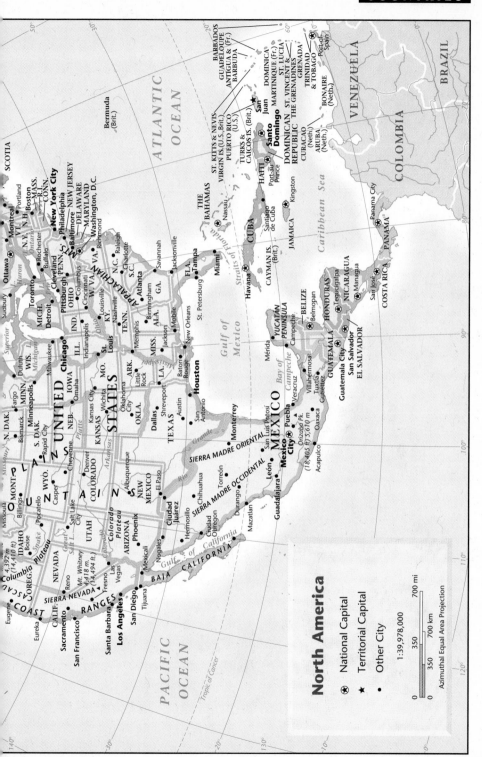

ATLANTIC OCEAN

PACIFIC OCEAN

Caribbean Sea

Gulf of Mexico

Bay of Campeche

Gulf of California

VENEZUELA

BRAZIL

COLOMBIA

**UNITED STATES**

**MEXICO**

CANADA

SCOTIA

Bermuda (Brit.)

THE BAHAMAS

CUBA

JAMAICA

HAITI

DOMINICAN REPUBLIC

CAYMAN IS. (Brit.)

BELIZE

GUATEMALA

EL SALVADOR

HONDURAS

NICARAGUA

COSTA RICA

PANAMA

ARUBA (Neth.)

CURAÇAO (Neth.)

BONAIRE (Neth.)

TURKS & CAICOS IS. (Brit.)

PUERTO RICO (U.S.)

VIRGIN IS. (U.S., Brit.)

ST. KITTS & NEVIS

ANTIGUA & BARBUDA

GUADELOUPE (Fr.)

DOMINICA

MARTINIQUE (Fr.)

ST. LUCIA

ST. VINCENT & THE GRENADINES

BARBADOS

GRENADA

TRINIDAD & TOBAGO

BAJA CALIFORNIA

SIERRA MADRE OCCIDENTAL

SIERRA MADRE ORIENTAL

YUCATÁN PENINSULA

APPALACHIAN MTS.

COAST RANGES

SIERRA NEVADA

CASCADE RANGE

Colorado Plateau

G R E A T P L A I N S

R O C K Y M O U N T A I N

Orizaba Pk. (18,405 ft) 5,610 m.

Mt. Whitney 4,418 m. (14,494 ft.)

4,392 m. (14,410 ft)

Great Salt Lake

Straits of Florida

Tropical of Cancer

**New York City**
**Philadelphia**
**Washington, D.C.**
**Baltimore**
Boston
Montreal
Ottawa
Toronto
Detroit
**Chicago**
Cleveland
Pittsburgh
Buffalo
Rochester
Portland
Montpelier
Columbus
Cincinnati
Louisville
Nashville
Memphis
Indianapolis
St. Louis
Kansas City
Omaha
Des Moines
Minneapolis
Milwaukee
Duluth
Fargo
Bismarck
Rapid City
Cheyenne
Denver
Wichita
Oklahoma City
Little Rock
Baton Rouge
New Orleans
Shreveport
**Dallas**
Austin
San Antonio
**Houston**
Jackson
Mobile
Birmingham
Atlanta
Charlotte
Raleigh
Richmond
Columbia
Savannah
Jacksonville
Tampa
Miami
St. Petersburg
Albuquerque
El Paso
**Phoenix**
Las Vegas
Salt Lake City
Boise
Pocatello
Missoula
Billings
Casper
Reno
Fresno
Sacramento
San Francisco
Eureka
Eugene
Santa Barbara
**Los Angeles**
San Diego
Tijuana
Mexicali
Nogales
Hermosillo
Ciudad Obregon
Chihuahua
**Ciudad Juárez**
Torreón
Durango
Mazatlán
Culiacán
León
**Guadalajara**
San Luis Potosí
**Monterrey**
Saltillo
Aguascalientes
**Mexico City**
**Puebla**
Veracruz
Oaxaca
Acapulco
Villahermosa
Tuxtla Gutiérrez
Mérida
Campeche
Belmopan
**Guatemala City**
**San Salvador**
Tegucigalpa
Managua
San José
Panama City
Nassau
Havana
Santiago de Cuba
Kingston
Port-au-Prince
**Santo Domingo**
San Juan
Port-of-Spain

N.Y.
VT.
N.H.
MASS.
R.I.
CONN.
NEW JERSEY
DELAWARE
MARYLAND
PENN.
W. VA.
VA.
N.C.
S.C.
GA.
FLA.
ALA.
MISS.
LA.
TENN.
KY.
OHIO
IND.
ILL.
MICH.
WIS.
MINN.
N. DAK.
S. DAK.
NEB.
IOWA
MO.
KANSAS
OKLA.
TEXAS
ARK.
COLORADO
WYO.
MONT.
IDAHO
UTAH
NEVADA
ARIZONA
NEW MEXICO
CALIF.
OREG.

Superior
Michigan
Huron
Ontario
Erie

Mississippi
Missouri
Platte
Arkansas
Rio Grande
Columbia
Colorado

## North America

1:39,978,000

⊕ National Capital

★ Territorial Capital

• Other City

| 0 | 350 | 700 mi |
| 0 | 350 | 700 km |

Azimuthal Equal Area Projection

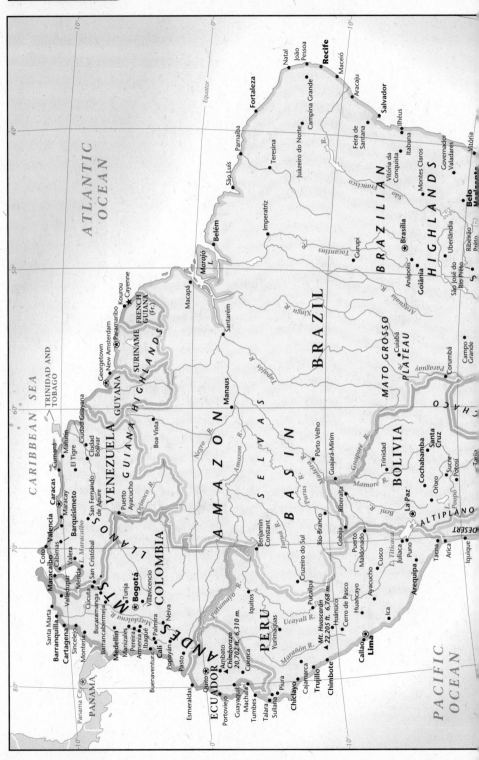

ATLANTIC OCEAN

CARIBBEAN SEA

PACIFIC OCEAN

Equator

TRINIDAD AND TOBAGO

Natal
João Pessoa
**Recife**
Maceió
Aracaju
**Salvador**
Ilhéus
Itabuna
**Fortaleza**
Campina Grande
Parnaíba
Feira de Santana
Vitória da Conquista
Governador Valadares
**Vitória**
Montes Claros
São Luís
Juàzeiro do Norte
Teresina
Uberlândia
**Belo Horizonte**
Imperatriz
**Belém**
Gurupi
✳ **Brasília**
Anápolis
São José do Rio Prêto
Ribeirão Prêto
Goiânia

Macapá
Marajó I.
Santarém

BRAZILIAN HIGHLANDS

Kourou
Cayenne
Paramaribo
New Amsterdam
Georgetown
FRENCH GUIANA (Fr.)
SURINAME
GUYANA

São Francisco R.
Tocantins R.
Xingu R.
Tapajós R.

BRAZIL

MATO GROSSO PLATEAU
Cuiabá
Campo Grande
Corumbá
Paraguay R.

CHACO

Manaus
Boa Vista
Negro R.
Amazon R.

AMAZON SELVAS BASIN

Araguaia R.
Madeira R.
Guaporé R.

Pôrto Velho
Guajará-Mirim
Trinidad
Santa Cruz
Cochabamba
Sucre
Potosí
Oruro
**La Paz**
BOLIVIA
Mamoré R.
Beni R.
Poopó

ALTIPLANO
DESERT

Ciudad Guayana
Cumaná
El Tigre
Ciudad Bolívar
Puerto Ayacucho
San Fernando de Apure
Maturín

GUIANA HIGHLANDS

VENEZUELA
LLANOS
Caracas
**Valencia**
Maracay
**Barquisimeto**
Orinoco R.

Santa Marta
**Barranquilla**
**Cartagena**
Sincelejo
Montería
Barrancabermeja
Coro
Cabimas
Valera
San Cristóbal
Mérida
L. Maracaibo
**Maracaibo**
Valledupar
Cúcuta
Bucaramanga
**Medellín**
Manizales
Pereira
Armenia
Ibagué
Tunja
**Bogotá**
Villavicencio
Neiva
**COLOMBIA**
Magdalena R.
Cali
Palmira
Popayán
Pasto
Buenaventura

ANDES MTS.

PANAMA
Panama City

Esmeraldas
**Quito** ✳
Portoviejo
Ambato
Chimborazo 20,702 ft. 6,310 m.
Guayaquil
Machala
Cuenca
**ECUADOR**
Tumbes
Talara
Sullana
Piura
**Chiclayo**
Cajamarca
**Trujillo**
**Chimbote**
Mt. Huascarán ▲ 22,205 ft. 6,768 m.
Iquitos
Putumayo R.
Marañón R.
Ucayali R.
Yurimaguas
Pucallpa
Cruzeiro do Sul
**PERU**
Huánuco
Cerro de Pasco
Huancayo
**Callao** ✳
**Lima**
Benjamin Constant
Juruá R.
Purus R.
Rio Branco
Cobija
Puerto Maldonado
Riberalta
Ica
Ayacucho
Cusco
L. Titicaca
Juliaca
Puno
**Arequipa**
Tacna
Arica
Iquique

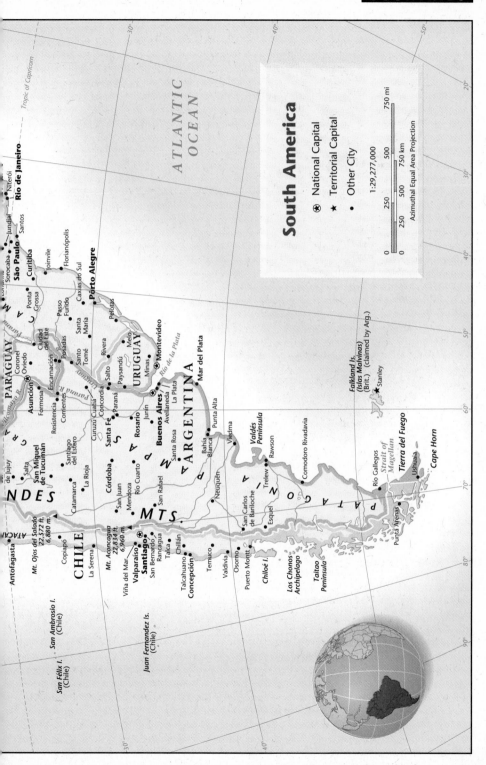

# South America

- ⊛ National Capital
- ★ Territorial Capital
- • Other City

1:29,277,000

| 0 | 250 | 500 | 750 mi |

| 0 | 250 | 500 | 750 km |

Azimuthal Equal Area Projection

ATLANTIC OCEAN

Tropic of Capricorn

Niterói
Rio de Janeiro
Santos
Jundiaí
Sorocaba
São Paulo
Curitiba
Joinvile
Florianópolis
Ponta Grossa
Passo Fundo
Caxias do Sul
Porto Alegre
Pelotas
Santa Maria

PARAGUAY
Asunción
Coronel Oviedo
Ciudad del Este
Encarnación
Formosa
Posadas
Santo Tomé
Resistencia
Corrientes
Curuzú Cuatiá
Concordia
Santa Fe
Paraná
Rosario
Junín
Avellaneda
Buenos Aires
La Plata
Santa Rosa

Paraná R.
Iguazú R.
Uruguay R.
Pilcomayo R.

Salto
Paysandú
Rivera
Melo
Minas
URUGUAY
Montevideo
Mar del Plata
Río de la Plata

Punta Alta
Bahía Blanca
Viedma
Valdés Peninsula
Rawson

ARGENTINA

Comodoro Rivadavia

Falkland Is.
(Islas Malvinas)
(Brit.) (claimed by Arg.)
★ Stanley

Neuquén
San Carlos de Bariloche
Esquel
Trelew

P A T A G O N I A

Río Gallegos
Strait of Magellan
Ushuaia
Tierra del Fuego
Cape Horn
Punta Arenas

de Jujuy
Salta
San Miguel de Tucumán
Santiago del Estero
Catamarca
La Rioja
Córdoba
San Juan
Mendoza
Río Cuarto
San Rafael

Antofagasta
ATACAMA
Mt. Ojos del Salado
22,572 ft.
6,880 m.
Copiapó
La Serena

CHILE

Mt. Aconcagua
22,834 ft.
6,960 m.
Viña del Mar
Valparaíso
Santiago
San Bernardo
Rancagua
Talca
Chillán
Talcahuano
Concepción
Temuco
Valdivia
Osorno
Puerto Montt
Chiloé I.
Los Chonos Archipelago
Taitao Peninsula

M T S.
A N D E S

San Félix I.
(Chile)
San Ambrosio I.
(Chile)

Juan Fernandez Is.
(Chile)

## Europe

⊛ National Capital

• Other City

1:22,107,000

| 0 | 250 | 500 mi |

| 0 | 250 | 500 km |

Azimuthal Equal Area Projection

ICELAND
Reykjavík • Akureyri

Arctic Circle

*Norwegian*    *Sea*

Faroe Is.
(Den.)

Shetland Is.
(Brit.)

Tromsø

Bodø

Trondheim

NORWAY

Sundsvall

SWEDEN

Bergen

Stavanger    Oslo ⊛

Uppsala
Stockholm ⊛
Linköping

Gotland

*Orkney
Is.*

*Hebrides*

Aberdeen

Glasgow • Edinburgh
Belfast

GREAT BRITAIN
Newcastle
(UNITED KINGDOM)

*Skagerrak*    *Kattegat*    Göteborg    Ölanc

Jutland    Århus
Copenhagen ⊛ Helsingborg
DENMARK    Odense • Malmö

Gdańsk
Szczecin

Dublin    Liverpool    Leeds
IRELAND    Manchester
Cork    Sheffield
Birmingham

*Irish
Sea*

*North
Sea*

Hamburg

Bremen
Hannover

Berlin ⊛

Poznań
Łó

Cardiff • Bristol

Amsterdam ⊛
NETHERLANDS

Elbe

Oder

Land's End    Portsmouth    London ⊛
*English Channel*    Rotterdam
Antwerp
Brussels    Essen
Channel Is.    Lille • ⊛    Cologne    GERMANY
(Brit.)    Le Havre    BELGIUM    Liège    Bonn
Brest    Rouen    LUXEMBOURG    Frankfurt
Paris ⊛    Luxembourg
Mannheim

Leipzig    Dresden

Wrocł

Prague ⊛    Katowice
CZECH REP.    Ostrava
Brno •    SLOVAK

Nantes •
*Loire*

Strasbourg    Stuttgart
Dijon    Munich •
Bern •    Linz    Vienna ⊛
FRANCE    Bratislava
*Rhine*    Zürich    AUSTRIA

*Danube*

*ATLANTIC
OCEAN*

*Bay
of
Biscay*

Bordeaux

Geneva •    SWITZERLAND    LIECHTENSTEIN
Lyon •    ALPS    Graz    Budap
HUNGA

Cabo Finisterre

Vigo •    Gijón •

Mt. Blanc
4807 m    Milan ⊛
(15,771 ft)    Turin • Verona    Venice
*Po*    Bologna    SLOVENIA
Ljubljana ⊛    Pécs
Zagreb ⊛

Porto •

Bilbao •

Toulouse •

Nice •
Marseille •
*Rhône*    Genoa    *DINARIC*    CROATIA
Toulon    MONACO    Florence    SAN    BOSNIA &
*Ligurian Sea*    *APENNINES*    MARINO    HERZEGOVI
Sarajevo •

Valladolid •
PORTUGAL    IBERIAN    Zaragoza •
Lisbon ⊛    *PYRENEES*
Pico de Aneto
3404 m    ANDORRA
(11,168 ft)
Badajoz •    PENINSULA
Córdoba •    SPAIN    Valéncia
Sevilla •
Granada •    Alicante •
Cádiz •    Málaga •
*Strait of
Gibraltar*    GIBRALTAR (Brit.)

Madrid ⊛

Barcelona

Corsica
(Fr.)

*Balearic Sea*
Majorca
Palma • Minorca
*Balearic Is.*
(Sp.)

Sardinia
(It.)

Elba

VATICAN    Rome ⊛
CITY
ITALY
Naples •    Salerno

*Adriatic*    Split •
Dubrovnik •
Podgori

Bari •

Co

*Tyrrhenian
Sea*    Cagliari •

Palermo •

*Ioni
Sea*

*Mediterranean*    *Sea*

Rabat ⊛
Casablanca •

Algiers ⊛

Tunis ⊛

Sicily    Catania • Mt. Etna
3323 m
(10,902 ft)
Valletta ⊛
MALTA

MOROCCO    A T L A S    M O U N T A I N S    ALGERIA    TUNISIA

*Sea*

Cabo de
São Vicente

Cabo Finisterre

40°    30°    20°    10°    0°    10°

60°

50°

40°

30°

10°

North Cape
Hammerfest
Nar'yan-Mar
Pechora
Barents Sea
*Ob*
*Irtysh*
na
Murmansk
KOLA PENINSULA
Apatity
*White Sea*
Ukhta
*Arctic Circle*
*Pechora*
U R A L
R U S S I A
Serov
Bereznіkі
Petropavl'
Luleå
Belomorsk
*Divina*
Syktyvkar
Yekaterinburg
FINLAND
Vaasa
*Lake Onega*
Kotlas
Perm'
*Kama*
M O U N T A I N S
Chelyabinsk
Qostanay
Petrozavodsk
Kirov
Izhevsk
Ufa
Magnitogorsk
Tampere
Lahti
*Lake Ladoga*
PLAIN
Vologda
Naberezhnyye Chelny
Helsinki
St. Petersburg
Cherepovets
Kazan
rku
nd
Tallinn
Novgorod
Yaroslavl'
Nizhniy Novgorod
50°
ESTONIA
Tartu
Ivanovo
Ul'yanovsk
Tol'yatti
Orenburg
Orsk
Pskov
EUROPEAN
Tver'
Samara
Aqtöbe
Riga
LATVIA
Moscow
Ryazan'
Penza
Oral
LITHUANIA
Daugavpils
Smolensk
Tula
Saransk
Volga
KAZAKHSTAN
Kaunas
USSIA
Vitsyebsk
Mahilyow
Tambov
Saratov
*Ural*
Aral Sea
iningrad
Vilnius
Minsk
Bryansk
Lipetsk
THERN
Hrodna
Homyel'
Kursk
Voronezh
Atyraü
UZBEKISTAN
Warsaw
Brest
BELARUS
Volgograd
*Don*
Astrakhan
Aqtaü
OLAND
Kiev
Kharkiv
Luhans'k
*Caspian*
ków
L'viv
UKRAINE
*Dnieper*
Donets'k
Rostov na Donu
*Dniester*
Dnipropetrovs'k
Zaporizhzhya
Makhachkala
TURKMENISTAN
ARPATHIAN
Chernivtsi
Kryvyy Rih
Mariupol'
*Sea*
Košice
MOLDOVA
Mykolayiv
*Sea of Azov*
Stavropol'
Groznyy
Debrecen
Iaşi
Chişinău
Odesa
Krasnodar
CAUCASUS
Krasnowodsk
40°
Timişoara
CRIMEA
Simferopol'
GEORGIA
vi Sad
ROMANIA
Ploieşti
Sevastopol'
T'bilisi
Baku
Belgrade
Bucharest
Constanţa
*Black Sea*
ARMENIA
AZERBAIJAN
*Danube*
Varna
Yerevan
GOSLAVIA
BULGARIA
Burgas
Trabzon
Sofia
Skopje
Plovdiv
Tabriz
ACEDONIA
ane
ANIA
Istanbul
Tehran
ALKAN
INSULA
Lárisa
Ankara
TURKEY
IRAN
GREECE
Izmir
ELOPONNESUS
Pátrai
Athens
Adana
IRAQ
Cyclades
Rhodes
Nicosia
SYRIA
*Euphrates*
Baghdad
*Sea of Crete*
Crete
Iráklion
CYPRUS
LEBANON
Beirut
Damascus
*Persian Gulf*

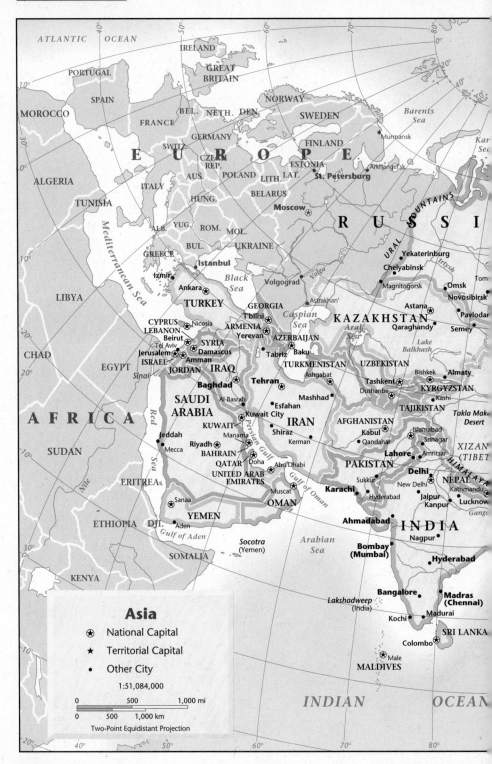

ATLANTIC OCEAN

IRELAND

PORTUGAL

GREAT
BRITAIN

SPAIN

MOROCCO

FRANCE

BEL. NETH. DEN.

NORWAY

SWEDEN

Barents
Sea

Murmansk

GERMANY

FINLAND

ALGERIA

SWITZ.

ITALY

CZE.
REP.

POLAND

AUS.

HUNG.

E    U    R    O    P    E

Arkhangel'sk

ESTONIA

St. Petersburg

LAT.

LITH.

TUNISIA

ALB.

YUG.

ROM.

MOL.

BELARUS

Moscow

R    U    S    S    I

BUL.

UKRAINE

GREECE

Mediterranean Sea

Volgograd

Volga

URAL MOUNTAINS

Yekaterinburg

LIBYA

Izmir

Istanbul

Black
Sea

Chelyabinsk

Irtysh

Tom

Magnitogorsk

Omsk

Ankara

TURKEY

GEORGIA

Astrakhan'

Caspian
Sea

KAZAKHSTAN

Novosibirsk

Astana

Pavlodar

CHAD

CYPRUS

Nicosia

T'bilisi

ARMENIA

Aral
Sea

Qaraghandy

Semey

LEBANON

Beirut

Tel Aviv

SYRIA

Yerevan

AZERBAIJAN

Baku

Lake
Balkhash

EGYPT

Jerusalem

Damascus

Tabriz

TURKMENISTAN

UZBEKISTAN

Bishkek

Almaty

ISRAEL

Amman

JORDAN

IRAQ

Ashgabat

Tashkent

KYRGYZSTAN

AFRICA

Baghdad

Tehran

Dushanbe

Kashi

SAUDI
ARABIA

Al-Basrah

Mashhad

TAJIKISTAN

Takla Mak.
Desert

Sinai

Esfahan

KUWAIT

Kuwait City

IRAN

AFGHANISTAN

Islamabad

XIZAN
(TIBE

SUDAN

Manama

Shiraz

Kabul

Srinagar

Jeddah

Riyadh

BAHRAIN

Kerman

Qandahar

Amritsar

HIMALAYA

Mecca

QATAR

Doha

PAKISTAN

Lahore

Delhi

Red
Sea

UNITED ARAB
EMIRATES

Abu Dhabi

Sukkur

New Delhi

NEPAL

Nile

ERITREA

Muscat

Gulf of Oman

Karachi

Hyderabad

Jaipur

Kathmandu

Lucknow

Kanpur

Ganges

Sanaa

OMAN

Ahmadabad

INDIA

ETHIOPIA

DJI.

Aden

YEMEN

Gulf of Aden

Arabian
Sea

Nagpur

SOMALIA

Socotra
(Yemen)

Bombay
(Mumbai)

Hyderabad

KENYA

Lakshadweep
(India)

Bangalore

Madras
(Chennai)

Kochi

Madurai

Colombo

SRI LANKA

## Asia

⊛ National Capital

★ Territorial Capital

• Other City

1:51,084,000

0        500        1,000 mi

0    500    1,000 km

Two-Point Equidistant Projection

Male

MALDIVES

INDIAN    OCEAN

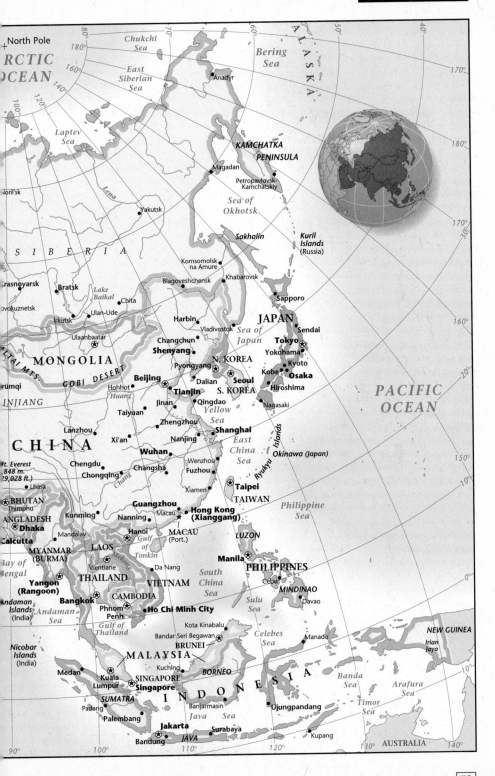

North Pole

ARCTIC
OCEAN

*Chukchi
Sea*

ALASKA

*Bering
Sea*

*East
Siberian
Sea*

Anadyr

*Laptev
Sea*

Noril'sk

*Lena*

*KAMCHATKA
PENINSULA*

Magadan

Petropavlovsk-
Kamchatskiy

Yakutsk

*Sea of
Okhotsk*

*Sakhalin*

*Kuril
Islands
(Russia)*

S I B E R I A

Krasnoyarsk

**Bratsk**

*Lake
Baikal*

Chita

Komsomolsk
na Amure

Khabarovsk

Blagoveshchensk

ovokuznetsk

Irkutsk

Ulan-Ude

Harbin

Vladivostok

Sapporo

*Sea of
Japan*

**JAPAN**

Sendai

Ulaanbaatar

Changchun

**Shenyang**

Pyongyang

**N. KOREA**

**Tokyo**

Yokohama

rümqi

**MONGOLIA**

*GOBI DESERT*

Hohhot

**Beijing**

Dalian

**Seoul**

Kyoto

Kobe

**Osaka**

INJIANG

TAI MTS.

**Tianjin**

**S. KOREA**

Hiroshima

Jinan

Qingdao

Nagasaki

**Huang**

Taiyuan

*Yellow
Sea*

**Lanzhou**

Xi'an

Zhengzhou

Nanjing

**Shanghai**

*East
China
Sea*

C H I N A

Mt. Everest
.848 m.
29,028 ft.)

Chengdu

Chongqing

*Chang*

Changsha

**Wuhan**

Wenzhou

Fuzhou

*Ryukyu Islands*

Okinawa (Japan)

**PACIFIC
OCEAN**

Lhasa

Xiamen

**Taipei**

**BHUTAN**
Thimphu

**Guangzhou**

Macau

**Hong Kong
(Xianggang)**

TAIWAN

*Philippine
Sea*

ANGLADESH

**Dhaka**

Kunming

Nanning

★

**MACAU**
(Port.)

alcutta

Mandalay

Hanoi

*Gulf
of
Tonkin*

*LUZON*

*Bay of
engal*

**MYANMAR
(BURMA)**

*Mekong*

**LAOS**

Da Nang

**Manila**

**PHILIPPINES**

Vientiane

**THAILAND**

**VIETNAM**

*South
China
Sea*

Cebu

*MINDINAO*

**Yangon
(Rangoon)**

**Bangkok**

**CAMBODIA**

*Sulu
Sea*

Davao

ndaman
Islands
(India)

*Andaman
Sea*

Phnom
Penh

**Ho Chi Minh City**

Kota Kinabalu

*Celebes
Sea*

Manado

*NEW GUINEA*

*Gulf of
Thailand*

Bandar Seri Begawan

*Irian
Jaya*

*Nicobar
Islands
(India)*

Medan

Kuching

**BRUNEI**

*BORNEO*

**MALAYSIA**

Kuala
Lumpur

**SINGAPORE**

**Singapore**

*Banda
Sea*

*Arafura
Sea*

*SUMATRA*

I N D O N E S I A

*Timor
Sea*

Padang

Banjarmasin

Ujungpandang

Palembang

*Java
Sea*

**Jakarta**

Surabaya

Kupang

**AUSTRALIA**

Bandung

*JAVA*

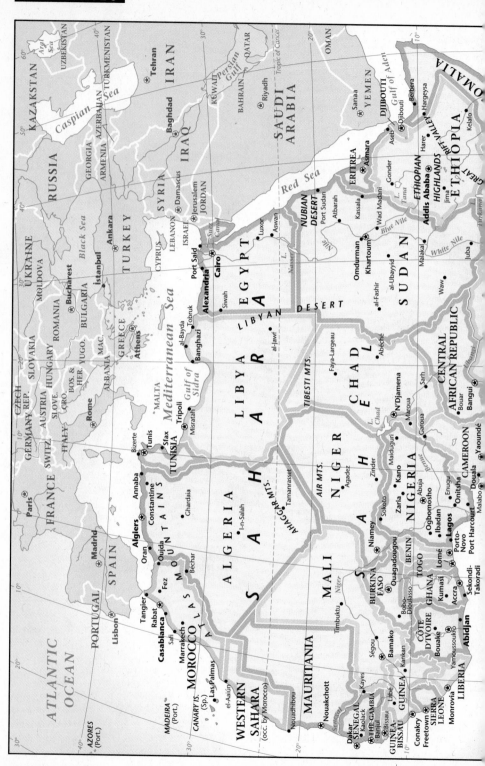

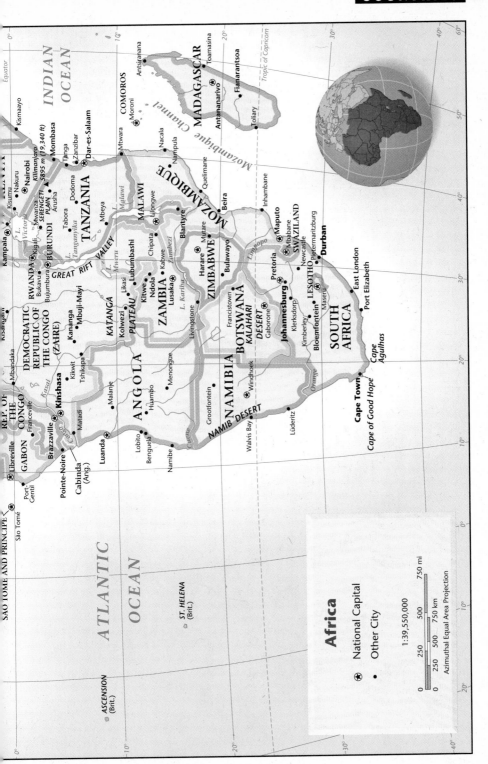

INDIAN OCEAN

Equator

Kismaayo

ATLANTIC OCEAN

SAO TOME AND PRINCIPE
São Tomé
Port Gentil
Libreville ⊛
GABON
Franceville
Brazzaville ⊛
Pointe-Noire
Cabinda (Ang.)

ASCENSION (Brit.)

ST. HELENA (Brit.)

⊛ Kampala
Nakuru ● Kisumu
L. Victoria
Kigali ⊛ RWANDA
BURUNDI
Bujumbura ⊛
Bukavu
Kananga
KATANGA
DEMOCRATIC REPUBLIC OF THE CONGO (ZAIRE)
REP. OF THE CONGO
Mbandaka
Kinshasa ⊛
Matadi
Kikwit
Tshikapa
Kasai
Luanda
Malanje
Lobito
Benguela
Namibe
ANGOLA
Huambo
Menongue

⊛ Nairobi
Kilimanjaro 5895 m (19,340 ft) ▲
Mombasa
Tanga
Zanzibar
Dar-es-Salaam
Mwanza
SERENGETI PLAIN
Arusha
Dodoma
TANZANIA
Tabora
Mbeya
GREAT RIFT VALLEY
L. Mweru
Lubumbashi
Likasi
Kolwezi
Ndola
Kitwe
ZAMBIA
Lusaka ⊛
Livingstone
L. Tanganyika
L. Malawi
MALAWI
Lilongwe
Chipata
Zambezi
Blantyre
L. Kariba
ZIMBABWE
Harare ⊛
Bulawayo
Francistown
BOTSWANA
KALAHARI DESERT
Gaborone
Mbuji-Mayi

COMOROS
Moroni ⊛
Mtwara
Nacala
Nampula
MOZAMBIQUE
Quelimane
Beira
Inhambane
Mozambique Channel
MADAGASCAR
Antsiranana
Toamasina
Antananarivo ⊛
Fianarantsoa
Toliary
Tropic of Capricorn

Maputo ⊛
Mbabane ⊛ SWAZILAND
Pietermaritzburg
Pretoria ⊛
Mutare
Limpopo
Newcastle
LESOTHO
Maseru ⊛
Johannesburg
Klerksdorp
Kimberley
Bloemfontein ⊛
SOUTH AFRICA
East London
Port Elizabeth
Durban
Pietermaritzburg
Orange
NAMIBIA
Windhoek ⊛
Grootfontein
Walvis Bay
Lüderitz
NAMIB DESERT
DESERT
Cape Town
Cape of Good Hope
Cape Agulhas

## Africa

⊛ National Capital
● Other City

1:39,550,000

0   250   500   750 mi
0   250   500   750 km

Azimuthal Equal Area Projection

75

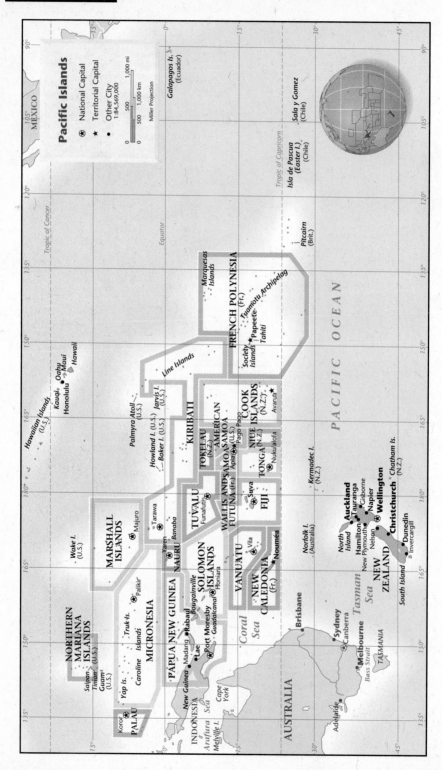

## Pacific Islands

⊛ National Capital
★ Territorial Capital
● Other City

1:84,569,000

0    500    1,000 mi
0  500  1,000 km

Miller Projection

MEXICO

Galapagos Is.
(Ecuador)

Sala y Gomez
(Chile)

Isla de Pascua
(Easter I.)
(Chile)

Tropic of Cancer

Equator

Tropic of Capricorn

Pitcairn
(Brit.)

Marquesas
Islands

FRENCH POLYNESIA
(Fr.)

Tuamotu Archipelago

Society
Islands    Papeete Tahiti

PACIFIC OCEAN

Line Islands

Hawaiian Islands
(U.S.)

Kauai
Oahu    Maui
Honolulu    Hawaii

Palmyra Atoll
(U.S.)

Jarvis I.
(U.S.)

Howland I. (U.S.)
Baker I. (U.S.)

KIRIBATI

AMERICAN
SAMOA
(U.S.)
Pago Pago

COOK
ISLANDS
(N.Z.)
Avarua ★

TOKELAU
(N.Z.)

ANDSAMOA
Apia

NIUE
(N.Z.)

Wake I.
(U.S.)

Tarawa

MARSHALL
ISLANDS
● Majuro

Banaba

TUVALU
Funafuti ⊛

WALLIS AND
FUTUNA (Fr.)

Suva

FIJI

TONGA
Nukuʻalofa

Kermadec I.
(N.Z.)

NORTHERN
MARIANA
ISLANDS
Saipan
Tinian (U.S.)
Guam
(U.S.)

Yap Is.    Truk Is.
Caroline    Islands    Palikir

MICRONESIA

Yaren ⊛
NAURU

SOLOMON
ISLANDS
Honiara ⊛
Bougainville
Guadalcanal

VANUATU
Vila

NEW
CALEDONIA
(Fr.)
Nouméa ⊛

Norfolk I.
(Australia)

PALAU
Koror
Palikir

PAPUA
NEW GUINEA

New Guinea
Madang
Lae
Port Moresby ⊛
Rabaul

Coral
Sea

Brisbane ●

INDONESIA

Arafura
Sea
Melville I.

Cape
York

AUSTRALIA

Adelaide ●

Sydney ⊛
Canberra

Melbourne ⊛

TASMANIA

Bass Strait

Tasman
Sea

North
Island
Hamilton
New Plymouth
Nelson

Auckland ●
Tauranga
Gisborne
Napier ●
Wellington ⊛

Christchurch ⊛

Chatham Is.
(N.Z.)

NEW
ZEALAND

South Island
Dunedin ●
Invercargill ●

# FLAGS of the
# COUNTRIES of the WORLD
## (Afghanistan-Dominican Republic)

AFGHANISTAN · ALBANIA · ALGERIA · ANDORRA · ANGOLA

ANTIGUA AND BARBUDA · ARGENTINA · ARMENIA · AUSTRALIA · AUSTRIA

AZERBAIJAN · THE BAHAMAS · BAHRAIN · BANGLADESH · BARBADOS

BELARUS · BELGIUM · BELIZE · BENIN · BHUTAN

BOLIVIA · BOSNIA AND HERZEGOVINA · BOTSWANA · BRAZIL · BRUNEI

BULGARIA · BURKINA FASO · BURUNDI · CAMBODIA · CAMEROON

CANADA · CAPE VERDE · CENTRAL AFRICAN REPUBLIC · CHAD · CHILE

CHINA · COLOMBIA · COMOROS · CONGO, DEM. REP. OF THE · CONGO, REP. OF THE

COSTA RICA · COTE D'IVOIRE · CROATIA · CUBA · CYPRUS

CZECH REPUBLIC · DENMARK · DJIBOUTI · DOMINICA · DOMINICAN REPUBLIC

# FLAGS of the COUNTRIES of the WORLD

## (Ecuador-Lithuania)

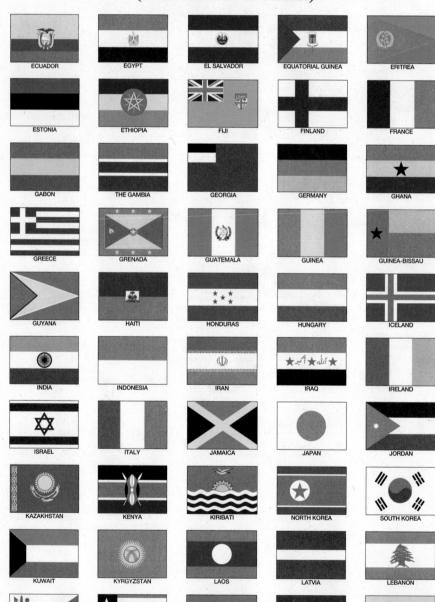

ECUADOR EGYPT EL SALVADOR EQUATORIAL GUINEA ERITREA

ESTONIA ETHIOPIA FIJI FINLAND FRANCE

GABON THE GAMBIA GEORGIA GERMANY GHANA

GREECE GRENADA GUATEMALA GUINEA GUINEA-BISSAU

GUYANA HAITI HONDURAS HUNGARY ICELAND

INDIA INDONESIA IRAN IRAQ IRELAND

ISRAEL ITALY JAMAICA JAPAN JORDAN

KAZAKHSTAN KENYA KIRIBATI NORTH KOREA SOUTH KOREA

KUWAIT KYRGYZSTAN LAOS LATVIA LEBANON

LESOTHO LIBERIA LIBYA LIECHTENSTEIN LITHUANIA

# FLAGS of the
# COUNTRIES of the WORLD
## (Luxembourg-Senegal)

LUXEMBOURG

MACEDONIA

MADAGASCAR

MALAWI

MALAYSIA

MALDIVES

MALI

MALTA

MARSHALL ISLANDS

MAURITANIA

MAURITIUS

MEXICO

MICRONESIA

MOLDOVA

MONACO

MONGOLIA

MOROCCO

MOZAMBIQUE

MYANMAR (BURMA)

NAMIBIA

NAURU

NEPAL

NETHERLANDS

NEW ZEALAND

NICARAGUA

NIGER

NIGERIA

NORWAY

OMAN

PAKISTAN

PALAU

PANAMA

PAPUA NEW GUINEA

PARAGUAY

PERU

PHILIPPINES

POLAND

PORTUGAL

QATAR

ROMANIA

RUSSIA

RWANDA

ST. KITTS AND NEVIS

ST. LUCIA

ST. VINCENT AND
THE GRENADINES

SAMOA

SAN MARINO

SÃO TOMÉ AND PRÍNCIPE

SAUDI ARABIA

SENEGAL

# FLAGS of the COUNTRIES of the WORLD

## (Seychelles-Zimbabwe)

SEYCHELLES

SIERRA LEONE

SINGAPORE

SLOVAKIA

SLOVENIA

SOLOMON ISLANDS

SOMALIA

SOUTH AFRICA

SPAIN

SRI LANKA

SUDAN

SURINAME

SWAZILAND

SWEDEN

SWITZERLAND

SYRIA

TAIWAN

TAJIKISTAN

TANZANIA

THAILAND

TOGO

TONGA

TRINIDAD AND TOBAGO

TUNISIA

TURKEY

TURKMENISTAN

TUVALU

UGANDA

UKRAINE

UNITED ARAB EMIRATES

UNITED KINGDOM (GREAT BRITAIN)

UNITED STATES

URUGUAY

UZBEKISTAN

VANUATU

VATICAN CITY

VENEZUELA

VIETNAM

YEMEN

YUGOSLAVIA

ZAMBIA

ZIMBABWE

# ENERGY: What It Is and Where It Comes From

**Y**ou can't touch or smell or taste energy, but you can observe what energy can *do*. You can feel that sunlight warms objects, and you can see that electricity lights up a light bulb, even if you can't see the heat or the electricity.

**What Is Energy?** Things that you see and touch every day use some form of energy to work: your body, a bike, a basketball, a car. Energy enables things to move. Scientists define **energy** as the ability to do work.

**Why Do We Need Energy to Do Work?** Scientists define **work** as a force moving an object. Scientifically speaking, throwing a ball is work, but studying for a test isn't! When you throw a ball, you use energy from the food you eat to do work on the ball. The engine in a car uses energy from gasoline to make the car move.

**Are There Different Kinds of Energy?** Yes, there are. When we rest or sleep we still have the ability to move. We do not lose our energy. We simply store it for another time. Stored energy is called **potential energy**. When we get up and begin to move around, we are using stored energy. As we move around and walk, our stored (potential) energy changes into **kinetic energy**, which is the energy of moving things. A parked car has potential energy. A moving car has kinetic energy. A sled stopped at the top of the hill has potential energy. As the sled goes down the hill, its potential energy changes to kinetic energy.

*potential energy*

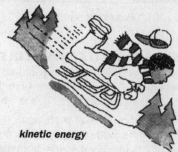

*kinetic energy*

**How Is Energy Created?** Energy cannot be created or destroyed, but it can be changed or converted into different forms. **Heat**, **light**, and **electricity** are forms of energy. Other forms of energy are **sound**, **chemical energy**, **mechanical energy**, and **nuclear energy**.

**Where Does Energy Come From?** All of the forms of energy we use come from the energy stored in **natural resources**. Sunlight, water, wind, petroleum, coal, and natural gas are natural resources. From these resources, we get heat and electricity.

# Turning NATURAL RESOURCES Into ENERGY

## THE SUN AND ITS ENERGY

Most of our energy comes from the sun. The sun is a big ball of glowing gases, made up mostly of hydrogen. Inside the sun, hydrogen atoms join together (through a process called nuclear fusion) and become helium. During the fusion process, large amounts of energy are released. This energy works its way to the sun's surface and then radiates out into space in the form of waves. These waves give us heat and light. The energy from the sun is stored in our food, which provides fuel for our bodies.

1. Plants absorb energy from the sun (solar energy) and convert absorbed energy to chemical energy for storage.

2. Animals eat plants and gain the stored chemical energy.

3. People eat plants and meat.

4. Food provides the body with energy to work and play.

## THE SUN STORES ITS ENERGY IN FOSSIL FUELS

The sun also provides the energy stored in fossil fuels. Coal, petroleum, and natural gas are **fossil fuels**. Fossil fuels come from the remains of ancient plants and animals over millions and millions of years. This is what happened:

**1.** Hundreds of millions of years ago, before people lived on Earth, trees and other plants absorbed energy from the sun, just as they do today.

**2.** Animals ate plants and smaller animals.

**3.** After the plants and animals died, they slowly became buried deeper and deeper underground.

**4.** After millions of years, they eventually turned into coal and petroleum.

Although the buried prehistoric plants and animals changed form over time, they still contained stored energy.

When we burn fossil fuels today, the stored energy from the sun is released in the form of heat. The heat is used to warm our homes and other buildings and produce electricity for our lights and appliances.

# How Does ENERGY GET to YOU?

## ENERGY FROM FOSSIL FUELS

Most of our energy comes from fossil fuels. Your home may be heated with oil or natural gas. You may have a kitchen stove that uses natural gas. Cars need gasoline to run. The diagram below shows how energy goes from a primary source (like coal or other fossil fuels) to a form of energy that you can use (like electricity).

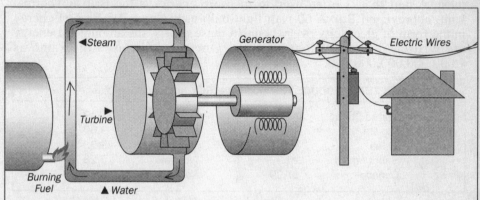

**1.** The **fossil fuel** is taken to a furnace, where it is burned. The **heat** produced by the burning fuel is used to heat water that flows through pipes. When the water boils, it becomes **steam**.

**2.** The steam is sent to a **turbine** (a wheel with blades). The steam pushes against the blades of the turbine and causes it to spin.

**3.** A shaft (a long, round bar) attached to the turbine turns a **generator**. Inside the generator, a spinning **magnet** produces **electricity** in coils nearby.

**4.** The electricity is sent by **wires** over long distances to homes and businesses. The electricity can then be used for lighting and for running appliances or machines.

## ENERGY FROM WATER

For centuries, people have been getting energy from rushing water. In a **hydroelectric plant**, water from rivers or dams is used to drive machinery like a turbine. The turbine is connected to a generator, which produces electricity.

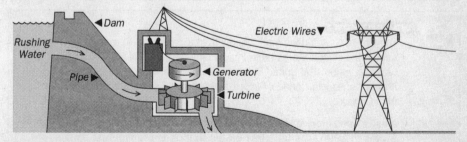

## NUCLEAR ENERGY

In **nuclear reactors**, uranium atoms are split into smaller atoms to produce heat. The heat is then used to produce electricity, just as the heat from burning coal is used.

# Who PRODUCES and USES the Most Energy?

**D**o you know that the United States produces more energy and uses more energy than any other country in the world? Below you can see which countries produced the most energy in 1996 and which countries used the most. A unit that is often used to measure energy is the British Thermal Unit, abbreviated Btu. A 60-watt light bulb uses about 205 Btus of energy in the form of electricity every hour. In these charts, the amounts of energy are written in quadrillions of Btus. One quadrillion is the same as 1,000,000,000,000,000.

**COUNTRIES THAT PRODUCE THE MOST ENERGY** (in quadrillion Btus)

| | | | |
|---|---|---|---|
| United States | 72.58 | Great Britain | 11.49 |
| Russia | 39.68 | Iran | 9.60 |
| China | 37.41 | India | 9.33 |
| Saudi Arabia | 20.39 | Norway | 9.28 |
| Canada | 17.29 | Venezuela | 8.84 |

**DID YOU KNOW?**

☑ Do you know which countries produce the most fossil fuels?

The country that produces the most crude oil is Saudi Arabia.
The country that produces the most natural gas is Russia.
The country that produces the most coal is China.

**COUNTRIES THAT USE THE MOST ENERGY** (in quadrillion Btus)

| | | | |
|---|---|---|---|
| United States | 93.36 | Canada | 12.20 |
| China | 37.04 | India | 11.55 |
| Russia | 25.98 | Great Britain | 10.05 |
| Japan | 21.37 | France | 9.87 |
| Germany | 14.44 | Italy | 7.63 |

**DID YOU KNOW?**

☑ The United States uses more energy than it produces. To meet its energy needs, the United States must import large amounts of fossil fuels from other countries. The United States gets its crude oil mainly from Saudi Arabia, Venezuela, Canada, Mexico, and Nigeria. It also imports natural gas from Canada.

☑ Alaska used more energy per person than any other state in the United States in 1995. The ten other states that used the greatest amount of energy per person were Louisiana, Wyoming, Texas, North Dakota, Kentucky, Alabama, West Virginia, Indiana, Montana, and Oklahoma.

# Will We Have ENOUGH ENERGY?

## WHERE DO WE GET ENERGY FROM?

In 1996, most of the energy used in the United States came from fossil fuels (about 38% from petroleum, 24% from natural gas, and 22% from coal). The rest came mostly from hydropower (water power) and nuclear energy. Fossil fuels are **nonrenewable** sources of energy. That means the amount of fossil fuel available for use is limited and that all this fuel might get used up after many years.

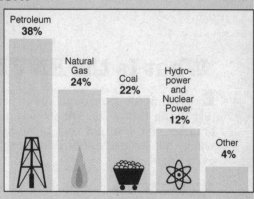

Petroleum **38%**

Natural Gas **24%**

Coal **22%**

Hydro-power and Nuclear Power **12%**

Other **4%**

## LOOKING FOR RENEWABLE RESOURCES

Scientists are trying to find more sources of energy that will reduce pollution and save some of the fossil fuels. People are using several types of **renewable resources**. Some of these forms of energy exist in an unlimited supply.

☑ **Solar power.** Solar power uses energy from sunlight. Solar panels can collect the sun's rays for heating. Solar cells can convert light energy directly into electricity.

☑ **Water from the ocean.** Ocean waves and tides can be used to drive generators to produce electricity.

☑ **The wind.** Old-fashioned windmills were used to drive machinery. Today, some people are using wind turbines to generate electricity.

☑ **Biomass energy.** Biomass includes wood from trees and other plants, animal wastes, and garbage. When these are burned or allowed to decay, they produce natural gas. Biomass energy is widely available and used in some parts of the world, although it is not unlimited.

☑ **Geothermal energy.** Geothermal energy is energy that comes from the hot, molten rock inside Earth. In certain parts of the world such as Iceland and New Zealand, people use this kind of energy for electricity and to heat buildings.

## SAVING ENERGY FOR TOMORROW

☑ Many businesses are trying to find ways to reuse heat from steam turbine generators.
☑ Recycling reduces the energy that would be used for making new products.
☑ Riding buses and trains, car pooling, and driving fuel-efficient cars reduces the use of fossil fuels.
☑ Using less heat, less hot water, and less air conditioning also helps save energy.

# What Is the ENVIRONMENT?

Everything that surrounds us is part of the environment. Not just living things like plants and animals, but also the air we breathe, the sunlight that provides warmth and energy, the water that we use in our homes, schools, and businesses, and even rocks.

 **WEB SITE** You can learn more about the environment at: http://www.nwf.org/nwf/kids/index.html

**People and the Environment.** People have existed for many thousands of years. For a long time people thought the Earth was so huge that it would always absorb any kind of pollution. And they thought that Earth's natural resources would never be used up.

Even prehistoric life affected the environment. People killed animals for food and built fires to cook food and keep themselves warm. They cut down trees for fuel, and their fires released gases into the air. In prehistoric times, though, there were so few people that their activities had little impact on the environment.

In modern times, the world's population has been growing very fast. In 1850 there were around 1 billion people in the world. In 1950 there were around 2.5 billion, and by 1997 there were more than 5.8 billion. Because there are so many people on the planet Earth, the things we do can affect the environment dramatically.

**Sharing the Earth.** People share the planet with trees, flowers, insects, fish, whales, dogs, and many other plants and animals. Each type (species) of animal or plant has its place on Earth, and each one is dependent on the others. Plants give off oxygen that animals need to breathe. Animals pollinate plants and spread their seeds. Animals eat plants and are in turn eaten by larger animals. When plants and animals die, they become part of the soil in which new plants, in their turn, take root and grow.

**The Earth Belongs to Everyone.** Many people are becoming more aware that some of the things humans do could seriously damage the planet and the animals and plants that live on it. Sometimes this damage can be reversed or slowed down. But it is often permanent. On the following pages you'll find facts about some parts of the environment, what is happening to them, and what can be done to clean up and protect our planet.

# What Is BIODIVERSITY?

Our planet, Earth, is shared by more than 5 million species of living things. Human beings of all colors, races, and nationalities make up just one species, *Homo sapiens*. All of the species together form the variety of life we call "biodiversity" (*bio* means "life" and *diversity* means "variety").

**How Many Species Are There?** This list of species is just a sampling of how diverse Earth is.

**BEETLES:** 290,000 species
**Fascinating Fact▶** There are more kinds of beetles than any other animal on Earth.

**FLOWERING PLANTS:** 250,000 species
**Fascinating Fact▶** The 750,000 species of insects and the 250,000 species of flowering plants depend on one another. The insects need the plants for food, the plants need the insects for pollination.

**EDIBLE PLANTS:** 30,000 species
**Fascinating Fact▶** Although 30,000 are edible, 90% of the world's food comes from only 20 species.

**ANTS:** 20,000 species
**Fascinating Fact▶** If you were to weigh all the insects on earth, ants would make up almost half of the total.

**BIRDS:** 9,040 species
**Fascinating Fact▶** More than 1,000 of these species are in danger of becoming extinct.

**BATS:** 1,000 species
**Fascinating Fact▶** There are more species of bats than of any other mammal.

**PET DOGS:** 1 species
**Fascinating Fact▶** Even though they can look very different, all dogs belong to the same species.

**HUMAN BEINGS:** 1 species
**Fascinating Fact▶** This one species holds the fate of all the other species in its hands. People can affect the environment more than any other type of living thing.

 **DID YOU KNOW?** Bats should be valued by humans rather than feared. These winged mammals are often killed because of superstition. Many of their habitats have been destroyed. But, except in rare cases, bats do not attack people. Some species help Earth's ecosystem by eating insects, such as mosquitoes, and by pollinating plants.

**Some Threats to Biodiversity.** Plants and animals are harmed by air, water, and land pollution, and their habitats are often destroyed by deforestation. For example, in recent years, large areas of rain forests have been cleared for wood, farmland, and cattle ranches, and people have become concerned that rain forests may be disappearing. Another threat is overharvesting, or the use of too many animals for food or other products. For example, the number of whales has been steadily declining, and some species of whales could eventually be wiped out entirely.

**Protecting Biodiversity.** Efforts to reduce pollutants in air, water, and soil, to preserve rain forests, and to limit deforestation and overharvesting help to preserve biodiversity. A few species that were endangered have increased sufficiently in number, so that they are no longer in danger of becoming extinct.

# GARBAGE and RECYCLING

**L**ook around. Everything you see will probably be replaced or thrown away someday. Skates, clothes, the toaster, the refrigerator, furniture—they may break or wear out, or you may get tired of them and want new ones sooner or later. Where will they go when they are thrown out? What kinds of waste will they create, and how will it affect the environment? The average person in the United States today produces more than 4 pounds of trash every day, and only 1 pound of that is recycled or composted.

## What Happens to the Things We Throw Away?

### LANDFILLS

Most of our trash goes to places called landfills. A **landfill** (or dump) is a low area of land that is filled with garbage. Most modern landfills are lined with a layer of plastic or clay to try to keep dangerous liquids from seeping out.

### The Problem with Landfills

There is so much trash that we are quickly running out of room for it. In less than ten years, all the landfills in more than half of the states of the United States will be full. Some of the household trash in landfills is hazardous. It includes batteries, paint, motor oil, and antifreeze. These things can poison land, air, and water.

### INCINERATORS

Another way to get rid of trash is to burn it. Trash is burned in a device like a furnace called an **incinerator**. Because incinerators can get rid of almost all of the bulk of the trash, some communities would rather use incinerators than landfills.

### The Problem with Incinerators

Leftover ash and smoke from burning trash may contain harmful chemicals, called **pollutants**. They can harm plants, animals, and people.

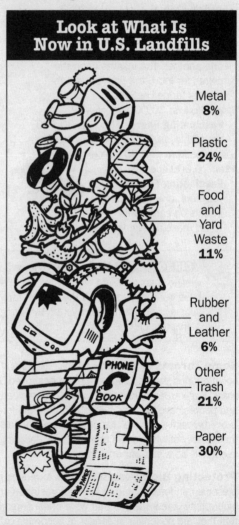

## Look at What Is Now in U.S. Landfills

Metal
**8%**

Plastic
**24%**

Food and Yard Waste
**11%**

Rubber and Leather
**6%**

Other Trash
**21%**

Paper
**30%**

# Reuse, Recycle, Reduce

When we reuse containers, batteries, paper, and other things, we can reduce the amount of garbage we create. When we recycle things like newspaper, glass, and plastics, we reduce the amount of garbage and provide materials for making other products. Here are some of the things we can do.

## PAPER

Use both sides of a piece of paper. Recycle newspapers, magazines, comic books, catalogs, and cardboard. Use cloth towels instead of paper towels.

## PLASTIC

Recycle soda bottles by returning them to the store. Refill or recycle detergent bottles and milk jugs. Wash food containers and use them to store leftovers or to store your collections or hobby things. Reuse plastic bags.

## GLASS

Reuse or recycle glass bottles and jars.

## CLOTHES

Give clothes to younger relatives, or donate used clothes to thrift shops. Cut torn, unwearable old clothes into rags to use instead of paper towels.

## METAL

Recycle aluminum cans and foil trays. Give the dry cleaner any wire clothes hangers you don't need.

## FOOD AND YARD WASTE

If you have a yard, make a compost heap for food scraps and grass clippings and leaves. A **compost heap** is a pile of food scraps, leaves, and other natural materials that decompose (rot) with the help of earthworms and tiny organisms. **Compost** can be used to fertilize soil and help plants grow.

## BATTERIES

Use rechargeable batteries for toys and games, radios, tape players, and flashlights. There are special rules for disposing of batteries, paints, and other harmful materials. Find out how your community wants people to dispose of them.

## What Is Made from RECYCLED MATERIALS?

☑ From **RECYCLED PAPER** we get newspapers, cereal boxes, wrapping paper, cardboard containers, insulation, and many other things.

☑ From **RECYCLED PLASTIC** we get soda bottles, tables, benches, bicycle racks, cameras, backpacks, carpeting, shoes, clothes, and many other things.

☑ From **RECYCLED STEEL** we get steel cans, cars, bicycles, nails, refrigerators and many other things.

☑ From **RECYCLED GLASS** we get glass jars, tiles, and many other things.

☑ From **RECYCLED RUBBER** we get bulletin boards, floor tiles, playground equipment, speed bumps, and many other things.

# The AIR We BREATHE

**A**ll human beings and animals need air to survive. Without air we would die. Plants also need air to live. Plants use sunlight and the carbon dioxide in air to make food, and then give off oxygen.

We all breathe the air that surrounds Earth. The air is composed mainly of gases: around 78% nitrogen, 21% oxygen, and 1% carbon dioxide, other gases, and water vapor. Human beings breathe more than 6 quarts of air every minute. Because air is so basic to life, it is very important to keep the air clean by reducing or preventing air pollution. Today, air pollution causes problems worldwide, such as **acid rain**, **global warming**, and the **breakdown of the ozone layer**.

Nitrogen 78%

Oxygen 21%

▲ Carbon Dioxide, Other Gases, Water Vapor 1%

**What Is Air Pollution and Where Does It Come From?** **Air pollution** is dirtying the air with chemicals or other materials that can injure health, the enjoyment of life, or the working of ecosystems. The major sources of air pollution are cars, trucks and buses, waste incinerators, factories, and some electric power plants, especially those that burn fossil fuels.

**What Is Acid Rain and Where Does It Come From?** **Acid rain** is a kind of air pollution. It is caused by chemicals that are released into the air and cause rain, snow, and fog to be more acidic than usual. The main sources of these chemicals are fumes from cars' exhaust pipes, and power plants that burn coal. When these chemicals mix with moisture and other particles in the air, they create sulfuric acid and nitric acid. The wind often carries these acids many miles before they fall to the ground in rain, snow, and fog, or even as dry particles.

**Why Worry About Air Pollution and Acid Rain?** Air pollution and acid rain can harm people, animals, and plants. Air pollution can cause our eyes to sting and can make some people sick. It can also damage crops and trees.

Air pollution (especially acid rain) is also harmful to water in lakes, often killing plants and fish that live there. Hundreds of lakes in the northeastern United States and 14,000 lakes in Canada are so acidic that fish can no longer live there. Acid rain has affected trees in U.S. national parks. In the Appalachian Mountains, for example, it has harmed spruce trees growing in the Shenandoah and Great Smoky Mountain National Parks. And it can turn buildings and statues black and damage them by eating away at metal, stone, and paint. Monuments and statues that have survived hundreds of years are suddenly disintegrating.

## Global Warming and the Greenhouse Effect

Many scientists believe that gases in the air are causing Earth's climate to become warmer. This is called **global warming**. If the climate becomes so warm that a great deal of ice near the north and south poles melts and more water goes into the oceans, many areas along the coasts may be flooded.

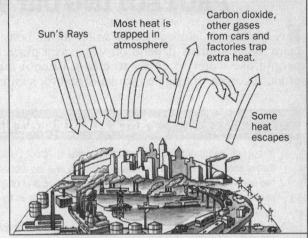

Sun's Rays

Most heat is trapped in atmosphere

Carbon dioxide, other gases from cars and factories trap extra heat.

Some heat escapes

In Earth's atmosphere there are tiny amounts of gases called **greenhouse gases**. These gases let the rays of the sun pass through to the planet, but they hold in the heat that comes up from the sun-warmed Earth—just as the glass of a greenhouse holds in the warmth of the sun.

As cities increased in size and population, factories and businesses also grew. People needed more and more electricity, cars, and other things that had to be manufactured. As industries in the world have increased, more greenhouse gases have been added to the atmosphere. These gases increase the thickness of the greenhouse "glass," causing too much heat to be trapped. This is called **the greenhouse effect**.

 **DID YOU KNOW?** More than 20% of the greenhouse gases that enter the atmosphere come from the United States. That is more than any other country.

## Good and Bad Ozone

**Good Ozone.** Another problem caused by air pollution involves a layer in the atmosphere high above Earth, called the **ozone layer**. The ozone layer protects us from the harsh rays of the sun. When refrigerators, air conditioners, and similar items are thrown away, gases from them (called chlorofluorocarbons or CFCs) rise into the air and destroy some of the ozone in this layer.

**Bad Ozone.** There is also ozone near the ground that forms when sunlight hits air pollutants from cars and smokestacks, causing smog. This ozone near the ground can be harmful.

## What Are We Doing to Reduce Air Pollution?

Many countries, including the United States, are trying to reduce air pollution. Today's cars can go farther on a gallon of gasoline than cars of 20 or 30 years ago, so that less gasoline has to be burned. In the United States, cars must have a special device to remove harmful chemicals from their smoke before it comes out of the tailpipe. More power plants and factories are putting devices on their smokestacks to catch harmful chemicals before they can enter the air. Many people are trying not to use more electricity than they really need, so that less coal will have to be burned to produce electricity. And in some places, power companies are using windmills or other equipment that does not pollute the air to make some of their electricity.

# PROTECTING Our WATER

Every plant and animal needs water for its body to work. Fish, frogs, and many other animals depend on water as a place to live. Besides drinking, people use water to cook, to clean, to cool machinery in factories, to produce power, to irrigate farmland, and for swimming and boating.

## Facts About WATER

☑ About two-thirds of the Earth's surface is water. About 97% of that is seawater, and 2% is frozen in glaciers and ice around the north and south poles. Only 1% is fresh water, and only part of that is close enough to the Earth's surface for us to use.

☑ If all of the water on Earth fit in a two-gallon bucket, just over two tablespoons would be available as fresh water.

☑ To stay healthy, people need to take in about $2\frac{1}{2}$ quarts of water a day from eating and drinking.

☑ Although the amount varies from place to place, the average American uses 183 gallons of water a day for things like cooking, washing, flushing, and watering the lawn.

☑ About 74% of the water used at home is used in the bathroom, about 21% is used for laundry and cleaning, and about 5% is used in the kitchen.

☑ A washing machine uses about 50 gallons of water for each load of wash.

☑ It takes 12 to 20 gallons of water to clean one load of dishes in a dishwasher.

☑ About 25-50 gallons of water are needed for a bath.

☑ A 10-minute shower can use up about 25-50 gallons of water. Some shower heads use 6-10 gallons of water a minute. Newer low-flow shower heads save water by using only about half that amount.

### What Is Threatening Our Water and What Are We Doing About It?
Water pollution and overuse of water are the major threats to our water.

**Water Pollution.** Water is said to be polluted when it is not fit for its intended uses, such as drinking, swimming, watering crops, or serving as a habitat. Polluted water can cause disease and kill fish and other animals. Some major water pollutants include sewage, chemicals from factories, fertilizers and weed killers, and leaking landfills. But water pollution is also being reduced in some areas. Some lakes are being cleaned up enough to restore plants and fish to them. Companies continue to look for better ways to get rid of wastes, and many farmers are trying new ways to grow crops without using fertilizers or chemicals that kill weeds or bugs.

**Overuse of Water.** It is important to try to conserve as much water as possible. Some modern plumbing supplies (like toilets and shower heads) are now designed to use less water. Many people take shorter showers, and they don't let the water run when they brush their teeth or wash dishes by hand. People concerned about water are also running dishwashers or washing machines only when they have a full load. They fix faucets that drip and don't water the lawn unless it really needs it.

# The IMPORTANCE of FORESTS

Trees and forests are very important to the environment. In addition to holding water, trees hold the soil in place. Trees use carbon dioxide and give off oxygen, which animals and plants need for survival. And they provide homes and food for millions of types of animals.

**Why Do We Cut Down Trees?** People cut down trees for many reasons. When the population grows, people cut down trees to clear space to build houses, schools, factories, and other buildings. People may clear land to plant crops and graze livestock. Sometimes all the trees in an area are cut and sold for lumber and paper.

**What Happens When Trees Are Cut Down?** Cutting down trees—usually to use the land for something besides a forest—is called **deforestation**. Although people often have good reasons for cutting down trees, deforestation can have serious effects. If animal habitats are destroyed, many species will become extinct. Because of deforestation, thousands of species in the Amazon rain forest in South America are being lost before scientists can even learn about them. (For more about rain forests, see page 164.)

Cutting down trees can also affect the climate. After rain falls on a forest, mist starts rising and new rain clouds are created. When forests are cut down, this cycle is disrupted, and the area eventually grows drier, causing a change in the local climate.

If huge areas of trees are cut down, the carbon dioxide they would have used builds up in the atmosphere and contributes to the greenhouse effect. And without trees to hold the soil and absorb water, rain washes topsoil away into rivers and reservoirs, a process called **soil erosion**. Farming on the poorer soil that is left can be very hard.

**What Are We Doing to Save Forests?** Many European countries are planting trees faster than they are cutting them down. Also, trees are being planted to restock woodland areas and to create forests in some countries where timber is scarce. In addition, communities and individuals are helping to save forests by recycling paper.

 **DID YOU KNOW?**

☑ Because changes in climate affect how much a tree grows each year, scientists can tell what the climate was like in years past (in some cases 4,000 years!) by examining a tree's annual rings.

☑ Some trees, such as the northern red oak and the junipers, resist pollution better than others.

☑ Of the forests in the lower 48 states that were standing before Europeans came to America, only 5% still stand. Most of this old growth forest is in the Pacific Northwest—in Washington, Oregon, and northern California.

☑ Each year, the average American uses enough wood and wood products to add up to one tree 100 feet tall.

☑ By the mid-1990s, more paper in the United States was being recycled than was sent to landfills.

# ENVIRONMENTAL GLOSSARY

**climate**
The average weather in a region of the world.

**compost heap**
A pile of food scraps and yard waste that is broken down by worms and tiny insects. The result looks like dirt. It can be used to enrich the soil.

**conservation**
The planned and wise use of water, forests, and other natural resources so they will not be wasted.

**deforestation**
The cutting down of most of the trees from forested land, usually so that the land can be used for something besides a forest.

**ecosystem**
A community of living things and the place where they live, such as a forest or pond.

**environment**
All living and non-living things in an area at a given time. The environment affects the growth of living things.

**extinction**
The disappearance of a type (species) of plant or animal from Earth. Some species become extinct because of natural forces, but many others are becoming endangered or threatened with extinction because of the activities of people.

**fossil fuel**
Anything that comes from once-living matter deep in the earth, such as oil, gas, and coal.

**global warming**
An increase in Earth's temperature due to a buildup of certain gases in the atmosphere.

**greenhouse effect**
Warming of Earth caused by certain gases (called **greenhouse gases**) that form a blanket in the atmosphere high over Earth. Small amounts of these gases keep Earth warm so we can live here, but the larger amounts produced by factories, cars, and burning trees may hold in too much heat and cause global warming.

**groundwater**
Water in the ground that flows in the spaces between soil particles and rocks. Groundwater supplies water for wells and springs.

**habitat**
The natural home of an animal or a plant.

**pollution**
Contamination of air, water, or soil by materials that can injure health, the quality of life, or the working of ecosystems.

**recycling**
Using something more than once, either just the way it is, or treated and made into something else.

**reforestation**
Planting new trees where other trees have been cut down.

**soil erosion**
The washing away or blowing away of topsoil. Trees and other plants hold the soil in place and help reduce the force of the wind. Soil erosion can happen when trees and plants are removed from the ground.

# How KIDS Can Help PROTECT the ENVIRONMENT

☑ *Recycle* as many things as possible: plastic, glass, papers, and clothes.

☑ *Save electricity* by turning off lights when you leave the room. Close the refrigerator door as quickly as possible. Don't stand with it open.

☑ *Save water* by not letting the water run when you brush your teeth. Take shorter showers. Don't leave water running when you're not using it.

☑ *Take care of things made from wood.* Remember that they come from trees. When you're finished with them, give them to someone else.

☑ Try products made from recycled materials.

## ENVIRONMENT PUZZLE

**Y**ou'll find most of these words on pages 90-94. Can you use them to solve the crossword puzzle below? (Answers are on page 303.)

| | | | |
|---|---|---|---|
| ACID | FUEL | OAK | SUN |
| AIR | GAS | OZONE | TREE |
| CLEAN | GLOBAL | PLANET | WATER |
| EXTINCT | KIDS | SOIL | WIND |
| FOSSIL | | | |

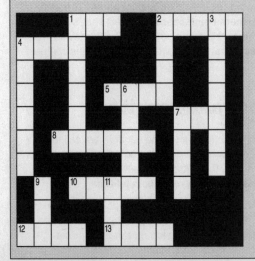

**ACROSS**

1. Nitrogen, found in our air, is a ___.
2. ___ covers about two thirds of the Earth.
4. Oil is a ___ that comes from deep in the earth.
5. ___ rain is a kind of air pollution.
7. Greenhouse gases hold in heat from the __.
8. Our ___ is Earth.
10. The layer of ___ in Earth's atmosphere helps protect us from the sun's rays.
12. The average American uses up enough wood products to add up to one 100-foot ___ every year.
13. ___ can help protect the environment by recycling everyday products.

**DOWN**

1. ___ warming is a change in Earth's climate.
2. The ___ can be used to help make electricity.
3. When a species dies out, it becomes __.
4. Anything that comes from once-living matter is a ___.
6. Our air and water should be ___ but often are not.
7. Trees hold ___ in place.
9. Without ___ we cannot survive.
11. The northern red ___ tree resists pollution better than most other trees.

# What Is a GLOBE?

**D**id you ever travel on a spaceship? Whether you know it or not, you're traveling right now on the spaceship called Planet Earth. Earth is always zooming through space and around the sun at very fast speeds.

A tiny model of Earth is called a **globe**. Like Earth, a globe is shaped like a ball or **sphere**. Although Earth isn't exactly a sphere because it gets flat at the top and bottom and bulges a little in the middle, a globe gives us the best idea of what Earth looks like. Because Earth is round, most flat maps do not show the shapes of the land masses exactly right. The shapes at the top and bottom usually look too big. For example, on a flat map the island of Greenland, which is next to North America, looks bigger than Australia, but it is really much smaller.

When you look at a ball or sphere, you can see only the half of it that is facing toward you. The drawing here shows half of a globe.

▼ North Pole

◀ 40 degrees north latitude

North America

◀ 20 degrees north latitude

◀ Equator

◀ 20 degrees south latitude

South America

◀ 40 degrees south latitude

▲ South Pole

### Which Hemisphere Do You Live In?

You can draw an imaginary line around the middle of Earth, like a belt. This is called the **equator**. The closer you get to the equator, the hotter it gets. The equator splits Earth into two halves called **hemispheres**. The part that's north of the equator is called the **northern hemisphere**. The part that's south of the equator is called the **southern hemisphere**. You can also divide Earth into the **western hemisphere** and the **eastern hemisphere**. The western hemisphere is the part shown on the globe above.

# Lines of Latitude and Longitude

Imaginary lines that run east and west around Earth, parallel to the equator, are called **parallels**. They tell you the **latitude** of a place, or how far it is from the equator. The equator is at 0 degrees latitude. As you go farther north or south, the latitude increases. The North Pole is at 90 degrees **north latitude**. The South Pole is at 90 degrees **south latitude**.

Imaginary lines that run north and south around the globe, from one pole to the other, are called **meridians**. These meridians tell you the degree of **longitude**, or how far east or west a place is from an imaginary line called the **Greenwich meridian** or **prime meridian**. That line runs through the city of Greenwich in England.

# How to READ a MAP

There are many different kinds of maps. **Physical maps** mainly show features that are part of nature, such as mountains, deserts, jungles, and grasslands. **Political** maps show features such as states and countries and the **boundaries** between them.

## DISTANCE

Of course the distances on a map are much smaller than the distances in the real world. The **scale** shows you how much smaller they are. In the map below, every inch on paper means a real distance of 10 miles.

## DIRECTION

Maps usually have a compass rose that shows you which way is north. On most maps, north is toward the top. On the map below, north is straight up. If you went from Westwood to Lake City you would be going almost exactly north. When north is straight up, east is to the right, and west is to the left.

## LOCATING PLACES

To help you locate places on a map, there often is a list, giving you a letter and number for each city or town. In the map below, you can find the first city on the list, Centerville, by drawing a straight line down from the letter E on top, and another line going across from the number 3 on the side. Centerville should be near the area where these two lines meet.

## SYMBOLS

Maps usually have different **symbols** in them. If you look along the side or bottom, you can find out what these symbols mean. At the bottom of this map, you can see the symbols for towns, roads, railroad tracks, and airports. Can you tell which are the two biggest cities or towns on the map? Can you find the airport and railroad? How would you get from the airport to Centerville by car?

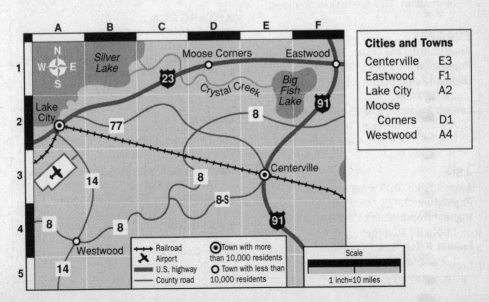

Cities and Towns

| | |
|---|---|
| Centerville | E3 |
| Eastwood | F1 |
| Lake City | A2 |
| Moose Corners | D1 |
| Westwood | A4 |

Railroad
Airport
U.S. highway
County road
Town with more than 10,000 residents
Town with less than 10,000 residents
Scale
1 inch=10 miles

# The CONTINENTS and OCEANS of the World

Almost two-thirds of Earth's surface is made up of water. The rest is land. **Oceans** are the largest areas of water. **Continents** are the largest pieces of land. The Earth has seven continents and four oceans. Many islands in the Pacific Ocean are not counted as part of any of the continents. In the table below, the highest point of each continent is the top of the highest mountain, and the lowest point is the place that is the farthest below sea level. See pages 65-76 for maps of the continents.

## CONTINENTS

### NORTH AMERICA
(including Mexico, Central America, and Caribbean islands)
**Area:** 9,400,000 square miles
**Population:** 464,000,000
**Highest Point:** Mount McKinley (Alaska), 20,320 feet
**Lowest Point:** Death Valley (California), 282 feet below sea level

### SOUTH AMERICA
**Area:** 6,900,000 square miles
**Population:** 329,000,000
**Highest Point:** Mount Aconcagua (Argentina), 22,834 feet
**Lowest Point:** Valdes Peninsula (Argentina), 131 feet below sea level

### EUROPE
**Area:** 3,800,000 square miles
**Population:** 801,000,000
**Highest Point:** Mount Elbrus (Russia), 18,510 feet
**Lowest Point:** Caspian Sea (Russia, Azerbaijan; eastern Europe and western Asia), 92 feet below sea level

### ASIA
**Area:** 17,400,000 square miles
**Population:** 3,477,000,000
**Highest Point:** Mount Everest (Nepal, Tibet), 29,028 feet
**Lowest Point:** Dead Sea (Israel, Jordan), 1,312 feet below sea level

### AFRICA
**Area:** 11,700,000 square miles
**Population:** 750,000,000
**Highest Point:** Mount Kilimanjaro (Tanzania), 19,340 feet
**Lowest Point:** Lake Assal (Djibouti), 512 feet below sea level

### AUSTRALIA
(including Australia, New Zealand, and islands that make up Oceania)
**Area:** 3,300,000 square miles
**Population:** 29,000,000
**Highest Point:** Mount Kosciusko (New South Wales), 7,310 feet
**Lowest Point:** Lake Eyre (South Australia), 52 feet below sea level

### ANTARCTICA
**Area:** 5,400,000 square miles
**Population:** Zero
**Highest Point:** Vinson Massif, 16,864 feet
**Lowest Known Point:** Bentley Subglacial Trench, 8,327 feet below sea level

## OCEANS

The facts about the oceans include their size and average depth.

**Pacific Ocean:** 64,186,300 square miles; 12,925 feet deep
**Atlantic Ocean:** 33,420,000 square miles; 11,730 feet deep
**Indian Ocean:** 28,350,500 square miles; 12,598 feet deep
**Arctic Ocean:** 5,105,700 square miles; 3,407 feet deep

# The TALLEST, LONGEST, HIGHEST, DEEPEST in the World

**Longest River:** Nile, in Egypt and Sudan (4,160 miles)

**Highest Waterfall:** Angel Falls, in Venezuela (3,212 feet)

**Tallest Mountain:** Mount Everest, in Tibet and Nepal (29,028 feet)

**Deepest Lake:** Lake Baykal, in Asia (5,315 feet)

**Biggest Lake:** Caspian Sea, in Europe and Asia (143,244 square miles)

**Biggest Desert:** The Sahara, in Africa (3,500,000 square miles)

**Biggest Island:** Greenland, in the Atlantic Ocean (840,000 square miles)

# Some Important REGIONS of the World

The regions of the world described below often appear in the news.

**BALKANS.** The Balkan region, in southeastern Europe, consists of Yugoslavia, Slovenia, Croatia, Bosnia and Herzegovina, Macedonia, and Albania. Bulgaria, southeastern Romania, northern Greece, and the portion of Turkey in Europe are also part of the Balkans. All the Balkan states were once part of the Ottoman Empire.

**CARIBBEAN.** The Caribbean region is centered on the Caribbean Sea, an arm of the Atlantic Ocean that lies south of the United States and north of South America. The Caribbean has thousands of islands. The largest groups are the Greater Antilles and the Lesser Antilles. Among countries in the Greater Antilles are Cuba, Haiti, the Dominican Republic, Jamaica, and the U.S. commonwealth of Puerto Rico. The Lesser Antilles include Dominica, Barbados, Grenada, and Trinidad and Tobago.

**CENTRAL AMERICA.** Central America is the region between Mexico and South America. It consists of Belize, Guatemala, Honduras, El Salvador, Nicaragua, Costa Rica, and Panama.

**EASTERN EUROPE.** Countries of Eastern Europe include Poland, the Czech Republic, Slovakia, Hungary, Romania, and Bulgaria. Three other Eastern European countries (Estonia, Latvia, and Lithuania) form a region known as the Baltic States.

**MIDDLE EAST.** One of the most famous regions in the news is the Middle East. The Middle East refers to Egypt and Libya (in northeast Africa), to Israel, Jordan, Lebanon, Syria, and Iraq, and to countries of the Arabian Peninsula: Saudi Arabia, Kuwait, Bahrain, Qatar, United Arab Emirates, Oman, and Yemen (all in southwestern Asia). The term "Middle East" sometimes also includes the other Islamic countries of North Africa: Morocco, Algeria, and Tunisia.

**SOUTHEAST ASIA.** The region of Southeast Asia lies east of India and south of China. It consists of 10 independent countries: Myanmar (Burma), Thailand, Vietnam, Laos, Cambodia, Malaysia, Singapore, the Philippines, Indonesia, and Brunei.

# Some FAMOUS European and American EXPLORERS

## EXPLORERS OF THE AMERICAS

**around 1000** — **Leif Ericson,** from Iceland, explored "Vinland," which may have been the coasts of northeast Canada and New England.

**1492 to 1504** — **Christopher Columbus,** from Italy, sailed four times to America and started colonies there.

**1513** — **Juan Ponce de León,** from Spain, explored and named Florida.

**1513** — **Vasco Núñez de Balboa,** from Spain, explored Panama and reached the Pacific Ocean.

**1519-36** — **Hernando Cortés,** from Spain, conquered Mexico and traveled as far as Baja California.

**1527-42** — **Alvar Núñez Cabeza de Vaca,** from Spain, explored the southwestern United States, Brazil, and Paraguay.

**1532-35** — **Francisco Pizarro,** from Spain, explored the west coast of South America and conquered Peru.

**1534-36** — **Jacques Cartier,** from France, sailed up the St. Lawrence River to the site of present-day Montreal.

**1539-42** — **Hernando de Soto,** from Spain, explored the southeastern United States and the lower Mississippi Valley.

**1603-13** — **Samuel de Champlain,** from France, traced the course of the St. Lawrence River and explored the northeastern United States.

**1609-10** — **Henry Hudson,** from England, explored the Hudson River, Hudson Bay, and Hudson Strait.

**1682** — **Robert Cavelier, sieur de La Salle,** from France, traced the Mississippi River to its mouth in the Gulf of Mexico.

**1804-6** — **Meriwether Lewis** and **William Clark,** from the United States, traveled from St. Louis along the Missouri and Columbia rivers to the Pacific Ocean and back.

## EXPLORERS OF ASIA AND THE PACIFIC

**1271-95** — **Marco Polo,** from Venice, Italy, traveled through Central Asia, India, China, and Indonesia.

**1519-21** — **Ferdinand Magellan,** from Portugal, sailed around the tip of South America and across the Pacific Ocean to the Philippines, where he died. His expedition continued around the world.

**1768-78** — **James Cook,** from England, charted the world's major bodies of water and explored Hawaii and Antarctica.

## EXPLORERS OF AFRICA

**1488** — **Bartolomeu Dias,** from Portugal, explored the Cape of Good Hope in southern Africa.

**1497-98** — **Vasco da Gama,** from Portugal, sailed farther than Dias, around the Cape of Good Hope to East Africa and India.

**1849-59** — **David Livingstone,** from Scotland, explored Southern Africa, including the Zambezi River and Victoria Falls.

# VOLCANOES

**A** **volcano** is a mountain or hill with an opening on top known as a **crater**. Every once in a while, hot melted rock (**magma**), gases, ash, and other material from inside the earth may blast out, or erupt, through the opening. The magma is called **lava** when it reaches the air. This red-hot lava may have a temperature of more than 2,000 degrees Fahrenheit. The hill or mountain is made out of lava and other materials that come out of the opening, and then cool off and harden. Some islands are really the tops of undersea volcanoes. The Hawaiian islands developed when volcanoes erupted under the Pacific Ocean. There have been many famous volcanic eruptions throughout history.

## Why Do Volcanoes Erupt?

More than 500 volcanoes have erupted over the centuries. Some have erupted many times. Volcanic eruptions come from pools of magma and other materials a few miles underground. The pools come from rock far below. After the rock melts and mixes with gases, it rises up through cracks and weak spots in the mountain.

### SOME FAMOUS VOLCANIC ERUPTIONS

| YEAR | VOLCANO (PLACE) | DEATHS (Approximate) |
|---|---|---|
| 79 | Mount Vesuvius (Italy) | 16,000 |
| 1586 | Kelut (Indonesia) | 10,000 |
| 1792 | Mount Unzen (Japan) | 14,500 |
| 1815 | Tambora (Indonesia) | 10,000 |
| 1883 | Krakatau or Krakatoa (Indonesia) | 36,000 |
| 1902 | Mount Pelée (Martinique) | 28,000 |
| 1980 | Mount St. Helens (U.S.) | 57 |
| 1982 | El Chichon (Mexico) | 1,880 |
| 1985 | Nevado del Ruiz (Colombia) | 23,000 |
| 1986 | Lake Nyos (Cameroon), | 1,700 |
| 1991 | Mt. Pinatubo (Philippines) | 800 |

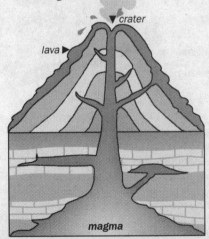

ash and gas ▶

▼ crater

lava ▶

magma

## Where Is the Ring of Fire?

There are volcanoes on the bottom of the ocean and on every continent. Many of the active volcanoes are found on land along the edges of the Pacific Ocean. These volcanoes are often called the **Ring of Fire.**

The Ring of Fire marks the boundary between the plates under the Pacific Ocean and the plates under the continents around the Pacific Ocean (North America, South America, Asia). The plates of Earth are explained on page 102 and can be seen on a map on page 103, under the section on Earthquakes.

# EARTHQUAKES

Earthquakes may be so weak that they are hardly felt, or they may be strong enough to do tremendous damage. There are thousands of earthquakes each year, but most of them are too small to be felt. About 1 in 5 can be felt, and about 1 in 500 causes damage.

▲ Damage after the 1989 earthquake in San Francisco, California

## What Causes Earthquakes?

The Earth's outer layer, its **crust**, is divided into huge pieces called **plates**. These plates, which are made of rock, are constantly moving —away from each other, toward each other, or past each other. A crack in Earth's crust between two plates is called a **fault**. Many earthquakes occur along faults where two plates collide as they move toward each other or grind together as they move past each other. Earthquakes along the **San Andreas Fault** in California are caused by the grinding of two plates.

## How Are Earthquakes Measured?

The strength of an earthquake is called its **magnitude**. The magnitude of an earthquake is registered on an instrument called a **seismograph** and is given a number on a scale called the **Richter scale**.

### RICHTER SCALE

The Richter scale goes from zero to more than 9. These numbers are used to describe the strength of an earthquake. Each number on the Richter scale is 10 times greater than the one before it. An earthquake measuring 6 on the Richter scale is 10 times stronger than an earthquake measuring 5 and 100 times stronger than one measuring 4. Earthquakes that register below 4 on the Richter scale are considered minor. Those of 4 or above are considered major.

*A seismograph* ▶

| MAGNITUDE | EFFECTS |
| --- | --- |
| 0-2 | Earthquake is recorded by instruments but is not felt by people. |
| 2-3 | Earthquake is felt slightly by a few people. |
| 3-4 | People feel tremors. Hanging objects like ceiling lights swing. |
| 4-5 | Earthquake causes some damage; walls crack; dishes and windows may break. |
| 5-6 | Furniture moves; earthquake seriously damages weak buildings. |
| 6-7 | Furniture may overturn; strong buildings are damaged; walls and buildings may collapse. |
| 7-8 | Many buildings are destroyed; underground pipes break; wide cracks appear in the ground. |
| Above 8 | Total devastation, including buildings and bridges; ground wavy. |

# Major Earthquakes of the 20th Century

The earthquakes listed below are among the largest and most destructive recorded in the 1900s. The list begins with recent earthquakes.

| YEAR | LOCATION | MAGNITUDE | DEATHS |
|------|----------|-----------|--------|
| 1997 | Iran (northern) | 7.5 | 1,560 |
| 1995 | Sakhalin Island (Russia) | 7.5 | 1,989 |
| 1995 | Japan (Kobe) | 6.9 | 5,502 |
| 1994 | United States (Los Angeles area) | 6.8 | 61 |
| 1993 | India (southern) | 6.3 | 9,748 |
| 1990 | Iran (northwestern) | 7.7 | 40,000 |
| 1989 | United States (San Francisco Bay area) | 7.1 | 62 |
| 1985 | Mexico (Michoacan) | 8.1 | 9,500 |
| 1976 | China (Tangshan) | 8.0 | 255,000 |
| 1976 | Guatemala | 7.5 | 23,000 |
| 1970 | Peru (northern) | 7.8 | 66,000 |
| 1960 | Chile (southern) | 9.5 | 5,000 |
| 1950 | India (Assam) | 8.7 | 1,530 |
| 1946 | Japan (Honshu) | 8.4 | 1,330 |
| 1939 | Chile (Chillan) | 8.3 | 28,000 |
| 1934 | India (Bihar-Nepal) | 8.4 | 10,700 |
| 1933 | Japan | 8.9 | 2,990 |
| 1927 | China (Nan-shan) | 8.3 | 200,000 |
| 1923 | Japan (Yokohama) | 8.3 | 143,000 |
| 1920 | China (Gansu) | 8.6 | 200,000 |
| 1906 | Chile (Valparaiso) | 8.6 | 20,000 |
| 1906 | United States (San Francisco) | 8.3 | 503 |

**DID YOU KNOW?**
Between December 16, 1811, and February 7, 1812, earthquakes near New Madrid, in Missouri, caused enormous damage in the midwestern United States. The earthquakes (estimated at about 8.7 on the Richter scale) were so powerful that they caused the Mississippi River to change its course.

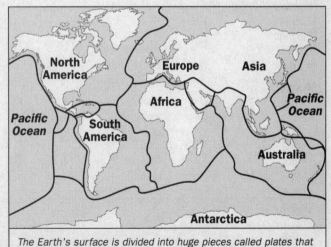

The Earth's surface is divided into huge pieces called plates that are constantly moving.

# GEOGRAPHy PUZZLE

## A DOUBLE PUZZLE IS TWICE THE FUN

**M**ost of the hidden words in this puzzle are from page 100. To find out what they are, first fill in the missing words in the sentences below, then locate them in the puzzle. The words go up, down, backward, forward, and diagonally. Some are used more than once. If you need help, you can find all the words in the word box at the bottom of the page. But it's more challenging to find them on your own. (Answers are on page 303.)

1. A river and a ___ ___ ___ are named for the English explorer Henry Hudson.
2. Christopher ___ ___ ___ ___ ___ ___ ___ ___ sailed to America four times.
3. Marco Polo's travels took him to China and ___ ___ ___ ___ ___.
4. ___ ___ ___ ___ Ponce de Leon named Florida.
5. ___ ___ ___ ___ ___ ___ ___ ___ ___ is both a country and a continent.
6. Leif ___ ___ ___ ___ ___ ___ ___ came across the ocean from Iceland.
7. Ferdinand ___ ___ ___ ___ ___ ___ ___ ___ sailed around the tip of South America.
8. Meriwether ___ ___ ___ ___ ___ and William Clark traveled from St. Louis to the Pacific Ocean and back.
9. In 1488, Bartholomeu ___ ___ ___ ___ explored the Cape of Good Hope.
10. Hernando de ___ ___ ___ ___ explored the lower Mississippi Valley.
11. David Livingstone explored southern ___ ___ ___ ___ ___ ___.
12. A shorter way to say "middle" is to use three letters, as in ___ ___ ___ -ocean.
13. A volcano is a ___ ___ ___ ___ ___ ___ ___ ___ topped by a crater.
14. European explorers had to cross an ___ ___ ___ ___ ___ to reach America.
15. To some explorers, America was the ___ ___ ___ World.
16. The Earth is our ___ ___ ___ ___ ___.

The leftover letters spell ___ ___ ___ ___ ___ ___ ___ ___ ___, a French explorer.

```
L  I  N  D  I  A  C  C  H
A  E  R  I  C  S  O  N  M
A  N  W  B  M  P  L  A  A
C  S  A  I  D  N  U  E  G
I  Y  O  U  S  E  M  C  E
R  L  A  T  J  W  B  O  L
F  D  L  R  O  W  U  I  L
A  I  L  A  R  T  S  U  A
N  M  O  U  N  T  A  I  N
```

| | | | |
|---|---|---|---|
| AFRICA | DIAS | LEWIS | NEW |
| AUSTRALIA | ERICSON | MAGELLAN | OCEAN |
| BAY | INDIA | MID | SOTO |
| COLUMBUS | JUAN | MOUNTAIN | WORLD |

# Learning About
# What's INSIDE Your BODY

**Y**our body is made up of many different parts that work together every minute of every day and night. The body is more amazing than any machine or computer. Machines don't eat, run, have feelings, read and learn, or do other things that you do. Even though everyone's body looks different outside, people have the same parts inside.

**DID YOU KNOW?**

- ☑ Your body is made up of billions of tiny living units called **cells.** Different kinds of cells have different tasks to do in the body.

- ☑ Cells that do similar work form **tissue,** like nerve tissue or bone tissue.

- ☑ Tissues that work together form **organs,** like the heart, lungs, and kidneys.

- ☑ The **skin** is the body's largest organ. It protects the internal organs from infection, injury, and harmful sunlight. It also helps control body temperature.

- ☑ Organs work together as **systems,** and each system has a separate job to do.

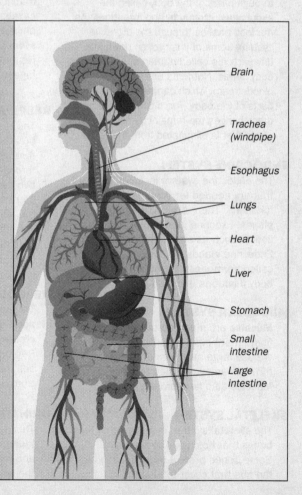

Brain

Trachea
(windpipe)

Esophagus

Lungs

Heart

Liver

Stomach

Small
intestine

Large
intestine

# What the Body's Systems Do

**E**ach system of the body has its own job. Some of the systems also work together in teams to keep you healthy and strong.

## CIRCULATORY SYSTEM

In the circulatory system, the **heart** pumps **blood**, which then travels through tubes, called **arteries**, to all parts of the body. The blood carries the oxygen and food that the body needs to stay alive. **Veins** carry the blood back to the heart.

## DIGESTIVE SYSTEM

The digestive system moves food through parts of the body called the **esophagus**, **stomach**, and **intestines**. As the food passes through the digestive system, some of it is broken down into tiny particles called nutrients, which the body needs. Nutrients enter the bloodstream, which carries them to all parts of the body. The digestive system then changes the remaining food into waste that is eliminated from the body.

## ENDOCRINE SYSTEM

The endocrine system includes **glands** that are needed for some body functions. There are two kinds of glands. Exocrine glands produce liquids such as sweat and saliva. Endocrine glands produce chemicals called **hormones**. Hormones control body functions, such as growth.

## MUSCULAR SYSTEM

**Muscles** are made up of elastic fibers that help the body move. We use large muscles to walk and run, and small muscles to smile. Muscles also help protect organs.

## SKELETAL SYSTEM

The skeletal system is made up of the **bones** that hold your body upright. Some bones protect organs, such as the ribs that cover the lungs.

## NERVOUS SYSTEM

The nervous system enables us to think, feel, move, hear, and see. It includes the **brain**, the **spinal cord**, and **nerves** in all parts of the body. Nerves in the spinal cord carry signals back and forth between the brain and the rest of the body. The brain tells us what to do and how to respond. The brain has three major parts. The **cerebrum** controls our thinking, speech, and vision. The **cerebellum** is responsible for physical coordination. The **brain stem** controls the body's respiratory, circulatory, and digestive systems.

## RESPIRATORY SYSTEM

The respiratory system allows us to breathe. Air comes into the body through the nose and mouth. It goes through the windpipe (or trachea) to two tubes (called bronchi), which carry air to the **lungs**. Oxygen from the air is taken in by tiny blood vessels in the lungs. The blood then carries oxygen to the cells of the body.

## REPRODUCTIVE SYSTEM

Through the reproductive system, adult human beings are able to create new human beings. Reproduction begins when a sperm cell from a man fertilizes an egg cell from a woman.

## URINARY SYSTEM

This system, which includes the **kidneys**, cleans waste from the blood and regulates the amount of water in the body.

# The TRUTH About COLDS

Colds are the most common illnesses we get. Schoolchildren often catch colds from one another—usually about 5 to 8 colds a year. Here are some mistakes, and some facts, about colds.

**Fiction:** In low temperatures, you can catch a cold by going outside without a coat.

**Fact:** It's smart to dress warmly when it's cold out. But colds are caused by viruses, and not cold weather. Washing your hands is a good way to avoid catching many viruses.

**Fiction:** Some vitamins and medicines cure colds.

**Fact:** While some vitamins and medicines may make you feel better for a while, there is no cure for the cold. It usually lasts about one or two weeks.

**Fiction:** You can cure a cold by staying home.

**Fact:** There is no cure for the cold. Enough sleep, drinking juices, and eating well will help you feel better.

# TAKE CARE of Your TEETH

If you want to chew food properly and speak clearly, it is important to keep your teeth healthy. Here are some tips for doing that.

- ☑ **Brush your teeth at least twice a day**—after every meal if you can.
- ☑ **Floss.** Use dental floss regularly to clean between your teeth.
- ☑ **Eat healthful foods.** Eating too many sweets and sodas causes cavities.
- ☑ **Visit your dentist** for a checkup and cleaning every six months.

**What Causes Cavities in Your Teeth?** Cavities are caused by tiny pieces of food left on or between the teeth after eating. These pieces of food combine with the natural bacteria in your mouth to form an acid. The acid slowly eats away the tooth's enamel and causes tooth decay, or cavities.

## Which Doctor Does What?

A **dentist** is a doctor who takes general care of your teeth.
An **orthodontist** is a doctor who straightens teeth.
A **pediatrician** is a doctor who takes care of children.
An **orthopedist** is a doctor who fixes broken bones.
A **dermatologist** is a doctor who treats skin problems and diseases.
A **cardiologist** is a doctor who treats people who have heart problems.
A **psychiatrist** is a doctor who helps people with emotional problems.

### DOCTOR PUZZLE

Using the letters in the word "cardiologist," see how many words you can make that have at least three letters. Plurals don't count. (Answers are on page 303.)

## SURPRISING FACTS About the Body

☑ **A newborn baby has more bones than an adult**. A baby's body has 350 bones, but an adult's body has 206 bones. That's because bones grow together to make fewer, larger bones as the baby grows up.

☑ **The largest bone in your body is your thigh bone** (or femur). The smallest bone in your body is the stirrup (or stapes), a tiny bone in your middle ear.

☑ **Children have 20 first teeth.** Adults have 32 teeth.

☑ **The human body has more than 650 muscles**.

☑ **The heart weighs less than one pound**. It beats about 100,000 times a day, and it pumps 2,000 gallons of blood in a day.

☑ **An adult's large intestine is about 5 feet long**. The small intestine, which is much narrower than the large one, is about 25 feet long.

☑ **Red blood cells live for about 120 days**. Then they are replaced by new ones. The bone cells in your body live for 25 to 30 years. Your brain cells live for a lifetime.

☑ **About 70% of the average-sized adult body is made up of water**.

☑ **It takes around 17 muscles to smile and around 43 to frown.**

# Staying Healthy With EXERCISE

**D**aily exercise is important for your good health, fitness, and appearance. Exercise makes you feel good. It helps you think better. And, believe it or not, it helps you sleep better and feel less tired and more relaxed. Once you start exercising regularly, you will feel stronger and keep improving at physical activities.

**What Happens When You Exercise?** When you exercise, you breathe more deeply and get more oxygen into your lungs with each breath. Your heart pumps more oxygen-filled blood to all parts of your body with each beat. Your muscles and joints feel more flexible. Exercise also helps you to stay at a healthy weight.

**What About People Who Don't Exercise?** People who don't exercise may have less strength and energy. They may not sleep well and may feel tired. And they may gain more weight than would be healthy.

**What Kind of Exercise Is Good?** Almost all kinds of activity that move the body around are good. Bicycling, dancing, skating, swimming, running, roller-blading, and playing soccer are a few ways to exercise and have fun at the same time.

# Which Foods Are the RIGHT FOODS?

To stay healthy, it is important to eat the right foods and to exercise. To help people choose the right foods for good health and fitness, the U.S. government developed the food pyramid shown below. The food pyramid shows the groups of foods that should be eaten every day.

The foods shown at the bottom (the largest part) of the pyramid are the foods to be eaten in the largest amounts. At the top are the foods to be eaten in the smallest amounts. The number of servings a person should eat depends on the person's age and body size. Younger, smaller people may eat fewer servings. Older, larger people may eat more. The meaning of "serving" is explained at the bottom of this page.

## FOOD GUIDE PYRAMID: A GUIDE TO DAILY FOOD CHOICES

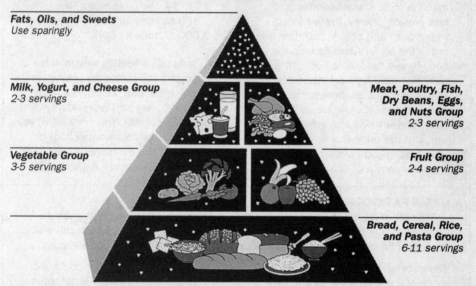

**Fats, Oils, and Sweets**
*Use sparingly*

**Milk, Yogurt, and Cheese Group**
*2-3 servings*

**Meat, Poultry, Fish, Dry Beans, Eggs, and Nuts Group**
*2-3 servings*

**Vegetable Group**
*3-5 servings*

**Fruit Group**
*2-4 servings*

**Bread, Cereal, Rice, and Pasta Group**
*6-11 servings*

## HOW MUCH FOOD IS IN A SERVING?

☑ **Milk, Yogurt, and Cheese Group**
1 serving = 1 cup of milk or yogurt; or $1\frac{1}{2}$ to 2 ounces of cheese

☑ **Meat, Poultry, Fish Group**
1 serving = 2 to 3 ounces of cooked lean meat, fish, or poultry; $\frac{1}{2}$ cup of cooked dry beans; 2 eggs; or 4 to 6 tablespoons of peanut butter

☑ **Vegetable Group**
1 serving = 1 cup of raw, leafy green vegetables; $\frac{1}{2}$ cup of other vegetables (cooked or chopped raw); or $\frac{3}{4}$ cup vegetable juice

☑ **Fruit Group**
1 serving = 1 medium apple, banana, or orange; $\frac{1}{2}$ cup of cooked, chopped, or canned fruit; or $\frac{3}{4}$ cup of fruit juice

☑ **Bread, Cereal, Rice and Pasta Group**
1 serving = 1 slice of bread; 1 ounce of ready-to-eat cereal; or $\frac{1}{2}$ cup of cooked cereal, rice, or pasta

# HEALTH TALK

Have you ever noticed the labels on the packages of food you and your family buy? The labels provide information people need to make healthy choices about the foods they eat. Below are some terms you may see on labels.

## NUTRIENTS ARE NECESSARY

**Nutrients** are the parts of food that the body can use. The body needs nutrients for growth, for energy, and to repair itself when something goes wrong. Carbohydrates, fats, proteins, vitamins, minerals, and water are different kinds of nutrients that are found in food. **Carbohydrates** and **fats** provide energy. **Proteins** help with growth and help to maintain and repair the body. **Vitamins** help the body to use food, help eyesight and skin, and help fight off infections. **Minerals** help build bones and teeth and work with the chemicals in the body. **Water** helps with growth and repair of the body. It also works with the blood and chemicals, and helps the body get rid of wastes.

## CALORIES COUNT

A **calorie** is a measure of the amount of energy we get from food. The government recommends the number of calories that should be taken in for different age groups. The number of calories recommended for children ages 7 to 10 is 2,400 a day. For ages 11 to 14, the government recommends 2,400 calories for girls every day and 2,800 calories for boys.

To maintain a **healthy weight**, it is important to balance the calories in the food you eat with the calories used by the body every day. Every activity uses up some calories. The more active you are, the more calories your body is burning. If you eat more calories than your body uses, you will gain weight.

## A LITTLE FAT GOES A LONG WAY

**A little bit of fat** is important for your body. It keeps your body warm. It gives the muscles energy. It helps keep the skin soft and healthy. But the body needs only a small amount of fat to do all these things—just one tablespoon of fat each day is enough.

**Cholesterol.** Eating too much fat can cause some people's bodies to produce too much of a chemical called **cholesterol** (ko-LESS-ter-all). This is a waxy substance that can build up over the years on the inside of arteries. Too much cholesterol keeps blood from flowing freely through the arteries and can cause serious health problems such as heart attacks.

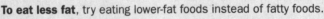

**To eat less fat**, try eating lower-fat foods instead of fatty foods.

| Some lower-fat foods: | Some fatty foods: |
|---|---|
| chicken or turkey hot dog | beef or pork hot dog |
| broiled chicken breast | fried hamburger |
| tuna fish canned in water | tuna fish canned in oil |
| pretzels | potato chips |
| low-fat or nonfat frozen yogurt | ice cream |
| plain popcorn (with no butter) | buttered popcorn |
| skim milk or 1% or 2% milk | whole milk |

# Say NO
# to DRUGS, ALCOHOL, and CIGARETTES

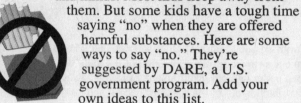

**D**rugs, alcohol, and cigarettes can do serious damage to people's bodies and minds. Most kids keep away from them. But some kids have a tough time saying "no" when they are offered harmful substances. Here are some ways to say "no." They're suggested by DARE, a U.S. government program. Add your own ideas to this list.

- ☑ **Say "No thanks."** (Say it again and again if you have to.)
- ☑ **Give reasons.** ("I don't like cigarettes" or "I'm going to soccer practice" or "I have asthma.")
- ☑ **Change the subject** or offer a better suggestion.
- ☑ **Walk away.** (Don't argue, don't discuss it. Just leave.)
- ☑ **Avoid the situation.** (If you are asked to a party where kids will be drinking, smoking, or using drugs, make plans to do something else instead.)
- ☑ **Find strength in numbers.** (Do things with friends who don't use harmful substances.)

## UNDERSTANDING AIDS

**What Is AIDS?** AIDS is a disease that is caused by a virus called HIV. AIDS attacks the body's immune system. The immune system is important because it helps the body fight off infections and diseases.

**How Do Kids Get AIDS?** A mother with AIDS may give it to her baby before the baby is born. Sometimes children (and adults, too) get AIDS from blood transfusions. But this happens less often, because blood banks now test all donations of blood for the AIDS virus.

**How Do Adults Get AIDS?** Adults get AIDS in two main ways: Having sex with a person who has AIDS, or sharing a needle used for drugs with a person who has AIDS.

**How Kids and Adults _Don't_ Get AIDS.** People _don't_ get AIDS from everyday contact with infected people at school, at home, or other places. People _don't_ get AIDS from clothes, telephones, or toilet seats, or from food prepared by someone with AIDS. Children _don't_ get AIDS from sitting near AIDS victims or from shaking hands with them.

**Is There a Cure for AIDS?** Not yet. But researchers are working to develop a vaccine to prevent AIDS or a drug to cure it. And new treatments are beginning to increase the lifespan of AIDS victims.

# Stay SAFE,
# PREVENT ACCIDENTS

**B**eing careful and using common sense are the best ways to avoid accidents. No one can prevent every accident. But some—especially those in the home, where most accidents happen—can be prevented. Here are some safety tips.

☑ **In the Kitchen.** Check with an adult about whether you can use a knife. Handle sharp knives carefully. Always cut away from your body and put the knife down in a safe place. To avoid fire, keep paper or cloth (like napkins or towels) away from the stove. Keep sharp objects and matches out of the reach of babies and little children.

☑ **In the Bathroom.** Use a rubber mat or other non-slip surface to keep you from slipping in the tub. Keep soap in a soap dish. Keep electrical appliances, such as radios and hair dryers, away from water.

☑ **In Every Room.** Everyone in your home should know all the exits in case of fire. If an accident happens, call an adult to help. Never let strangers into your home. Don't give your name or address to strangers over the phone. Don't let anyone know if you are home alone.

☑ **On Bikes and Skates.** Wear a helmet. When skating, wear wrist, elbow, and knee guards. Be alert. Look for traffic and watch for bikes, skaters, and people walking. Learn the safety laws for cars. They apply to others on the road, too.

☑ **In Cars.** Always wear a seat belt. Don't distract the driver; don't jump around.

☑ **On the Street.** Watch for traffic. Look both ways. Cross only at corners. Stay on the curb until the light turns green and the "Walk" sign is on. Don't fool around near traffic.

## BE READY for Any EMERGENCY

**1. Tape a list of emergency numbers** near the phone or on the refrigerator. Numbers to include are:

- your parents' or guardians' telephone numbers at work

- the telephone number of a relative or other adult who lives nearby.

- the numbers of your family doctor, a nearby hospital, the fire department, and the police department.

Emergency phone numbers can often be found inside the front cover of your local telephone book.

**2. Remember 911.** The number 911 is a special phone number for emergencies only. When a person who needs help right away calls 911, the operator asks the caller for his or her name and address and what the emergency is. Then the operator quickly sends the police, an ambulance, and, if needed, the fire department. Dial 0 (Operator) if your town doesn't have 911, and ask the operator for help.

# Legal or Public HOLIDAYS in the United States

There are no legal holidays for the whole United States. The U.S. government decides which days are holidays for its workers and for Washington, D.C. Each state picks its own holidays, but most states celebrate those listed below. On legal holidays, most banks and schools are closed, and so are many offices. Since 1971, Washington's Birthday (now often celebrated as Presidents' Day), Memorial Day, Columbus Day, and Veterans Day have been celebrated on a Monday so that many people can have a three-day weekend.

**New Year's Day.** Countries the world over celebrate the new year, although not always on January 1. The Chinese New Year falls between January 10 and February 19. In ancient Egypt, the New Year began around mid-June, when the Nile river overflowed and watered the crops.

**Martin Luther King, Jr., Day.** Observed on the third Monday in January, this holiday marks the birth (January 15, 1929) of the African-American civil rights leader Martin Luther King, Jr.

**Washington's Birthday or Presidents' Day.** On the third Monday in February, Americans often celebrate the births of both George Washington (born February 22, 1732) and Abraham Lincoln (born February 12, 1809).

**Memorial Day or Decoration Day.** Memorial Day, observed on the last Monday in May, is set aside to remember all those who died in United States wars.

**Fourth of July or Independence Day.** July 4 is the anniversary of the day in 1776 when the American colonies declared their independence from England. Kids and grownups celebrate with bands and parades, picnics, barbecues, and fireworks.

**Labor Day.** Labor Day, the first Monday in September, honors the workers of America. It was first celebrated in 1882.

**Columbus Day.** Celebrated on the second Monday in October, Columbus Day is the anniversary of October 12, 1492, the day when Christopher Columbus was traditionally thought to have discovered America.

**Election Day.** Election Day, the first Tuesday after the first Monday in November, is a legal holiday in some states.

**Veterans Day.** Veterans Day, November 11, honors the veterans of United States wars. First called Armistice Day, it marked the armistice (agreement) that ended World War I. This was signed on the 11th hour (11 A.M.) of the 11th day of the 11th month of 1918.

**Thanksgiving.** Celebrated on the fourth Thursday in November, Thanksgiving Day was first observed by the Pilgrims in 1621 as a harvest festival and a day for thanks and feasting.

**Christmas.** Christmas is both a religious holiday and a legal holiday. (See p. 180.)

## HOLIDAYS in 1999

| Holiday | Date in 1999 | Day |
|---|---|---|
| New Year's Day | January 1 | Friday |
| Martin Luther King, Jr., Day | January 18 | Monday |
| Washington's Birthday | February 15 | Monday |
| Memorial Day | May 31 | Monday |
| Independence Day | July 4 | Sunday |
| Labor Day | September 6 | Monday |
| Columbus Day | October 11 | Monday |
| Election Day | November 2 | Tuesday |
| Veterans Day | November 11 | Thursday |
| Thanksgiving | November 25 | Thursday |
| Christmas | December 25 | Saturday |

## Some Other SPECIAL HOLIDAYS

**Valentine's Day** February 14 is a day for sending cards or gifts to people you love.

**Arbor Day** To remind us of how they protect the environment, we plant trees on Arbor Day. Each state observes the day at different times in the spring, depending on the state's climate.

**Halloween** In ancient Britain, Druids lit fires and wore grotesque costumes on October 31 to scare off evil spirits. Today, "trick or treating" children collect candy and other sweets. Some also collect money for UNICEF, the United Nations Children's Fund.

**Mother's Day and Father's Day** Mothers are honored on the second Sunday in May. Fathers are honored on the third Sunday in June.

**Kwanzaa** Originally an African harvest festival, Kwanzaa is a week-long African-American celebration beginning on December 26. Candles are lit every night.

## HOLIDAYS AROUND THE WORLD

**Children's Day** In Japan, May 5 is set aside to honor children.

**Canada Day** Canada's national holiday, July 1, commemorates the union of Canadian provinces under one government in 1867.

**Chinese New Year** China's most important holiday falls between January 21 and February 9 every year. Celebrations include lively parades, fireworks, and traditional family meals.

**Boxing Day** December 26 is a holiday in Britain, and also in Australia, Canada, and New Zealand. On this day, at one time, Christmas gifts were distributed in boxes to servants, tradespeople, and the poor.

**Independence Day** Mexico celebrates September 16 as its national holiday.

# Some Major INVENTIONS

Some of the world's most important inventions were developed before history was written. These include tools and the wheel, the ability to make and control fire, and the ability to make pottery. More recent inventions help us to travel faster, communicate better, and live longer.

## INVENTIONS THAT TAKE US FROM ONE PLACE TO ANOTHER

Automobiles made travel easier, and jet planes allowed ordinary people to see the world.

| Year | Invention | Inventor | Country |
|------|-----------|----------|---------|
| 1785 | parachute | Jean Pierre Blanchard | France |
| 1807 | steamboat | Robert Fulton | U.S. |
| 1829 | steam locomotive | George Stephenson | England |
| 1852 | safety elevator | Elisha G. Otis | U.S. |
| 1885 | bicycle | James Starley | England |
| 1885 | motorcycle | Goltlieb Daimler | Germany |
| 1891 | escalator | Jesse W. Reno | U.S. |
| 1892 | automobile (gasoline) | Charles E. Duryea & J. Frank Duryea | U.S. |
| 1894 | submarine | Simon Lake | U.S. |
| 1895 | diesel engine | Rudolf Diesel | Germany |
| 1903 | propeller airplane | Orville & Wilbur Wright | U.S. |
| 1939 | helicopter | Igor Sikorsky | U.S. |
| 1939 | turbojet airplane | Hans von Ohain | Germany |
| 1969 | supersonic passenger airplane (Concorde) | Aérospatiale & British Aircraft Corp. | France & England |

## INVENTIONS THAT HELP US LIVE HEALTHIER AND LONGER LIVES

Penicillin and other antibiotics help fight some illnesses. CAT scanners and X rays help doctors look inside our bodies to see if anything is wrong.

| Year | Invention | Inventor | Country |
|------|-----------|----------|---------|
| 1780 | bifocal lenses for glasses | Benjamin Franklin | U.S. |
| 1819 | stethoscope | René T.M.H. Laënnec | France |
| 1842 | anesthesia (ether) | Crawford W. Long | U.S. |
| 1895 | X ray | Wilhelm Roentgen | Germany |
| 1922 | insulin | Sir Frederick G. Banting | Canada |
| 1929 | penicillin | Alexander Fleming | Scotland |
| 1954 | antibiotic for fungal diseases | Rachel F. Brown & Elizabeth L. Hazen | U.S. |
| 1955 | polio vaccine | Jonas E. Salk | U.S. |
| 1973 | CAT scanner | Godfrey N. Hounsfield | England |

## INVENTIONS THAT HELP US COMMUNICATE WITH ONE ANOTHER

The pen, pencil, and printing press, fax, phone, and computer are all ways of exchanging messages, information, and ideas.

| Year | Invention | Inventor | Country |
| --- | --- | --- | --- |
| A.D. 105 | paper | Ts'ai Lun | China |
| 1447 | movable type | Johann Gutenberg | Germany |
| 1795 | modern pencil | Nicolas Jacques Conté | France |
| 1837 | telegraph | Samuel F.B. Morse | U.S. |
| 1845 | rotary printing press | Richard M. Hoe | U.S. |
| 1867 | typewriter | Christopher L. Sholes, Carlos Glidden, & Samuel W. Soulé | U.S. |
| 1876 | telephone | Alexander G. Bell | U.S. |
| 1888 | ballpoint pen | John Loud | U.S. |
| 1913 | modern radio receiver | Reginald A. Fessenden | U.S. |
| 1937 | xerography copies | Chester Carlson | U.S. |
| 1942 | electronic computer | John V. Atanasoff & Clifford Berry | U.S. |
| 1944 | auto sequence computer | Howard H. Aiken | U.S. |
| 1947 | transistor | William Shockley, Walter H. Brattain, & John Bardeen | U.S. |
| 1955 | fiber optics | Narinder S. Kapany | England |
| 1965 | word processor | IBM | U.S. |
| 1979 | cellular telephone | Ericsson Company | Sweden |

## INVENTIONS THAT MAKE OUR LIVES EASIER

| Year | Invention | Inventor | Country |
| --- | --- | --- | --- |
| 1800 | electric battery | Alessandro Volta | Italy |
| 1827 | matches | John Walker | England |
| 1831 | lawn mower | Edwin Budding & John Ferrabee | England |
| 1834 | refrigeration | Jacob Perkins | England |
| 1846 | sewing machine | Elias Howe | U.S. |
| 1851 | cylinder (door) lock | Linus Yale | U.S. |
| 1879 | electric light bulb | Thomas A. Edison | U.S. |
| 1886 | dishwasher | Josephine Cochran | U.S. |
| 1891 | zipper | Whitcomb L. Judson | U.S. |
| 1901 | washing machine | Langmuir Fisher | U.S. |
| 1903 | windshield wipers | Mary Anderson | U.S. |
| 1907 | vacuum cleaner | J. Murray Spangler | U.S. |
| 1911 | air conditioning | Willis H. Carrier | U.S. |
| 1924 | frozen packaged food | Clarence Birdseye | U.S. |
| 1947 | microwave oven | Percy L. Spencer | U.S. |
| 1948 | Velcro | Georges de Mestral | Switzerland |
| 1969 | cash machine (ATM) | Don Wetzel | U.S. |
| 1971 | food processor | Pierre Verdon | France |

 **DID YOU KNOW?** Thomas Alva Edison (1847-1931) claimed more than 1,000 inventions. Among them are early motion pictures, an electric light bulb, and a talking doll.

## INVENTIONS THAT ENTERTAIN US

Books, games, the radio, and television have entertained us in our homes for many years. Newer inventions like VCRs and CD players also entertain us today.

| Year | Invention | Inventor | Country |
|------|-----------|----------|---------|
| 1709 | piano | Bartolomeo Cristofori | Italy |
| 1877 | phonograph | Thomas A. Edison | U.S. |
| 1877 | microphone | Emile Berliner | U.S. |
| 1888 | portable camera | George Eastman | U.S. |
| 1893 | moving picture viewer | Thomas A. Edison | U.S. |
| 1894 | motion picture projector | Charles F. Jenkins | U.S. |
| 1899 | tape recorder | Valdemar Poulsen | Denmark |
| 1923 | television* | Vladimir K. Zworykin* | U.S. |
| 1951 | flexible kite | Gertrude Rogallo & Francis Rogallo | U.S. |
| 1963 | audiocassette | Phillips Corporation | Netherlands |
| 1969 | videotape cassette | Sony | Japan |
| 1972 | compact disc (CD) | RCA | U.S. |
| 1972 | video game (Pong) | Noland Buschnel | U.S. |
| 1979 | Walkman | Sony | Japan |

*Others who helped invent television include Philo T. Farnsworth (1926) and John Baird (1928).*

### A MISTAKE THAT WORKED

Some inventions are created by accident. Walter E. Diemer (1905-1998) was an accountant for a chewing gum company. In his free time, he experimented with ways to make gum chewier. Instead, he came up with something that bubbled—the first batch of bubble gum. He made it pink because that was the only food coloring he had.

## INVENTIONS THAT HELP US EXPAND OUR UNIVERSE

| Year | Invention | Inventor | Country |
|------|-----------|----------|---------|
| 1250 | magnifying glass | Roger Bacon | England |
| 1590 | 2-lens microscope | Zacharias Janssen | Netherlands |
| 1608 | telescope | Hans Lippershey | Netherlands |
| 1714 | mercury thermometer | Gabriel D. Fahrenheit | Germany |
| 1926 | rocket engine | Robert H. Goddard | U.S. |
| 1930 | cyclotron (atom smasher) | Ernest O. Lawrence | U.S. |
| 1943 | Aqua Lung | Jacques-Yves Cousteau & Emile Gagnan | France |
| 1953 | bathyscaphe | August Piccard | France |
| 1977 | space shuttle | NASA | U.S. |

### NATIONAL INVENTORS HALL OF FAME

If you would like to learn more about inventions and the people who created them, or try to make your own invention, visit Inventure Place, National Inventors Hall of Fame, 221 S. Broadway St., Akron, Ohio, 44308. Phone: (216) 762-4463.

# ABBREVIATIONS

**A**bbreviations are short forms of words or phrases. We use abbreviations all the time because they save us time in both writing and speaking. Acronyms are abbreviations made out of the first letters of several words. An acronym can be pronounced as a word. NASA is an acronym for National Aeronautics and Space Administration.

### TITLES
We almost always use abbreviations before and after people's names.
For example, Mr., Mrs., Ms., Miss, Jr., and Sr.

### TECHNICAL TALK
Special fields have their own abbreviations.

**Sports.** Professional football teams belong to the NFL (National Football League). Pro hockey teams are part of the NHL (National Hockey League). Baseball players score RBIs (runs batted in). MVP in any sport stands for Most Valuable Player.

**Cooking.** Cooks measure their ingredients by the tsp. (teaspoon), tbs. or tbsp. (tablespoon), oz. (ounce), or lb. (pound).

**Computers.** Computer users talk about a PC (personal computer) and CD-ROM (Compact Disk-Read Only Memory) and send each other e-mail (electronic mail). They often use the abbreviation "www" when logging onto the World Wide Web, which they also call "the Web."

**Navigation.** Navigators use N, S, E, and W to refer to compass directions.

## ABBREVIATIONS PUZZLE

**C**an you match each of these phrases with their abbreviations?
(Answers are on page 303.)

| | |
|---|---|
| 1. World Wide Web | a. UFO |
| 2. as soon as possible | b. WYSIWYG |
| 3. alternating current | c. DA |
| 4. absent without leave | d. ATM |
| 5. automated teller machine | e. ESP |
| 6. district attorney | f. AWOL |
| 7. what you see is what you get | g. RFD |
| 8. rural free delivery | h. WWW |
| 9. extrasensory perception | i. AC |
| 10. unidentified flying object | j. ASAP |

# Words That SOUND ALIKE or Almost Alike

When words sound similar, sometimes their spellings and meanings are confusing. Words that sound alike are called **homophones**.

### BRAKE OR BREAK
A **brake** is a device for slowing or stopping a vehicle. A **break** is a brief rest period (a lunch break).

### CAPITAL OR CAPITOL
A **capital** is the city where a country or state government is located. The **capitol** is the building where a legislative body meets.

### DESERT OR DESSERT
A **desert** is a hot, sandy area where few plants can grow. **Dessert** is fruit, ice cream, or something else eaten at the end of a meal.

### EMIGRATE OR IMMIGRATE
To **emigrate** means to move away from a country. To **immigrate** means to move to a country. (Ana emigrated from Brazil. She immigrated to the United States.)

### FAIR OR FARE
A **fair** is an exhibition or show. **Fair** also means better than poor, but less than good. **Fare** is the cost of a ride on a public vehicle like a bus, train, plane, or taxi.

### FLOUR OR FLOWER
Cakes and breads are made with **flour**. A **flower** is a blossom.

### HOARSE OR HORSE
If your voice is **hoarse**, it's rough or harsh. A **horse** is an animal that can gallop quickly.

### ITS OR IT'S
**Its** is the possessive form of "it" (the bird flapped its wings). **It's** is a contraction of "it is."

### PRINCIPAL OR PRINCIPLE
A **principal** is the person in charge of a school. **Principal** also means first in importance. A **principle** is a basic idea that a person believes in deeply.

### STATIONARY OR STATIONERY
**Stationary** means fixed in one place. **Stationery** means paper and envelopes to write on.

### THEIR, THEY'RE, OR THERE
**Their** is the possessive form of "they." **They're** is a contraction of "they are." **There** means at or in that place. (They're going to put their packages there on the table.)

# NEW WORDS

**E**nglish is a language that is always changing. New words become part of the vocabulary, while other words become outdated. The new words may come from television shows, books, even slang first used on the street. Here are some words that have recently been added to dictionaries.

**blow off** • to refuse to deal with, or to fail to show up for
(She blew off Jenny and went to the movies with Emily.)

**channel surfing** • rapidly changing TV channels, usually with a remote control
(Jim channel surfed so he could watch three games at a time on TV.)

**cineplex** • a building that contains several movie theaters
(We spent the day at the cineplex watching one movie after another.)

**grunge** • music that mixes rock and roll, punk rock, and heavy metal; kinds of clothes worn by fans of this music
(Some kids wear grunge clothes and listen to grunge music.)

**morph** • to change to a different form
(The cartoon characters morph from ordinary kids into cartoon superheroes.)

# IDIOMS: Words That Are Not As They Seem

Idioms are groups of words (phrases) that cannot be understood just by knowing the meaning of each of the words. This often makes them particularly puzzling to people learning a new language. Some idioms are hard to understand even in your own language. Here are some common idioms, with their meanings.

**ALL ABOUT CLOTHES**
**fit like a glove:** fit or suit perfectly
**fill someone's shoes:** take someone else's place, do another person's job
**cap in hand:** in a humble or respectful manner
**get hot under the collar:** become angry
**keep under one's hat:** keep secret, keep to oneself
**in one's stocking feet:** wearing stockings or socks, but not shoes

**IT'S ALL IN THE GAME**
**to play games:** to fool someone or keep the truth from someone
**to be on the ball:** to be alert or quick to catch on or understand
**get the ball rolling:** get something started
**to be off base:** to be wrong
**right off the bat:** immediately, first thing
**skate on thin ice:** be in a dangerous or risky situation

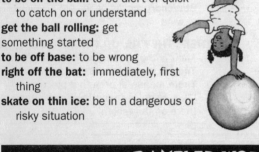

**COLORFUL EXPRESSIONS**
**in the black:** making a profit, not in debt
**out of the blue:** unexpectedly, without warning
**to be green with envy:** to be extremely envious
**to see red:** to become very angry
**to wave a white flag:** to indicate, in battle, that you wish to surrender

## SCRAMBLED WORD PUZZLE

Unscramble the tiles to find out which idiom they contain. (Answers are on page 304.)

1. | LOV | LI | FIT | E | AG | KE |

Idiom: _____ _____ _____ _____

2. | B | HE | LU | T | E | T | OF | OU |

Idiom: _____ _____ _____ _____

3. | HT | RIG | TH | OFF | EB | AT |

Idiom: _____ _____ _____ _____

# Where Do ENGLISH WORDS Come From?

**E**ach new ethnic group that immigrated to the United States brought its own traditions and customs. Many of their foods and customs were adopted by Americans, and so were the words that described them. Here are some food words and the languages they came from.

**from Arabic:**
apricot, candy, coffee, couscous, lime, sherbet, spinach, sugar, syrup, tuna

**from Chinese:**
chopsticks, chow, chow mein, soy, tea, wok, wonton

**from French:**
bouillon, casserole, chowder, crepe, croissant, croutons, mayonnaise, menu, mousse, omelette, quiche, tart

**from German:**
delicatessen, frankfurter, hamburger, pretzel, pumpernickel, sauerkraut, seltzer

**from Italian:**
bologna, broccoli, lasagna, minestrone, pasta, pizza, salami, spaghetti

**from Japanese:**
sukiyaki, sushi, tempura, teriyaki, tofu

**from Spanish:**
avocado, burrito, chili, chocolate, cocoa, garbanzo, maize, tamale, tomato, tortilla

**from Yiddish:**
bagel, blintze, knish, nosh

## LANGUAGE PUZZLE

**H**idden in this puzzle are words to do with foods and eating. The words have become part of the English language, but they come from other languages. The words go up, down, backward, forward, and diagonally. Some letters are used more than once. (Answers are on page 304.)

**WORD LIST**

| APRICOT | PASTA | SPAGHETTI | TEA |
|---------|-------|-----------|-----|
| BAGEL | PIZZA | SUGAR | TEMPURA |
| MAIZE | SAUERKRAUT | SYRUP | TOFU |
| MENU | SOY | TART | WOK |

```
T   A   R   T   E   M   P   U   R   A
S   P   A   G   H   E   T   T   I   Z
Y   R   A   G   U   S   O   Y   B   Z
R   I   U   J   A   P   P   A   A   I
U   C   F   N   A   M   G   E   S   P
P   O   O   S   E   E   W   O   K   A
E   T   T   N   L   M   A   I   Z   E
S   A   U   E   R   K   R   A   U   T
```

The leftover letters spell the language that gave us sukiyaki and sushi:

_ _ _ _ _ _ _ _

# Writing a LETTER

**D**id you know there are different kinds of letters? A letter or note to a friend or relative is informal, and you can write it any way you like. But a letter to an official person—say, your mayor or the head of a company—is a formal letter and should include your name and address, the date, the address of the person you're writing to, and an ending such as "Sincerely yours" or "Yours truly." Below are examples of a formal letter to a company and two informal letters, one written on a computer for e-mail.

222 Fifth Street
Small Town, RI 02898

January 24, 1998

Joan Smith, President
The Totally Rad Skate Company
123 Zip Street
Whoops, CA  90086

Dear Ms. Smith:

   I saved up a long time—at least a year—to buy a pair of your best skates. So it was disappointing that they broke after I just used them twice. One wheel fell off! Luckily I was just putting on my skates when that happened.

   The store where I bought them won't take back the skates. They said I must have broken the wheel. But, honest, I was very careful. Please tell me what to do.  Please get back to me as soon as you can. Thank you for your help.

Sincerely yours,

Darren

Darren Lewis

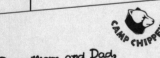

Dear Mom and Dad,
Camp is fun. My team won at volleyball. My friend Billy got poison ivy.

Love,
Bobby

Ride Home

Send    Compose    Send Later    Delete

From: MiaGal
Date: Sept. 15, 1998, 11:05:24 EST
To: CoolCathi
Subject: Band Practice

Hi! I'm going to band practice after school tomorrow. Are you? If you are, can you give me a ride home? Please e-mail back before 9 tonight. Thanks.

# LANGUAGES of the WORLD

Would you have guessed that Mandarin, the principal language of China, is the world's most spoken language? You may find more surprises in the chart below, which lists languages spoken in 1997 by at least 50,000,000 native speakers (those for whom the language is their first language, or mother tongue) and some of the places where they are spoken.

Konnichi wa! (Japanese)

## PRINCIPAL LANGUAGES OF THE WORLD

| LANGUAGE | WHERE SPOKEN | NATIVE SPEAKERS |
|---|---|---|
| Mandarin | China, Taiwan | 863,000,000 |
| Hindi* | India | 357,000,000 |
| Spanish | Spain, Latin America | 352,000,000 |
| English | U.S., Canada, Britain | 335,000,000 |
| Bengali* | India, Bangladesh | 200,000,000 |
| Arabic | Arabian Peninsula | 200,000,000 |
| Portuguese | Portugal, Brazil | 173,000,000 |
| Russian | Russia | 168,000,000 |
| Japanese | Japan | 125,000,000 |
| German | Germany | 99,000,000 |
| French | France, Canada, Haiti | 75,000,000 |
| Malay-Indonesian | Indonesia | 57,000,000 |

Hello! (English)

*Hindi and Bengali are spoken in different parts of India.

¡Hola! (Spanish)

# Which LANGUAGES Are SPOKEN in the UNITED STATES?

Since the beginning of American history, immigrants have come to the United States from all over the world and brought their native languages with them. That's why so many Americans speak a language other than English at home. Here are some of the languages other than English that are spoken by 200,000 or more Americans.

| LANGUAGE USED AT HOME | SPEAKERS OVER 5 YEARS OLD | LANGUAGE USED AT HOME | SPEAKERS OVER 5 YEARS OLD |
|---|---|---|---|
| 1. Spanish | 17,339,000 | 11. Japanese | 428,000 |
| 2. French | 1,702,000 | 12. Greek | 388,000 |
| 3. German | 1,547,000 | 13. Arabic | 355,000 |
| 4. Italian | 1,309,000 | 14. Hindi, Urdu, | |
| 5. Chinese | 1,249,000 | & related | |
| 6. Tagalog | 843,000 | languages | 331,000 |
| 7. Polish | 723,000 | 15. Russian | 242,000 |
| 8. Korean | 626,000 | 16. Yiddish | 213,000 |
| 9. Vietnamese | 507,000 | 17. Thai | 206,000 |
| 10. Portuguese | 430,000 | 18. Persian | 202,000 |

# Why Do We Need LAWS?

**D**id you ever wonder what your day would be like if there weren't any rules to follow? What if you could go to school any time you wanted? And what if there were no traffic lights or stop signs for crossing the street?

Life would be difficult and confusing without rules. We all need them. Governments, businesses, organizations, and families make rules so that people don't get hurt and are not treated unfairly.

The rules that a government makes are called laws. The government has the power to punish people who break a law. But U.S. laws assume that a person is innocent until proven guilty in the courts.

Laws are made to:

- ☑ Protect people from getting hurt
- ☑ Help people to be treated fairly
- ☑ Help people do their jobs properly
- ☑ Help people know how to act in public

## WHAT HAPPENS WHEN YOU BREAK THE LAW?

**Kids**. When children under 18 years old are accused of breaking the law, they are arrested by the police and usually must appear in **juvenile court**. This court has no jury. A judge decides whether or not there is strong enough evidence that the child has broken the law. If there is enough evidence, the judge decides how the child should be punished or helped. Sometimes the judge lets the child go home, but still under the watch of authorities. This is called **probation**. In other cases, a judge may decide that a child cannot be helped by juvenile court and should be tried as an adult in criminal court. This usually happens when a child who has broken the law several times in the past is accused of a very serious crime.

**Adults**. When an adult breaks the law, the offense may be minor or it may be serious. An adult who gets a parking ticket, a relatively minor crime, may have to pay a fine or may decide to go to court to argue against the ticket.

An adult who is accused of a serious crime would be arrested and have to appear in court. A trial might result if the evidence against the person seems strong enough. At the trial, a government lawyer, called a **prosecutor**, would present the case against the accused person (called the **defendant**). A person who is **acquitted**, or found "not guilty," is free to go home. If the defendant is **convicted**, or found "guilty," he or she will get a punishment, or a **sentence**, such as having to go to prison for a specific length of time.

For very serious crimes, 38 U.S. states allow defendants who are convicted to be sentenced to death.

## LAWS YOU CAN NO LONGER BREAK

Here are some laws in different states that people were supposed to follow a long time ago. You can see why these laws are no longer on the books.

- ☑ In Massachusetts, a dachshund could not be kept as a pet dog.
- ☑ In California, a permit was needed to set a trap for a mouse.
- ☑ In Louisiana, it was illegal to lead a bear around with a rope.
- ☑ In Michigan, it was illegal to hitch a crocodile to a fire hydrant.
- ☑ In Waterville, Maine, it was illegal to blow your nose in public.

## GROWN-UPS HAVE RIGHTS AND SO DO KIDS

All people have rights. This means that no one should be treated unfairly. It means that everyone should be free to do certain things. In the United States many years ago, the government made a list of these rights. This list is part of the U.S. Constitution and is called the **Bill of Rights**.

The Bill of Rights says that people in the United States have the right to belong to any religion they choose and to say and write whatever they believe, even if it is against the government. The police cannot search people or go into their houses, unless they have a good reason and get special permission. And anyone who is arrested has the right to a lawyer and a fair trial.

## RIGHTS FOR CHILDREN

Under the laws in the United States, children do not have all the rights that adults do. Children cannot drive a car or vote. They must go to school and live with their parents or legal guardian. Children do have some special rights, such as the right to be taken care of by their parents.

▲ Child workers in Myanmar

## WHEN CHILDREN DON'T HAVE RIGHTS: CHILD LABOR

Like many children around the world, you probably have chores to do. You must go to school, just as adults go to jobs. And you have to do homework. This is all within the law and not an abuse of children's rights.

But in some parts of the world, many children do not attend school. Instead, millions of children work in factories and fields. They may do backbreaking, often dangerous, work from early morning to late at night. UNICEF, the United Nations Children's Fund, estimates that 250 million children around the world work. This is a big problem in Asia, Africa, and Latin America. Even in the United States, from $2\frac{1}{2}$ to $3\frac{1}{2}$ million children work. These are usually the children of migrant workers, people who move from place to place depending on the season, picking fruits and vegetables.

The families of many child laborers could not survive without the money children bring home. This poverty is a big obstacle to stopping child labor.

# HISTORY of MONEY

**Why Did People Start Using Money?** People first started using money in order to trade. A farmer who had cattle might want to have salt to preserve meat or cloth to make clothing. For this farmer, a cow became a "medium of exchange"—a way of getting things that the farmer did not make or grow. Cattle became a form of money. Whatever people agreed to use for trade became the earliest kinds of money.

**What Objects Have Been Used as Money Throughout History?** You may be surprised by some of the items that people have used every day as money. What does the form of money tell you about a society and its people?

- ☑ knives, rice, and spades in China around 3000 B.C.
- ☑ cattle and clay tablets in Babylonia around 2500 B.C.
- ☑ wampum (beads) and beaver fur by American Indians of the northeast around A.D. 1500
- ☑ tobacco by early American colonists around 1650
- ☑ whales' teeth by the Pacific peoples on the island of Fiji, until the early 1900s

**The First Paper Money.** By the time of the Middle Ages in Europe (about A.D. 800-1100), gold had become a popular medium for trade. But gold was heavy and difficult to carry, and European cities and the roads of Europe at that time were dangerous places to carry large amounts of gold. So merchants and goldsmiths began issuing notes promising to pay gold to the person carrying the note. These "promissory notes" were the beginning of paper money in Europe. Paper money was probably also invented in China, where the explorer Marco Polo saw it in the 1280s.

**Why Did Governments Get Interested in Issuing Money?** The first government to make coins that looked alike and use them as money is thought to be the Greek city-state of Lydia in the 7th century B.C. These Lydian coins were actually bean-shaped lumps made from a mixture of gold and silver.

The first government in Europe to issue paper money that looked alike was France in the early 18th century. Governments were interested in issuing money because the money itself had value. If a government could gain control over the manufacture of money, it could increase its own wealth—often simply by making more money.

Today, money throughout the world is issued only by governments. In the United States, the Department of the Treasury and the U.S. Mint make all the paper money and coins we use. Nowadays, we also use checks and credit cards to pay for things we buy. These are not thought of as real money but more as "promises to pay."

# MONEY TALK:
## An Economics Glossary

### ATM or automated teller machine
An electronic machine in a public place where customers of a bank can withdraw cash from their accounts or make deposits by using a special plastic card.

### bank
A business establishment in which people and businesses keep money in savings accounts or checking accounts.

### bond
A certificate issued by a government or a business to a person or business from whom it has borrowed money. A bond promises to pay back the borrowed money with interest.

### CD or certificate of deposit
A kind of bank savings account that earns a fixed rate of interest over a specific period of time.

### cost of living
The average cost of the basic needs of life, including food, clothing, housing, medical care, and other services.

### debt
Something that is owed.

### depression
A period of severe economic decline. In a depression, many people are unemployed, many businesses fail, and people buy less. The last depression in the United States came in the 1930s.

### FDIC or Federal Deposit Insurance Corporation
A government agency created in 1933 to protect deposits when a bank fails. The FDIC guarantees to insure deposits up to $100,000 if they are in a bank that is a member of the FDIC.

### GDP or Gross Domestic Product
The total value of all goods made and services performed within a particular country during a period of time, usually one year.

### goods and services
**Goods** refer to real items such as cars, TVs, VCRs, wristwatches, clothes, and so on. **Services** refer to work that is done for other people. Firefighters, nurses, waiters, actors, and lawyers all perform services.

### inflation
An increase in the level of prices.

### interest
The amount of money a borrower pays to borrow money. A bank pays interest on a savings account.

### money
Paper and coins that are issued by the government and are used in exchange for all goods and services.

### recession
A period of economic decline. During a recession, more people become unemployed, some businesses fail, and people buy less than usual. A recession is not as severe as a depression.

### stock
A share in a corporation. A corporation sells shares to individuals or other companies to raise money. The shares may increase or decrease in value. When the company makes a profit, it pays the stockholder a "dividend," or a part of the money.

# Making Money: THE U.S. MINT

**What Is the U.S. Mint?** The U.S. Mint is responsible for making all U.S. coins. It also safeguards the Treasury Department's stored gold and silver at Fort Knox, KY. The U.S. Mint was founded in 1792 and today is a part of the U.S. Treasury Department. The U.S. Mint's headquarters are in Washington, D.C. Local branches that produce coins are located in Philadelphia, PA; Denver, CO; San Francisco, CA; and West Point, NY.

Another division of the Treasury Department—the Bureau of Engraving and Printing, also in Washington, D.C—designs, engraves, and prints all U.S. paper money.

**What Kinds of Coins Does the Mint Make?** The U.S. Mint makes all the pennies, nickels, dimes, quarters, half dollars, and dollar coins that Americans use each day. These coins are made of a mixture of metals. For example, dimes, quarters, half dollars, and dollar coins look like silver but are a mixture of copper, nickel, and silver. The U.S. Mint also makes special coins honoring famous people and special events.

**Where Can I Get Information About the Mint?** Write to the United States Mint, Customer Service Center, 10003 Derekwood Lane, Lanham, MD 20706. Telephone: (202) 283-COIN. The Mint also offers free public tours at some of its facilities.

**Whose Portraits Are on Our Money?** On the front of all U.S. paper money are portraits of presidents and other famous Americans. Presidents also appear on the most commonly used coins. Starting in 1999, five new quarters will be coined every year. Each one will feature the design of a different state. The quarters will be introduced in the same order as states entered the Union.

| Denomination | Portrait |
|---|---|
| 1¢ | Abraham Lincoln, 16th U.S. President |
| 5¢ | Thomas Jefferson, 3rd U.S. President |
| 10¢ | Franklin Delano Roosevelt, 32nd U.S. President |
| 25¢ | George Washington, 1st U.S. President |
| $1 | George Washington, 1st U.S. President |
| $2 | Thomas Jefferson, 3rd U.S. President |
| $5 | Abraham Lincoln, 16th U.S. President |
| $10 | Alexander Hamilton, 1st U.S. Treasury Secretary |
| $20 | Andrew Jackson, 7th U.S. President |
| $50 | Ulysses S. Grant, 18th U.S. President |
| $100 | Benjamin Franklin, colonial inventor and U.S. patriot |

**Paper Money.** Bills larger than $100 stopped being made in 1969. In 1996 the United States printed a new $100 bill with many features to help prevent counterfeiting. A new $50 bill was printed in 1997, and a new $20 bill was being issued in 1998. Over the next few years, other bills are being changed.

 **WEB SITE** Read more about money on the Internet at:
http://www.ustreas.gov/kids

# How Much MONEY Is in CIRCULATION in the United States?

**A**s of March 31, 1997, the total amount of money in circulation was $444,533,960,595 (more than 400 billion dollars). About 25 billion dollars was in coins, the rest in paper money. The following chart shows the number of bills of each kind in circulation.

| Kind (Denomination) | Value of Money in Circulation | Number of Bills in Circulation | |
|---|---|---|---|
| $1 bills | $6,253,758,057 | 6,253,758,057 | |
| $2 bills | $1,097,154,754 | 548,577,377 | |
| $5 bills | $7,344,374,165 | 1,468,874,833 | |
| $10 bills | $13,383,913,360 | 13,338,391,336 | |
| $20 bills | $81,874,792,100 | 4,093,739,605 | |
| $50 bills | $46,627,618,500 | 932,552,370 | |
| $100 bills | $264,019,434,500 | 2,640,194,345 | |

# What Are EXCHANGE RATES?

**W**hen one country exports goods to another, the payment from the country buying the goods must be changed into the currency of the country selling them. An **exchange rate** is the price of one currency in terms of another. For example, 1 U.S. dollar could buy 6 French francs in 1998. Exchange rates change as a nation's economy becomes stronger or weaker. This chart compares the exchange rates in 1970 and 1998 between the U.S. dollar and the currency of five of the country's biggest trading partners. The more foreign money the dollar can buy, the better the exchange rate for Americans.

about 520 yen

$4.00

U.S.     Japan

| | $1 BOUGHT: | |
|---|---|---|
| COUNTRY | IN 1970 | IN 1998 |
| France | 6 francs | 6 francs |
| Germany | $3\frac{3}{5}$ marks | $1\frac{4}{5}$ marks |
| Great Britain | $\frac{2}{5}$ pound | $\frac{3}{5}$ pound |
| Italy | 600 lire | 1,800 lire |
| Japan | 350 yen | 130 yen |

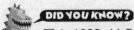

**DID YOU KNOW?**

☑ In 1998, 11 European countries agreed to a new currency called the euro. It will eventually replace the individual currencies of these countries.

☑ Most products that arrive in the United States from other countries or are sent to other countries by the United States travel by ship. The busiest ports in 1995 were in South Louisiana; Houston, Texas; New York and New Jersey; Baton Rouge, Louisiana; and Valdez, Alaska.

# BUDGETS

A budget is a plan that estimates how much money a person, a business, or a government will receive during a particular period of time, how much money will be spent and what it will be spent on, and how much money will be left over (if any).

## A FAMILY BUDGET

Does your family have a budget? Do you know what your family spends money on? Do you know where your family's income comes from? The chart below shows some sources of income and typical yearly expenses for a family's budget.

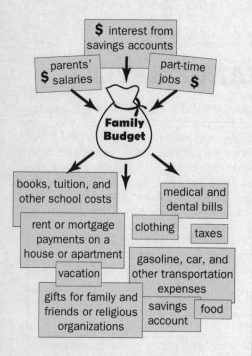

interest from savings accounts

parents' salaries

part-time jobs

**Family Budget**

books, tuition, and other school costs

medical and dental bills

rent or mortgage payments on a house or apartment

clothing

taxes

vacation

gasoline, car, and other transportation expenses

gifts for family and friends or religious organizations

savings account

food

### A Balanced Budget

A budget is **balanced** when the amount of money you receive equals the amount of money you spend. A budget is **unbalanced** when the amount of money you spend is greater than the amount of money you have.

## MAKING YOUR OWN BUDGET

Imagine that you are given a weekly allowance of $10. With this money you must pay for things like snacks and magazines and also try to save up for special things you may want. A budget will help you plan how to do this. Here are examples of things you might want to put in your budget:

### Possible Purchases and Cost

Snacks: $.75 each
Rental of a video movie: $3.00
Magazine: $2.00

### Savings:

For gifts: $.50 - $3.00
For something special for yourself (like a basketball, an audiocassette, a video game, or tickets to a concert): $1.00 or more.

On the lines below, list the items you want along with their price. You may also add any other items that interest you—and their prices. And don't forget to include any money you want to save.

| Item | Amount |
| --- | --- |
| | |
| | |
| | |
| | |
| | |

Savings

Now total all your purchases and savings: _____

**Is your budget balanced?** Is the amount you plan to spend and save equal to the amount of your "income" ($10)?

# THE U.S. BUDGET

Businesses take in money by making and selling products or by providing services. But what about the government? Where does the government's income come from? And what are the government's biggest expenses?

## WHERE DOES THE U.S. GOVERNMENT GET MONEY?

The chart below shows where the U.S. government got its money from in the 1997 budget year.

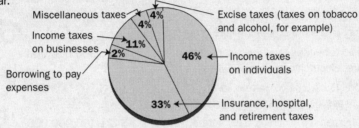

Miscellaneous taxes — 4%

Excise taxes (taxes on tobacco and alcohol, for example)

Income taxes on businesses — 11%

4%

Borrowing to pay expenses — 2%

46% — Income taxes on individuals

33% — Insurance, hospital, and retirement taxes

## WHERE DOES THE U.S. GOVERNMENT SPEND MONEY?

The chart below shows some of the major ways the U.S. government spent money during the 1997 budget year.

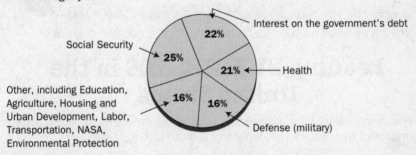

22% — Interest on the government's debt

Social Security — 25%

21% — Health

Other, including Education, Agriculture, Housing and Urban Development, Labor, Transportation, NASA, Environmental Protection — 16%

16% — Defense (military)

---

## THE GOVERNMENT IS STARTING TO BALANCE ITS BUDGET

The U.S. government has been trying to balance its budget for a long time. Every year from 1969 to 1997 the government spent more money than it took in through taxes. The difference between the higher amount spent and the amount taken in each year is called the **budget deficit**. Most economists say that paying interest on a large debt hurts our economy. Cutting the debt may mean raising taxes or cutting programs that many citizens depend on. But the budget deficit has been going down since 1993. And in 1998, for the first time in many years, officials are expecting to take in more money than is spent. This would be a budget **surplus**.

| YEAR | $ TAKEN IN | $ SPENT | DEFICIT |
|------|-----------|---------|---------|
| 1992 | $1.092 trillion | $1.382 trillion | $–290 billion |
| 1993 | $1.153 trillion | $1.408 trillion | $–255 billion |
| 1994 | $1.257 trillion | $1.460 trillion | $–203 billion |
| 1995 | $1.350 trillion | $1.514 trillion | $–164 billion |
| 1996 | $1.453 trillion | $1.560 trillion | $–107 billion |
| 1997 | $1.579 trillion | $1.602 trillion | $–23 billion |

# What Do AMERICANS BUY?

The chart below shows how Americans spent their money in 1996.

| CATEGORY | AMOUNT SPENT |
|---|---|
| Medical and dental care | $912,800,000,000 |
| Food and tobacco | $805,700,000,000 |
| Housing | $787,200,000,000 |
| Transportation expenses (such as cars, gasoline, and train, bus, and plane tickets) | $602,200,000,000 |
| Household expenses (such as telephone, furniture, electricity, kitchen supplies) | $591,900,000,000 |
| Recreation (such as books, magazines, toys, videos, sports events, amusement parks) | $431,100,000,000 |
| Personal expenses (such as baby sitters, lawn care, house cleaning, lawyers) | $421,100,000,000 |
| Clothing and jewelry | $336,300,000,000 |
| Religious and charitable contributions | $150,500,000,000 |
| School tuition and other educational expenses | $119,600,000,000 |
| Personal care (such as haircuts, health clubs) | $75,700,000,000 |

# Leading BUSINESSES in the United States

The following chart lists the leading American business in many different categories and the money the company took in during 1996.

**Airplanes**
Lockheed Martin, $26,875,000,000

**Banks**
Citicorp, $32,605,000,000

**Beverages**
Coca-Cola, $18,546,000,000

**Cars and Other Motor Vehicles**
General Motors, $168,369,000,000

**Chemicals**
E. I. du Pont de Nemours, $39,689,000,000

**Clothing**
Nike, $6,471,000,000

**Computers and Office Equipment**
IBM, $75,947,000,000

**Electronics and Electrical Equipment**
General Electric, $79,179,000,000

**Entertainment**
Walt Disney, $18,739,000,000

**Food and Drug Stores**
Kroger, $25,171,000,000

**Industrial and Farm Equipment**
Caterpillar, $16,522,000,000

**Medicines and Drugs**
Johnson & Johnson, $21,620,000,000

**Petroleum Refining**
Exxon, $119,434,000,000

**Retail Stores**
Wal-Mart Stores, $106,147,000,000

**Rubber and Plastic Products**
Goodyear Tire and Rubber, $13,113,000,000

**Soap and Cosmetics**
Procter & Gamble, $35,284,000,000

**Telecommunications**
AT&T, $74,525,000,000

**Toys, Sporting Goods**
Mattel, $3,786,000,000

# What Kinds of JOBS Do Americans Have?

How are Americans employed? Each year the U.S. Department of Labor publishes information on employment in the United States. The following chart shows the number of men and women who worked full-time in different kinds of jobs during 1997. The column with weekly earnings shows the mid-range of earnings. This means that many people in each kind of job earned more than this amount and many earned less.

| JOBS | NUMBER OF WORKERS | WEEKLY EARNINGS |
|---|---|---|
| **Managers and professionals** (for example, business executives and supervisors, doctors, lawyers, teachers, nurses) | | |
| Men | 14,359,000 | $875 |
| Women | 13,893,000 | $632 |
| **Sales people, technicians, administrative workers** (including clerical workers) | | |
| Men | 10,239,000 | $588 |
| Women | 16,552,000 | $403 |
| **People who repair things, precision workers, crafts people** | | |
| Men | 10,511,000 | $569 |
| Women | 984,000 | $382 |
| **Machine operators and laborers, assemblers** | | |
| Men | 11,709,000 | $436 |
| Women | 3,630,000 | $313 |
| **Service jobs** (for example, police and firefighters, waiters, cooks, hairdressers) | | |
| Men | 5,071,000 | $372 |
| Women | 5,101,000 | $282 |
| **Farming, forestry, and fishing** | | |
| Men | 1,331,000 | $302 |
| Women | 198,000 | $257 |

## OCCUPATIONS THAT ARE GROWING
Below is a list of some of the fastest-growing occupations in the United States:

**Computer science field:** computer programmers and scientists, systems analysts, desktop publishing specialists

**Health and medical field:** home health aides, medical assistants and secretaries, physical and occupational therapy assistants, technicians

**Teaching:** teachers' aides, high school teachers, and special education teachers

**Human services:** social workers, child care workers, gardeners and groundskeepers

**Paralegals**

# TRADE

**W**hen companies or countries buy and sell their products or services to other companies or countries, we call this **trade**. **Exports** are goods that one country *sells* to another country. **Imports** are goods that one country *buys* from another country. The United States trades with many other countries. It exports and imports goods.

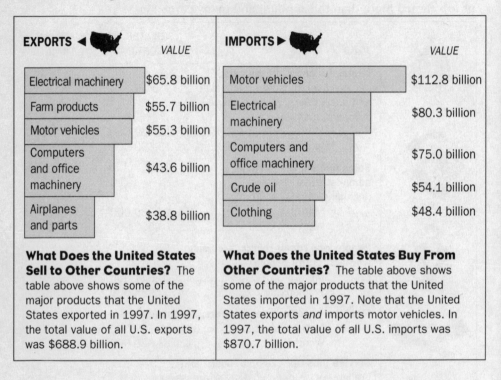

| EXPORTS | VALUE |
|---|---|
| Electrical machinery | $65.8 billion |
| Farm products | $55.7 billion |
| Motor vehicles | $55.3 billion |
| Computers and office machinery | $43.6 billion |
| Airplanes and parts | $38.8 billion |

| IMPORTS | VALUE |
|---|---|
| Motor vehicles | $112.8 billion |
| Electrical machinery | $80.3 billion |
| Computers and office machinery | $75.0 billion |
| Crude oil | $54.1 billion |
| Clothing | $48.4 billion |

**What Does the United States Sell to Other Countries?** The table above shows some of the major products that the United States exported in 1997. In 1997, the total value of all U.S. exports was $688.9 billion.

**What Does the United States Buy From Other Countries?** The table above shows some of the major products that the United States imported in 1997. Note that the United States exports *and* imports motor vehicles. In 1997, the total value of all U.S. imports was $870.7 billion.

**Who Are America's Leading Trading Partners?** In 1997, the countries with which the United States traded most were: Canada, Japan, Mexico, Germany, China, and Great Britain.

**Why Do Americans Buy Foreign-made Products?** Americans buy products from abroad that (1) they do not make for themselves or (2) that are less expensive or better-made than products made in the United States. For example, the United States imports most of its clothing because foreign-made products are less expensive.

**What Happens If a Country Imports More Than It Exports?** When the United States sells to other countries (or exports), other countries pay the United States for the goods. When the United States buys from other countries (or imports), it makes payments to them. It is best for a country to export more than it imports, or to export and import an equal amount. When a country imports more than it exports, it has what is called a **trade deficit**. The United States imports more than it exports and has a trade deficit. That means it is spending more money abroad for foreign-made products than it is getting from selling American-made products overseas.

# 20 MOVIE HITS OF 1997

Some of these are older movies that were shown again.

*Men in Black (PG-13)*
*The Lost World: Jurassic Park (PG-13)*
*Liar, Liar (PG-13)*
*Star Wars (PG)*
*My Best Friend's Wedding (PG-13)*
*Titanic (PG-13)*
*Batman & Robin (PG-13)*
*George of the Jungle (PG)*
*Hercules (G)*
*Flubber (PG)*
*The Empire Strikes Back (PG)*

*Jungle 2 Jungle (PG)*
*Anastasia (G)*
*Bean (PG-13)*
*Return of the Jedi (PG)*
*Mouse Hunt (PG)*
*101 Dalmatians (G)*
*The Little Mermaid (G)*
*Home Alone 3 (PG)*
*That Darn Cat (G)*

▲ *The Lost World: Jurassic Park*

▲ *Anastasia*

# 20 Popular
# KIDS' VIDEOS OF 1997

*Bambi*
*The Hunchback of Notre Dame*
*Wallace and Gromit: A Close Shave*
*The Aristocats*
*The Land Before Time IV*
*Schoolhouse Rock: America Rock*

*Oliver & Company*
*Aladdin and the King of Thieves*
*Mary-Kate & Ashley: Hotel-Who-Done-It*
*Mary-Kate & Ashley: Case of the U.S. Navy Mystery*
*Sesame Street: Best of Elmo*
*Mary-Kate & Ashley: Case of the Volcano Adventure*

*Fun and Fancy Free*
*Pooh's Grand Adventure*
*Pocahontas*
*The Wallace and Gromit Gift Set*
*Schoolhouse Rock: Grammar Rock*
*Goosebumps: The Werewolf of Fever Swamp*
*The Lion King*
*Sleeping Beauty*

135

# Some Popular MOVIES

***Snow White and the Seven Dwarfs*** (1937). This Disney classic was the first movie-length cartoon ever released. Since the late 1980s, Disney's new animated movies, such as *Beauty and the Beast, Aladdin, The Lion King,* and *Pocahontas,* have been popular with adults almost as much as with kids.

***The Wizard of Oz*** (1939). This movie made Judy Garland a star and "Over the Rainbow" a hit song. During the movie's filming, however, some people wanted to cut the song, thinking that it slowed down the action.

***The Sound of Music*** (1965). Winner of 5 Academy Awards, including Best Picture, this musical tells the story of Maria Von Trapp, whose plans to become a nun change when she becomes the governess to 7 children and falls in love with their father. (G)

***Star Wars*** (1977). Luke Skywalker, Princess Leia, and others battle Darth Vader and the forces of evil in a thriller set in outer space. Two sequels, *The Empire Strikes Back* (1980) and *The Return of the Jedi* (1983), were also huge hits. (PG)

***E.T. The Extra-Terrestrial*** (1982). A heart-warming tale about a boy and a space alien whose deep relationship helps them both to grow. "E.T., phone home" became the catchphrase for the year. (G)

***Home Alone*** (1990). An 8-year-old kid left home alone by accident outwits the bad guys all by himself but decides that, in the end, he'd rather have his family back. (PG)

***Jurassic Park*** (1993). A thriller about dinosaurs created in a lab from DNA found in fossils and put on a Caribbean island as the attraction in what is supposed to be a secure park. The park turns out to be a very scary place. (PG-13)

***The Lost World: Jurassic Park*** (1997). Action-filled sequel to *Jurassic Park*, and even scarier. Realistic-looking dinosaurs on an island stampede and attack people, and a T. Rex escapes to the city of San Diego. (PG-13)

## MOVIE-MAKING TALK

**cameo**
A brief appearance in a movie by a major star, usually in a rather unimportant role.

**dubbing**
Adding sound to a scene or a movie that has already been shot. Films are often dubbed when they are shown in countries where the language is different from the language the movie was originally shot in.

**editing**
The process of choosing which part of the scenes filmed will actually make it into the final movie and putting them together in order. Editing also involves combining the finished movie with the sound track.

**extra**
An actor who is hired by the day to play a small non-speaking part, such as someone in a crowd.

**freeze-frame**
A camera shot that seems to stop in an instant all the action on the screen.

**outtake**
A shot filmed by the camera operator but not used in the final movie.

**rushes**
The first prints of a day's shooting. The prints are developed in a rush and given to the director, so that he or she can see how well the movie is coming along. Rushes are also called *dailies.*

# TELEVISION RATINGS

**I**n 1997 the television industry came up with ratings to help parents choose programs that are OK for kids to watch. The ratings may be followed by a letter such as (V) for violence or (L) for bad language.

**TV-Y**      For all children—including those age 6 or younger.

**TV-Y7**    For children over age 7, especially those who can tell the difference between what is real and what is make-believe.

**TV-G**     General audience—suitable for all ages. Program has little or no violence.

**TV-PG**   Parental guidance suggested. Program may contain violence or bad language.

**TV-14**    Parents strongly warned. Program contains very violent or adult material.

**TV-M**     For adults—program may not be suitable for children under 17.

## Popular VIDEO GAMES in 1997

*Nintendo 64*
  *Mario Kart 64*
  *Star Fox 64 with Rumble Pak*
  *Super Mario 64*
  *Diddy Kong Racing*
  *Goldeneye 007*

*Sony Playstation Final Fantasy VII*
*Sony Playstation NFL Gameday '98*
*Nintendo 64*
  *Star Wars: Shadow of the Empire*
  *Madden NFL '98*
*Sony Playstation Crash Bandicoot*

## Popular TV SHOWS in 1997-1998

▲ *The cast of Seinfeld*

**AGES 6-11**
1. Sabrina, the Teenage Witch (TV-G)
2. Teen Angel (TV-G)
3. You Wish (TV-G)
4. Boy Meets World (TV-G)
5. Wonderful World of Disney (TV-G)
6. King of the Hill (TV-PG)
7. The Simpsons (TV-PG)
8. Seinfeld (TV-PG)
9. Home Improvement (TV-G)
10. Hiller and Diller (TV-G)

**AGES 12-17**
1. Seinfeld (TV-PG)
2. The Simpsons (TV-PG)
3. King of the Hill (TV-PG)
4. Dawson's Creek (TV-14) (rating varies)
5. Sabrina, the Teenage Witch (TV-G)
6. Boy Meets World (TV-G)
7. E.R. (TV-PG)
8. Friends (TV-PG)
9. Home Improvement (TV-G)
10. Teen Angel (TV-G )

(SOURCE: *Nielsen Media Research*)

**DID YOU KNOW?** After nine years, *Seinfeld*, the hit TV series starring Jerry Seinfeld, went off the air in May 1998. Almost 80 million people watched the last episode. The show was about Jerry, a comedian, and his group of wacky friends. They liked to say the show was about "nothing."

# PEOPLE to KNOW

**H**undreds of young actors and actresses appear in TV shows and movies. But some really stand out. Here are three of today's most popular stars.

## LEONARDO DICAPRIO

▲ Leonardo DiCaprio

Is Leonardo DiCaprio the hottest young actor around? Thousands of teenaged movie fans would answer a loud "yes!" to that question. The 23-year-old teen idol, called Leo by his friends, became even more popular when the hit movie *Titanic* was released in late 1997. *Titanic* has made more money than any other movie ever. One reason seems to be that Leo is among its stars. Some of his fans, especially teenaged girls, have seen the movie three or four times!

Born November 11, 1974, in Los Angeles, DiCaprio started his career when he was 5, on the children's TV show *Romper Room*. At 14, he appeared in an ad for toy cars. But it wasn't until 1991 that he really started being noticed. That's when he played a homeless boy in *Growing Pains*, a popular TV series. "He just lit up the place," one of his co-stars said.

When he was filming *The Man in the Iron Mask*, which came out in 1998, fans followed him everywhere. What's next? "He's not just a pretty face," a movie reviewer said. "He's an excellent actor who is getting better all the time."

## SARAH MICHELLE GELLAR

▲ Sarah Michelle Gellar

Sarah Michelle Gellar has been in front of a camera since she was 4 years old. Born April 14, 1977, in New York City, she started her career in a commercial for a hamburger chain. Today, she's the star of *Buffy the Vampire Slayer*, a popular television series.

When she's not working on the show, she's making movies and giving interviews, spending time with her friends, eating pizza, and giving even more interviews. "Phew! I'm tired and I complain sometimes," she said in one interview. "But this is my career and I love it."

People who work with Sarah say she gives every role more than 100 percent. So plan on seeing more of the girl who, one reporter said, "made TV fun to watch again."

## WILL SMITH

▲ Will Smith

Born September 25, 1968, in Philadelphia, Will Smith is famous both as an actor and as a singer. He's starred in *The Fresh Prince of Bel-Air* on TV and in such mega-hit movies as *Independence Day* (1996) and *Men in Black* (1997). He was also part of a popular rap act, DJ Jazzy Jeff and the Fresh Prince. In 1998, he won a Grammy for the *Men in Black* theme song.

On New Year's Eve 1997, Will got married to another star, Jada Pinkett. They met in 1990 when Jada tried out for a role as the star's girlfriend in *The Fresh Prince*. The people making the series said she was too short. (She is 5 feet tall and Will Smith is 6 feet 2 inches.) The show is now history. But Jada and Will are just at the beginning of their story, and their friends predict they're in for a very long run.

# Visiting the
# PAST and the FUTURE

**I**f you like to learn new things and have fun at the same time, museums are the places to go. Some museums, such as children's museums, have exhibits on many subjects, and some have exhibits in which you can learn a lot about one subject. In another kind of museum, you can walk in a village and watch people from an earlier century work and go about their daily lives. This type of museum is called a historic restoration.

The ancient Greeks were the first people to have public museums open to everyone. The oldest museum in the United States in continuous existence is the Charleston Museum, founded in South Carolina in 1773 to gather material on the natural history of that colony. The United States now has more than 7,700 museums. A few children's museums, ethnic museums, museums of entertainment, and historic restorations are listed below.

Many libraries have a *Directory of Museums in the United States*, and some museums also have home pages on the Internet.

 **WEB SITE** To check out museums in your community and elsewhere go to: http://www.museumca.org/usa

## Children's Museums

**Children's Museum, Inc.,** *Boston, Massachusetts*. Has a full-size Japanese house, a Latino market, plus displays on Native Americans.

**Children's Museum of Indianapolis,** *Indianapolis, Indiana*. Has natural science exhibits, including a walk-through limestone cave; computer center; old-fashioned railway depot with a 19th-century locomotive and caboose; exhibits about people around the world, including interactive videos.

**Children's Museum of Manhattan,** *New York, New York*. Displays of interest for kids on natural history, science, and art.

**Children's Museum,** *Portland, Oregon*. Hands-on displays on transportation, natural history, and toys.

**Los Angeles Children's Museum,** *Los Angeles, California*. Exhibits on health and city life; has a TV studio.

# Museums of Entertainment

**Country Music Hall of Fame and Museum,** Nashville, Tennessee
Celebrates country music's history and stars.

**Graceland,** Memphis, Tennessee
The 14-acre estate of the King of Rock 'n' Roll, Elvis Presley. Every year, hundreds of thousands of people visit Graceland.

**Museum of Television and Radio,** New York, New York
Contains 15,000 radio and 35,000 TV tapes from the 1920s to the present.

# Ethnic Museums

Here are some museums that show the culture and history of groups of people who share traditions and customs.

**Arthur M. Sackler Gallery**, and the **Freer Gallery of Art**, Washington, D.C
Displays paintings and other art objects from China, Japan, India, and other Asian countries.

**California African-American Museum**, Los Angeles, California
Displays art, books, and photographs on African-American culture.

▲ Chinese jar

**Heard Museum**, Phoenix, Arizona
Displays art by Native Americans and artists from Africa, Asia, Oceania, and the Upper Amazon.

**University of Texas Institute of Texan Cultures**, San Antonio, Texas
Exhibits showing contributions of 24 ethnic groups.

▲ Native American bowl

**Jewish Museum**, New York, New York
Exhibits covering 40 centuries of Jewish history and culture.

**Museum of African-American History**, Detroit, Michigan
Features include a large model of a slave ship, inventions by African-Americans, music by black composers, and the space suit worn by the first U.S. black female astronaut.

**National Museum of the American Indian**, New York, New York
A branch of the Smithsonian Institution, this museum features displays on the ways of life and the history of Native Americans.

## A NEW CENTER FOR ART

**The Getty Center**, Los Angeles, California

The Getty Center, which had been in nearby Malibu, opened in new headquarters in December 1997, after 14 years of planning and building. The museum, which has five different buildings, is one of the largest and most advanced in the world. It features paintings, furniture, and photographs. Special shades run by a computer control the amount of light in each part of the museum. The exhibits are meant to make looking at and understanding art both easy and enjoyable.

# Museums of Natural History

Museums of natural history contain exhibits of things found in nature. These include animals, rocks, and fossils of prehistoric animals and plants. Natural history museums allow you close-up looks at life-size models of coal mines, dinosaurs, desert and prairie life, or even whales.

**Academy of Natural Sciences of Philadelphia**, Philadelphia, Pennsylvania
**American Museum of Natural History**, New York, New York
**Carnegie Museum of Natural History**, Pittsburgh, Pennsylvania
**Denver Museum of Natural History**, Denver, Colorado
**Field Museum of Natural History**, Chicago, Illinois
**Museum of Comparative Zoology**, Cambridge, Massachusetts
**Museum of the Rockies**, Bozeman, Montana
**National Museum of Natural History**, Smithsonian Institution, Washington, D.C.
**New Mexico Museum of Natural History and Science**, Albuquerque, New Mexico
**University of Nebraska State Museum**, Lincoln, Nebraska

# Historic Restorations

These houses or parts of cities or towns have been restored to look the way they did many years ago.

**Colonial Williamsburg**, Williamsburg, Virginia
  The restored 18th-century capital of Virginia.
**Henry Ford Museum and Greenfield Village**, Dearborn, Michigan
  More than 80 historic buildings and more than 1 million objects on American history.
**Mystic Seaport**, Mystic, Connecticut
  Re-creation of a 19th-century New England whaling village, including ships and a museum.
**Old Sturbridge Village**, Sturbridge, Massachusetts
  Re-creation of a New England farming community of the 1830s.
**Plimoth Plantation, Inc.**, Plymouth, Massachusetts
  Re-creation of the Pilgrims' first settlement in the New World.
**St. Augustine Historic District**, St. Augustine, Florida
  Includes the Oldest House (Gonzalez-Alvarez House),
  showing life in St. Augustine over 400 years.

*Scene from a historic restoration* ▼

# MUSIC and MUSIC MAKERS

## CLASSICAL MUSIC

People often think of classical music as serious music. Often more complex than other types of music, classical music is based on European musical traditions that go back several hundred years. Common forms of classical music include the symphony, chamber music, opera, and ballet music. **Famous early classical composers:** Johann Sebastian Bach, Ludwig van Beethoven, Johannes Brahms, Franz Joseph Haydn, Wolfgang Amadeus Mozart, Franz Schubert, Peter Ilyich Tchaikovsky. **Famous modern classical composers:** Aaron Copland, Virgil Thomson, Charles Ives, Igor Stravinsky.

## CHAMBER MUSIC

Chamber music is written for a small group of musicians, often only three (a trio) or four (a quartet), to play together. In chamber music, each instrument plays a separate part.

A **string quartet** (music written for two violins, viola, and cello) is an example of chamber music. Other instruments, such as a piano, are sometimes part of a chamber group.

## SYMPHONY

A symphony is music written for an orchestra. The parts of a symphony are called **movements**.

## OPERA

An opera is a play whose words are sung to music. The music is played by an orchestra. The words of an opera are called the **libretto**, and a long song sung by one character (like a speech in a play) is called an **aria**. **Famous operas:** *Madama Butterfly* (Giacomo Puccini); *Aida* (Giuseppe Verdi); *Porgy and Bess* (George Gershwin).

## VOICE

There are six common types of voices, three for men and three for women. Women's voices usually range from *soprano* (highest) to *mezzo-soprano* (middle) to *alto* (lowest). Men's voices range from *tenor* (highest) to *baritone* (middle) to *bass* (lowest).

## MUSICAL NOTATION

These are some of the symbols composers use when they write music.

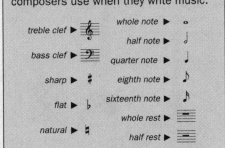

treble clef ▶

bass clef ▶

sharp ▶ ♯

flat ▶ ♭

natural ▶ ♮

whole note ▶ 𝅝

half note ▶ 𝅗𝅥

quarter note ▶ ♩

eighth note ▶ ♪

sixteenth note ▶ 𝅘𝅥𝅯

whole rest ▶

half rest ▶

 **DID YOU KNOW?** **Ludwig van Beethoven** started to go deaf in his twenties. By the end of his life, he had completely lost his hearing, yet he continued to compose and play music. **Wolfgang Amadeus Mozart** was only eight years old when he wrote his first symphony. **Johann Sebastian Bach** came from a well-known musical family. Over the course of about 300 years, more than 30 of his relatives made their living as musicians.

# More MUSIC and MUSIC MAKERS

## BLUES

The music called "the blues" developed from work songs and religious folk songs (spirituals) sung by African-Americans. It was introduced early in the 1900s by African-American musicians, especially the composer W. C. Handy. Blues songs are usually sad.

**Famous blues performers:** Ma Rainey, Bessie Smith, Billie Holiday, Buddy Guy, B. B. King, Muddy Waters. (A type of jazz is also called "the blues.")

## JAZZ

Jazz is a form of American music with roots in the work songs, spirituals, and folk music of African-Americans. Some kinds of jazz are created as they are played (improvised). Jazz began in the south in the early 1900s.

**Famous jazz performers:** Louis Armstrong, Fats Waller, Jelly Roll Morton, Duke Ellington, Benny Goodman, Billie Holiday, Sarah Vaughan, Ella Fitzgerald, Dizzy Gillespie, Charlie Parker, Miles Davis, Thelonious Monk, Wynton Marsalis.

## COUNTRY MUSIC

**American** country music is based on Southern mountain music. Blues, jazz, and other musical styles have also influenced it. Country music became popular through the *Grand Ole Opry* radio show in Nashville, Tennessee, during the 1920s.

**Famous country performers:** Johnny Cash, Dolly Parton, Willie Nelson, Garth Brooks, Travis Tritt, Vince Gill, Reba McEntire.

## ROCK (also known as rock 'n' roll)

Rock music, which started in the 1950s, is based on black rhythm and blues and country music. It often uses electronic instruments and equipment. Folk rock, punk, heavy metal, and alternative music are types of rock music.

**Famous rock musicians:** Elvis Presley, Bob Dylan, the Beatles, Janis Joplin, The Rolling Stones, Joni Mitchell, Bruce Springsteen, Aerosmith, R.E.M., Pearl Jam, Alanis Morissette, Jewel.

## POP MUSIC

Pop music (short for popular music) puts more emphasis on melody (tune) than does rock and has a softer beat.

**Famous pop singers:** Frank Sinatra, Barbra Streisand, Whitney Houston, Madonna, Michael Jackson, Mariah Carey, Boyz II Men, Brandy, Celine Dion.

## RAP MUSIC

Rap is music in which words are spoken or chanted at a fast pace and are backed by music that emphasizes strong rhythm rather than melody. It was created by African-Americans in inner cities. Rap lyrics show strong feelings and may be about anger and violence.

**Famous rappers:** Coolio, LL Cool J, TLC, The Fugees.

▼ *Spice Girls. In May 1998, Ginger Spice, second from left, left the group.*

## TOP ALBUMS OF 1997

1. *Spice,* Spice Girls
2. *Pieces of You,* Jewel
3. *No Way Out,* Puff Daddy & the Family
4. *Sevens,* Garth Brooks
5. *Middle of Nowhere,* Hanson

# INSTRUMENTS of the ORCHESTRA

The instruments of an orchestra are divided into four groups, or sections: string, woodwind, brass, and percussion. In an orchestra with 100 musicians, usually more than 60 play string instruments. The rest play woodwinds, brasses, or percussion instruments.

## STRINGS

Stringed instruments make sounds when the strings are either stroked with a bow or plucked with the fingers. The violin, viola, cello, bass, and harp are stringed instruments used in an orchestra. The guitar, banjo, balalaika, mandolin, koto, and dulcimer are other examples of stringed instruments.

## WOODWINDS

Woodwind instruments are long and round and hollow inside. They make sounds when air is blown into them through a mouth hole or a reed. The clarinet, flute, oboe, bassoon, and piccolo are woodwinds.

## BRASSES

Brass instruments are also hollow inside. They make sounds when air is blown into a mouthpiece shaped like a cup or a funnel. The trumpet, French horn, trombone, and tuba are brasses.

## PERCUSSION INSTRUMENTS

Percussion instruments make sounds when they are struck. The most common percussion instrument is the drum, which comes in many forms. Other percussion instruments include cymbals, triangles, gongs, bells, and xylophone. Keyboard instruments, like the piano, are sometimes thought of as percussion instruments.

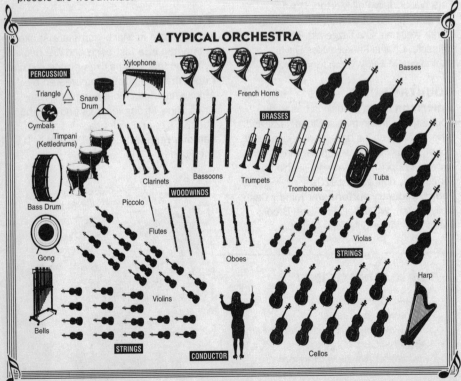

A TYPICAL ORCHESTRA

## MUSIC PUZZLE

**T**ry matching music makers with the kind of music for which they're best known. If you need to, look back on pages 142 and 143 for help. (Answers are on page 304.)

1. Brandy
2. Marsalis
3. Mozart
4. McEntire
5. Jewel
6. Coolio

a. rock
b. symphony
c. country
d. jazz
e. pop
f. rap

# AMERICAN MUSICAL THEATER

**A**merican musicals are plays known for their lively music and songs, comedy routines, dancing, colorful costumes, and elaborate stage sets. Tony (Antoinette Perry) Awards are given every year to outstanding Broadway plays. (Broadway is the theater district of New York City, which includes the street named Broadway and several surrounding blocks.) Some famous Broadway musicals are listed below. The date after the name of the play is the year it opened on Broadway.

**Annie** (1977), by Charles Strouse and Martin Charnin. Tony Award 1977.

**Annie Get Your Gun** (1946), by Irving Berlin.

**Anything Goes** (1930), by Cole Porter.

**Beauty and the Beast** (1994), by Alan Menken, Howard Ashman, and Tim Rice.

**Bring in 'da Noise, Bring in 'da Funk** (1996), by George C. Wolfe, Savion Glover, Daryl Waters, Zane Mark, and Ann Duquesnay.

**Carousel** (1945), by Richard Rodgers and Oscar Hammerstein II.

**Cats** (1982), by Andrew Lloyd Webber. Tony Award 1983.

**A Chorus Line** (1975), by Marvin Hamlisch and Edward Kleban. Tony Award 1976.

**Evita** (1979), by Andrew Lloyd Webber and Tim Rice. Tony Award 1980.

**Fiddler on the Roof** (1964), by Jerry Bock and Sheldon Harnick. Tony Award 1965.

**Grease** (1972), by Jim Jacobs and Warren Casey.

**Hello, Dolly!** (1964), by Jerry Herman. Tony Award 1964.

**The King and I** (1952), by Richard Rodgers and Oscar Hammerstein II. Tony Award 1952.

**Kiss Me Kate** (1948), by Cole Porter. Tony Award 1949.

**The Lion King** (1997), by Elton John, Tim Rice, Mark Mancina, Roger Allers, and Irene Meechi.

**The Music Man** (1957), by Meredith Willson. Tony Award 1958.

**My Fair Lady** (1956), by Alan Jay Lerner and Frederick Loewe. Tony Award 1957.

**Oklahoma!** (1943), by Richard Rodgers and Oscar Hammerstein II.

**The Pajama Game** (1954), by Richard Adler and Jerry Ross. Tony Award 1955.

**Rent** (1996), by Jonathan Larson. Tony Award 1996.

**Show Boat** (1927), by Jerome Kern and Oscar Hammerstein II.

**The Sound of Music** (1959), by Richard Rodgers and Oscar Hammerstein II.

**South Pacific** (1949), by Richard Rodgers and Oscar Hammerstein II. Tony Award 1950.

**West Side Story** (1957), by Leonard Bernstein and Stephen Sondheim.

# DANCE

In dance, the body performs patterns of movement, usually to music or rhythm. Dance may be a form of art, or part of a religious ceremony. Or it may be done just for fun.

Ballet, modern dance, folk dance, and social dance are all important kinds of dance.

## BALLET

Ballet is a kind of dance that is based on formal steps. Ballet movements are often graceful and flowing. Ballets are almost always danced to music. They are performed for an audience and often tell a story. In the 15th century, ballet was part of the elaborate entertainment that was performed for the rulers of Europe. In the 1600s, professional dance companies existed, but without women. Women's parts were danced by men wearing masks. In the 1700s dancers wore bulky costumes and shoes with high heels. Women danced in hoopskirts—and so did men! In the 1800s ballet steps and costumes began to look the way they do now. In fact, many of the most popular ballets today date back to the middle or late 1800s.

### SOME FAMOUS BALLETS

**Swan Lake.** First danced in St. Petersburg, Russia, in 1895. Perhaps the most popular ballet ever, *Swan Lake* is the story of a prince and his love for a maiden who was turned into a swan by an evil magician.

**The Nutcracker.** When this ballet was first performed in St. Petersburg, Russia, in 1892, it was a colossal flop. It has since become so popular that it is danced in many places every year at Christmastime.

**The Sleeping Beauty** is based on the fairy tale *The Sleeping Beauty.* The ballet was first danced in St. Petersburg in 1890.

**Jewels.** This ballet by the American choreographer George Balanchine was first performed in New York City in 1967. In *Jewels,* the dancers do not dance to a story. They explore patterns and movement of the human body.

**The River.** This 1970 ballet by Alvin Ailey is danced to music by the famous jazz musician Duke Ellington. It has been described as a ballet of imaginative movement and a celebration of life.

### NOTED BALLET DANCERS
Anna Pavlova (1885-1931)
Vaslav Nijinsky (1890-1950)
Margot Fonteyn (1919-1991)
Arthur Mitchell (born 1934)
Rudolph Nureyev (1938-1993)
Mikhail Baryshnikov (born 1948)

### NOTED CHOREOGRAPHERS
Marius Petipa (1818-1910)
Michel Fokine (1880-1942)
George Balanchine (1904-1983)
Agnes de Mille (1908-1993)
Jerome Robbins (born 1918)
Kenneth MacMillan (1929-1992)

## MODERN DANCE

Modern dance differs from classical ballet in many ways. It is often less concerned with graceful, flowing movement and with stories. Modern dance steps are often not performed in traditional ballet. Dancers may put their bodies into awkward, angular positions and turn their backs on the audience. Many modern dances are based on ancient art, such as Greek sculpture, or on dance styles found in Africa and Asia.

**Noted Modern Dancers and Choreographers**. Many of the most important modern dance choreographers, including those on this list, are also dancers.

| | |
|---|---|
| Alvin Ailey (1931-1989) | Martha Graham (1894-1991) |
| Trisha Brown (born 1936) | Mark Morris (born 1956) |
| Merce Cunningham (born 1919) | Paul Taylor (born 1930) |
| Isadora Duncan (1878-1927) | Twyla Tharp (born 1941) |

**FOLK DANCE.** Folk dance is the term for a dance that is passed on from generation to generation and that is part of the culture or way of life of people from a particular country or ethnic group. Virginia reel (American), czardas (Hungarian), jig, and the Israeli hora are some folk dances.

**SOCIAL DANCE.** Social dance is the name for dances done just for fun by ordinary people. They are not made up by professionals and not usually danced by trained dancers for an audience. Instead, they are danced at parties and clubs. Social dancing has been around since at least the Middle Ages, when it was popular at fairs and festivals. In the 1400s social dance was part of fancy court pageants. It developed into dainty dances like the minuet and the waltz during the 1700s. New dances in the 20th century include the Charleston, the lindy, the twist, and the tango, as well as disco dancing, break dancing, and line dances such as the macarena and electric slide.

▲ Folk dancing

## DANCE TALK

**arabesque** (ar-a-BESK)
A ballet pose in which the dancer balances on one leg, puts the other behind, toes pointed, and extends one arm in front and the other behind, creating the illusion of a straight line from fingertip in front to toe in back.

**choreographer** (core-e-OG-ra-fer)
The person who makes up the steps to be danced.

**corps de ballet** (core de bal-LAY)
The group of dancers, usually less experienced, who dance together, with or without the stars of the ballet.

**position**
The way that dancers place their arms and feet. In ballet there are five standard positions for the arms and five for the feet.

**prima ballerina** (PREE-ma)
In ballet, a woman who is one of the star dancers in her company and who takes on leading roles.

**pas de deux** (pa de DU)
A part of a ballet in which a man and a woman dance a duet together.

# Numerals in ANCIENT CIVILIZATIONS

**P**eople have been counting since the earliest of times. This is what some early numerals looked like.

| Modern | 1 | 2 | 3 | 4 | 5 | 6 | 7 | 8 | 9 | 10 | 20 | 50 | 100 |
|---|---|---|---|---|---|---|---|---|---|---|---|---|---|
| Egyptian | I | II | III | IIII | III/II | III/III | IIII/III | IIII/IIII | IIII/IIIII | ∩ | ∩∩ | ∩∩∩∩∩ | 9 |
| Baby-lonian | Υ | ΥΥ | ΥΥΥ | ΥΥ/Υ | ΥΥΥ/ΥΥ | ΥΥΥ/ΥΥΥ | ΥΥΥΥ/ΥΥΥ | ΥΥΥΥ/ΥΥΥΥ | ΥΥΥΥΥ/ΥΥΥΥ | ‹ | ‹‹ | ‹‹‹ | ‹Υ‹ |
| Greek | A | B | Γ | Δ | E | F | Z | H | θ | I | K | N | P |
| Mayan | • | •• | ••• | •••• | — | ⋅⁻ | ⁻⁻ | ••• | •••• | ═ | 👁 | ⋯ | ◎ |
| Chinese | 一 | 二 | 三 | 四 | 五 | 六 | 七 | 八 | 九 | 十 | 二十 | 五十 | 百 |
| Hindu | I | ૨ | ૩ | ૪ | ૫ | ૬ | ૭ | ૮ | ૯ | 10 | ૨0 | ૪0 | 100 |
| Arabic | / | ૨ | ૩ | ૪ | ૬ | ૪ | v | ᴧ | ૧ | /0 | ૨0 | ૪0 | /00 |

# ROMAN NUMERALS

**R**oman numerals are still used today. The symbols used to represent different numbers are the letters I (1), V (5), X (10), L (50), C (100), D (500), and M (1,000). If one Roman numeral is followed by a larger one, the first is subtracted from the second. For example, the numeral IX means 10 − 1 = 9. Think of it as "one less than ten." On the other hand, if one Roman numeral is followed by another that is equal or smaller, add them together. Therefore, VII means 5 + 1 + 1 = 7.

| 1 | I | 11 | XI | 30 | XXX | 400 | CD |
|---|---|---|---|---|---|---|---|
| 2 | II | 12 | XII | 40 | XL | 500 | D |
| 3 | III | 13 | XIII | 50 | L | 600 | DC |
| 4 | IV | 14 | XIV | 60 | LX | 700 | DCC |
| 5 | V | 15 | XV | 70 | LXX | 800 | DCCC |
| 6 | VI | 16 | XVI | 80 | LXXX | 900 | CM |
| 7 | VII | 17 | XVII | 90 | XC | 1,000 | M |
| 8 | VIII | 18 | XVIII | 100 | C | | |
| 9 | IX | 19 | XIX | 200 | CC | | |
| 10 | X | 20 | XX | 300 | CCC | | |

Can you write the year on the front cover of this book in Roman numerals? The answer is on page 304.

# The PREFIX Tells the Number

**E**ach number listed below has one or more prefixes used to form words that include that number. Knowing which number the prefix stands for helps you to understand the meaning of the word. For example, a unicycle has one wheel. A triangle has three sides. An octopus has eight tentacles. Next to the prefixes are some examples of words that use these prefixes.

| | | |
|---|---|---|
| 1 | uni-, mon-, mono- | unicycle, unicorn, monarch, monotone |
| 2 | bi- | bicycle, binary, binoculars, bifocals |
| 3 | tri- | tricycle, triangle, trilogy, triplet |
| 4 | quadr-, tetr- | quadrangle, quadruplet, tetrahedron |
| 5 | pent-, penta- | pentagon, pentathlon |
| 6 | hex-, hexa- | hexagon |
| 7 | hepta- | heptathlon |
| 8 | oct-, octa-, octo- | octave, octet, octopus, octagon |
| 9 | nona- | nonagon |
| 10 | dec-, deca- | decade, decibel, decimal |
| 100 | cent- | centipede, century |
| 1000 | kilo- | kilogram, kilometer |
| million | mega- | megabyte, megahertz |
| billion | giga- | gigabyte, gigawatt |

# Reading and Writing LARGE NUMBERS

**B**elow is the name of a number and the number of zeros that would follow it when the number is written out.

**A googol! What's a googol?!**

| | | |
|---|---|---|
| ten: | 1 zero | 10 |
| hundred: | 2 zeros | 100 |
| thousand: | 3 zeros | 1,000 |
| ten thousand: | 4 zeros | 10,000 |
| hundred thousand: | 5 zeros | 100,000 |
| million: | 6 zeros | 1,000,000 |
| ten million: | 7 zeros | 10,000,000 |
| hundred million: | 8 zeros | 100,000,000 |
| billion: | 9 zeros | 1,000,000,000 |
| trillion: | 12 zeros | 1,000,000,000,000 |
| quadrillion: | 15 zeros | 1,000,000,000,000,000 |
| quintillion: | 18 zeros | 1,000,000,000,000,000,000 |
| sextillion: | 21 zeros | 1,000,000,000,000,000,000,000 |
| septillion: | 24 zeros | 1,000,000,000,000,000,000,000,000 |

Look below to see how numbers larger than these would be written:

| | |
|---|---|
| octillion has 27 zeros | decillion has 33 zeros |
| nonillion has 30 zeros | googol has 100 zeros |

# How Many SIDES and FACES Do They Have?

**W**hen a figure is flat (two-dimensional), it is a **plane figure**. When a figure takes up space (three-dimensional), it is a **solid figure**. The flat surface of a solid figure is called a **face**. Plane and solid figures come in many different shapes.

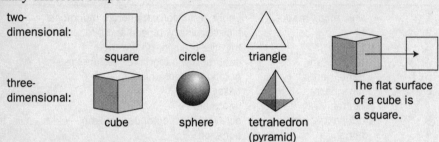

two-dimensional:　square　circle　triangle

The flat surface of a cube is a square.

three-dimensional:　cube　sphere　tetrahedron (pyramid)

**WHAT ARE POLYGONS?** A polygon is a two-dimensional figure that has three or more straight sides (called line segments). A square is a polygon. Polygons have different numbers of sides—and each has a different name. If the sides of a polygon are all the same length and all the angles between the sides are equal, the polygon is called regular. If the sides are of different lengths or the angles are not equal, the polygon is called irregular. Below are some regular and irregular polygons.

| NAME AND NUMBER OF SIDES | REGULAR | IRREGULAR | NAME AND NUMBER OF SIDES | REGULAR | IRREGULAR |
|---|---|---|---|---|---|
| triangle - 3 | | | heptagon - 7 | | |
| quadrilateral or tetragon - 4 | | | octagon - 8 | | |
| pentagon - 5 | | | nonagon - 9 | | |
| hexagon - 6 | | | decagon - 10 | | |

**WHAT ARE POLYHEDRONS?** A polyhedron is a three-dimensional figure with four or more faces. Each face on a polyhedron is a polygon. Below are some polyhedrons with many faces.

tetrahedron
4 faces

hexahedron
6 faces

octahedron
8 faces

dodecahedron
12 faces

icosahedron
20 faces

## NUMBERS PUZZLES

### HOW LONG IS THE LONGEST RIVER IN THE WORLD?

If you fill in the numbers below and add or subtract (whichever is asked for), you will learn the length of the longest river in the world. Hint: If you use a calculator, the puzzle will be much easier, but less of a challenge. (Answers are on page 305.)

Write down the number of pounds in a ton (see page 285) ＿＿＿＿＿

Add the height (in feet) of the Empire State Building (page 34) + ＿＿＿＿＿

= ＿＿＿＿＿

Add the total number of endangered species (page 20) + ＿＿＿＿＿

= ＿＿＿＿＿

Subtract the number of countries in the world (page 42) – ＿＿＿＿＿

= ＿＿＿＿＿

Add the number of senators in the U.S. Senate (page 220) + ＿＿＿＿＿

= ＿＿＿＿＿

Subtract the number of sides on a hexagon (page 150) – ＿＿＿＿＿

= ＿＿＿＿＿

Subtract the number of days in a week – ＿＿＿＿＿

The answer is the length of the world's longest river in miles = ＿＿＿＿＿

### WHAT IS THE WORLD'S LONGEST RIVER AND WHERE DOES IT FLOW?

Can you decode the name of the longest river and the countries it flows through? (Answers are on page 305.)

A=1, B=2, C=3, D=4, E=5, F=6, G=7, H=8, I=9, J=10, K=11, L=12, M=13, N=14, O=15, P=16, Q=17, R=18, S=19, T=20, U=21, V=22, W=23, X=24, Y=25, Z=26

The name of the longest river in the world is

| ＿＿＿ | ＿＿＿ | ＿＿＿ | ＿＿＿ | | ＿＿＿ | ＿＿＿ | ＿＿＿ | ＿＿＿ | ＿＿＿ |
|---|---|---|---|---|---|---|---|---|---|
| 14 | 9 | 12 | 5 | | 18 | 9 | 22 | 5 | 18 |

＿＿ ＿＿ ＿＿ ＿＿ ＿＿ and ＿＿ ＿＿ ＿＿ ＿＿ ＿＿ in ＿＿ ＿＿ ＿＿ ＿＿ ＿＿ ＿＿
5   7   25   16   20     19   21   4   1   14     1   6   18   9   3   1

### MAGIC SQUARE

Can you place the numbers 3 through 11 (using each number only once) in the boxes below so that any three numbers in a row across, down, or diagonally will add up to 21? The number 7 has been placed to help you get started. (One possible answer is given on page 305.)

|  |  |  |
|---|---|---|
|  |  |  |
|  | 7 |  |
|  |  |  |

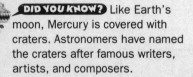

# The SOLAR SYSTEM

**N**ine planets, including Earth, travel around the sun. These planets, together with the sun, form the **solar system**.

## THE SUN IS A STAR

Did you know that the sun is a star, like the other stars you see at night? It is a typical, medium-size star. But because the sun is closer to us than any other star, we can study it in great detail. The diameter of the sun is 864,000 miles—more than 100 times Earth's diameter. The gravity of the sun is nearly 28 times the gravity of Earth.

**How Hot Is the Sun?** The temperature of the sun's surface is close to 11,000°F, and the inner core may reach temperatures near 35 million degrees! The sun provides enough light and heat energy to support all forms of life on our planet.

## THE PLANETS ARE IN MOTION

The planets move around the sun along oval-shaped paths called **orbits**. Each planet travels in its own orbit. One complete path around the sun is called a **revolution**. Earth takes one year, or 365 ¼ days, to make one revolution around the sun. Planets that are farther away from the sun take longer. Some planets have one or more **moons**. A moon orbits a planet in much the same way that the planets orbit the sun.

Each planet also spins (or rotates) on its axis. An **axis** is an imaginary line running through the center of a planet. The time it takes for one rotation of the planet Earth on its axis equals one day. Below are some other facts about the planets and the symbol for each planet.

---

### I. MERCURY
**Average distance from the sun:**
  36 million miles
**Diameter:** 3,032 miles
**Time to revolve around the sun:** 88 days
**Time to rotate on its axis:**
  58 days, 15 hours, 30 minutes
**Number of moons:** 0

**DID YOU KNOW?** Like Earth's moon, Mercury is covered with craters. Astronomers have named the craters after famous writers, artists, and composers.

### 2. VENUS
**Average distance from the sun:**
  67 million miles
**Diameter:** 7,521 miles
**Time to revolve around the sun:**
  224.7 days
**Time to rotate on its axis:** 243 days
**Number of moons:** 0

**DID YOU KNOW?** The surface of Venus is covered with thick clouds. Its atmosphere of carbon dioxide traps heat. The temperature of Venus can reach close to 900°F.

---

# The Solar System

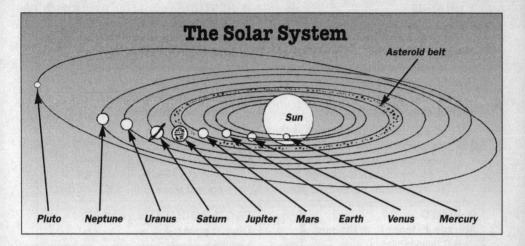

Asteroid belt

Sun

Pluto   Neptune   Uranus   Saturn   Jupiter   Mars   Earth   Venus   Mercury

## 3. EARTH

**Average distance from the sun:**
93 million miles
**Diameter:** 7,926 miles
**Time to revolve around the sun:**
365 ¹/₄ days
**Time to rotate on its axis:**
23 hours, 56 minutes, 4.2 seconds
**Number of moons:** 1

 **DID YOU KNOW?** Earth's path around the sun is nearly 600 million miles long. To make the trip in one year, Earth travels more than 66,000 miles per hour.

## 4. MARS

**Average distance from the sun:**
142 million miles
**Diameter:** 4,213 miles
**Time to revolve around the sun:**
687 days
**Time to rotate on its axis:**
24 hours, 37 minutes, 22 seconds
**Number of moons:** 2

**DID YOU KNOW?** Mars is the home of Olympus Mons, the largest volcano found in the solar system. It stands about 17 miles high, with a crater 50 miles wide.

## 5. JUPITER

**Average distance from the sun:**
484 million miles
**Diameter:** 88,732 miles
**Time to revolve around the sun:**
11.9 years
**Time to rotate on its axis:**
9 hours, 55 minutes, 30 seconds
**Number of moons:** 16

 **DID YOU KNOW?** The Galileo spacecraft has snapped pictures showing that one of Jupiter's moons, Io, has more than 80 volcanoes.

## 6. SATURN

**Average distance from the sun:**
888 million miles
**Diameter:** 74,975 miles
**Time to revolve around the sun:**
29.5 years
**Time to rotate on its axis:**
10 hours, 30 minutes
**Number of moons:** at least 22

 **DID YOU KNOW?** Saturn's famous rings are made of billions of chunks of ice and some rock. The rings stretch out to about 170,000 miles in diameter and are estimated to be no more than 10 miles thick.

## 7. URANUS

**Average distance from the sun:**
1.8 billion miles
**Diameter:** 31,763 miles
**Time to revolve around the sun:** 84 years
**Time to rotate on its axis:**
17 hours, 14 minutes
**Number of moons:** at least 17

**DID YOU KNOW?** Uranus was the first planet discovered with a telescope, by William Herschel in 1781. Its surface is covered with greenish clouds of methane gas.

## 8. NEPTUNE

**Average distance from the sun:**
2.8 billion miles
**Diameter:** 30,603 miles
**Time to revolve around the sun:**
164.8 years
**Time to rotate on its axis:**
16 hours, 6 minutes
**Number of moons:** 8

**DID YOU KNOW?** Neptune's largest moon is called Triton. At about −390°F, Triton is the coldest place in the solar system.

## 9. PLUTO

**Average distance from the sun:**
3.6 billion miles
**Diameter:** 1,413 miles
**Time to revolve around the sun:**
247.7 years
**Time to rotate on its axis:**
6 days, 9 hours, 18 minutes
**Number of moons:** 1

**DID YOU KNOW?** Pluto's orbit is so strangely shaped that, since 1977, Pluto has been closer to the sun than Neptune. In March 1999, Pluto will move beyond Neptune once again.

## FACTS ABOUT THE PLANETS

**Largest planet:** Jupiter
**Smallest planet:** Pluto
**Planet closest to the sun:** Mercury
**Planet that comes closest to Earth:**
Venus (Every 19 months, Venus gets closer to Earth than any other planet.)
**Fastest-moving planet:** Mercury
(107,000 miles per hour)
**Slowest-moving planet:** Pluto (10,600 miles per hour)
**Warmest planet:** Venus
**Coldest planet:** Pluto
**Planet with the most moons:** Saturn

# The Moon

Earth's satellite—the moon—is the only other body in the solar system that people have traveled to. The moon is about 238,900 miles from Earth. It is 2,160 miles in diameter and has no atmosphere. Its dusty surface is covered with deep craters. It takes the same amount of time for the moon to rotate on its axis as it does to orbit Earth (27 days, 7 hours, 43 minutes). For this reason, one side of the moon is always facing Earth. The moon has no light of its own, but reflects light from the sun. The lighted part of the moon we can see from Earth is called a phase. It takes the moon about $29\frac{1}{2}$ days to go through all of its phases, from new moon to full moon and back to new moon. Below are some of these phases.

| New Moon | Crescent Moon | First Quarter | Full Moon | Last Quarter | Crescent Moon | New Moon |

**DID YOU KNOW?** In 1998 the Lunar Prospector, a U.S. spacecraft, found strong evidence of some water, in the form of ice, at the moon's poles. Scientists hoped there might be enough water to help people live on the moon for periods of time.

# Comets, Asteroids, and Satellites

**B**esides the planets and their moons, there are thousands of other objects in the solar system. These include comets, asteroids, and satellites.

**Comets** are fast-moving chunks of ice, dust, and rock that form long tails of gas as they move nearer to the sun. One of the most well-known is **Halley's Comet**. It can be seen about every 76 years and will appear again in the year 2061.

**Asteroids** (or minor planets) are solid chunks of rock or metal that range in size from very small, like grains of sand, to very large. **Ceres**, the largest, is about 600 miles across. Thousands of asteroids orbit the sun between the planets Mars and Jupiter.

**Satellites** are objects that move in an orbit around a planet. Moons are natural satellites. Satellites made by humans are used as space stations and astronomical observatories. They are also used to photograph Earth's surface and to transmit communications signals.

**DID YOU KNOW?** **Ganymede**, one of Jupiter's moons, is the largest natural satellite. It is larger than Mercury and, like Earth, has oxygen in its atmosphere, frozen water, and a magnetic field. **Europa**, another moon of Jupiter, has an atmosphere and both liquid and frozen water.

# What Is an Eclipse?

A **solar eclipse** occurs when the moon moves between the sun and Earth, casting a shadow over part of Earth. When the moon completely blocks out the sun, it is called a **total solar eclipse**. When this happens, a halo of gas can be seen around the sun. This halo of gas is called the **corona**.

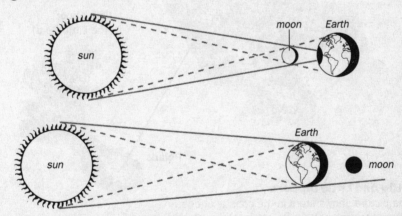

Sometimes Earth casts a shadow on the moon. This is called a **lunar eclipse**. Usually, a lunar eclipse lasts longer than a solar eclipse. The moon remains visible, but becomes dark, often with a reddish tinge (from sunlight that is bent through Earth's atmosphere).

### 1998 to 2002—Total Solar Eclipses and Where They Can Be Seen
**August 11, 1999:** Can be seen mainly in Europe, Middle East, and India.
**June 21, 2001:** Will be seen over the Atlantic Ocean, Africa, and Madagascar.
**December 4, 2002:** Will be seen in southern Africa, over the Indian Ocean, and in Australia.

# CONSTELLATIONS: Pictures in the Sky

Thousands of years ago, ancient astronomers grouped stars together to form pictures. These groupings, or the areas of sky that they cover, are known as **constellations**. Astronomers all over the world named the constellations after animals or mythological figures or tools. Many of the constellations we know today were named by the people living in ancient Greece and Rome. But many constellations could not be seen from that part of the world. Some constellations were named later, when Europeans began traveling to different parts of the world and saw many other constellations. Also, cultures in different parts of the world have sometimes grouped the same stars into different constellations.

In 1930, the International Astronomical Union established a standard set of 88 constellations, which cover the entire sky that is visible from Earth. Astronomers use constellations as a quick way to locate other objects. For example, from Earth, the other planets moving around the sun appear in different constellations at different times.

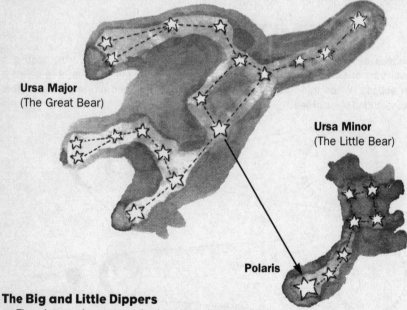

Ursa Major
(The Great Bear)

Ursa Minor
(The Little Bear)

Polaris

### The Big and Little Dippers

The picture shows stars in the constellations
thought to resemble bears—Ursa Major (Great Bear)
and Ursa Minor (Little Bear). The tail and hips of the Great Bear are also
known as the Big Dipper. Ursa Minor is also known as the Little Dipper.

### The North Star

Throughout history, people have been using the stars to guide them in their travels.
Polaris, the last star in the handle of the Little Dipper, shines to the north and is called
the North Star. The two stars at the end of the bowl of the Big Dipper always point in
the direction of Polaris, making it easy to find.

# Looking for LIFE BEYOND EARTH

For years scientists have tried to discover if there is life on other planets in our solar system or life elsewhere in the universe. They look for signs of what is needed for life on Earth—basics like water and proper temperature.

## WHAT SCIENTISTS HAVE LEARNED SO FAR

**Mars and Jupiter.** In 1996, two teams of scientists examined two meteorites that may have come from **Mars** and found evidence that some form of life may have existed on Mars billions of years ago. In 1997 and 1998, photographs of Europa, a moon of **Jupiter**, showed areas of a liquid ocean under an icy surface. This may be a sign that Europa had an ocean sometime in the far-distant past. Scientists wonder: Where there was water, could there have been life?

**New Planets.** In 1996, astronomers believed they found several new planets traveling around stars very far away from our sun. Scientists do not think life exists on these planets. They are so close to their sun that they would be too hot. But scientists are hoping to find other stars with planets around them that might support life.

## AND THE SEARCH CONTINUES

**NASA** (the National Aeronautics and Space Administration) has a program to search for signs of life on Mars. By the year 2005, eight missions are scheduled to go to the red planet. Some will fly around Mars taking pictures, while others will land there to study soil and rocks and to look for living things. Two earlier missions, *Mars Pathfinder* and *Mars Global Surveyor*, launched in 1996, already reached Mars in 1997.

Another program that searches for life on other worlds is called **SETI**. SETI (an acronym for Search for Extraterrestrial Intelligence) uses powerful radio telescopes to look for life elsewhere in the universe.

**Question:** Is there life elsewhere in the universe? **Answer:** No one knows yet.

# EXPLORING the SOLAR SYSTEM

American exploration into space began in January 1958, when the United States launched the *Explorer I* satellite into orbit. In October 1958, NASA was formed to explore space for scientific purposes. NASA uses both unmanned spacecraft and astronauts. Below are some important U.S. unmanned missions. The year in parentheses shows when each one was launched.

**Mariner 2** (1962)
First successful flyby of Venus.
**Mariner 4** (1964)
First probe to reach Mars, 1965.
**Pioneer 10** (1972)
First probe to reach Jupiter, 1973.
**Mariner 10** (1973)
Only U.S. probe to Mercury, 1974.
**Viking 1** and **2** (1975)
Landed on Mars in 1976.
**Voyager 1** (1977)
Reached Jupiter in 1979 and Saturn in 1980.
**Voyager 2** (1977)
Reached Jupiter in 1979, Saturn in 1981, Uranus in 1986, Neptune in 1989.

**Pioneer Venus 1** (1978)
Operated in Venus orbit 14 years.
**Magellan** (1989)
After mapping Venus, *Magellan* burned up in its atmosphere in 1994.
**Galileo** (1989)
Scheduled to pass by Jupiter 7 times in 1998.
**Mars Pathfinder** (1996)
Landed on Mars, sent a roving vehicle *(Sojourner)* to explore the surface.
**Cassini** (1997)
Expected to reach Saturn in 2004.
**Lunar Prospector** (1998)
Began yearlong orbit just a few miles above the moon's surface.

# Heavenly QUESTIONS and ANSWERS

## What Is a Galaxy?

A **galaxy** is a group of billions of stars that are held together by gravity. A galaxy also contains interstellar gas and dust. There may be about 50 billion galaxies in the universe. The galaxy we live in is called the **Milky Way**. The sun and every star we see at night are just a few of the 200 billion stars in the Milky Way. The Milky Way is so large that the light from a star along the edge of the galaxy would take about 100,000 years to reach the other side. Astronomers measure the distance between stars and between galaxies in light-years. One **light-year** is the distance that light travels in one year. Light travels about 186,282 miles in one second. In one year, light travels about 5.9 trillion miles.

 **DID YOU KNOW?** The Hubble Space Telescope discovered a huge star in 1997. It is 10 million times brighter than the sun.

## What Are Meteors, Meteorites, and Meteor Showers?

On a clear night, you may see a sudden streak of light in the sky. It may be caused by chunks of rock or metal called **meteoroids** speeding through space. When a meteoroid enters Earth's atmosphere, friction with air molecules causes it to burn brightly. The streak we see is called a **meteor**, or **shooting star**.

Many meteoroids follow in the path of a comet as it orbits the sun. As these meteoroids enter Earth's atmosphere, large numbers of meteors can be seen coming from about the same point in the sky. These streaks are called **meteor showers**. If a meteoroid is large enough to reach the ground without burning up completely, it is called a **meteorite**.

 **DID YOU KNOW?** The largest known meteorite was found in Namibia in 1920. It is 9 feet long, 8 feet wide and weighs around 65 tons. The largest meteorite that can be seen in a museum is at the American Museum of Natural History in New York City. It weighs over 68,000 pounds and was found in Greenland in 1897.

## What Is a Black Hole?

Stars have limited life spans. Our sun, which is a star, is about 5 billion years old. It is expected to last another 5 billion years. **Black holes** cannot be seen, but astronomers believe they are what remain at the end of the life of very rare stars.

Eventually some stars merely stop shining, while others explode. Many astronomers believe that when a star explodes it may leave behind a chunk of matter as heavy as our sun yet only a few miles across. The force of gravity of this tiny star is so strong that nothing that comes close to it can escape its pull, not even light. These tiny stars are called black holes.

## How Did the Universe Begin?

Most astronomers believe that the universe began in a massive explosion 10 to 20 billion years ago and that it has been expanding ever since. This is called the **big bang theory**. Some believe that the universe will keep expanding forever. Others believe that the expansion will slow down over billions of years and that gravity will begin to cause the universe to collapse.

# ASTRONAUTS in OUTER SPACE

The rapid entry of the United States into space in 1958 was in response to the Soviet Union's launching of its satellite *Sputnik I* into orbit on October 4, 1957. In 1961, three years after NASA was formed, President John F. Kennedy promised Americans that the United States would land a person on the moon by the end of the 1960s. As promised, NASA landed the first person on the moon in July 1969. Since then, many astronauts have made trips into outer space. The following time line gives some of the major flights of astronauts into space, including the Apollo flights to the moon.

**1961** — On April 12, Soviet cosmonaut Yuri Gagarin, in *Vostok 1*, became the **first human to orbit Earth**. On May 5, U.S. astronaut Alan B. Shepard Jr. of the *Mercury 3* mission became the **first American in space**.

**1962** — On February 20, U.S. astronaut John H. Glenn Jr. of *Mercury 6* became the **first American to orbit Earth**.

**1963** — From June 16 to 19, the Soviet spacecraft *Vostok 6* carried the **first woman in space**, Valentina V. Tereshkova.

**1965** — On March 18, Soviet cosmonaut Aleksei A. Leonov became the **first person to walk in space**. He spent 10 minutes outside the spaceship. On December 15, U.S. *Gemini 6A* and *7* (with astronauts) became the **first vehicles to rendezvous** (approach and see each other) **in space**.

**1966** — On March 16, U.S. *Gemini 8* became the **first craft to dock with** (become attached to) **another vehicle** (an unmanned Agena rocket).

**1967** — On January 27, a fire in a U.S. Apollo spacecraft on the ground killed astronauts Virgil I. Grissom, Edward H. White, and Roger B. Chaffee. On April 23, *Soyuz 1* crashed to the Earth, killing Soviet cosmonaut Vladimir Komarov.

**1969** — On July 20, after successful flights of *Apollo 8, 9,* and *10,* **U.S. Apollo 11's lunar module Eagle landed on the moon's surface** in the area known as the Sea of Tranquillity. Neil Armstrong became the **first person ever to walk on the moon**.

**1970** — In April, *Apollo 13* astronauts returned safely to Earth after an explosion damaged their spacecraft and prevented them from landing on the moon.

**1971** — In July and August, U.S. *Apollo 15* astronauts tested the **Lunar Rover** on the moon.

**1972** — In December, *Apollo 17* was the sixth and **final U.S. space mission to land successfully on the moon**.

▲ *Lunar Rover on the Moon*

**1973** — On May 14, the U.S. put its **first space station, Skylab, into orbit**. Crews worked in Skylab until January 1974, when the last crew left.

**1975** — On July 15, the U.S. launched *Apollo 18* and the U.S.S.R. launched *Soyuz 19*. Two days later, the **American and Soviet spacecraft docked**, and for several days their crews worked and spent time together in space. This was NASA's last space mission with astronauts until the space shuttle.

# COOPERATION in SPACE: The Space Shuttle and the Space Station

In an effort to reduce costs, NASA developed the space shuttle program during the 1970s. The U.S. space shuttle became the first reusable spacecraft. Earlier space capsules could not be used again after returning to Earth, but the space shuttle lands on a runway like an airplane and can be launched again at a later date. On space shuttle missions, astronauts perform many experiments, test equipment, and sometimes place satellites into orbit.

The European Space Agency, which was formed by some European countries in 1975, constructed the Spacelab scientific laboratory. Spacelab first rode a space shuttle in 1983. In 1986, the Soviet Union launched its successful *Mir* space station. By the mid-1990s, the United States and Russia were sharing projects in space.

**1977** — On August 12, the first shuttle, **Enterprise**, took off from the back of a 747 jet airliner.

**1981** — On April 12, **Columbia** was launched and became the first shuttle to reach Earth's orbit.

**1983** — In April, NASA began using a third shuttle, **Challenger**. Two more **Challenger** flights in 1983 included astronauts Sally K. Ride and Guion S. Bluford Jr., the first American woman and African-American man in space. On November 28, **Columbia** was launched carrying the scientific laboratory Spacelab.

▲ *Space Shuttle*

**1984** — In August, the shuttle **Discovery** was launched for the first time.

**1985** — In October, the shuttle **Atlantis** was launched for the first time.

**1986** — On January 28, after 24 successful shuttle missions, **Challenger** exploded 73 seconds after takeoff. Astronauts Dick Scobee, Michael Smith, Ellison Onizuka, Judith Resnik, Greg Jarvis, and Ron McNair, and teacher Christa McAuliffe all died. In February, the Soviet space station **Mir** was launched into orbit.

**1987** — On December 21, Soyuz TM-4 cosmonauts Vladimir Titov, Muso Manarov, and Anatoly Levchenko arrived at **Mir**. They stayed for one year, until December 21, 1988.

**1988** — In September, more than two years after the **Challenger** disaster, new safety procedures led to the successful launch of **Discovery**.

**1990** — On April 24, the **Hubble Space Telescope** was launched from **Discovery**, but the images sent back to Earth were fuzzy.

**1992** — In May, NASA launched a new shuttle, **Endeavour**.

**1993** — In December, a crew aboard **Endeavour** repaired the Hubble telescope.

**1995** — In March, an American astronaut traveled in a Russian spacecraft and joined cosmonauts on **Mir**. In June, **Atlantis** docked with **Mir** for the first time, and they orbited Earth while joined together.

**1996** — In March, Shannon Lucid joined the **Mir** crew. She spent 188 days in space, setting the record for all American and all female astronauts.

**1998** — Astronaut Andrew Thomas in January became the last U.S. astronaut to join the **Mir** crew.

# The ZODIAC

**T**he **zodiac** is an imaginary belt (or path) that goes around the sky. The orbits of the sun, the moon, and most of the planets are within the zodiac. The zodiac is divided into 12 equal sections called signs. Each section is named for the constellation that in ancient times occupied most of its space. Below are the symbols and signs of the zodiac.

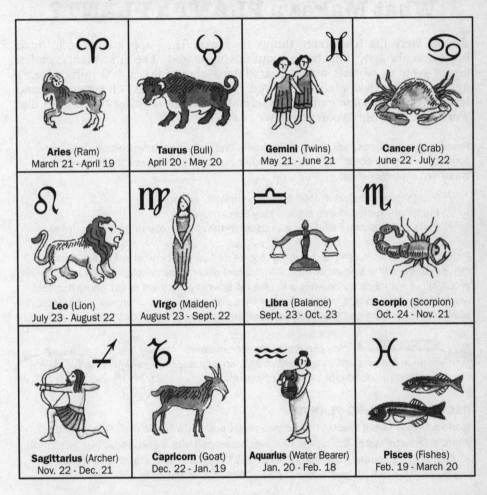

| | | | |
|---|---|---|---|
| **Aries** (Ram) March 21 - April 19 | **Taurus** (Bull) April 20 - May 20 | **Gemini** (Twins) May 21 - June 21 | **Cancer** (Crab) June 22 - July 22 |
| **Leo** (Lion) July 23 - August 22 | **Virgo** (Maiden) August 23 - Sept. 22 | **Libra** (Balance) Sept. 23 - Oct. 23 | **Scorpio** (Scorpion) Oct. 24 - Nov. 21 |
| **Sagittarius** (Archer) Nov. 22 - Dec. 21 | **Capricorn** (Goat) Dec. 22 - Jan. 19 | **Aquarius** (Water Bearer) Jan. 20 - Feb. 18 | **Pisces** (Fishes) Feb. 19 - March 20 |

## Who Is Interested in the Signs of the Zodiac?

The stars in the constellations interest both astronomers and astrologers. **Astronomers** are scientists who study the sky, including the stars, planets, moons, comets, asteroids, and meteors. Astronomers study what these are made of, how they behave, what they measure, how fast they move, and what gases they are made up of. **Astrologers** are not scientists. Astrologers believe that the positions and movements of the sun, the moon, and the planets have an influence on the lives of people on Earth and can be used to predict the future.

# PLANTS

# What Makes a PLANT a PLANT?

**P**lants were the first living things on Earth. They appeared around three billion years ago, long before animals appeared. The first plants, called algae, grew in or near water. Years later—about 300 or 400 million years ago—the first land plants appeared. These were ferns, club mosses, and horsetails. After these came plants that bear cones (**conifers**) and trees that were ancestors of the palm trees we see today.

Flowers, grass, weeds, oak trees, palm trees, and poison ivy have certain things in common with each other and with every other plant. All plants have the following three important characteristics:

- ☑ Plants create their own food from air, sunlight, and water.
- ☑ Plants are rooted in one place—they don't move around.
- ☑ Plant cells contain cellulose, a substance that keeps plants rigid and upright.

Plants need air, water, light, and warmth to grow. Not all plants need soil or the same climate, or the same amount of light, warmth, and water. A cactus plant needs a lot of heat and light but not much water, while a fir tree will grow in a northern forest where it is cold much of the year and light is limited. Water lilies are really rooted in the soil underwater, while water hyacinths just float on the water's surface and grow to about two feet above it.

 **DID YOU KNOW?** You can grow plants from some common foods, such as a sweet potato, an avocado pit, grapefruit seeds, or the tops of carrots.

## RECORD-BREAKING PLANTS
**World's Oldest Living Plants:** Bristlecone pine trees in California (4,700 years old)
**World's Tallest Plants:** The tallest tree ever measured was a eucalyptus tree in Victoria, Australia, measuring 435 feet in 1872. The tallest tree now standing is a giant sequoia tree in Redwood National Park, California, standing at 365 feet.

 **DID YOU KNOW?** You can tell how old a tree is by looking at its rings. Rings are the irregularly shaped circles you see on the stump of a tree that has been cut down. As a tree gets taller, it also gets wider, and each year that a tree grows outward is marked by a ring. A year with a good growing season leaves a thicker ring than a year that is too dry or cold. From the size of tree rings, scientists can tell what the climate was like years and years ago.

162

# PLANT TALK

**agronomy**
The growing of plants for food.

**fertilizer**
A natural or chemical substance applied to the soil to help plants grow bigger and faster.

**herb**
A plant used for flavoring or seasoning, for its scent, or as medicine. Mint, lavender, and rosemary are all herbs.

**horticulture**
The growing of plants for beauty.

**house plant**
A plant that is grown indoors. Many plants that are grown outdoors in tropical and desert regions have become popular as house plants.

**hybrid**
A plant that has been scientifically combined with another plant or has been changed to make it more beautiful, larger, stronger, or better in some other way. Many roses are hybrids.

**hydroponics**
A way of growing plants in a nutritional liquid rather than in soil.

**mulch**
A covering of bark, compost (decomposed garbage), hay, or other substance used to conserve water and control weeds. Mulch can also provide nutrients for plants and keep plants warm in winter.

**native**
A plant that has always grown in a certain place, rather than being brought there from somewhere else. Corn is native to North America.

**photosynthesis**
The process that allows plants to make their own food from air, sunlight, and water.

**phototropism**
The turning of plants toward the light.

**propagation**
The reproduction of plants. Plants can be reproduced from seeds, or by dividing the roots of a plant, or sometimes by simply placing a piece of the leaf on soil.

**terrarium**
A glass box containing small plants and animals, such as moss, ferns, lizards, and turtles.

**transplant**
A plant that is dug up and moved from one place to another.

**wildflower**
A flowering plant that grows on its own in the wild, rather than being planted by a person.

*A wildflower* ▲

**evergreen**
A tree that keeps its leaves or needles all year long.

**deciduous**
A tree that loses its leaves in autumn and gets new ones in the spring.

▲ *A deciduous tree*

**annual**
A plant that grows, flowers, and dies in one year. Most annuals produce seeds that can be planted the following spring.

**biennial**
A plant that takes two years to mature. The first year the plant produces a stem and leaves, and the second year it produces flowers and seeds.

**perennial**
A plant that stops growing and may look dead in the fall, but comes back year after year.

# WHERE DO PLANTS GROW?

**P**lants grow nearly everywhere except near the South and North Poles.

## FORESTS
**Where Evergreens Grow.** Forests cover much of Earth's land surface. Evergreens, such as pines, hemlocks, firs, and spruces, grow in the cool forest regions farthest from the equator. These trees are called **conifers** because they produce cones.

**Temperate Forests.** Temperate forests have warm, rainy summers and cold, snowy winters. Here **deciduous trees** (which lose their leaves in the fall and grow new ones in the spring) join the evergreens. Temperate forests are home to maple, oak, beech, and poplar trees, and to wildflowers and shrubs. These forests are found in eastern United States, southeastern Canada, northern Europe and Asia, and southern Australia.

**Tropical Rain Forests.** Still closer to the equator are the tropical rain forests, home to the greatest variety of plants on Earth. The temperature never falls below freezing except on the mountain slopes. About 60 to 100 inches of rain fall each year. Tropical trees stay green all year. They grow close together, shading the ground. There are several layers of trees. The top, emergent layer has trees that can reach 200 feet in height. The canopy, which gets lots of sun, comes next, followed by the understory. The forest floor, covered with roots, gets little sun and many plants cannot grow there.

Tropical rain forests are found mainly in Central America, South America, Asia, and Africa. They once covered more than 8 million square miles. Today, because of destruction by humans, fewer than 3.4 million square miles remain. More than half the plant and animal species in the world live there. Foods such as bananas and pineapples first grew there. Woods such as mahogany and teak also come from rain forests. Many kinds of plants there are used to make medicines.

When rain forests are burned, carbon dioxide is released in the air. This adds to the greenhouse effect (see page 91). As forests are destroyed, the soil also slowly wears away, so there is nothing to keep heavy rain from flooding the ground.

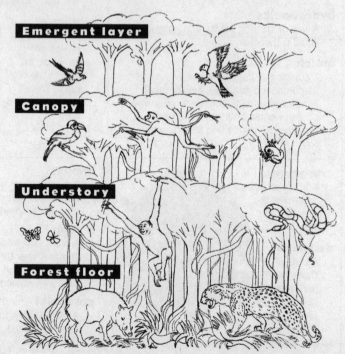

Emergent layer

Canopy

Understory

Forest floor

## TUNDRA AND ALPINE REGION

The northernmost regions of North America, Europe, and Asia surrounding the Arctic Ocean are called the **tundra**. The temperature rarely rises above 45 degrees Fahrenheit, and it is too cold for trees to grow there. Most tundra plants are mosses and lichens that hug the ground for warmth. A few wildflowers and small shrubs also grow where the soil thaws for about two months of the year. This kind of climate and plant life also exists on top of the highest mountains (the Himalayas, Alps, Andes, Rockies), where small Alpine flowers also grow.

**What Is the Tree Line?** On mountains in the north (such as the Rockies) and in the far south (such as the Andes), there is an altitude above which trees will not grow. This is the **tree line** or **timberline**. Above the tree line, you can see low shrubs and small plants, like Alpine flowers. As you move farther from the poles to the edge of the tundra, small dwarfed and twisted trees begin to appear. This is the start of the forest region.

## DESERTS

The driest areas of the world are the **deserts**. They can be hot or cold, but they also contain an amazing number of plants. Cactuses and sagebrush are native to dry regions of North and South America. The deserts of Africa and Asia contain plants called euporbias. Dates have grown in the deserts of the Middle East and North Africa for thousands of years. In the southwestern United States and northern Mexico, there are many types of cactuses, including prickly pear, barrel, and saguaro.

## GRASSLAND

The areas of the world that are too dry to have green forests, but not dry enough to be deserts, are called **grasslands**. The most common plants found there are grasses. Cooler grasslands are found in the Great Plains of the United States and Canada, in the steppes of Europe and Asia, and in the pampas of Argentina. The drier grasslands are used for grazing cattle and sheep. In the **prairies**, where there is a little more rain, important grains, such as wheat, rye, oats, and barley are grown. The warmer grasslands, called **savannas**, are found in central and southern Africa, Venezuela, southern Brazil, and Australia. Most savannas have moist summers and cool, dry winters.

# Fascinating Plants

### Plants That "Eat" Bugs

Bugs sometimes eat plants. But did you know that some plants trap insects and eat them? These are "carnivorous plants." The **pitcher-plant**, **Venus's-flytrap**, and **sundew** are three examples. Most carnivorous plants live in poor soils, where they don't get enough nourishment. They digest their prey very slowly over a long period of time.

### Flowering Stones

Plants have ways of protecting themselves. For example, **Lithops** (or flowering stones) are plants in the South African desert that look like small, gray stones. They are much less likely to be eaten by animals than something that looks green and delicious.

# The LARGEST and SMALLEST PLACES in the WORLD

If someone asks you what the largest country is, you would have to ask that person another question before you could answer: Do you mean the country with the largest area or the country with the largest population (most people)? The world's largest country in area is Russia. The world's biggest country in population is China. Vatican City is the smallest country in area and population. Below are lists of the world's largest and smallest countries and largest cities, with their populations in 1997.

## Total Population of the World in 1997: 5,852,000,000

| LARGEST COUNTRIES (Most People) | |
|---|---|
| Population | Country |
| 1,221,592,000 | China |
| 967,613,000 | India |
| 267,955,000 | United States |
| 209,774,000 | Indonesia |
| 164,511,000 | Brazil |
| 147,987,000 | Russia |
| 132,185,000 | Pakistan |
| 125,717,000 | Japan |
| 125,340,000 | Bangladesh |
| 107,129,000 | Nigeria |
| 97,563,000 | Mexico |
| 84,068,000 | Germany |
| 76,104,000 | Philippines |
| 73,977,000 | Vietnam |
| 67,540,000 | Iran |
| 64,792,000 | Egypt |
| 63,528,000 | Turkey |
| 59,451,000 | Great Britain |
| 58,851,000 | Thailand |
| 58,733,000 | Ethiopia |
| 58,470,000 | France |
| 57,534,000 | Italy |
| 50,685,000 | Ukraine |
| 47,440,000 | Congo |
| 46,822,000 | Myanmar |

| SMALLEST COUNTRIES (Fewest People) | |
|---|---|
| Population | Country |
| 811 | Vatican City |
| 10,000 | Nauru |
| 10,000 | Tuvalu |
| 17,000 | Palau |
| 25,000 | San Marino |
| 31,000 | Liechtenstein |

### LARGEST CITIES (Most People)

Here are the 10 cities in the world that have the most people. Numbers include people from the whole built-up area around each city (the metropolitan area).

| City, Country | Population |
|---|---|
| Tokyo, Japan | 27,000,000 |
| Mexico City, Mexico | 16,562,000 |
| São Paulo, Brazil | 16,533,000 |
| New York City, U.S. | 16,332,000 |
| Bombay, India | 15,138,000 |
| Shanghai, China | 13,584,000 |
| Los Angeles, U.S. | 12,410,000 |
| Calcutta, India | 11,923,000 |
| Buenos Aires, Argentina | 11,802,000 |
| Seoul, South Korea | 11,609,000 |

# POPULATION of the UNITED STATES

## Total Population of the United States in 1997: 267,636,061

| Population of the STATES and DISTRICT OF COLUMBIA in 1997 | | | |
|---|---|---|---|
| **Rank & State Name** | **Population** | **Rank & State Name** | **Population** |
| 1. California | 32,268,301 | 27. Oklahoma | 3,317,091 |
| 2. Texas | 19,439,337 | 28. Connecticut | 3,269,858 |
| 3. New York | 18,137,226 | 29. Oregon | 3,243,487 |
| 4. Florida | 14,653,945 | 30. Iowa | 2,852,423 |
| 5. Pennsylvania | 12,019,661 | 31. Mississippi | 2,730,501 |
| 6. Illinois | 11,895,849 | 32. Kansas | 2,594,840 |
| 7. Ohio | 11,186,331 | 33. Arkansas | 2,522,819 |
| 8. Michigan | 9,773,892 | 34. Utah | 2,059,148 |
| 9. New Jersey | 8,052,849 | 35. West Virginia | 1,815,787 |
| 10. Georgia | 7,486,242 | 36. New Mexico | 1,729,751 |
| 11. Virginia | 7,425,183 | 37. Nevada | 1,676,809 |
| 12. North Carolina | 6,733,996 | 38. Nebraska | 1,656,870 |
| 13. Massachusetts | 6,117,520 | 39. Maine | 1,242,051 |
| 14. Indiana | 5,864,108 | 40. Idaho | 1,210,232 |
| 15. Washington | 5,610,362 | 41. Hawaii | 1,186,602 |
| 16. Missouri | 5,402,058 | 42. New Hampshire | 1,172,709 |
| 17. Tennessee | 5,368,198 | 43. Rhode Island | 987,429 |
| 18. Wisconsin | 5,169,677 | 44. Montana | 878,810 |
| 19. Maryland | 5,094,289 | 45. South Dakota | 737,973 |
| 20. Minnesota | 4,685,549 | 46. Delaware | 731,581 |
| 21. Arizona | 4,554,966 | 47. North Dakota | 640,883 |
| 22. Louisiana | 4,351,769 | 48. Alaska | 609,311 |
| 23. Alabama | 4,319,154 | 49. Vermont | 588,978 |
| 24. Kentucky | 3,908,124 | 50. District of Columbia | 528,964 |
| 25. Colorado | 3,892,644 | 51. Wyoming | 479,743 |
| 26. South Carolina | 3,760,181 | | |

## THE LARGEST CITIES IN THE UNITED STATES

Cities grow and shrink in population. Below is a list of the largest cities in the United States in 1996 compared with their populations in 1950. Can you find the six cities that increased in population? The four that decreased?

| Rank & City | 1996 | 1950 |
|---|---|---|
| 1. New York, NY | 7,380,906 | 7,891,957 |
| 2. Los Angeles, CA | 3,553,638 | 1,970,358 |
| 3. Chicago, IL | 2,721,547 | 3,620,962 |
| 4. Houston, TX | 1,744,058 | 596,163 |
| 5. Philadelphia, PA | 1,478,002 | 2,071,605 |
| 6. San Diego, CA | 1,171,121 | 334,387 |
| 7. Phoenix, AZ | 1,159,014 | 106,818 |
| 8. San Antonio, TX | 1,067,816 | 408,442 |
| 9. Dallas, TX | 1,053,392 | 434,462 |
| 10. Detroit, MI | 1,000,272 | 1,849,568 |

▲ New York City

# Taking the Census: EVERYONE COUNTS

## WHAT IS A CENSUS?

Every ten years the United States government counts the people who live in the United States. This is called taking the census. The census is taken to find out how many people live in the United States, where they live, how old they are, what they do, how much money they earn, the number of children in families, and other things about them.

## WHEN WAS THE FIRST U.S. CENSUS TAKEN?

The first census was taken in 1790, after the American Revolution. That year there were 3,929,200 people in the United States. Most of the people then lived in the eastern part of the country, on farms or in small towns.

## WHEN WILL THE NEXT CENSUS COME?

Plans are now being made for the next census, which will be taken in the year 2000.

## WHY DO WE NEED TO BE COUNTED?

☑ **Congress.** The number of representatives from each state in the U.S. House of Representatives is determined by the population of each state.

☑ **National government.** Census information helps the national government make plans to provide public services such as health care, highways, and parks.

☑ **State and local governments.** Census information helps state and local governments decide local questions, such as whether to build more schools for children or homes for elderly people.

☑ **Private companies.** It gives private companies information that helps them—such as how many people use cars, refrigerators, baby food, and other products; how many people read newspapers; and where these people live.

## WHAT DOES THE LATEST CENSUS TELL US ABOUT THE UNITED STATES?

☑ By 1990, the population had increased to 248,709,873.

☑ More than half of the people in the United States live in the southern and western sections of the country.

☑ About 80% of Americans live in cities or suburbs.

☑ The United States is known for its large population that includes people of different races and nationalities.

The chart below shows how many Americans called themselves white, black, Asian, American Indian, and Hispanic in the 1990 census. The percentages add up to more than 100% because Hispanics may be of Mexican, Puerto Rican, Cuban or Spanish descent, or they may have roots in other Spanish-speaking countries of the Caribbean, or in Central or South America. Hispanics may be of any race.

**White,** 199,686,070 .............................80%

**Black,** 29,986,060 ...............................12%

**Hispanic,** 22,354,059 .............................9%

**Asian,** 7,276,662......................................3%
(including the Pacific Islands)

**American Indian,** 1,959,234 ....................1%
(including Eskimo, or Aleut)

**Other race,** 9,804,847 .............................4%
(people who said "other race")

# COUNTING THE FIRST AMERICANS

## WHERE DID THEY COME FROM?

American Indians, also called Native Americans, lived in North and South America long before the first European explorers arrived. Their ancestors are thought to have come from northeast Asia more than 20,000 years ago. American Indians are not one people, but many different peoples, each with their own traditions and way of life.

## HOW MANY WERE THERE IN THE BEGINNING?

It is believed that many millions of Indians lived in the Americas before Columbus came. About 850,000 lived in what is now the United States.

## HOW MANY ARE THERE NOW?

During the 17th, 18th, and 19th centuries, disease and wars with white settlers and soldiers caused the death of thousands of American Indians. By 1910 there were only about 220,000 left in the United States. Since then, the American Indian population has increased dramatically. In 1990, the last year a census was taken, the total number of Native Americans was close to 2 million.

## WHERE DO NATIVE AMERICANS LIVE?

Below are the states with the largest Native American populations.

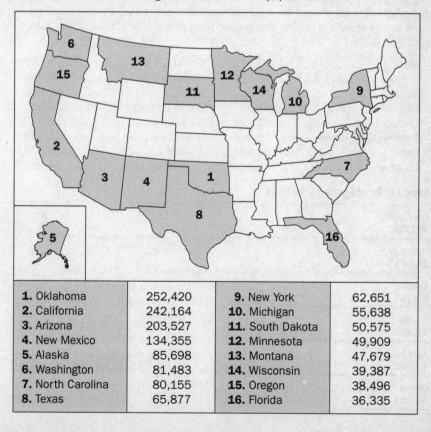

| | | | | |
|---|---|---|---|---|
| 1. Oklahoma | 252,420 | | 9. New York | 62,651 |
| 2. California | 242,164 | | 10. Michigan | 55,638 |
| 3. Arizona | 203,527 | | 11. South Dakota | 50,575 |
| 4. New Mexico | 134,355 | | 12. Minnesota | 49,909 |
| 5. Alaska | 85,698 | | 13. Montana | 47,679 |
| 6. Washington | 81,483 | | 14. Wisconsin | 39,387 |
| 7. North Carolina | 80,155 | | 15. Oregon | 38,496 |
| 8. Texas | 65,877 | | 16. Florida | 36,335 |

# The MANY FACES of America: IMMIGRATION

You have probably heard it said that America is a nation of immigrants. Many Americans are descended from Europeans, Africans, or Asians. Do you know someone who was born in another country?

### Why Do People Come to the United States?
Have you ever wondered why so many people leave their native country and come and live in the United States? It isn't usually because they don't love their own country. Most people are very attached to the place where they were born. Immigrants come to America for many reasons: to live in freedom, to worship as they choose, to escape poverty, to make a better life for themselves and their children.

Millions of people have immigrated to the United States from all over the world—more than 40 million since 1820. Much of the art we see or the music we hear, and many of the scientific discoveries and inventions we use, foods we eat, and languages we speak were introduced to us by people who came from other countries.

### What Countries Do Immigrants Come From?
Immigrants come to the United States from many countries. Below are some of the countries immigrants came from in 1996. The name of the country is followed by the number of immigrants. In 1996, immigration from all countries to the United States totaled 915,900.

| | | | |
|---|---|---|---|
| Mexico | 163,572 | Russia | 19,668 |
| Philippines | 55,876 | Jamaica | 19,089 |
| India | 44,859 | Haiti | 18,386 |
| Vietnam | 42,067 | North and South Korea | 18,185 |
| China | 41,728 | El Salvador | 17,903 |
| Dominican Republic | 39,604 | Canada | 15,825 |
| Cuba | 26,466 | Poland | 15,772 |
| Ukraine | 21,079 | Colombia | 14,283 |

### Where Do Immigrants Settle?

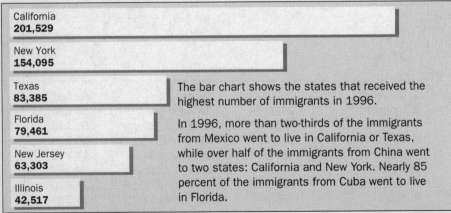

California
**201,529**

New York
**154,095**

Texas
**83,385**

Florida
**79,461**

New Jersey
**63,303**

Illinois
**42,517**

The bar chart shows the states that received the highest number of immigrants in 1996.

In 1996, more than two-thirds of the immigrants from Mexico went to live in California or Texas, while over half of the immigrants from China went to two states: California and New York. Nearly 85 percent of the immigrants from Cuba went to live in Florida.

# Becoming an AMERICAN CITIZEN: NATURALIZATION

When a foreign-born person becomes a citizen of the United States, we say the person has become **naturalized.** To apply for American citizenship, a person

- ☑ Must be at least 18 years old.
- ☑ Must have lived legally in the United States for at least 5 years.
- ☑ Must be able to understand English if under the age of 55.
- ☑ Must be of good moral character.
- ☑ Must show knowledge of the history and form of government of the United States.

# ELLIS ISLAND and THE STATUE OF LIBERTY

### ELLIS ISLAND: THE GATEWAY TO AMERICA

Until this century, people could immigrate freely to the United States. They piled on to ships and came, hoping to find a better life. Between 1892 and 1924, more than 12 million people came into the country by passing through Ellis Island, a huge immigration center in New York harbor. There they were screened for certain contagious diseases and some sick people were sent back, but most immigrants were allowed to stay.

Immigrants who passed through Ellis Island came from many places—Italy, Russia, Hungary, Austria, Germany, England, Ireland, Sweden, Greece, Norway, Turkey, Scotland, the West Indies, Poland, Portugal, France, and others.

**Ellis Island as a Museum.** As an immigration center, Ellis Island was closed in 1954. But in 1990, it reopened as a museum to tell the story of the immigrants who helped make the United States a great country. The names of many of the immigrants who came through Ellis Island are inscribed on a wall in their memory.

**THE STATUE OF LIBERTY.** Many of the immigrants who steamed into New York harbor passed by the Statue of Liberty. Set on her own island, the "Lady With the Lamp" was given to the United States by France and has served as a symbol of freedom and a welcome to Americans-to-be since she was erected in 1886. In 1903, a poem by the U.S. poet Emma Lazarus was inscribed at the base of the statue. Two of its lines read: "Give me your tired, your poor, your huddled masses yearning to breathe free...."

# ENTERTAINMENT AWARDS

**W**ho is your favorite movie actor or actress? What is your all-time favorite film? If you are interested in the movies, you probably know that an Oscar is a golden statuette that is awarded for the year's best actor, best actress, best movies, and so on. The Oscar presentations are watched on television by millions of people all over the world. Among other awards given every year for the best in entertainment are the Grammys, the Emmys, and the Tonys.

## ACADEMY AWARDS: THE OSCARS

The Oscars are given every year by the Academy of Motion Picture Arts and Sciences for the best in movies. Here are some of the films and people that won Oscars in 1998.

▲ Scene from the Academy Award winning motion picture Titanic

**Best Picture:** *Titanic*

**Best Actor:** Jack Nicholson in *As Good As It Gets*

**Best Actress:** Helen Hunt in *As Good As It Gets*

**Best Supporting Actor:** Robin Williams in *Good Will Hunting*

**Best Supporting Actress:** Kim Basinger in *L.A. Confidential*

**Best Director:** James Cameron for *Titanic*

**Best Original Screenplay:** Ben Affleck, Matt Damon, *Good Will Hunting*

**Best Original Song:** "My Heart Will Go On," from *Titanic*

**Best Original Musical Score:** *The Full Monty*

**Best Visual Effects:** *Titanic*

**Best Costume Design:** *Titanic*

**Best Makeup:** *Men in Black*

**DID YOU KNOW?** Walt Disney won 20 Oscars during his career—more than anyone else. The youngest person ever to receive an Oscar was Shirley Temple. She won an honorary Oscar in 1934 at the age of 5. The oldest was Jessica Tandy. In 1990, at the age of 80, she won an Oscar for Best Actress in the film *Driving Miss Daisy*.

# THE GRAMMYS

Grammys are awards given out each year by the National Academy of Recording Arts and Sciences for the best in popular music. Some of the winners in 1998 were:

**Best Record and Best Song:** "Sunny Came Home," Shawn Colvin
**Best Album:** *Time Out of Mind*, Bob Dylan
**Best New Artist:** Paula Cole
**Best Rock Group:** The Wallflowers, "One Headlight"
**Best Rock Album:** *Blue Moon Swamp*, John Fogerty
**Best Rock Song:** *"One Headlight,"* Jakob Dylan
**Best Rhythm-and-Blues Song:** "I Believe I Can Fly," R. Kelly
**Best Rap Soloist:** Will Smith, "Men in Black"
**Best Rap Album:** *No Way Out,* Puff Daddy & the Family
**Best Country Group:** Alison Krauss & Union Station, "Looking in the Eyes of Love"
**Best Country Album:** *Unchained*, Johnny Cash
**Best Contemporary Folk Album:** *Time Out of Mind*, Bob Dylan
**Best Musical Album for Children:** *All Aboard!*, John Denver
**Best Nonmusical Album for Children:** *Winnie-the-Pooh*, Charles Kuralt

▲ *Shawn Colvin*

# THE EMMYS

The Emmy Awards are given each year by the Academy of Television Arts and Sciences. Here are some of the major winners for the 1996-1997 season for primetime (the evening from 8 PM to 11 PM).

**Best Drama Series:** *Law & Order* (NBC)
**Best Actor in a Drama Series:** Dennis Franz, in *NYPD Blue* (ABC)
**Best Actress in a Drama Series:** Gillian Anderson, in *The X-Files* (Fox)
**Best Comedy Series:** *Frasier* (NBC)
**Best Actor in a Comedy Series:** John Lithgow, in *3rd Rock From the Sun* (NBC)
**Best Actress in a Comedy Series:** Helen Hunt, in *Mad About You* (NBC)
**Best Miniseries:** *Prime Suspect 5: Errors of Judgment* (PBS)

# THE TONYS

The Antoinette Perry Awards, known as the "Tonys," are annual awards given to the best Broadway plays and to those who write them, act in them, and direct them. Winners for the 1997-1998 season were:

**Best Play:** *Art*
**Best Musical:** *The Lion King*
**Best Musical Revival:** *Cabaret*
**Leading Actor in a Play:** Anthony LaPaglia
**Leading Actress in a Play:** Marie Mullen
**Leading Actor in a Musical:** Alan Cumming
**Leading Actress in a Musical:** Natasha Richardson

# Other PRIZES and AWARDS

## NOBEL PRIZES

The Nobel Prizes are named after Alfred B. Nobel (1833-1896), a Swedish scientist who left money to be awarded every year to people who have helped humankind. Albert Einstein, the world-famous German-born physicist, won the physics prize in 1921. The Polish-French scientist Marie Curie won two Nobel Prizes—one in physics in 1903 (with Pierre Curie, her husband, and Henry Becquerel) and one in chemistry in 1911. Prizes are also given for medicine-physiology, literature, economics, and peace.

The Nobel Peace Prize goes to a person or group that the judges think did the most during the past year to help achieve peace. In 1997, the prize went to an American, Jody Williams, and to the International Campaign to Ban Landmines, a group she works with.

## PULITZER PRIZES

The Pulitzer Prizes are named after Joseph Pulitzer (1847-1911), a journalist and publisher, who gave the money to set them up. The prizes are given yearly in the United States for journalism, drama, literature, and music.

## SPINGARN MEDAL

The Spingarn Medal was set up in 1914 by Joel Elias Spingarn, then the leader of the National Association for the Advancement of Colored People (NAACP). It is awarded every year by the NAACP for the highest achievement by a black American. Here are some of the winners and the year they won.

1998: Civil rights activist
Myrlie Evers-Williams
1997: Journalist Carl T. Rowan
1996: Professor and former judge
A. Leon Higginbotham, Jr.
1995: Historian John Hope Franklin
1994: Writer and poet Maya Angelou

1991: General Colin Powell
1985: Actor Bill Cosby
1979: Civil rights activist
Rosa Parks
1975: Baseball player Hank Aaron
1957: Civil rights leader
Martin Luther King, Jr.

## THE MEDAL OF HONOR

The Medal of Honor is the highest award that is given by the government of the United States. It is a military award for extraordinary personal bravery in war against an enemy. The first Medals of Honor were awarded in 1863. By the middle of 1998, 3,428 Medals of Honor had been awarded.

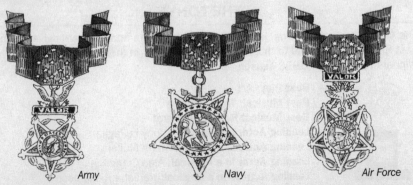

Army          Navy          Air Force

# HALLS OF FAME

**H**alls of fame are special museums created to honor people who are best in their field. The first hall of fame, which was opened in 1900 in New York City, honors great Americans from President George Washington to agricultural scientist George Washington Carver (who developed peanut butter), from early feminist Susan B. Anthony to composer and marching band leader John Philip Sousa.

Below are some well-known halls of fame. For others, look at the pages on Sports and Inventions.

▲ *Abraham Lincoln*

## HALL OF FAME FOR GREAT AMERICANS
Bronx Community College
University Avenue and
W. 181st Street
Bronx, NY 10453

Founded in 1900, this hall of fame honors well-known Americans for their work as political leaders, scientists, artists, writers, soldiers, inventors, and humanitarians.

## NATIONAL COWBOY HALL OF FAME AND WESTERN HERITAGE CENTER
1700 NE 63rd Street
Oklahoma City, OK 73111

**WEB SITE** http://www.cowboyhalloffame.org

Honors many of the pioneers who helped to develop the American West.

## NATIONAL WOMEN'S HALL OF FAME
76 Fall Street
Seneca Falls, NY 13148

**WEB SITE** http://www.great women.org

▲ *Susan B. Anthony*

Honors American women who have made great contributions to their country. Holds essay and poster contests and sponsors special activities for school groups.

## ROCK AND ROLL HALL OF FAME AND MUSEUM
1 Key Plaza
Cleveland, OH 44114

**WEB SITE** http://www.rockhall.com

Opened in 1995, this hall honors famous rock-and-roll artists and the people who influenced their music. In order to be included in the Hall of Fame, musicians must have recorded their first song at least 25 years ago. The museum honors current rockers.

---

## PRIZES MATCHING PUZZLE

Try to match the name, in the first column, with the award in the second column. The names and awards can be found on pages 172-175. (Answers are on page 305.)

| | |
|---|---|
| 1. Myrlie Evers-Williams | a. Emmy |
| 2. *Mad About You* | b. Nobel Prize |
| 3. Abraham Lincoln | c. Spingarn |
| 4. Matt Damon | d. Hall of Fame |
| 5. Marie Curie | e. Grammy |
| 6. Jakob Dylan | f. Oscar |

# CONTESTS

**S**ome kids like to compete in soccer or gymnastics. Others like to enter contests for making posters, writing stories, or creating science projects. And others prefer not to compete at all. If you like contests, there are many kinds to choose from. Some contests appear in magazines or newspapers, and you can enter them on your own. Others are run only through schools.

## MAGAZINE CONTESTS

If you like history, *The American History Magazine for Young People* runs a contest each year asking readers (ages 8-14) to create a short video, poster, or essay telling why they think a particular person played an important role in history. If you like science projects, the magazine *Odyssey, Science That Is Out of This World* holds contests in which kids do artwork, write science fiction stories, or design science projects. For more information on either contest, you may contact: Cobblestone Publishing, 30 Grove Street, Peterborough, NH 03458. Phone: (800) 821-0115

Other magazines also hold contests for kids or print kids' original stories, poems, opinions, artwork, photographs, and even jokes and riddles. Some of them are: *Contact, Highlights for Children, Sports Illustrated for Kids, Stone Soup: The Magazine by Young Writers and Artists,* and *Zillions.* You can look for these and others in your library.

## CONTESTS THROUGH SCHOOLS

**National Spelling Bee.** Are you a good speller? A company named Scripps Howard runs spelling bees for kids 15 years old and under. Winners go on to county contests, and then possibly to the National Spelling Bee in Washington, D.C. For information, a school principal may contact: The Scripps Howard National Spelling Bee, PO Box 371541, Pittsburgh, PA 15251. Phone: (513) 977-3040

**WEB SITE** http://www.spellingbee.com

**Contests in Photography, Writing, Music, and Art.** Do you like to take photographs, write stories or poems, compose music, or create art? If so, contests through the PTA (Parent Teacher Association) Reflections Program may interest you. The contests are based on a different theme each year, and entries may be in photography, writing, music, or art. Students compete from local to national levels. For information, a school PTA may contact: National PTA Reflections Program, 330 North Wabash Avenue, Suite 2100, Chicago, IL 60611. Phone: (312) 670-6782

**National Geography Bee.** How would you like to test your knowledge of geography? The National Geographic Society sponsors The National Geography Bee. In this contest, fourth through eighth graders compete on local, state, and national levels by answering oral and written questions about geography. For information, a school principal may write to: National Geography Bee, National Geographic Society, 1145 17th Street N.W., Washington, D.C., 20036.

# RELIGION
## Around the WORLD

**H**ave you ever asked yourself questions like these: How did the universe begin? Why are we here on earth? What happens to us after we die? For many people, religion is a way of answering such questions. Believing in a God or gods, or in a Divine Being, is one way of making sense of the world around us. Religions can also help guide people's lives. More than 5 billion people all over the world belong to some religious group. Different religions have different beliefs. For example, Christians, Jews, and Muslims believe in one God, while Hindus believe in many gods. On this page and the next page are some facts about the world's major religions.

### CHRISTIANITY

**Who Started Christianity?** Jesus Christ, in the first century. He was born in Bethlehem between 8 B.C. and 4 B.C. and died about A.D. 29.

**What Do Christians Believe?** That there is one God. That Jesus Christ is the Son of God, who came on earth and died to save humankind.

**How Many Are There?** Christianity is the world's biggest religion. In 1997 there were almost 2 billion Christians, in nearly all parts of the world. Nearly one billion of the Christians were **Roman Catholics**, who follow the leadership of the pope in Rome. Other groups of Christians include **Orthodox Christians**, who accept most of the same teachings as Roman Catholics but do not follow the pope as their leader, and **Protestants**, who often disagree with Catholic teachings. Protestants rely especially on the Bible, as well as insights of the laity (members of the church who are not ordained as clergy). They are divided into many different groups that have different beliefs.

### JUDAISM

**Who Started Judaism?** Abraham is considered the founder of Judaism. He lived around 1300 B.C.

**What Do Jews Believe?** That there is one God who created the universe and rules over it. That they should be faithful to God and carry out God's commandments.

**How Many Are There?** In 1997, there were about 14 million Jews, spread around the world. Many live in Israel or the United States.

**What Kinds Are There?** In the United States there are three main kinds: **Orthodox**, **Conservative**, and **Reform**. Orthodox Jews are the most traditional. Traditional means that they follow strict laws about how they dress, what they can eat, and how they conduct their lives. Conservative Jews follow many of the traditions. Reform Jews are the least traditional.

## ISLAM

**Who Started Islam?** Muhammad, the Prophet, in A.D. 610.

**What Do Muslims Believe?** People who believe in Islam are known as Muslims. The word "Islam" means submission to God. Muslims believe (1) that there is no other god than God; (2) that Muhammad is the prophet and lawgiver of his community; (3) that they should pray five times a day, fast during the month of Ramadan, give to the poor, and once during their life make a pilgrimage to Mecca in Saudi Arabia if they can afford it.

**How Many Are There?** In 1997, there were about 1 billion Muslims, mostly in parts of Africa and Asia. The two main branches of Muslims are: **Sunni Muslims**, who make up some 80% of all Muslims today, and **Shiite Muslims**, who broke away in a dispute over leadership after Muhammad died in 632.

## HINDUISM

**Who Started Hinduism?** No one person. Aryan invaders of India, around 1500 B.C., brought their own beliefs with them, which were mixed with the beliefs of the people who already lived in India.

**What Do Hindus Believe?** That there are many gods and many ways of worshipping. That people die and are reborn many times as another living thing. That there is a universal soul or principle known as *Brahman*. That the goal of life is to escape the cycle of birth and death and become part of the *Brahman*. This is achieved by leading a pure and good life.

**How Many Are There?** In 1997, there were nearly 800 million Hindus, mainly in India and places where people from India have gone to live.

**What Kinds Are There?** There are many kinds of Hindus, who worship different gods or goddesses.

## BUDDHISM

**Who Started Buddhism?** Gautama Siddhartha (the Buddha), around 525 B.C.

**What Do Buddhists Believe?** Buddha taught that life is filled with suffering. In order to be free of that suffering, believers have to give up worldly possessions and worldly goals and try to achieve a state of perfect peace known as *nirvana*.

**How Many Are There?** In 1997, there were more than 320 million Buddhists, mostly in Asia.

**What Kinds Are There?** There are two main kinds. **Theravada** ("Path of the Elders") **Buddhism,** the older kind, is more common in southern Asia. **Mahayana** ("Great Vessel") **Buddhism** is more common in northern Asia.

# RELIGIOUS MEMBERSHIP
## in the United States

**D**id you know that Protestants are the largest religious group in the United States, and that Catholics are the second largest? In the box below you can see how many people belong to the major religious groups. These numbers are estimates, because no one knows exactly how many people belong to each group.

| Protestants | | | | over 100 million |
|---|---|---|---|---|
| Including: | Baptists | 37 million | Mormons | 5 million |
| | Methodists | 13 million | Presbyterians | 4 million |
| | Pentecostals | 10 million | Episcopalians | 3 million |
| | Lutherans | 8 million | Reformed Churches | 2 million |

| Roman Catholics | 60 million |
|---|---|

| Jews | 6 million |
|---|---|

| Orthodox Christians | 6 million |
|---|---|

| Muslims | 4 million |
|---|---|

# RELIGIOUS TEXTS

**E**very religion has its writings or sacred texts that set out its laws and beliefs. Among them are:

### THE BIBLE
**The Old Testament.** Also known as the Hebrew Bible, this is a collection of laws, history, and other writings that are holy books for Jews and also for Christians. The first five books of the Old Testament are known by Jews as the Torah. These contain the stories of creation and the beginnings of human life, as well as the laws handed down by the prophet Moses.

**The New Testament.** A collection of Gospels (stories about Jesus), epistles (letters written to guide the early Christians), and other writings. The Old Testament and New Testament together make up the Bible that is read by Christians.

### THE KORAN
The Koran (al-Qur'an in Arabic) sets out the main beliefs and practices of Islam, the religion of Muslims. Muslims believe that the Koran was revealed by God to the prophet Muhammad through the angel Gabriel.

### THE BHAGAVAD GHITA
The Bhagavad Ghita is one of several Hindu religious writings. Part of a long poem about war, it is familiar to almost every Hindu. In it the god Krishna, in the form of a man, drives the chariot of Prince Arjuna into battle and teaches him about how to live.

# MAJOR HOLY DAYS
# for Christians, Jews, and Muslims

## CHRISTIAN HOLY DAYS

|  | 1998 | 1999 | 2000 |
|---|---|---|---|
| Ash Wednesday | February 25 | February 17 | March 28 |
| Good Friday | April 10 | April 2 | April 21 |
| Easter Sunday | April 12 | April 4 | April 23 |
| Easter for Orthodox Churches | April 19 | April 11 | April 30 |
| Christmas | December 25 | December 25 | December 25 |

## JEWISH HOLY DAYS
The Jewish holy days begin at sundown and end at sundown. The days listed below are the first night of the observance.

|  | 1998 (5758-59) | 1999 (5759-60) | 2000 (5760-5761) |
|---|---|---|---|
| Passover | April 10 | March 31 | April 19 |
| Rosh Hashanah (New Year) | September 20 | September 10 | September 29 |
| Yom Kippur | September 29 | September 19 | October 8 |
| Chanukah | December 13 | December 3 | December 21 |

## ISLAMIC (MUSLIM) HOLY DAYS

|  | 1998-99 (1419) | 1999-2000 (1420) | 2000-2001 (1421) |
|---|---|---|---|
| Muharram 1 (New Year) | April 27 | April 17 | April 6 |
| Mawlid (Birthday of Muhammad) | July 6 | June 26 | June 14 |
| Ramadan 1 | December 20 | December 9 | November 27 |
| Id al-Adha Dhu al-Hijjah 10 | March 28 | March 16 | March 5 |

# CHEMICAL ELEMENTS

**P**eople, dogs, butterflies, flowers, rocks, air, water, CDs, baseball cards, telephones—everything we see and use is made up of "basic ingredients" called **elements**. There are 112 elements. Most of them have been found in nature. Some have been created in laboratories. The charts below show the elements found in Earth's crust and those found in the atmosphere:

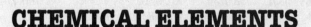

**Elements Found in Earth's Crust**
(percent by weight)

Iron, Calcium, Sodium, Potassium, Others — 17%
Aluminum — 8%
Oxygen 47%
Silicon 28%

**Elements Found in the Atmosphere**
(percent by volume)

Argon, Carbon Dioxide, Others — 1%
Oxygen 21%
Nitrogen 78%

**How Can Scientists Tell One Element From Another?** The smallest possible piece of an element that has all the properties of the original element is called an **atom**. Each tiny atom is made up of even smaller particles called **protons**, **neutrons**, and **electrons**.

To tell one element from another, scientists count the number of protons in an atom. The total number of protons is called the element's **atomic number**. All of the atoms of an element have the same number of protons and electrons, but some atoms have a different number of neutrons. For example, carbon–12 has 6 protons and 6 neutrons, and carbon–13 has 6 protons and 7 neutrons.

We call the amount of matter in an atom its **atomic mass**. Carbon–13 has a greater atomic mass than carbon–12. The average atomic mass of all of the different atoms of the same element is called the element's **atomic weight**. Every element has a different atomic number and a different atomic weight.

**Chemical Symbols Are Scientific Shorthand.** When scientists write the names of elements, they often use a symbol instead of spelling out the full name. Just as we sometimes use $ instead of writing "dollars," scientists write O for oxygen and He for helium. The symbol for each element is one or two letters. The symbols usually come from the English name for the element (C for carbon). The symbols for some of the elements come from the element's Latin name. For example, the symbol for gold is Au, which is short for *Aurum,* the Latin word for gold.

# A LOOK at Some COMMON ELEMENTS

The table below shows some common elements with their symbol, atomic number, atomic weight, the year they were discovered, and some of their common uses.

| NAME OF ELEMENT | SYMBOL | ATOMIC NUMBER | ATOMIC WEIGHT | YEAR FOUND | COMMON USE |
|---|---|---|---|---|---|
| Hydrogen | H | 1 | 1.01 | 1766 | in welding |
| Helium | He | 2 | 4.00 | 1868 | inflate balloons |
| Carbon | C | 6 | 12.01 | B.C. | pencils, diamonds |
| Nitrogen | N | 7 | 14.01 | 1772 | fertilizers |
| Oxygen | O | 8 | 16.00 | 1774 | breathing |
| Fluorine | F | 9 | 19.00 | 1771 | toothpastes |
| Neon | Ne | 10 | 20.18 | 1898 | electric signs |
| Sodium | Na | 11 | 22.99 | 1807 | in salt |
| Aluminum | Al | 13 | 26.98 | 1825 | soda cans |
| Silicon | Si | 14 | 28.09 | 1823 | in sand |
| Sulfur | S | 16 | 32.06 | B.C. | matches |
| Chlorine | Cl | 17 | 35.45 | 1774 | purifies water, in salt |
| Calcium | Ca | 20 | 40.08 | 1808 | in bones |
| Iron | Fe | 26 | 55.85 | B.C. | steel, magnets |
| Copper | Cu | 29 | 63.55 | B.C. | water pipes, wire |
| Silver | Ag | 47 | 107.87 | B.C. | jewelry, dental fillings |
| Gold | Au | 79 | 196.97 | B.C. | jewelry, coins |
| Mercury | Hg | 80 | 200.59 | B.C. | in thermometers |
| Lead | Pb | 82 | 207.19 | B.C. | in car batteries |

**ELEMENTS ARE ALL AROUND US.** Neon signs light up store windows. Car batteries contain lead. Soda cans are made from aluminum. Chips using silicon are found in computers. Jewelry is made from gold and silver.

When elements join together, they form **compounds**. Water is a compound made up of hydrogen and oxygen. Salt is a compound made up of sodium and chlorine. Many things we use at home or in school are compounds.

| Common Name | Contains the Compound | Contains the Elements |
|---|---|---|
| Vinegar | Acetic acid | carbon, hydrogen, oxygen |
| Chalk | Calcium carbonate | calcium, carbon, oxygen |
| Soda bubbles | Carbon dioxide | carbon, oxygen |
| Rust | Iron oxide | iron, oxygen |
| Baking soda | Sodium bicarbonate | sodium, hydrogen, carbon, oxygen |
| Toothpaste | Sodium fluoride | sodium, fluorine |

# MINERALS, ROCKS, and GEMS

## WHAT ARE MINERALS?

**Minerals** are natural solid materials in the soil that were never alive. All of the land on our planet and even the ocean floor rest on a layer of rock made up of minerals. Minerals have also been found on other planets, on our moon, and in meteorites that landed on Earth. Some minerals, such as gold and silver, are made up entirely of one element. But most minerals are formed from two or more elements joined together. The most common mineral is quartz, which is made of silicon and oxygen and is found all over the world. Sand is made up mostly of quartz. Graphite, which is used in pencils, is another common mineral. Other minerals, like diamonds, are very rare and valuable. Oddly enough, diamonds and graphite are different forms of the same element—carbon.

## WHAT ARE ROCKS?

**Rocks** are combinations of minerals. There are three kinds of rocks:

1. **Igneous rocks** are rocks that form from melted minerals in the Earth that cool and become solid. Granite is an igneous rock made from quartz, feldspar, and mica.
2. **Sedimentary rocks** are rocks that usually form in sea and river beds from tiny pieces of other rocks, sand, and shells that get packed together. It takes millions of years for these pieces to form sedimentary rocks. Limestone is a kind of sedimentary rock.
3. **Metamorphic rock**. Over millions of years, the heat and pressure inside Earth can change the minerals in igneous and sedimentary rocks. When the minerals in a rock change, the new rock is called a **metamorphic rock**. Marble is a metamorphic rock formed from limestone.

## WHAT ARE GEMS?

Most **gems** are minerals that have been cut and polished to be used as jewelry or other kinds of decoration. Some gems are not minerals. A pearl is a gem that is not a mineral, because it comes from an oyster, which is a living thing. The most valued gems—diamonds, emeralds, rubies, and sapphires—are minerals called **precious stones**. Below are some popular gems, the kind of mineral each one is, the elements each is made up of, and the usual colors for the gem.

| Gem Name | Mineral | Element It Is Made Of | Usual Colors |
|---|---|---|---|
| Amethyst | quartz | silicon, oxygen | purple |
| Diamond | carbon | carbon | bluish white |
| Emerald | beryl | beryllium, silicon, aluminum, oxygen | green |
| Opal | opal | silicon, oxygen | red, green, blue |
| Ruby | corundum | aluminum, oxygen | red |
| Sapphire | corundum | aluminum, oxygen | blue |

 **DID YOU KNOW?** Some minerals glow in the dark. Those that change color under ultraviolet light—like diamonds, opals, and rubies—are called **fluorescent minerals**. Fluorescent minerals that glow in the dark even after ultraviolet light is taken away are called **phosphorescent minerals**.

# ANSWERS to Some
# SCIENCE QUESTIONS

## WHY DO ICE CUBES FLOAT?

What happens when you put ice in water? It floats! Ice floats because it is less tightly packed, less dense, than water (a liquid). The atoms of most substances are more tightly packed in the solid state than in the gas or liquid states. Water is different. At 212 degrees Fahrenheit (100 degrees Celsius) or higher, water is a gas called steam. Below 212 degrees Fahrenheit it becomes a liquid. As water is cooled the groups of atoms start squeezing together up to a point. At 39 degrees Fahrenheit (4 degrees Celsius), they spread out to link in a special way. At 32 degrees Fahrenheit (0 degrees Celsius), water finally becomes the solid called ice. Its atoms spread apart some more as the water freezes.

## WHAT CAUSES FROST PATTERNS ON WINDOWS IN WINTER?

Have you ever seen feathery patterns of frost on windows in very cold weather? When water vapor in the air comes in contact with the extremely cold glass of a window, the water vapor immediately turns to ice. The ice forms on the windows in patterns of ice crystals.

## WHAT IS A MAGNET?

Have you ever seen paper clips or pins sliding toward a magnet and then sticking to it? Magnets have two areas, called **poles**, where magnetic effects are strongest. A bar magnet has a pole at each end. Around each pole is a region called a **magnetic field**. A magnetic field cannot be seen, but it can be felt when another magnet enters the field or when something with iron in it, such as a paper clip or a pin, enters the magnetic field. Such an object will then become attracted to one of the magnet's poles.

## HOW DO MAGNETS REACT TO OTHER MAGNETS?

Magnets have two poles. One is called the north pole and the other is called the south pole. The north pole of one magnet will attract the south pole of another magnet—in other words, opposites attract. But when the north poles of two magnets are brought near each other, they will push away (repel) each other. Magnets can have different shapes and can be made of different materials.

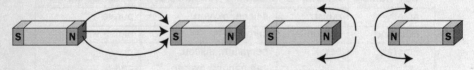

**DID YOU KNOW?** Do you know that Earth is a giant magnet whose magnetic field exists at all locations? Like a bar magnet, Earth has two magnetic poles—one of them is near the geographical north pole and the other is near the geographical south pole. If you have ever used a compass, you have seen that the compass needle always points in the same direction—toward the north—no matter which way you turn. The needle is a small bar magnet that can rotate easily. The needle points north because the north pole of the magnet is attracted to the magnetic pole of Earth near the geographical north pole.

# Some FAMOUS SCIENTISTS

**Archimedes** (about 287 B.C.-212 B.C.), a Greek mathematician who discovered that heavy objects could be moved with little force. He was one of the first people to test his ideas with experiments.

*Moving heavy blocks ▶ with a wheelbarrow.*

**Nicolaus Copernicus** (1473-1543), a Polish scientist known as the founder of modern astronomy. He believed that Earth and other planets revolved around the sun.

**Galileo Galilei** (1564-1642), an Italian astronomer who, like Copernicus, believed that the sun was at the center of the solar system, and that the planets revolved around it. He also proved that all objects, whether heavy or light, fall at the same rate.

**Sir Isaac Newton** (1642-1727), a British scientist famous for discovering the laws of gravity. He also discovered that sunlight is made up of all the colors of the rainbow.

**Edward Jenner** (1749-1823), a British doctor who discovered a way to prevent smallpox by injecting healthy people with cowpox vaccine. Today's vaccines work in a similar way.

**Michael Faraday** (1791-1867), a British scientist who discovered that magnets can be used to create electricity in copper wires. His discoveries enable us to produce massive amounts of electricity.

**Charles Darwin** (1809-1882), a British scientist best known for his theory of evolution. According to this theory, living creatures slowly develop over millions of years.

**Gregor Johann Mendel** (1822-1884), an Austrian monk who discovered the laws of heredity by showing how characteristics are passed from one generation of plants to the next.

**Louis Pasteur** (1822-1895), a French chemist who discovered a process called pasteurization, in which heat is used to kill germs.

**Marie Curie** (1867-1934), a Polish-French physical chemist known for discovering radium, which is used to treat certain diseases.

**Albert Einstein** (1879-1955), a German-American physicist who developed a revolutionary theory about the relationships between time, space, matter, and energy.

▲ *Pasteurized milk*

**Francis Crick** (born 1916) and **Maurice Wilkins** (born 1916) of England and **James D. Watson** (born 1928) of the United States, who worked out the structure of DNA, the basic chemical that controls inheritance in all living cells.

**DID YOU KNOW?** Emily Rosa of Loveland, Colorado, designed a science experiment that was described in an important medical journal in 1998. She did the project for her fourth-grade science fair when she was only nine years old. People called healers say they can heal some ailments by changing a body's energy field through "therapeutic touch." But the healers she tested could not tell whether her hand was hidden behind a screen or not. This showed that they could not detect a body's energy field.

# Some LIGHT and SOUND Subjects

## WHAT IS LIGHT?

Light is a form of energy that travels in **rays**. Light rays generally move in straight lines, at a speed of 186,000 miles per second through empty space. It takes over 8 minutes for the light from the sun to reach Earth. Light also moves through materials like water and glass, but more slowly.

## WHAT IS A RAINBOW?

The light we usually see (visible light) is made up of colors called the **spectrum**. The colors of the spectrum are red, orange, yellow, green, blue, indigo, and violet. White light is formed from a mixture of all the colors of the spectrum. A prism can separate the colors in a beam of white light. When you see a rainbow, the tiny water droplets in the air are separating the white light into the spectrum.

## WHERE DOES SOUND COME FROM?

When objects vibrate quickly back and forth in the air, they create **sound**. The vibrating objects cause the molecules in the air around the objects to move. As the molecules move, the vibrations travel through the air in **waves**. These sound waves move outward in every direction from the place where they started—like ripples in a pond moving away from the point where a pebble is dropped.

## WHAT CAN YOU HEAR IN OUTER SPACE?

Sound waves have to have a medium to move through. Usually air serves as the medium. But sounds can also travel through water, wood, glass, and other materials. In outer space, where there is no air or other medium for sound waves to travel through, there is no sound. Astronauts in space communicate with Earth over radio waves, not sound waves.

## HOW LOUD ARE THOSE SOUNDS?

The loudness of a sound (called **volume**) is measured in **decibels**. The volume depends on how many air molecules are vibrating and how strongly they are vibrating. The quietest sound that can be heard has a value of zero decibels. The louder the sound, the higher the decibel level.

**0 decibels**
faintest sound heard

**10-20 decibels**
rustling leaves

**20-30 decibels**
whispering

**50-70 decibels**
conversation

**80-100 decibels**
heavy traffic and trains

**100-120 decibels**
loud music

**140-150 decibels**
nearby jet engine

# SCIENCE MUSEUMS

Seeing is believing—and you made it happen! If you like hands-on exhibits and like to learn about science, here are a few museums in the United States that you might be able to visit sometime. Look in the INDEX under Museums to find information about museums dealing with natural history and computers.

**National Air and Space Museum,** Washington, D.C. Houses the Wright brothers' plane, Charles Lindbergh's *Spirit of St. Louis*, and *Skylab*, as well as many other planes and rockets.

**California Museum of Science and Industry,** Los Angeles, California. Includes a giant electromagnet activated by visitors; exhibits on electricity, earthquakes, computer-assisted design, aerospace, and health sciences.

**Museum of Science and Industry,** Chicago, Illinois. Includes a reproduction of a coal mine, as well as displays to help visitors learn more about health, human intelligence, and how people live.

**The Franklin Institute Science Museum,** Philadelphia, Pennsylvania. Includes an exhibit on the environment called Earth Quest; a giant heart people can walk through; exhibits on astronomy (including an observatory), communications, mathematics, shipbuilding, and railroads. Features many hands-on exhibits.

**Liberty Science Center,** Liberty State Park, Jersey City, New Jersey. Features more than 250 interactive exhibits and an OMNIMAX theater. A ferry to the Statue of Liberty and Ellis Island Museum is also in Liberty State Park.

**Southwest Museum of Science and Technology, The Science Place and TI Founders IMAX Theater,** Dallas, Texas. Includes hands-on science exhibits; water and sound experiments; an exhibit on special effects in movies; mathematical puzzles, and a planetarium.

**Exploratorium,** San Francisco, California. Interactive hands-on exhibits.

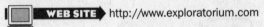 **WEB SITE** ➤ http://www.exploratorium.com

# SIGNS AND SYMBOLS

 **SIGNS AND SYMBOLS**

**S**igns and symbols give us information at a glance. Many signs indicate where something is located, such as a hospital or rest rooms. Others give commands, such as Stop or Yield. Still others warn us of danger. Long ago, when most people did not know how to read, simple pictures and symbols were used on signs to help strangers find the shops in a town. Each sign shown here uses a symbol to refer to something so that you do not have to read a language to understand what is meant.

Telephone

Gasoline

Hospital

First Aid

Drug Store

Handicapped Access

Men's Rest Room

Women's Rest Room

Food

Lodging

Airport

Information

Library

School Zone

No Bicycles

Picnic Area

Camping

Swimming

Fishing

Hiking Trail

No Smoking

Flammable

Poison

Radioactive

Explosives

# Road Signs

 Stop

 One Way

 No Entry

 No Parking

 Right Turn

 No Left Turn

 Hill

 Signal Ahead

 No U Turn

 Pedestrian Crossing

 Deer Crossing

 Railroad Crossing

 Road Work Ahead

 Cross Road

 Winding Road

 Slippery Road

 Divided Highway

 Yield

 Merging Traffic

# Some Useful Symbols

 Dollar

 Cent

 Percent

 Ampersand (and)

 Prescription

 Copyright

 Registered Trademark

 Male

 Female

 Plus or Minus

 Is Equal To

 Is Not Equal To

 Is Less Than

 Is Greater Than

 Parentheses

189

# BRAILLE

Blind people read with their fingers using a system of raised dots called Braille. Braille was developed by Louis Braille (1809-1852) in France in 1826, when he was a teenager. The Braille alphabet, numbers, punctuation, and speech sounds are represented by 63 different combinations of 6 raised dots arranged in a grid like this:

| 1 | 4 |
|---|---|
| 2 | 5 |
| 3 | 6 |

All the letters in the basic Braille alphabet are lowercase. Special symbols are added to show that what follows is a capital letter or a number. The light circles on the grid below show the raised dots.

## BRAILLE ALPHABET AND NUMBERS

a  b  c  d  e  f  g  h  i  j  k  l  m

n  o  p  q  r  s  t  u  v  w  x  y  z

cap  #  1  2  3  4  5  6  7  8  9  0

# SIGN LANGUAGE

Many people who are deaf or hearing-impaired, and cannot hear spoken words, talk with their fingers instead of their voices. To do this, they use a system of manual signs (the manual alphabet), or finger spelling, in which the fingers are used to form letters and words. Originally developed in France by Abbe Charles Michel De l'Epee in the late 1700s, the manual alphabet was later brought to the United States by Laurent Clerc (1785-1869), a Frenchman who taught people who were deaf.

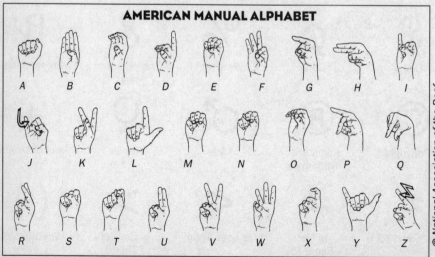

### AMERICAN MANUAL ALPHABET

A  B  C  D  E  F  G  H  I

J  K  L  M  N  O  P  Q

R  S  T  U  V  W  X  Y  Z

© National Association of the Deaf

# SEDOC REHTO DNA SEGASSEM TERCES

**C**an you guess what the title of this page says? If you look closely, you will see that it is "secret messages and other codes" written backwards. This is one simple way to create a secret code. Different kinds of codes have been used since ancient times to keep military plans secret. Secret codes are still used today by the military, by banks for ATM machines, and in many other places. The science of writing and reading secret messages is called **cryptography.**

## CIPHERS

One system of cryptography is called **ciphers**. In this system, letters are rearranged in different ways or letters may be substituted for other letters. In the examples below, you can see four ways that ciphers are used to hide the sentence "WANT TO GO SKATING TOMORROW?"

**1.** Changing the spaces: WA NTTOG OSK ATIN GTOM ORR OW?

**2.** Writing the sentence backward: WORROMOT GNITAKS OG OT TNAW?

**3.** Writing the sentence using the alphabet from Z to A instead of A to Z, so that A=Z, B=Y, C=X, D=W, and so on: DZMG GL TL HPZGRMT GLNLIILD?

**4.** Writing the sentence using an alphabet with the letters rearranged, for example, X V O R A N G E B C D F H I J K L M P Q S T U W Y Z (X=A, V=B, O=C, R=D, and so on): UXIQ QJ GJ PDXQBIG QJHJMMJU?

## NUMBERS FOR LETTERS

Numbers can also be used in place of some or all of the letters of the alphabet. If you know that 1=W, 2=D, 3=O, 4=H, 5=L, 6=E, 7=A, 8=M, and 9=F, you can read the message below.

46553 9R38 T46 13R52 7587N7C 93R KI2S.

## SECRET MESSAGE PUZZLE

**T**o decipher (figure out) this secret message, look at the telephone buttons. Notice that most buttons contain one number and three letters. Let A=2, B=2, and C=(2). Do the same thing with the other buttons, so that D=3, E=3, and F=(3), and so on. If you need Q and Z, let Q=*, and Z=#. Now can you crack the code for this sentence? (Answers are on page 305.)

843(7)3 7243(7) 273 (3)(4)(5)(5)33 9(4)84 (3)2(2)8(7).

| 1 | ABC 2 | DEF 3 |
|---|---|---|
| GHI 4 | JKL 5 | MNO 6 |
| PRS 7 | TUV 8 | WXY 9 |
| * | OPER 0 | # |

# BASEBALL

In 1997 the Florida Marlins scored two exciting firsts. By defeating the Cleveland Indians in a tense, seven-game World Series, they became world champions in just their fifth year of existence. No expansion team had ever won the World Series so soon. In addition, the Marlins entered the playoffs as a "wild card" team and became the first non-division winner to emerge as champions.

Inter-league play (between teams in different leagues) started up in the 1997 season and was a big success. Also, two sluggers made a run at Roger Maris's all-time record of 61 home runs in a season. Seattle's Ken Griffey, Jr., wound up with 56, while Mark McGwire hit 58. McGwire, however, reached that lofty total with two teams, hitting 34 with the Oakland A's, then another 24 with the St. Louis Cardinals. Amid all that, Cal Ripken, Jr., of the Orioles ran his incredible record playing streak to 2,477 straight games.

## FINAL 1997 STANDINGS

**AMERICAN LEAGUE**

| Eastern Division | Won | Lost |
|---|---|---|
| Baltimore Orioles | 98 | 64 |
| New York Yankees* | 96 | 66 |
| Detroit Tigers | 79 | 83 |
| Boston Red Sox | 78 | 84 |
| Toronto Blue Jays | 76 | 86 |
| **Central Division** | **Won** | **Lost** |
| Cleveland Indians | 86 | 75 |
| Chicago White Sox | 80 | 81 |
| Milwaukee Brewers | 78 | 83 |
| Minnesota Twins | 68 | 94 |
| Kansas City Royals | 67 | 94 |
| **Western Division** | **Won** | **Lost** |
| Seattle Mariners | 90 | 72 |
| Anaheim Angels | 84 | 78 |
| Texas Rangers | 77 | 85 |
| Oakland Athletics | 65 | 97 |

*Wild card team

**NATIONAL LEAGUE**

| Eastern Division | Won | Lost |
|---|---|---|
| Atlanta Braves | 101 | 61 |
| Florida Marlins* | 92 | 70 |
| New York Mets | 88 | 74 |
| Montreal Expos | 78 | 84 |
| Philadelphia Phillies | 68 | 94 |
| **Central Division** | **Won** | **Lost** |
| Houston Astros | 84 | 78 |
| Pittsburgh Pirates | 79 | 83 |
| Cincinnati Reds | 76 | 86 |
| St. Louis Cardinals | 73 | 89 |
| Chicago Cubs | 68 | 94 |
| **Western Division** | **Won** | **Lost** |
| San Francisco Giants | 90 | 72 |
| Los Angeles Dodgers | 88 | 74 |
| Colorado Rockies | 83 | 79 |
| San Diego Padres | 76 | 86 |

*Wild card team

## PLAYOFF RESULTS

**Division Series**
Baltimore defeated Seattle 3-1
Cleveland defeated New York Yankees 3-2

**Championship Series**
Cleveland defeated Baltimore 4-2

**Division Series**
Atlanta defeated Houston 3-0
Florida defeated San Francisco 3-0

**Championship Series**
Florida defeated Atlanta 4-2

**WORLD SERIES**—Florida defeated Cleveland 4 games to 3

## 1997 MAJOR LEAGUE LEADERS
### Most Valuable Players
**American League:** Ken Griffey, Jr., Seattle Mariners
**National League:** Larry Walker, Colorado Rockies
### Cy Young Award Winners (Top Pitcher)
**American League:** Roger Clemens, Toronto Blue Jays
**National League:** Pedro Martinez, Montreal Expos
### Rookies of the Year
**American League:** Nomar Garciaparra, Boston Red Sox
**National League:** Scott Rolen, Philadelphia Phillies
### Batting Champs
**American League:** Frank Thomas, Chicago White Sox, .347
**National League:** Tony Gwynn, San Diego Padres, .372
### Home Run Leaders*
**American League:** Ken Griffey, Jr., Seattle Mariners, 56
**National League:** Larry Walker, Colorado Rockies, 49
### Runs Batted In (RBI) Leaders
**American League:** Ken Griffey, Jr., Seattle Mariners, 147
**National League:** Andres Galarraga, Colorado Rockies, 140
### Most Pitching Victories
**American League:** Roger Clemens, Toronto Blue Jays, 21
**National League:** Denny Neagle, Atlanta Braves, 20
*Mark McGwire hit 58 home runs playing in both leagues.

▲ *Mark McGwire hit 58 home runs—34 in the American League for the Oakland Athletics, 24 in the National League for the St. Louis Cardinals.*

**DID YOU KNOW?**

☑ At the age of 37, Tony Gwynn seems to be getting better and better. In 1997, the San Diego Padres right fielder led the majors with a .372 batting average. He also had the most hits (220), was second in doubles (49), hit 17 homers, and drove home a career-best 119 runs. By winning his eighth National League batting crown, he tied Honus Wagner for the most in league history.

☑ Major League Baseball expanded again in 1998. The Arizona Diamondbacks began play in the National League, and the Tampa Bay Devil Rays in the American League, for a total of 30 teams. So that each league would have an even number of teams, the Milwaukee Brewers moved to the National League. Now the National League has 16 teams, while the American League has 14.

 **WEB SITE** For more information go to http://www.majorleaguebaseball.com

---

## BASEBALL HALL OF FAME
The National Baseball Hall of Fame and Museum opened in 1939, in Cooperstown, New York. To be nominated for membership, players must be retired from baseball for five years. **Address:** PO Box 590, Cooperstown, NY 13326. **Phone:** (607) 547-7200; toll-free: (888) 425-5633
**WEB SITE** www.baseballhalloffame.org

---

## LITTLE LEAGUE
Little League Baseball is the largest youth sports program in the world. It began in 1939 in Williamsport, Pennsylvania, with 30 boys playing on 3 teams. By 1997, 3 million boys and girls ages 5 to 18 were playing on 200,000 Little League teams in 90 countries.

 **WEB SITE** For more information go to http://www.littleleague.org

# BASKETBALL

Basketball began in 1891 in Springfield, Massachusetts, when Dr. James Naismith invented it using peach baskets as hoops. Big-time professional basketball was born in 1949, when the National Basketball Association (NBA) was formed. In the 1997-1998 season, there were 29 NBA teams.

## Professional Basketball

### FINAL 1997-1998 NBA STANDINGS

**EASTERN CONFERENCE**

| Atlantic Division | Won | Lost |
|---|---|---|
| Miami Heat | 55 | 27 |
| New York Knicks | 43 | 39 |
| New Jersey Nets | 43 | 39 |
| Washington Wizards | 42 | 40 |
| Orlando Magic | 41 | 41 |
| Boston Celtics | 36 | 46 |
| Philadelphia 76ers | 31 | 51 |

| Central Division | Won | Lost |
|---|---|---|
| Chicago Bulls | 62 | 20 |
| Indiana Pacers | 58 | 24 |
| Charlotte Hornets | 51 | 31 |
| Atlanta Hawks | 50 | 32 |
| Cleveland Cavaliers | 47 | 35 |
| Detroit Pistons | 37 | 45 |
| Milwaukee Bucks | 36 | 46 |
| Toronto Raptors | 16 | 66 |

**WESTERN CONFERENCE**

| Midwest Division | Won | Lost |
|---|---|---|
| Utah Jazz | 62 | 20 |
| San Antonio Spurs | 56 | 26 |
| Minnesota Timberwolves | 45 | 37 |
| Houston Rockets | 41 | 41 |
| Dallas Mavericks | 20 | 62 |
| Vancouver Grizzlies | 19 | 63 |
| Denver Nuggets | 11 | 71 |

| Pacific Division | Won | Lost |
|---|---|---|
| Seattle SuperSonics | 61 | 21 |
| Los Angeles Lakers | 61 | 21 |
| Phoenix Suns | 56 | 26 |
| Portland Trail Blazers | 46 | 36 |
| Sacramento Kings | 27 | 55 |
| Golden State Warriors | 19 | 63 |
| Los Angeles Clippers | 17 | 65 |

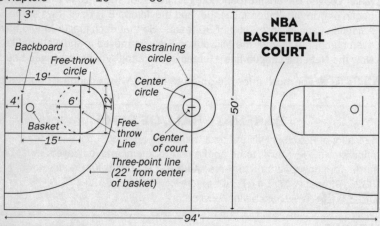

### CONFERENCE FINALS

**Eastern Conference:** Chicago Bulls defeated Indiana Pacers, 4 games to 3.
**Western Conference:** Utah Jazz defeated Los Angeles Lakers, 4 games to 0.

### NBA FINALS

Chicago Bulls defeated Utah Jazz, 4 games to 2. Michael Jordan, Finals MVP for the sixth time, led the Bulls to their third straight title and their sixth in eight years.

## HIGHLIGHTS OF THE 1997-1998 BASKETBALL SEASON

**Most Valuable Player:** Michael Jordan, Chicago Bulls
**Defensive Player of the Year:** Dikembe Mutombo, Atlanta Hawks
**Rookie of the Year:** Tim Duncan, San Antonio Spurs
**Coach of the Year:** Larry Bird, Indiana Pacers
**Scoring Leader:** Michael Jordan, Chicago Bulls

| | | |
|---|---|---|
| **Games:** 82 | **Points:** 2,357 | **Average:** 28.7 |

**Rebounding Leader:** Dennis Rodman, Chicago Bulls

| | | |
|---|---|---|
| **Games:** 80 | **Rebounds:** 1,201 | **Average:** 15.0 |

**Assists Leader:** Rod Strickland, Washington Wizards

| | | |
|---|---|---|
| **Games:** 76 | **Assists:** 801 | **Average:** 10.5 |

**Steals Leader:** Mookie Blaylock, Atlanta Hawks

| | | |
|---|---|---|
| **Games:** 70 | **Steals:** 183 | **Average:** 2.61 |

**Blocked Shots Leader:** Marcus Camby, Toronto Raptors

| | | |
|---|---|---|
| **Games:** 63 | **Blocks:** 230 | **Average:** 3.65 |

**WEB SITE** You can have fun and find out more facts about basketball at the Web site for the National Basketball Association: http://www.nba.com

---

## BASKETBALL HALL OF FAME

The Naismith Memorial Basketball Hall of Fame was founded in 1959 to honor great basketball players, coaches, referees, and other people who have made important contributions to the game. Named after the inventor of basketball, the museum features exhibits on the history of the game.

**Address:** 1150 West Columbus Avenue, Springfield, MA 01101-0179.

**Phone:** (413) 781-5759.

**WEB SITE** http://www.hoophall.com

---

**DID YOU KNOW?**

▲Tim Duncan

☑ In 1997-1998, Tim Duncan of the San Antonio Spurs put together one of the greatest rookie years ever. Playing with poise and stamina in all 82 games, Duncan finished 13th in scoring (21.1), fourth in field goal percentage (.549), third in rebounding (11.9), and sixth in block shots (2.51). He was a unanimous choice as the league's Rookie of the Year.

☑ Michael Jordan added to his reputation as basketball's all-time greatest player by winning a record 10th NBA scoring title in 1997-1998.

## THE TIME HAS COME FOR WOMEN'S BASKETBALL

Basketball has grown more and more popular. And the number of fans of women's college basketball has increased. So it seems as if the time for women's professional basketball has finally come. Even before the U.S. team won the gold medal at the 1996 Summer Olympics in Atlanta, plans were afoot for two new pro leagues for women. The American Basketball League began play in October 1996. The Women's National Basketball Association had its first tip-off in June 1997. Both leagues have TV contracts and many fans, and have been showing a high level of play. With top stars such as Rebecca Lobo, Sheryl Swoopes, Dawn Staley, Cynthia Cooper, Nikki McCray, and Lisa Leslie, women's pro basketball looks as if it's here to stay.

# College Basketball

College basketball has become a huge sport. The National Collegiate Athletic Association (NCAA) Tournament began in 1939. Today, it is a spectacular 64-team extravaganza that is considered the national championship tournament. The Final Four weekend, when the semi-finals and finals are played, is one of the most watched sports events in the United States. The NCAA Tournament for women's basketball began in 1982. Since then, the popularity of the women's game has grown by leaps and bounds.

## THE 1998 NCAA TOURNAMENT RESULTS

**MEN'S FINAL FOUR RESULTS**
**Semi-Finals:**
   Kentucky, 86, Stanford, 65 OT
   Utah, 65, North Carolina, 59
**Championship Game:**
   Kentucky, 78, Utah, 69

**DID YOU KNOW?** By defeating Utah in an action-packed title game, the Kentucky Wildcats won their seventh national championship—second only to UCLA's eleven—and their second in the last three years. The Wildcats, under first-year coach Tubby Smith, became known as the Comeback 'Cats. Against Duke in the Regional Final, they trailed by 17 and won. Facing Stanford in the semi-finals, they were down by 10 at halftime, yet prevailed. And in the title game with the Utes, Kentucky again found itself behind by 10 at intermission, but came on to win the game and the championship.

**WOMEN'S FINAL FOUR RESULTS**
**Semi-Finals:**
   Louisiana Tech, 84, North Carolina St., 65
   Tennessee, 86, Arkansas, 58
**Championship Game:**
   Tennessee, 93, Louisiana Tech, 75

**DID YOU KNOW?** The Tennessee Lady Vols won their third national championship in a row and their sixth overall. The Lady Vols destroyed their opponents in the semi-final and championship games and also set an NCAA record by completing a 39-0 season. No college team had ever won that many games while undefeated. And no women's team had ever won six national titles. Led by their All-American and national player of the year, Chamique Holdsclaw, the Lady Vols blew the final game open early and led by 23 points at halftime. The best ever? Maybe. These Lady Vols are surely the greatest of their era.

### BOOST/NAISMITH AWARD WINNERS 1997-1998

**MEN**
**Player of the Year:** Antawn Jamison, North Carolina
**Coach of the Year:** Bill Guthridge, North Carolina

**WOMEN**
**Player of the Year:** Chamique Holdsclaw, Tennessee ▶
**Coach of the Year:** Pat Summitt, Tennessee

# FOOTBALL

American football began as a college sport. The first game that was like today's football took place between Yale and Harvard in New Haven, Connecticut, on November 13, 1875. The sport was largely shaped by Walter Camp in the 1880s. He reduced the number of players to 11 on each side and started the idea of having each play begin from the line of scrimmage. He also introduced the concept of "downs" and was the first to have the field lined with chalk every 5 yards.

## Professional Football

The 1997 National Football League season saw great individual performances, as well as a major upset in the biggest game of all, the Super Bowl. In the regular season, Detroit's superstar running back, Barry Sanders, became just the third player in NFL history to rush for more than 2,000 yards. He then joined Green Bay quarterback Brett Favre as co-winner of the league's Most Valuable Player award.

When Favre's Green Bay Packers rolled through the playoffs to Super Bowl XXXII, they were heavy favorites to beat the wild card Denver Broncos. After all, the NFC had won the last 13 championships. Denver's great veteran quarterback, John Elway, had been the loser in three of those games. But this time, the underdogs came out on top. With Terrell Davis running for 157 yards and Elway playing clutch ball, the Broncos won, 31-24, giving the American Football Conference its first Super Bowl victory in 14 years.

### FINAL NFL STANDINGS FOR THE 1997 SEASON

**National Football Conference**

| Eastern Division | Won | Lost | Tied |
|---|---|---|---|
| New York Giants | 10 | 5 | 1 |
| Washington Redskins | 8 | 7 | 1 |
| Philadelphia Eagles | 6 | 9 | 1 |
| Dallas Cowboys | 6 | 10 | 0 |
| Arizona Cardinals | 4 | 12 | 0 |
| **Central Division** | **Won** | **Lost** | **Tied** |
| Green Bay Packers | 13 | 3 | 0 |
| Tampa Bay Buccaneers* | 10 | 6 | 0 |
| Detroit Lions* | 9 | 7 | 0 |
| Minnesota Vikings* | 9 | 7 | 0 |
| Chicago Bears | 4 | 12 | 0 |
| **Western Division** | **Won** | **Lost** | **Tied** |
| San Francisco 49ers | 13 | 3 | 0 |
| Carolina Panthers | 7 | 9 | 0 |
| Atlanta Falcons | 7 | 9 | 0 |
| New Orleans Saints | 6 | 10 | 0 |
| St. Louis Rams | 5 | 11 | 0 |

*Wild card team

**American Football Conference**

| Eastern Divison | Won | Lost | Tied |
|---|---|---|---|
| New England Patriots | 10 | 6 | 0 |
| Miami Dolphins* | 9 | 7 | 0 |
| New York Jets | 9 | 7 | 0 |
| Buffalo Bills | 6 | 10 | 0 |
| Indianapolis Colts | 3 | 13 | 0 |
| **Central Division** | **Won** | **Lost** | **Tied** |
| Pittsburgh Steelers | 11 | 5 | 0 |
| Jacksonville Jaguars* | 11 | 5 | 0 |
| Tennessee Oilers | 8 | 8 | 0 |
| Cincinnati Bengals | 7 | 9 | 0 |
| Baltimore Ravens | 6 | 9 | 1 |
| **Western Division** | **Won** | **Lost** | **Tied** |
| Kansas City Chiefs | 13 | 3 | 0 |
| Denver Broncos* | 12 | 4 | 0 |
| Seattle Seahawks | 8 | 8 | 0 |
| Oakland Raiders | 4 | 12 | 0 |
| San Diego Chargers | 4 | 12 | 0 |

*Wild card team

### 1997 CONFERENCE CHAMPIONSHIP GAMES
**National Football Conference:** Green Bay Packers 23, San Francisco 49ers 10
**American Football Conference:** Denver Broncos 24, Pittsburgh Steelers 21

### SUPER BOWL XXXII, January 25, 1998, San Diego's Qualcomm Stadium
Denver Broncos 31, Green Bay Packers 24

## NFL FOOTBALL FIELD

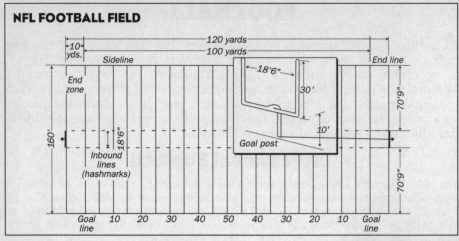

## TOP NFL PERFORMERS OF 1997

**Rushing Leader:** Barry Sanders, Detroit Lions
   **Carries:** 335; **Yards:** 2,053; **Average:** 6.1
**Passing Leader:** Steve Young, San Francisco 49ers
   **Passing Attempts:** 356; **Passing Completions:** 241
   **Passing Yards:** 3,029
   **Passing Completion Percentage:** 67.7
   **Touchdown Passes:** 19; **Passes Intercepted:** 6
   **Quarterback Rating:** 104.7
**Pass Receiving Leader:** (tie) Herman Moore, Detroit Lions; Tim
Brown, Oakland Raiders
   **Catches:** 104 each; **Yards:** Moore 1,293, Brown, 1,408
   **Average:** Moore 12.4; Brown 13.5

▲ *Barry Sanders*

**The following awards were all chosen by the Associated Press**
   **Most Valuable Player:** (tie) Brett Favre, Green Bay Packers; Barry Sanders, Detroit Lions
   **Offensive Player of the Year:** Barry Sanders, Detroit Lions
   **Defensive Player of the Year:** Dana Stubblefield, San Francisco 49ers
   **Coach of the Year:** Jim Fassel, New York Giants
   **Offensive Rookie of the Year:** Warrick Dunn, Tampa Bay Buccaneers
   **Defensive Rookie of the Year:** Peter Boulware, Baltimore Ravens

 **DID YOU KNOW?**

☑ A football is 11 to 11¼ inches long and weighs 14-15 ounces. It is oval in
shape and somewhat pointed at the ends. It is made up of an inflated bladder
covered with pebbled grain leather.

 **WEB SITE** You can reach the NFL at http://www.nfl.com

## PRO FOOTBALL HALL OF FAME

Football's Hall of Fame was founded in 1963 by the National Football League
to honor outstanding players, coaches, and contributors. To be nominated,
players must be retired for 5 years. **Address:** Pro Football Hall of Fame, 2121
George Halas Drive, Canton, OH 44708. **Phone:** (330) 456-8207.
**WEB SITE** http://www.profootballhof.com

# College Football

College football is one of America's most colorful and exciting sports. The National Collegiate Athletic Association (NCAA), which was founded in 1906, oversees college football today. There is no tournament to determine the best team in college football. The national champion is chosen by several football polls, which sometimes disagree.

| 1997 TOP 10 COLLEGE TEAMS | | | |
|---|---|---|---|
| Chosen by the Associated Press Poll and the USA Today/ESPN Poll | | | |
| Rank AP | USA Today/ESPN | Rank AP | USA Today/ESPN |
| 1. Michigan | Nebraska | 6. North Carolina | Florida |
| 2. Nebraska | Michigan | 7. Tennessee | Kansas St. |
| 3. Florida St. | Florida St. | 8. Kansas St. | Tennessee |
| 4. Florida | North Carolina | 9. Washington St. | Washington St. |
| 5. UCLA | UCLA | 10. Georgia | Georgia |

## THE BOWL GAMES

Post-season "bowl" games held on or near New Year's Day have become a great part of college football tradition. The Bowl Alliance, which includes the Sugar, Fiesta, and Orange Bowls, has been formed to try to get the best matchups in these bowls, with the hope that one will determine the national champion. The Rose Bowl is the oldest bowl game. It was first played in 1902. There are now some 18 bowl games.

## SOME 1997 SEASON BOWL RESULTS

**Sugar Bowl** (New Orleans, Louisiana): Florida 31, Ohio State 14
**Rose Bowl** (Pasadena, California): Michigan 21, Washington State 16
**Cotton Bowl** (Dallas, Texas): UCLA 29, Texas A&M 23
**Orange Bowl** (Miami, Florida): Nebraska 42, Tennessee 17
**Fiesta Bowl** (Tempe, Arizona): Kansas State 35, Syracuse 18

**HEISMAN TROPHY.** The Heisman Trophy is given to the most outstanding college football player in the United States. It was first presented in 1935. The 1997 winner was cornerback Charles Woodson of Michigan. Not only was Woodson dominant at his position, but he also became the first primarily defensive player to win the coveted award. In winning, Woodson upset the two favorites, quarterbacks Peyton Manning of Tennessee and Ryan Leaf of Washington State.

▲ *Charles Woodson*

## COLLEGE FOOTBALL HALL OF FAME

The College Football Hall of Fame was established in 1955 by the National Football Foundation. To be nominated, a player must be out of college 10 years and must have been a first team All-American pick by a major selector. Coaches must be retired 3 years. **Address:** 111 South St. Joseph Street, PO Box 11146, South Bend, IN 46601. **Phone:** (219) 235-9999.

**WEB SITE** http://collegefootball.org

# GAMES: CHESS and Other BOARD GAMES

**C**hess is a game of skill for two players. The aim is to checkmate, or trap, the opponent's king. Chess was probably invented around the 6th or 7th century A.D. in India. From there it moved into Persia (now Iran); the word *chess* comes from the Persian word *shah*, which means king. Today, there are national chess contests for children, and many schools have chess clubs. For further information, contact the U.S. Chess Federation, 3054 NYS Route 9W, New Windsor, NY 12553. Phone: 914-562-8350.

**WEB SITE** http://www.uschess.org

## THE BOARD AND THE CHESSMEN

Chess is played on a chessboard divided into 64 squares, alternately light and dark in color, arranged in 8 rows of 8. No matter what colors the squares and chessmen really are, they are always called white and black. White always moves first, then white and black take turns, moving only one chessman at a time. Each player begins the game with 16 chessmen: 8 pieces (the king, the queen, 2 bishops, 2 knights, and 2 rooks) and 8 pawns. When a chessman lands on a space occupied by an opponent's piece or pawn, that piece or pawn is captured and removed from the board.

## THE MOVES

Each piece or pawn has particular moves it can make, as are described below. The number (or point value) after each chessman gives an idea of how powerful it is:

queen       rook

knight      bishop

pawn        king

**queen** (9): moves any number of squares in any direction—forward or backward, side to side, or diagonally

**rook** (5): moves any number of squares forward or backward, or side to side

**knight** (3): moves two squares forward or backward and one square to either side, or one forward or backward and two to the side (the knight is the only chessman that can jump over others)

**bishop** (3): moves any number of squares diagonally forward or diagonally backward

**pawn** (1): first moves one or two squares; otherwise, moves one square straight ahead, except when it moves diagonally forward to capture another chessman

**king:** moves one square in any direction; is not given a point value

When a player moves a chessman into position to capture the opponent's king, he or she says "check" and the opponent must block the move or must move the king to safety; otherwise, the king is "checkmated" and the game is over.

## CHESS CHAMPIONS

👤 In 1851, Adolf Anderssen of Germany became the first world chess champion.

👤 In 1858, Paul Morphy became the first American world champion.

👤 In 1866, Wilhelm Steinitz of Austria became the first official world champion.

👤 In 1958, 14-year-old Bobby Fischer became the youngest-ever "grandmaster," one of the world's top players. He was world champion from 1972 to 1975.

👤 In 1994, at 14, Peter Leko of Hungary became the world's youngest grandmaster.

👤 Current world champions are Garry Kasparov and Anatoly Karpov, both of Russia.

☑ In March 1998, Hikaru Nakamura, age 10, became the youngest United States chess National Master ever. Fewer than 1 out of every 100 players of any age ever become qualified to be National Masters.

☑ In 1996 and 1997 chess champion Garry Kasparov played a computer named Deep Blue. In 1996 he beat Deep Blue, 3 games to 1, with 2 draws. But in 1997 Deep Blue surprised the world by defeating Kasparov, 2 games to 1, with 3 draws.

# Some Other Board Games

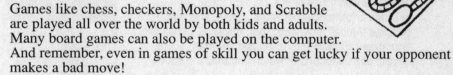

**W**e play board games to have fun, but they also sharpen our mental skills. Games can teach us how to win without gloating and how to lose without being too disappointed. Some games are based on skill. Others depend only on the throw of dice. For most, winning takes a mixture of skill and luck.

Games like chess, checkers, Monopoly, and Scrabble are played all over the world by both kids and adults. Many board games can also be played on the computer. And remember, even in games of skill you can get lucky if your opponent makes a bad move!

**Backgammon**, a game for two players, was played in ancient Egypt, Greece, and Rome. Each player has 15 pieces to move around the board, and the skill is in deciding which pieces to move. Getting the right numbers when you throw the dice can also help make you a winner. To win the game, you must be the first to get all your pieces off the board.

**Checkers** is a game of skill. A form of checkers was played in ancient Egypt and Greece. The game is played by two players on a board with alternating light and dark squares. The goal is to capture all the opponent's pieces by jumping. To do so, you have to think ahead and take advantage of your opponent's mistakes.

**Parcheesi**, a game for two, three, or four players, is based on pachisi, a game played thousands of years ago in India. It is a mixture of skill and luck. Each player has four counters, and the one who gets them all into the center of the board first wins.

**Monopoly**, a game for two or more players, is one of the best-selling games of the 20th century. It involves both skill and luck. The skill is in making choices. Should you buy Water Works? How many houses should you put on Boardwalk? The luck is in throwing the dice and landing on the right places.

Monopoly was created in the 1930s by Charles P. Darrow, who took the names for places in the game from streets in Atlantic City, New Jersey.

**Scrabble** is a crossword game for two, three, or four players, played on a board with tiles that are letters. It had its beginnings in the 1930s with a game called Criss-Cross Words, which was invented by Alfred Butts.

To win at Scrabble, it helps to be a good speller and have a big vocabulary. The lucky part is picking up the letters you need at the right time. Scrabble is also available in Braille for blind players.

# GOLF

Golf began in Scotland as early as the 1400s. The first golf course in the United States opened in 1888. Since then, the sport has grown to include both men's and women's professional tours. And millions play golf just for fun.

The men's tour is guided by the Professional Golf Association (PGA). The four major championships, with the year they were first played, are:

British Open (1860)　　　　　PGA Championship (1916)
United States Open (1895)　　Masters Championship (1934)

The women's tour is guided by the Ladies Professional Golf Association (LPGA). The major championships are:

United States Open (1946)　　　　　　　Nabisco Dinah Shore Championship (1972)
McDonalds LPGA Championship (1955)　Du Maurier Classic (1973)

**DID YOU KNOW?**

☑ Tiger Woods burst onto the professional golf scene in 1996, at the age of only 20. He started out by winning three of his first nine pro tournaments. Then in April 1997, he won the Masters (his first major) in a record-setting performance. His youth, talent, and mixed heritage (African-American, Thai, Chinese, Caucasian, and American Indian) have helped get many young people and minorities to watch and play the sport.

☑ Mark O'Meara won his first major event by winning the 1998 Masters Championship. He sank a 20-foot putt to clinch his victory.

▲ Tiger Woods

**WEB SITE** For more information: www.pga.com
www.lpga.com

# GYMNASTICS

It takes strength, coordination, and grace to become a top gymnast. Although the sport goes back to ancient Greece, modern-day gymnastics began in Sweden in the early 1800s. The sport has been part of the Olympics since 1896. There is also an annual World Gymnastics Championship meet.

## GYMNASTIC EVENTS

### FOR WOMEN
1. All-Around
2. Side Horse Vault
3. Asymmetrical (Uneven) Bars
4. Balance Beam
5. Floor Exercises
6. Team Combined Exercises
7. Rhythmic All-Around

### FOR MEN
1. All-Around
2. Horizontal Bar
3. Parallel Bars
4. Rings
5. Long Horse Vault
6. Side Horse (Pommel Horse)
7. Floor Exercises
8. Team Combined Exercises

**DID YOU KNOW?**

☑ The trampoline and tumbling will be gymnastics medal events for the first time at the 2000 Summer Olympic Games in Sydney, Australia.

# ICE HOCKEY

**I**ce hockey began in Canada in the mid-1800s. By the beginning of the 1900s, hockey was becoming a major Canadian sport. The National Hockey League was formed in 1916 and has been in operation ever since. In the 1997-1998 season, there were 26 teams in the NHL, 20 in the United States and 6 in Canada.

 **WEB SITE** To learn more about NHL hockey try:
http://www.nhl.com

## FINAL 1997-1998 STANDINGS

### EASTERN CONFERENCE

| Northeast Division | W | L | T | Pts |
|---|---|---|---|---|
| Pittsburgh Penguins | 40 | 24 | 18 | 98 |
| Boston Bruins | 39 | 30 | 13 | 91 |
| Buffalo Sabres | 36 | 29 | 17 | 89 |
| Montreal Canadiens | 37 | 32 | 13 | 87 |
| Ottawa Senators | 34 | 33 | 15 | 83 |
| Carolina Hurricanes | 33 | 41 | 8 | 74 |

| Atlantic Division | W | L | T | Pts |
|---|---|---|---|---|
| New Jersey Devils | 48 | 23 | 11 | 107 |
| Philadelphia Flyers | 42 | 29 | 11 | 95 |
| Washington Capitols | 40 | 30 | 12 | 92 |
| New York Islanders | 30 | 41 | 11 | 71 |
| New York Rangers | 25 | 39 | 18 | 68 |
| Florida Panthers | 24 | 43 | 15 | 63 |
| Tampa Bay Lightning | 17 | 55 | 10 | 44 |

### WESTERN CONFERENCE

| Central Division | W | L | T | Pts |
|---|---|---|---|---|
| Dallas Stars | 49 | 22 | 11 | 109 |
| Detroit Red Wings | 44 | 23 | 15 | 103 |
| St. Louis Blues | 45 | 29 | 8 | 98 |
| Phoenix Coyotes | 35 | 35 | 12 | 82 |
| Chicago Blackhawks | 30 | 39 | 13 | 73 |
| Toronto Maple Leafs | 30 | 43 | 9 | 69 |

| Pacific Division | W | L | T | Pts |
|---|---|---|---|---|
| Colorado Avalanche | 39 | 26 | 17 | 95 |
| Los Angeles Kings | 38 | 33 | 11 | 87 |
| Edmonton Oilers | 35 | 37 | 10 | 80 |
| San Jose Sharks | 34 | 38 | 10 | 78 |
| Calgary Flames | 26 | 41 | 15 | 67 |
| Anaheim Mighty Ducks | 26 | 43 | 13 | 65 |
| Vancouver Canucks | 25 | 43 | 14 | 64 |

## CONFERENCE FINALS

**Eastern Conference:** Washington Capitols defeated Buffalo Sabres, 4 games to 2.

**Western Conference:** Detroit Red Wings defeated Dallas Stars, 4 games to 2.

**NHL CHAMPIONSHIP:** Detroit Red Wings defeated Washington Capitols, 4 games to 0.

**DID YOU KNOW?** They call him the *Dominator*, and with good reason. Dominik Hasek of the Buffalo Sabres has simply become the best goaltender in the hockey world. Hasek was the NHL's Most Valuable Player in 1996-1997, and was even better the next year. Not only did he lead all NHL goalies with 13 shutouts in 1997-1998, but in mid-season he went to Nagano, Japan, and led his native Czech Republic to the hockey gold medal at the Winter Olympic Games. At Nagano, Hasek gave up just six goals in six games, turning away the best players in the world.

▲ *Dominik Hasek*

## HOCKEY HALL OF FAME

The Hockey Hall of Fame was opened in 1961 to honor hockey greats.

**Address:** BCE Place, 30 Yonge Street, Toronto, Ontario, Canada M5E 1X8.

**Phone:** (416) 360-7735.

**WEB SITE** http://www.hhof.com

# The OLYMPIC GAMES

The first Olympic Games were played in Greece more than 2,500 years ago. They began in 776 B.C. and featured just one event—a footrace. The ancient Greeks later added boxing, wrestling, chariot racing, and the pentathlon (which consists of five different events). The ancient Olympic Games were held every four years for more than 1,000 years, until A.D. 393, when a Roman Emperor stopped them. The modern Olympic Games were organized by a French educator named Baron Pierre de Coubertin. In 1894, he helped set up the International Olympic Committee, which organized the Games.

## SOME OLYMPIC FIRSTS

1896 — **The first modern Olympic Games were held in Athens, Greece.** Thirteen countries and 311 athletes took part.

1900 — **Women competed in the Olympic Games for the first time.**

1908 — **For the first time, medals were awarded to the first three people to finish each event**—a gold medal for first place, a silver medal for second, and a bronze medal for third.

1920 — **The Olympic flag was raised for the first time, and the Olympic oath was introduced.** The five interlaced rings of the flag represent: Africa, America, Europe, Asia, and Australia.

1924 — **The Winter Olympics, featuring skiing and skating events, were held for the first time.**

1928 — **The Olympic flame was introduced at the Olympic Games.** The flame is carried by runners in a relay, from Olympia in Greece to the site of where the Games are played. It traveled by air for the first time in 1956, when the Games were held in Australia.

1994 — **Starting with the 1994 Winter Olympics, the winter and summer Games have been held two years apart,** instead of in the same year.

## A SUCCESSFUL WINTER OLYMPICS

The 1998 Winter Olympic Games at Nagano, Japan, were a huge success. About 3,000 athletes and officials from 72 nations took part. At stake were medals in 68 events, with the competition leading to many outstanding and courageous performances. Among nations, Germany led the way with 12 gold and 29 total medals. The United States won 6 golds and took a total of 13 medals. Among the best individual achievements was the gold medal in figure skating by 15-year-old Tara Lipinski of the United States

▲ Hermann Maier

and the gold in the super giant slalom by Austria's Hermann Maier. Maier took his gold just three days after walking away from a frightening fall in the downhill that would have put a lesser athlete out of action. In team sports, the United States took a pair of medals (silver and bronze) in luge for the first time ever, and the U.S. women's ice hockey team ripped through the competition unbeaten to bring home the gold.

# SITES OF OLYMPIC GAMES

## WINTER GAMES:
1998—Nagano, Japan
2002—Salt Lake City, Utah

## SUMMER GAMES:
2000—Sydney, Australia
2004—Athens, Greece

## OLYMPIC SPORTS

### 1996 SUMMER OLYMPIC SPORTS

| | | |
|---|---|---|
| Archery | Football (Soccer) | Softball |
| Badminton | Gymnastics | Swimming |
| Baseball | Rhythmic | Synchronized |
| Basketball |   Gymnastics |   Swimming |
| Boxing | Judo | Table Tennis |
| Canoe/Kayak | Modern Pentathlon | Team Handball |
| Cycling |   (cross-country | |
| Diving |   riding, fencing, | Tennis |
| Equestrian |   pistol shooting, | Track and Field |
|   (dressage, |   swimming, | Volleyball |
|   show |   cross-country | |
|   jumping, |   running—one | Water Polo |
|   3-day event) |   event per day for | Weight Lifting |
| |   5 days) | Wrestling |
| Fencing | Rowing | Yachting |
| Field Hockey | Shooting | |

### 1998 WINTER OLYMPIC SPORTS

| | | |
|---|---|---|
| Biathlon | Ice Hockey | Freestyle Skiing |
|   (cross-country | Luge (Toboggan) | Nordic Skiing |
|   skiing, rifle | Figure Skating |   Cross-Country |
|   marksmanship) | |   Ski Jumping |
| Bobsled | Speed Skating |   Nordic Combined |
| Curling | Alpine Skiing | Snowboarding |

**DID YOU KNOW?**

☑ At the 1998 Winter Games, U.S. skier Picabo Street won a gold medal in the super giant slalom just two weeks after suffering a concussion in a serious fall while competing in Sweden. She had already overcome major knee surgery in December 1996 to make the U.S. team.

☑ The Paralympic Games are for international athletes who are wheelchair bound, are blind, or have other physical disabilities. These Games, which are held after the Summer and the Winter Olympic Games in the same city, took place for the first time in 1960. At the 1998 Paralympic Games in Nagano, Japan, 571 athletes from 32 nations competed for medals in over 30 events.

# SKATING

**P**eople have enjoyed ice skating for hundreds of years. The first ice skates were made from animal bones ground to a smooth, flat surface. Wooden skates with iron blades appeared in the Netherlands around the 13th or 14th century. Steel skating blades appeared around 1860 and allowed skaters to move quickly and with more control.

## FIGURE SKATING

There are two types of competitive ice skating—figure skating and speed skating. Figure skating, which is almost like ballet, is judged by the way the skaters perform certain turns and jumps and by the creative difficulty of their programs. There are singles competitions for both men and women, pairs skating, and ice dancing.

## 1998 WORLD CHAMPIONSHIPS

The figure skating World Championships took place in Minneapolis, Minnesota, in spring 1998. Below are the winners for the singles competition.

|  | Women's Singles | Men's Singles |
|---|---|---|
| **Gold Medal:** | Michelle Kwan (U.S.) | Alexei Yagudin (Russian) |
| **Silver Medal:** | Irina Slutskaya (Russian) | Todd Eldredge (U.S.) |
| **Bronze Medal:** | Maria Butyrskaya (Russian) | Evgeni Plushenko (Russian) |

**DID YOU KNOW?** When Tara Lipinski won the World Championship in 1997 at age 14, she became the youngest champion ever, a month younger than Sonja Henie, who won back in 1927. Then, in the 1998 Winter Olympic Games at Nagano, Japan, Lipinski did it again. She was trailing her favored teammate, 17-year-old Michelle Kwan, after the short program. But after Kwan skated a long program that was safe, Tara dazzled the judges, and a worldwide audience, with a display of exciting skating. She took the gold medal, becoming not only the youngest gold medalist ever in skating, but the youngest person ever to win an individual gold at the Winter Olympics.

▲ *Tara Lipinski*

## AMERICA'S OLYMPIC CHAMPIONS

Below are America's Olympic gold medalists in singles competition:

**Men:** Dick Button (1948, 1952), Hayes Alan Jenkins (1956), David Jenkins (1960), Scott Hamilton (1984), Brian Boitano (1988).

**Women:** Tenley Albright (1956), Carol Heiss (1960), Peggy Fleming (1968), Dorothy Hamill (1976), Kristi Yamaguchi (1992), Tara Lipinski (1998).

## SPEED SKATING

Speed skating is a race around an oval track. The traditional track is 400 meters around, with two lanes. The skaters, who skate two at a time, are racing the clock. The winner is the skater with the fastest time of any competitor. Speed skating for men became part of the Winter Olympics in 1924, for women in 1960. Men compete in five events: the 500 meters, 1,000 meters, 1,500 meters, 5,000 meters, and 10,000 meters. Women also compete in five events: the 500 meters, 1,000 meters, 1,500 meters, 3,000 meters, and 5,000 meters.

# SOCCER

Soccer, which is called football in many countries, is the number one sport worldwide. It is estimated that soccer is played by more than 100 million people in over 150 countries. The first rules for the game were published in 1863 by the London Football Association. Since then, the sport has spread rapidly from Europe to almost every part of the world.

According to the 1996 National Soccer Participation Survey, there are now some 17 million children and adults playing soccer in the United States. More than 13 million are under the age of 18—the sport is growing fast among the young. Among youngsters between the age of 6 and 11, soccer is now the second most popular sport, after basketball.

## MAJOR LEAGUE SOCCER

Major League Soccer took a giant step as a professional soccer league in the United States by completing its second successful season in 1997. In two years, more than 6 million fans have watched the 10 league teams play 32 regular-season games and playoffs. In 1997, Washington D.C. United won its second straight MLS championship with a 2-1 victory over the Colorado Rapids in the title game. Preki of Kansas City was the league's leading scorer and Most Valuable Player. Brad Friedel of Columbus was the top goalkeeper. The 1998 MLS season began on March 15, with two new teams—the Miami Fusion and the Chicago Fire.

## THE WORLD CUP

The biggest world soccer tournament is the World Cup. It is held every four years. Teams from more than 100 nations compete, and the top 24 teams represent their countries in a three-week-long tournament. In 1994, the World Cup tournament was held in the United States for the first time. Brazil was the tournament winner for a record fourth time, defeating Italy in the final, 3-2, with the game decided by penalty kicks.

▲ Preki

The 1998 World Cup was hosted by France. The 2002 World Cup will be co-hosted by Japan and South Korea.

### DID YOU KNOW?

☑ Major League Soccer set the all-time attendance record for a United States-based professional soccer league game at the Rose Bowl in Pasadena, California, on June 16, 1996. That day, 92,216 fans watched the Los Angeles Galaxy win a 3-2 shootout victory over the Tampa Bay Mutiny.

☑ His real name is Edson Arantes do Nascimento, but the soccer world knows him as Pele. A native of Brazil, Pele retired as a player in 1977. He is still considered by many the greatest soccer player who ever lived. Since his retirement, he has been a worldwide ambassador for the sport.

☑ A standard soccer ball is made of leather and is between 27 and 28 inches in circumference. Unlike basketball, young players can use a smaller ball. For kids 8 years old or younger, a ball of 23 to 24 inches in circumference is recommended. For kids 9 to 12, a ball of 25 to 26 inches is often used.

# SPECIAL OLYMPICS

The Special Olympics is the world's largest program of sports training and athletic competition for children and adults with mental retardation. Founded in 1968, Special Olympics International has offices in all 50 U.S. states and Washington, D.C., and in many countries throughout the world. The organization offers year-round training and competition to nearly 1.5 million athletes in more than 140 countries.

The first Special Olympics competition was held in Chicago in 1968. After holding national events in individual countries, Special Olympics International holds World Games. The World Games alternate between summer and winter sports every two years. The 1997 Special Olympics World Winter Games were held in Toronto and Collingwood, Canada, in February. The 1999 World Summer Games will be held in North Carolina.

### SPECIAL OLYMPICS OFFICIAL SPORTS
**Winter:** alpine and cross-country skiing, figure and speed skating, floor hockey
**Summer:** aquatics, athletics (track and field), basketball, bowling, cycling, equestrian, gymnastics, roller skating, soccer, softball, tennis, volleyball, golf
**Demonstration sports:** badminton, powerlifting, table tennis, team handball, sailing

For more information on the Special Olympics, contact Special Olympics International Headquarters, 1325 G Street, Washington, D.C. 20005. Phone: (202) 628-3630.
**WEB SITE** http://www.specialolympics.org

# SWIMMING

Competitive swimming as an organized sport began in the second half of the 19th century. When the modern Olympic Games began in Athens, Greece, in 1896, the only racing stroke was the breaststroke. Today, men and women at the Olympics swim the backstroke, breaststroke, butterfly, and freestyle, in events ranging from 50 meters to 1,500 meters.

▲ *Amy Van Dyken*

**OLYMPIC GOLD FOR THE U.S.** At the 1996 Olympic Games in Atlanta, U.S. men and women swimmers won 13 gold medals. The biggest story was unheralded Amy Van Dyken, who became the first American woman in history to win four gold medals in a single Olympics. Van Dyken was first in the 50-meter freestyle and 100-meter butterfly, and took two more gold medals as part of two American relay teams.

### SOME GREAT U.S. OLYMPIC SWIMMERS
☑ **Johnny Weissmuller** won three gold medals at the 1924 and 1928 Games. He later became even more famous playing Tarzan in movies.
☑ **Mark Spitz** won two gold medals in relays at the 1968 Games. He returned in 1972 to make Olympic swimming history by winning seven gold medals.
☑ **Janet Evans**, at age 17, won three gold medals at the 1988 Olympics in Seoul, South Korea. In 1992, she won another gold and a silver in Barcelona, Spain.
☑ **Matt Biondi** won seven medals at the 1988 Olympics, including five golds.

# TENNIS

The modern game of tennis began in 1873 when a British officer, Major Walter Wingfield, developed it from the earlier game of court tennis. In 1877, the first championship matches were held at the old Wimbledon Grounds near London. The United States Lawn Tennis Association was founded in 1881, and that same year the first United States men's championships were held at Newport, Rhode Island. Six years later the first women's championships took place in Philadelphia.

## GRAND SLAM TOURNAMENTS

Today, professional tennis players from all over the world compete in dozens of tournaments. The four most important, called the **grand slam** tournaments, are the Australian Open, the French Open, the All-England (Wimbledon) Championships, and the United States Open. There are separate competitions for men and women in singles and doubles. There are also mixed doubles, where men and women team together.

## MEN'S AND WOMEN'S SINGLES CHAMPIONS

### 1998 Australian Open Finals
**Men:** Petr Korda (Czech Republic) defeated Marcelo Rios (Chile), 6-2, 6-2, 6-2.
**Women:** Martina Hingis (Switzerland) defeated Conchita Martinez (Spain), 6-3, 6-3.

### 1997 Wimbledon Finals
**Men:** Pete Sampras (U.S.) defeated Cedric Piloine (France), 6-4, 6-2, 6-4.
**Women:** Martina Hingis (Switzerland) defeated Jana Novotna (Czech Republic), 2-6, 6-3, 6-3.

### 1997 United States Open Finals
**Men:** Patrick Rafter (Australia) defeated Greg Rusedski (Great Britain, 6-3, 6-2, 4-6, 7-5.
**Women:** Martina Hingis (Switzerland) beat Venus Williams (U.S.), 6-0, 6-4.

### 1997 French Open Finals
**Men:** Gustavo Kuerten (Brazil) defeated Sergi Bruguera (Spain), 6-3, 6-4, 6-2.
**Women:** Iva Majoli (Croatia) defeated Martina Hingis (Switzerland), 6-4, 6-2.

**RANKINGS FOR 1997.** The Association of Tennis Professionals (ATP) and the Women's Tennis Association (WTA) now keep computer rankings of all the players on the tour. The final top five rankings for men and women in 1997 were as follows:

**Women**
1. Martina Hingis, Switzerland
2. Jana Novotna, Czech Republic
3. Lindsay Davenport, United States
4. Amanda Coetzer, South Africa
5. Monica Seles, United States

**Men**
1. Pete Sampras, United States
2. Patrick Rafter, Australia
3. Michael Chang, U.S.
4. Jonas Bjorkman, Sweden
5. Yevegeny Kafelnikov, Russia

**DID YOU KNOW?** When she won the 1997 Australian Open at the age of 16, Martina Hingis became the youngest person to win a Grand Slam event in over a century. Since then, the Swiss teenager has taken the tennis world by storm. She went on to win three of the next four Grand Slams, including the Australian Open again in 1998. Ranked number one all this time, Hingis seems destined to become one of tennis's all-time greats.

◄ Martina Hingis

# What Are TIME ZONES?

The length of a day is 24 hours—the time it takes Earth to complete one rotation on its axis. The system we use to tell time is called **standard time**. In standard time, Earth is divided into 24 time zones. They run north to south, from the North Pole to the South Pole. To figure out the time in a particular zone, count the number of zones east or west of the **prime meridian**, or 0 degrees, which runs through Greenwich, England. When it is midnight, or 0 hour, in Greenwich, it is 5 hours earlier in New York, because New York is 5 zones away. Forty-eight states are in 4 of the 24 time zones (Alaska and Hawaii are in different time zones).

**WHEN IT IS 12 NOON IN NEW YORK, IT IS**

12 noon in Atlanta, Georgia
11 A.M. in St. Louis, Missouri
11 A.M. in Dallas, Texas
10 A.M. in Denver, Colorado
9 A.M. in Los Angeles, California
8 A.M. in Juneau, Alaska
7 A.M. in Honolulu, Hawaii

## HOW LONG DID IT TAKE?

**1492** — Christopher Columbus's first trip across the Atlantic Ocean, from Spain to San Salvador, took 70 days.

**1650s** — It took 50 days to sail from London, England, to Boston, Massachusetts.

**1829** — The first Atlantic Ocean crossing by a ship powered in part by steam (*Savannah*, sailing from Savannah, Georgia, to Liverpool, England) took 29 days.

**1903** — The first flight in a heavier-than-air craft was made by Wilbur Wright at Kitty Hawk, North Carolina, and lasted for 59 seconds.

**1927** — Charles Lindbergh flew from New York to Paris in 33 hours, 29 minutes, 30 seconds in the first nonstop flight across the Atlantic Ocean by one person.

**1961** — The flight of the first U.S. satellite carrying an astronaut (Alan Shepard, Jr.) lasted 15 minutes.

**1990s** — Passengers can fly by supersonic plane, the Concorde, between London and New York in only $3\frac{1}{2}$ hours.

# CALENDARS

## WHAT IS A CALENDAR?

Calendars divide time into units, such as days, weeks, months, and years. Calendar divisions are based on movements of Earth and on the sun and the moon. A day is the average time it takes for one rotation of Earth on its axis (24 hours). A year is the average time it takes for one revolution of Earth around the sun ($365\frac{1}{4}$ days).

## EARLIEST CALENDAR: The Egyptian Calendar

In ancient times, calendars were based upon the movements of the moon across the sky. The ancient Egyptians were the first to develop a solar calendar, a calendar based on the movements of the sun.

## ROMAN CALENDARS: The Julian and Gregorian Calendars

At first the ancient Romans had a calendar with a year of 304 days, but it was not a solar calendar and became confusing. Later, in 45 B.C., the emperor Julius Caesar decided to use a calendar based on the movements of the sun. This calendar, called the **Julian calendar**, fixed the normal year at 365 days and added one day every fourth year (leap year). The Julian calendar also established the months of the year and the days of the week.

The Julian calendar was used until A.D. 1582, when it was revised by Pope Gregory XIII, because the Julian calendar year was 11 minutes and 14 seconds longer than the solar year. Pope Gregory shortened the calendar year slightly to match the solar year. This new calendar, called the **Gregorian calendar,** is the one we use today in the United States.

## OTHER CALENDARS: Jewish and Islamic Calendars

Other calendars are also used. The Jewish calendar, which starts in the year 3761 B.C., is the official calendar of the State of Israel. The year 1999 is equivalent to the year 5759-5760 on the Jewish calendar, beginning at Rosh Hashanah (New Year). The Islamic calendar starts counting years in A.D. 622. The year 1999 is equivalent to the year 1419-1420 on the Islamic calendar, beginning at Muharram (New Year).

**DID YOU KNOW?** Stonehenge, the ancient stone monument in Salisbury, England, is between 3,000 and 5,000 years old. Most scientists think it was used to predict the positions of the sun and moon—a kind of huge calendar.

| BIRTHSTONES | | | | | |
|---|---|---|---|---|---|
| January | Garnet | May | Emerald | September | Sapphire |
| February | Amethyst | June | Pearl | October | Opal |
| March | Aquamarine | July | Ruby | November | Topaz |
| April | Diamond | August | Peridot | December | Turquoise |

# UNITED NATIONS

The United Nations (UN) was established in 1945 after World War II to promote world peace and cooperation. The UN conducts its business in six official languages: Arabic, Chinese, English, French, Russian, and Spanish. The first members of the UN were the 50 countries that met and signed its charter. The charter was officially approved on October 24, 1945. By the middle of 1998, 185 countries (most of the world) were members.

**The UN has set these goals. Not all of them have been achieved.**

☑ To keep worldwide peace and security.

☑ To develop friendly relations among countries.

☑ To help countries cooperate in solving economic, social, cultural, and humanitarian problems.

☑ To promote respect for human rights and basic freedoms.

☑ To be a center that helps countries to achieve these goals.

# How the UN Is ORGANIZED

The work of the United Nations is carried out almost all over the world. It is done through six main organs, each with a different purpose. The Secretary-General is the chief officer of the UN.

## GENERAL ASSEMBLY

The General Assembly can discuss any problem important to the world. The Assembly admits new members to the UN, appoints the Secretary-General, and decides the UN's budget. It meets once a year for three months, but emergency meetings can be called at any time.

**Who Are Its Members?** All members of the UN are represented in the General Assembly.

**How Do Members Vote?** When the General Assembly votes, each country—whether large or small, rich or poor—has one vote. Two thirds of the members must agree for a resolution to be decided.

## SECURITY COUNCIL

The Security Council discusses questions of peace and security.

**Who Are Its Members?** The Security Council is made up of 5 permanent members (China, France, Great Britain, Russia, and the United States) and 10 members that are elected by the General Assembly for two-year terms.

**How Do Members Vote?** To pass a resolution, at least 9 of the 15 members, including all the permanent members, must vote "yes." If any permanent member vetoes (votes "no" on) the resolution, it is not passed.

## UN SECRETARIES-GENERAL AND THEIR TERMS IN OFFICE

The Secretary-General is the chief officer of the United Nations, appointed by the General Assembly for a five-year term.

1997- ..............Kofi Annan, Ghana
1992-1996 ......Boutros Boutros-Ghali, Egypt
1982-1991 ......Javier Perez de Cuellar, Peru
1972-1981 ......Kurt Waldheim, Austria

1961-1971 ......U Thant, Burma (Myanmar)
1953-1961 ......Dag Hammarskjold,
               Sweden
1945-1952 ......Trygve Lie, Norway

On January 12, 1998, Louise Fréchette of Canada became the first person to be named Deputy Secretary General of the UN.

 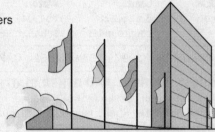

**DID YOU KNOW?** The headquarters for the UN is located in New York City, but the land and the buildings are not part of the United States. The United Nations is an international zone, with its own flag, post office, stamps, and security.

To get more information about the United Nations, you can write to the Public Inquiries Unit, Room GA-57, United Nations, NY 10017 or call the UN at (212) 963-4475.

 **WEB SITE** Information can be found on-line at:
http://www.pbs.org/tal/un

## INTERNATIONAL COURT OF JUSTICE

The International Court of Justice, or World Court, is the highest court of law for legal disputes between countries. When countries have a dispute, they can take their case before the International Court of Justice, which is located at The Hague, Netherlands. Countries that come before the Court must promise to obey the decision of the judges.

**Who Are Its Members?** There are 15 judges on the Court, each from a different country, elected by the General Assembly and the Security Council.

## SECRETARIAT

The Secretariat is the UN staff that carries out the day-to-day operations of the United Nations. Its head is the Secretary-General, currently Kofi Annan. Members of the Secretariat collect background information for the delegates to study and help carry out UN decisions.

## ECONOMIC AND SOCIAL COUNCIL

The Economic and Social Council deals with world problems such as trade, economic development, industry, population, children, food, education, health, and human rights. The Council works closely with many commissions and special agencies, such as FAO (Food and Agriculture Organization), UNICEF (United Nations International Children's Fund), and WHO (World Health Organization).

**Who Are Its Members?** It has 54 member countries elected by the General Assembly for three-year terms.

## TRUSTEESHIP COUNCIL

The Trusteeship Council was formed to watch over the people living in territories that were placed under UN trust until they could become independent.

**Who Are Its Members?** Its members are the permanent members of the Security Council.

# United States: FACTS & FIGURES

| AREA | Land:<br>3,536,278<br>square miles | Water:<br>251,041<br>square miles | Total:<br>3,787,319<br>square miles |
|---|---|---|---|

**POPULATION** (1997): 267,636,061  **CAPITAL:** Washington, D.C.

### LARGEST, HIGHEST, AND OTHER STATISTICS

**Largest state:** Alaska (656,424 square miles)
**Smallest state:** Rhode Island (1,545 square miles)
**Northernmost city:** Barrow, Alaska (71°17' north latitude)
**Southernmost city:** Hilo, Hawaii (19°44' north latitude)
**Easternmost city:** Eastport, Maine (66°59'05" west longitude)
**Westernmost city:** Atka, Alaska (174°20' west longitude)
**Highest town:** Climax, Colorado (11,360 feet)
**Lowest town:** Calipatria, California (184 feet below sea level)
**Oldest national park:** Yellowstone National Park (Idaho, Montana, Wyoming), 2,219,791 acres, established 1872
**Largest national park:** Wrangell-St. Elias, Alaska (8,323,618 acres)
**Longest river:** Mississippi-Missouri-Red Rock (3,710 miles)
**Deepest lake:** Crater Lake, Oregon (1,932 feet)
**Highest mountain:** Mount McKinley, Alaska (20,320 feet)
**Lowest point:** Death Valley, California (282 feet below sea level)
**Rainiest spot:** Mt. Waialeale, Hawaii (average annual rainfall 460 inches)
**Tallest building:** Sears Tower, Chicago, Illinois (1,450 feet)
**Tallest structure:** TV tower, Blanchard, North Dakota (2,063 feet)
**Longest bridge span:** Verrazano-Narrows Bridge, New York (4,260 feet)
**Highest bridge:** Royal Gorge, Colorado (1,053 feet)

### INTERNATIONAL BOUNDARY LINES OF THE U.S.

U.S.-Canadian border.....................................3,987 miles (excluding Alaska)
Alaska-Canadian border .................................1,538 miles
U.S.-Mexican border (Rio Grande) ..................1,933 miles
Atlantic coast................................................2,069 miles
Gulf of Mexico coast......................................1,631 miles
Pacific coast .................................................7,623 miles
Arctic coast, Alaska.......................................1,060 miles

**TERRITORIAL SEA OF THE U.S.** The territorial sea of the United States is the surrounding waters that the country claims as its own. A proclamation issued by President Ronald Reagan on December 27, 1988, stated that the territorial sea of the United States extends 12 nautical miles from the shores of the country.

# SYMBOLS of the UNITED STATES

## THE MOTTO

The U.S. motto, "In God We Trust," was originally put on coins during the Civil War (1861-1865). It disappeared and reappeared on various coins until 1955, when Congress ordered it placed on all paper money and coins.

## THE GREAT SEAL OF THE UNITED STATES

The Great Seal of the United States shows an American bald eagle with a ribbon in its mouth bearing the Latin words "e pluribus unum" (one out of many). In its talons are the arrows of war and an olive branch of peace. On the back of the Great Seal is an unfinished pyramid with an eye (the eye of Providence) above it. The seal was approved by Congress on June 20, 1782.

## THE FLAG

The flag of the United States has 50 stars (one for each state) and 13 stripes (one for each of the original 13 states). It is called unofficially the "Stars and Stripes." The first U.S. flag was commissioned by the Second Continental Congress in 1777 but did not exist until 1783, after the American Revolution. Historians are not certain who designed the Stars and Stripes. Many different flags are believed to have been used during the American Revolution.

The flag of 1777 was used until 1795. In that year President George Washington ordered that a new flag have 15 stripes, alternate red and white, and 15 stars on a blue field. In 1818, Congress directed that the flag have 13 stripes and that a new star be added for each new state of the Union. The last star was added in 1960 for the state of Hawaii.

| 1777 | 1795 | 1818 |

## PLEDGE OF ALLEGIANCE TO THE FLAG

"I pledge allegiance to the flag of the United States of America and to the republic for which it stands, one nation under God, indivisible, with liberty and justice for all."

## NATIONAL ANTHEM: "THE STAR-SPANGLED BANNER"

"The Star-Spangled Banner" was a poem written in 1814 by Francis Scott Key as he watched British ships bombard Fort McHenry, Maryland, during the War of 1812. It became the National Anthem by an act of Congress in 1931. Although it has four stanzas, the one most commonly sung is the first stanza. The music to "The Star-Spangled Banner" was originally a tune called "Anacreon in Heaven."

# The U.S. GOVERNMENT and How It Works

## THE U.S. CONSTITUTION: The Foundation of American Government

The Constitution is the document that created the present government of the United States. It was written in 1787 and went into effect in 1789. It establishes the three branches of the U.S. government, which are the executive (headed by the president), the legislative (the Congress), and the judicial (the Supreme Court and other federal courts). The first 10 amendments to the Constitution (the Bill of Rights) explain the basic rights of all American citizens.

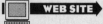 **WEB SITE** You can find the Constitution on-line at:
http://www.usia.gov/usa/aboutusa/consteng.htm

## The Preamble to the Constitution

The Constitution begins with a short statement called the **Preamble**. The Preamble states that the government of the United States was established by the people.

> "We, the people of the United States, in order to form a more perfect Union, establish justice, insure domestic tranquility, provide for the common defense, promote the general welfare, and secure the blessings of liberty to ourselves and our posterity do ordain and establish this Constitution for the United States of America."

## The Articles

The original Constitution contained seven articles. The first three articles of the Constitution establish the three branches of the U.S. government.

### Article 1, Legislative Branch

ARTICLE 1 creates the Senate and House of Representatives and describes their functions and powers.

### Article 2, Executive Branch

ARTICLE 2 creates the office of the President and the Electoral College and lists their powers and responsibilities.

### Article 3, Judicial Branch

ARTICLE 3 creates the Supreme Court and gives Congress the power to create lower courts. The powers of the courts and certain crimes are defined.

### Article 4, The States

ARTICLE 4 discusses the relationship of states to one another and to citizens. Defines their powers.

### Article 5, Amending the Constitution

ARTICLE 5 describes how the Constitution may be amended (changed).

### Article 6, Federal Law

ARTICLE 6 makes the Constitution the supreme law of the land over state laws and constitutions.

### Article 7, Ratifying the Constitution

ARTICLE 7 establishes how to ratify (approve) the Constitution.

# AMENDMENTS TO THE CONSTITUTION

The creators of the Constitution understood that the Constitution might need to be amended, or changed, in the future. Article 5 describes how the Constitution may be amended. In order to pass, an amendment must be approved by a two-thirds majority in the House of Representatives and a two-thirds majority in the Senate. An amendment must then be approved by three-fourths of the states (38 states). Between 1791 and 1995 the Constitution was amended 27 times.

## The Bill of Rights: The First Ten Amendments

The first ten amendments were adopted in 1791 and contain the basic freedoms Americans enjoy as a people. These amendments are known as the Bill of Rights. They are summarized below.

1. Guarantees freedom of religion, speech, and the press
2. Guarantees the right of the people to have firearms
3. Guarantees that soldiers cannot be lodged in private homes except with consent of the owner
4. Protects citizens against being searched or having their property searched or taken away by the government without a good reason
5. Protects rights of people on trial for crimes
6. Guarantees people accused of crimes the right to a speedy public trial by jury
7. Guarantees people the right to a trial by jury for other kinds of cases
8. Prohibits cruel and unusual punishments
9. States that specific rights listed in the Constitution do not take away rights that may not be listed
10. Establishes that powers not granted specifically to the federal government are reserved for state governments or the people

## Other Important Amendments

**13 (1865):** Abolishes slavery in the United States

**14 (1868):** Establishes the Bill of Rights as protection against actions by a state government; guarantees equal protection under the law for all citizens

**15 (1870):** Guarantees that a person of any race or color cannot be denied the right to vote

**19 (1920):** Grants women the right to vote

**22 (1951):** Limits the president to two four-year terms of office

**24 (1964):** Outlaws the poll tax (a tax people had to pay before they could vote) in federal elections. (The poll tax had been used to keep African-Americans in the South from voting.)

**25 (1967):** Grants the president the power to appoint a new vice president, with the approval of Congress, if a vice president dies or leaves office in the middle of a term

**26 (1971):** Lowers the voting age to eighteen

# The Executive Branch:
# The PRESIDENT and the CABINET

The executive branch of the federal government is headed by the president of the United States. It also consists of the vice president, people who work for the president or vice president, the major departments of the government, and many special agencies. The cabinet is made up of the vice president, the heads of the major departments, and a few other important officials. It meets when the president asks for its advice. As head of the executive branch, the president is responsible for enforcing the laws passed by Congress. The president is also commander in chief of all U.S. armed forces. The chart below shows how the executive branch is organized.

## PRESIDENT
### VICE PRESIDENT

### CABINET DEPARTMENTS

| | | | |
|---|---|---|---|
| State | Interior | Health and Human Services | Transportation |
| Treasury | Agriculture | | Energy |
| Defense | Commerce | Housing and Urban Development | Education |
| Justice | Labor | | Veterans Affairs |

## How Long Does the President Serve?
The president serves a four-year term, starting on January 20. No president can be elected more than twice.

## What Happens If the President Dies?
If the president dies in office or cannot complete the term, the vice president becomes president. If the president is disabled, the vice president can become acting president until the president is able to work again. The next person to become president after the vice president would be the Speaker of the House of Representatives. A person who finishes more than two years of a president's term can be elected to only one more term.

 **WEB SITE** The White House has an address on the World Wide Web especially for kids. It is:

http://www.whitehouse.gov/WH/kids/html/home.html

 **DID YOU KNOW?** You can use that site to "tour" the White House and learn about the First Family.

**E-MAIL** You can send e-mail to the president at:

president@whitehouse.gov

▲ The White House, home of the U.S. president

# The Judicial Branch:
# The SUPREME COURT

The highest court in the United States is the **Supreme Court**. It consists of nine justices who are appointed for life by the president with the approval of the Senate. Eight of the nine members are called associate justices. The ninth is the chief justice, who presides over the Court's meetings.

**What Does the Supreme Court Do?** The Supreme Court's major responsibilities are to review federal laws, actions of the president, treaties of the United States, and laws passed by state governments to be sure that they do not conflict in any way with the U.S. Constitution. The Supreme Court carries out these responsibilities by deciding cases that come before it. This process is known as **judicial review**. If the Supreme Court finds that a law or action violates the Constitution, the justices declare it **unconstitutional**.

**The Supreme Court's Decision Is Final**. Most cases must go through other federal courts or state courts before they go to the Supreme Court. The Supreme Court is the final court for a case, and the justices usually decide which cases they will review. After the Supreme Court hears a case, it may agree or disagree with the decision by an earlier court. When the Supreme Court makes a ruling, its decision is final, and all people involved in the case must abide by it.

**Who Is on the Supreme Court?** Below are the nine justices sitting on the Supreme Court for its 1997–1998 session.

**Back row** (from left to right): Ruth Bader Ginsburg, David H. Souter, Clarence Thomas, Stephen Breyer.
**Front row** (from left to right): Antonin Scalia, John Paul Stevens, Chief Justice William H. Rehnquist, Sandra Day O'Connor, Anthony M. Kennedy.

**DID YOU KNOW?** In 1967, Thurgood Marshall became the first African-American to serve on the Supreme Court. He served until 1991. In 1981, Sandra Day O'Connor became the first woman to serve on the Court.

# The Legislative Branch: CONGRESS

The Congress of the United States is the legislative branch of the federal government. Congress's major responsibility is to pass the laws that govern the country. It is the president's responsibility to enforce them. Congress consists of two parts—the Senate and the House of Representatives. They are known as the houses of Congress.

 **WEB SITE** You can reach the Senate and the House on-line at:

http://www.house.gov
http://www.senate.gov

### THE SENATE

The Senate has 100 members, two from each state. Senators are elected for six-year terms. The framers (writers) of the Constitution created the Senate so that one house of Congress could provide equal representation for each state, whether the state is large or small. Thus, the state with the greatest population (California) has two senators, the same number as the state with the smallest population (Wyoming).

In addition to passing laws, the Senate has the responsibility of approving people the president appoints for certain jobs, for example, cabinet members and Supreme Court justices. The Senate must approve all treaties by at least a two-thirds vote. It also has the responsibility under the Constitution of putting on trial high-ranking federal officials who have been impeached (see box below) by the House of Representatives.

### THE HOUSE OF REPRESENTATIVES

The House of Representatives has 435 members. The number of representatives a state has is determined by the state's population, so California has many more representatives than Wyoming. Each state is entitled to at least one representative— no matter how small its population. The first House of Representatives in 1789 had 65 members. As the country's population grew, the number of representatives increased. The total membership has been fixed at 435 since the 1910 census.

---

## What Impeachment Means

A president, vice president, and other high-ranking officials of the United States (for example, federal judges) can be formally charged by the House of Representatives and removed from office for committing treason, bribery, or other serious crimes. Under the Constitution, the House of Representatives has the sole authority to impeach federal officials accused of crimes. "Impeachment" means that the House of Representatives formally charges a federal official with committing a crime. Once an official has been impeached (charged with a crime), he or she must be tried by the Senate. If the Senate finds the official guilty of the charges, he or she is then removed from office.

In 1868, the House impeached President Andrew Johnson, but he was acquitted (found not guilty) after a trial in the Senate. In 1974, a House committee recommended that the House of Representatives impeach President Richard Nixon, but before a vote was taken, President Nixon resigned.

---

# The House of Representatives— State by State

Each state has the following number of representatives in the House:

| | | |
|---|---|---|
| Alabama ...................7 | Minnesota................8 | Texas......................30 |
| Alaska ......................1 | Mississippi ..............5 | Utah .........................3 |
| Arizona ....................6 | Missouri ..................9 | Vermont....................1 |
| Arkansas .................4 | Montana ..................1 | Virginia ..................11 |
| California ..............52 | Nebraska .................3 | Washington ..............9 |
| Colorado .................6 | Nevada ....................2 | West Virginia...........3 |
| Connecticut..............6 | New Hampshire ........2 | Wisconsin ...............9 |
| Delaware .................1 | New Jersey.............13 | Wyoming..................1 |
| Florida ...................23 | New Mexico .............3 | |
| Georgia..................11 | New York...............31 | |
| Hawaii .....................2 | North Carolina........12 | |
| Idaho........................2 | North Dakota ...........1 | |
| Illinois ...................20 | Ohio .......................19 | |
| Indiana ..................10 | Oklahoma ...............6 | |
| Iowa .........................5 | Oregon ....................5 | |
| Kansas.....................4 | Pennsylvania ..........21 | |
| Kentucky...................6 | Rhode Island............2 | |
| Louisiana.................7 | South Carolina .........6 | |
| Maine.......................2 | South Dakota ...........1 | |
| Maryland .................8 | Tennessee ...............9 | |
| Massachusetts ......10 | | |
| Michigan................16 | | |

The District of Columbia (Washington, D.C.) has one nonvoting member of the House of Representatives.

# How Congress Makes Laws

### 1. Senators and Representatives Propose a Bill.

A proposed law is called a bill. Any member of Congress may propose (introduce) a bill. A bill is introduced in each house of Congress. The House of Representatives and the Senate consider a bill separately. A member of Congress who introduces a bill is known as the bill's *sponsor*.

### 2. House and Senate Committees Consider the Bill.

The bill is then sent to appropriate committees for consideration. A committee is made up of a small number of members of the House or Senate. A bill relating to agriculture, for example, would be sent to the agriculture committees in the House and in the Senate. When committees are considering a bill, they hold hearings at which people can speak for or against the bill.

### 3. Committees Change the Bill.

The committees then consider the bill and change it as they see fit. They vote on the bill.

### 4. The Bill Is Debated in the House and Senate.

If the committees vote in favor of the bill, it goes to the full House and Senate, where it is debated and changed further. The House and Senate then vote on the bill.

### 5. From the House and Senate to Conference Committee.

If the House and the Senate pass different versions of the same bill, the bill must then go to a "conference committee," where differences between the two versions must be worked out. A conference committee is a special committee made up of Senate and House members who meet to resolve the differences in versions of the same bill.

### 8. What If the President Doesn't Sign the Bill?

Sometimes the president does not approve of a bill and refuses to sign it. This is called vetoing the bill. A bill that has been vetoed goes back to Congress, where the members can vote on it again. If the House and the Senate pass the bill again with a two-thirds majority vote, the bill becomes law. This is called overriding the president's veto. A new law, called a line-item veto, allows the president to veto parts of some bills. This law has been challenged, and the Supreme Court could decide that it is not allowed under the Constitution.

### 6. Final Vote in the House and Senate.

The conference committee version is then voted on by the House and the Senate. In order for a bill to become a law, it must be approved in exactly the same form by a majority of members of both houses of Congress and signed by the president.

### 7. The President Signs the Bill Into Law.

If the bill passes both houses of Congress, it then goes to the president for his signature. Once the president signs a bill, it becomes law.

# Major GOVERNMENT AGENCIES

Government agencies have a variety of functions. Some set rules and regulations or enforce laws. Others investigate or gather information. Some major agencies are listed below, along with what they try to do.

## Central Intelligence Agency (CIA)

Gathers secret information on other countries and their leaders.

## Consumer Product Safety Commission

Examines the products that people buy to see that they are safe.

## Environmental Protection Agency (EPA)

Enforces laws on clean air and water and is responsible for cleaning up hazardous waste sites.

## Equal Employment Opportunity Commission (EEOC)

Makes sure that people are not discriminated against when they apply for a job and when they are at work.

## Federal Aviation Administration (FAA)

Watches over the airline industry and establishes safety rules.

## Federal Bureau of Investigation (FBI)

Investigates federal crimes and collects statistics on crime in the United States.

## Federal Communications Commission (FCC)

Issues licenses to radio and TV stations and makes broadcasting rules.

## Federal Emergency Management Agency (FEMA)

Helps local communities recover from disasters such as hurricanes, earthquakes, and floods.

## Federal Trade Commission (FTC)

Makes sure that businesses operate fairly and that they obey the law.

## Library of Congress

The main library of the United States, collects most of the books published in the United States. It also has many historic documents and photographs.

## National Foundation on the Arts and the Humanities

Gives government money to museums and artists.

## Occupational Safety and Health Administration (OSHA)

Makes sure that places where people work are safe and will not harm their health.

## Peace Corps

Sends American volunteers to foreign countries for two years to help with special projects such as teaching and farming.

## Securities and Exchange Commission (SEC)

Makes sure that the stock market operates fairly and obeys the laws.

# ELECTIONS: Electing the PRESIDENT and VICE PRESIDENT

**Y**ou may be amazed to learn that the president and vice president of the United States are not really elected in November on Election Day. They are actually elected in December by 538 people called the Electoral College.

## WHAT IS THE ELECTORAL COLLEGE?

The system for electing presidents was established by the U.S. Constitution in 1789. Each state must choose a group of "electors," equal to the total number of senators and representatives the state sends to Congress. For example, Missouri has 9 representatives and 2 senators and thus has 11 electors. The District of Columbia has 3 electors. Electors from the 50 states and the District of Columbia are called the Electoral College. Despite its name, the Electoral College is not a school. It is a group of people (usually members of political parties) who officially elect the president and vice president.

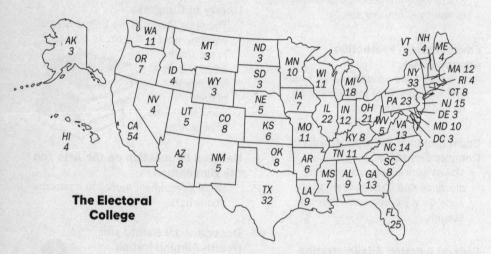

**The Electoral College**

## HOW ARE THE PRESIDENT AND VICE PRESIDENT ELECTED?

Every four years on Election Day in November, the names of the candidates for president and vice president appear on the voting machine or ballot. Voters select the people they prefer. When a voter pulls the lever for president, he or she is really choosing a group of electors who have promised to support (are "pledged to") the voter's presidential candidate. The names of the electors are not usually shown on the voting machine.

After the election polls close, each state begins counting the votes cast for each presidential and vice presidential candidate. The electors in the Electoral College, who are pledged to the candidate with the most votes in each state, meet in their home state in December. There, they officially cast their ballots for president and vice president. To be elected, a candidate must receive a majority of the Electoral College votes, or 270 votes. The results are announced in Congress the following January. If no candidate receives 270 electoral votes, the election goes to the House of Representatives, where the president is selected from the top three candidates. In the 1996 presidential election, the Electoral College cast 379 votes for Bill Clinton and 159 votes for Bob Dole.

# Using a VOTING MACHINE

**A**lthough some people in the United States still vote on paper ballots, most people now vote on voting machines. There are different kinds of voting machines, but they all work in the same basic way. When the voter goes into the voting booth, he or she pulls a master lever that locks the machine. The voter sees the names of the candidates from different political parties and pulls a small lever next to the candidate the voter chooses for each office. The votes are then recorded in the machine when the voter pulls the master lever back into its original position.

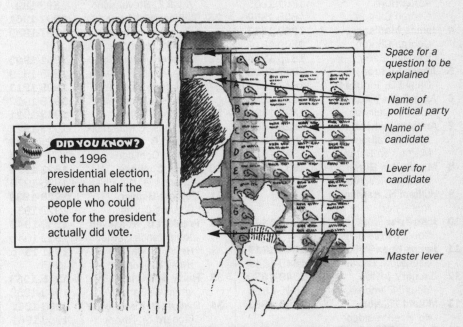

Space for a question to be explained

Name of political party

Name of candidate

Lever for candidate

Voter

Master lever

**DID YOU KNOW?**
In the 1996 presidential election, fewer than half the people who could vote for the president actually did vote.

## WHO CAN VOTE IN THE UNITED STATES: A TIME LINE

**1789** — The U.S. Constitution is adopted in 1789, and all states allow white men who own land to vote. In New Jersey, women who own land are also allowed to vote.

**1807** — New Jersey ends women's right to vote.

**1830s** — All states allow all white men to vote, even those who don't own land.

**1848** — At a convention in Seneca Falls, New York, women call for the right to vote.

**1870** — The Fifteenth Amendment to the Constitution is adopted, guaranteeing the right to vote to men regardless of race or color.

**1890s** — Some states allow women to vote in state and local elections (but not elections for president or members of Congress).

**1920** — The Nineteenth Amendment to the Constitution is adopted, guaranteeing women the right to vote in all elections.

**1964** — The Civil Rights Act of 1964 bans the use of literacy tests and poll taxes, which were used to prevent African-Americans from voting.

**1971** — The Twenty-sixth Amendment to the Constitution is adopted, lowering the age from 21 to 18.

# PRESIDENTS and VICE PRESIDENTS of the UNITED STATES

| PRESIDENT / VICE PRESIDENT | YEARS IN OFFICE | | PRESIDENT / VICE PRESIDENT | YEARS IN OFFICE |
|---|---|---|---|---|
| 1 George Washington | **1789-1797** | 22 | Grover Cleveland | **1885-1889** |
| John Adams | 1789-1797 | | Thomas A. Hendricks | 1885 |
| 2 John Adams | **1797-1801** | 23 | Benjamin Harrison | **1889-1893** |
| Thomas Jefferson | 1797-1801 | | Levi P. Morton | 1889-1893 |
| 3 Thomas Jefferson | **1801-1809** | 24 | Grover Cleveland | **1893-1897** |
| Aaron Burr | 1801-1805 | | Adlai E. Stevenson | 1893-1897 |
| George Clinton | 1805-1809 | 25 | William McKinley | **1897-1901** |
| 4 James Madison | **1809-1817** | | Garret A. Hobart | 1897-1899 |
| George Clinton | 1809-1812 | | Theodore Roosevelt | 1901 |
| Elbridge Gerry | 1813-1814 | 26 | Theodore Roosevelt | **1901-1909** |
| 5 James Monroe | **1817-1825** | | Charles W. Fairbanks | 1905-1909 |
| Daniel D. Tompkins | 1817-1825 | 27 | William Howard Taft | **1909-1913** |
| 6 John Quincy Adams | **1825-1829** | | James S. Sherman | 1909-1912 |
| John C. Calhoun | 1825-1829 | 28 | Woodrow Wilson | **1913-1921** |
| 7 Andrew Jackson | **1829-1837** | | Thomas R. Marshall | 1913-1921 |
| John C. Calhoun | 1829-1832 | 29 | Warren G. Harding | **1921-1923** |
| Martin Van Buren | 1833-1837 | | Calvin Coolidge | 1921-1923 |
| 8 Martin Van Buren | **1837-1841** | 30 | Calvin Coolidge | **1923-1929** |
| Richard M. Johnson | 1837-1841 | | Charles G. Dawes | 1925-1929 |
| 9 William H. Harrison | **1841** | 31 | Herbert Hoover | **1929-1933** |
| John Tyler | 1841 | | Charles Curtis | 1929-1933 |
| 10 John Tyler | **1841-1845** | 32 | Franklin D. Roosevelt | **1933-1945** |
| No Vice President | | | John Nance Garner | 1933-1941 |
| 11 James Knox Polk | **1845-1849** | | Henry A. Wallace | 1941-1945 |
| George M. Dallas | 1845-1849 | | Harry S. Truman | 1945 |
| 12 Zachary Taylor | **1849-1850** | 33 | Harry S. Truman | **1945-1953** |
| Millard Fillmore | 1849-1850 | | Alben W. Barkley | 1949-1953 |
| 13 Millard Fillmore | **1850-1853** | 34 | Dwight D. Eisenhower | **1953-1961** |
| No Vice President | | | Richard M. Nixon | 1953-1961 |
| 14 Franklin Pierce | **1853-1857** | 35 | John F. Kennedy | **1961-1963** |
| William R. King | 1853 | | Lyndon B. Johnson | 1961-1963 |
| 15 James Buchanan | **1857-1861** | 36 | Lyndon B. Johnson | **1963-1969** |
| John C. Breckinridge | 1857-1861 | | Hubert H. Humphrey | 1965-1969 |
| 16 Abraham Lincoln | **1861-1865** | 37 | Richard M. Nixon | **1969-1974** |
| Hannibal Hamlin | 1861-1865 | | Spiro T. Agnew | 1969-1973 |
| Andrew Johnson | 1865 | | Gerald R. Ford | 1973-1974 |
| 17 Andrew Johnson | **1865-1869** | 38 | Gerald R. Ford | **1974-1977** |
| No Vice President | | | Nelson A. Rockefeller | 1974-1977 |
| 18 Ulysses S. Grant | **1869-1877** | 39 | Jimmy Carter | **1977-1981** |
| Schuyler Colfax | 1869-1873 | | Walter F. Mondale | 1977-1981 |
| Henry Wilson | 1873-1875 | 40 | Ronald Reagan | **1981-1989** |
| 19 Rutherford B. Hayes | **1877-1881** | | George Bush | 1981-1989 |
| William A. Wheeler | 1877-1881 | 41 | George Bush | **1989-1993** |
| 20 James A. Garfield | **1881** | | Dan Quayle | 1989-1993 |
| Chester A. Arthur | 1881 | 42 | Bill Clinton | **1993-** |
| 21 Chester A. Arthur | **1881-1885** | | Al Gore | 1993- |
| No Vice President | | | | |

# PRESIDENTS of the UNITED STATES and Their FAMILIES

### 1. GEORGE WASHINGTON (1789-1797)
**Political Party:** Federalist
**Born:** Feb. 22, 1732, at Wakefield, Westmoreland County, Virginia
**Married:** Martha Dandridge Custis (1731-1802); no children
**Died:** Dec. 14, 1799; buried at Mount Vernon, Fairfax County, Virginia
**Early Career:** Soldier; head of the Virginia militia; commander in chief of the Continental Army; chairman of Constitutional Convention (1787)

### 2. JOHN ADAMS (1797-1801)
**Political Party:** Federalist
**Born:** Oct. 30, 1735, in Quincy, Massachusetts
**Married:** Abigail Smith (1744-1818); 3 sons, 2 daughters
**Died:** July 4, 1826; buried in Quincy, Massachusetts
**Early Career:** Lawyer; delegate to Continental Congress; signer of the Declaration of Independence; first vice president

### 3. THOMAS JEFFERSON (1801-1809)
**Political Party:** Democratic-Republican
**Born:** Apr. 13, 1743, at Shadwell, Albemarle County, Virginia
**Married:** Martha Wayles Skelton (1748-1782); 1 son, 5 daughters
**Died:** July 4, 1826; buried at Monticello, Albemarle County, Virginia
**Early Career:** Lawyer; member of the Continental Congress; author of the Declaration of Independence; governor of Virginia; first secretary of state; author of the Virginia Statute on Religious Freedom

### 4. JAMES MADISON (1809-1817)
**Political Party:** Democratic-Republican
**Born:** Mar. 16, 1751, at Port Conway, King George County, Virginia
**Married:** Dolley Payne Todd (1768-1849); no children
**Died:** June 28, 1836; buried at Montpelier, Orange County, Virginia
**Early Career:** Member of the Virginia Constitutional Convention (1776); member of the Continental Congress; major contributor to the U.S. Constitution; writer of the *Federalist Papers*; secretary of state

### 5. JAMES MONROE (1817-1825)
**Political Party:** Democratic-Republican
**Born:** Apr. 28, 1758, in Westmoreland County, Virginia
**Married:** Elizabeth Kortright (1768-1830); 2 daughters
**Died:** July 4, 1831; buried in Richmond, Virginia
**Early Career:** Soldier; lawyer; U.S. senator; governor of Virginia; secretary of state

### 6. JOHN QUINCY ADAMS (1825-1829)
**Political Party:** Democratic-Republican
**Born:** July 11, 1767, in Quincy, Massachusetts
**Married:** Louisa Catherine Johnson (1775-1852); 3 sons, 1 daughter
**Died:** Feb. 23, 1848; buried in Quincy, Massachusetts
**Early Career:** Diplomat; U.S. senator; secretary of state

### 7. ANDREW JACKSON (1829-1837)
**Political Party:** Democratic
**Born:** Mar. 15, 1767, in New Lancaster County, South Carolina
**Married:** Rachel Donelson Robards (1767-1828); no children
**Died:** June 8, 1845; buried in Nashville, Tennessee
**Early Career:** Lawyer; U.S. representative and senator; Indian fighter; general in the U.S. Army

### 8. MARTIN VAN BUREN (1837-1841)
**Political Party:** Democratic
**Born:** Dec. 5, 1782, at Kinderhook, New York
**Married:** Hannah Hoes (1783-1819); 4 sons
**Died:** July 24, 1862; buried at Kinderhook, New York
**Early Career:** Governor of New York; secretary of state; vice president

### 9. WILLIAM HENRY HARRISON (1841)
**Political Party:** Whig
**Born:** Feb. 9, 1773, at Berkeley, Charles City County, Virginia
**Married:** Anna Symmes (1775-1864); 6 sons, 4 daughters
**Died:** Apr. 4, 1841; buried in North Bend, Ohio
**Early Career:** First governor of Indiana Territory; superintendent of Indian affairs; U.S. representative and senator

### 10. JOHN TYLER (1841-1845)
**Political Party:** Whig
**Born:** Mar. 29, 1790, in Greenway, Charles City County, Virginia
**Married:** Letitia Christian (1790-1842); 3 sons, 5 daughters
        Julia Gardiner (1820-1889); 5 sons, 2 daughters
**Died:** Jan. 18, 1862; buried in Richmond, Virginia
**Early Career:** U.S. representative and senator; vice president

### 11. JAMES KNOX POLK (1845-1849)
**Political Party:** Democratic
**Born:** Nov. 2, 1795, in Mecklenburg County, North Carolina
**Married:** Sarah Childress (1803-1891); no children
**Died:** June 15, 1849; buried in Nashville, Tennessee
**Early Career:** U.S. representative; Speaker of the House; governor of Tennessee

### 12. ZACHARY TAYLOR (1849-1850)
**Political Party:** Whig
**Born:** Nov. 24, 1784, in Orange County, Virginia
**Married:** Margaret Smith (1788-1852); 1 son, 5 daughters
**Died:** July 9, 1850; buried in Louisville, Kentucky
**Early Career:** Indian fighter; general in the U.S. Army

### 13. MILLARD FILLMORE (1850-1853)
**Political Party:** Whig
**Born:** Jan 7, 1800, in Cayuga County, New York
**Married:** Abigail Powers (1798-1853); 1 son, 1 daughter
        Caroline Carmichael McIntosh (1813-1881); no children
**Died:** Mar. 8, 1874; buried in Buffalo, N.Y.
**Early Career:** Teacher; lawyer; U.S. representative; vice president

### 14. FRANKLIN PIERCE (1853-1857)
**Political Party:** Democratic
**Born:** Nov. 23, 1804, in Hillsboro, New Hampshire
**Married:** Jane Means Appleton (1806-1863); 3 sons
**Died:** Oct. 8, 1869, in Concord, New Hampshire
**Early Career:** U.S. representative, senator

### 15. JAMES BUCHANAN (1857-1861)
**Political Party:** Democratic
**Born:** Apr. 23, 1791, near Mercersburg, Pennsylvania
Never Married
**Died:** June 1, 1868, in Lancaster, Pennsylvania
**Early Career:** U.S. representative; secretary of state

### 16. ABRAHAM LINCOLN (1861-1865)
**Political Party:** Republican
**Born:** Feb. 12, 1809, in Larue, Kentucky
**Married:** Mary Todd (1818-1882); 4 sons
**Died:** Apr. 15, 1865; buried in Springfield, Illinois
**Early Career:** Lawyer; U.S. representative

### 17. ANDREW JOHNSON (1865-1869)
**Political Party:** Republican
**Born:** Dec. 29, 1808, in Raleigh, North Carolina
**Married:** Eliza McCardle (1810-1876); 3 sons, 2 daughters
**Died:** July 31, 1875; buried in Greeneville, Tennessee
**Early Career:** State representative and senator; U.S.
    representative; governor of Tennessee; U.S. senator;
    vice president

### 18. ULYSSES S. GRANT (1869-1877)
**Political Party:** Republican
**Born:** Apr. 27, 1822, in Point Pleasant, Ohio
**Married:** Julia Dent (1826-1902); 3 sons, 1 daughter
**Died:** July 23, 1885; buried in New York City
**Early Career:** Army officer; commander of Union forces during
    Civil War

### 19. RUTHERFORD B. HAYES (1877-1881)
**Political Party:** Republican
**Born:** Oct. 4, 1822, in Delaware, Ohio
**Married:** Lucy Ware Webb (1831-1889); 7 sons, 1 daughter
**Died:** Jan. 17, 1893; buried in Fremont, Ohio
**Early Career:** Lawyer; general in Union Army; U.S. representative;
    governor of Ohio

### 20. JAMES A. GARFIELD (1881)
**Political Party:** Republican
**Born:** Nov. 19, 1831, in Orange, Cuyahoga County, Ohio
**Married:** Lucretia Rudolph (1832-1918); 4 sons, 1 daughter
**Died:** Sept. 19, 1881; buried in Cleveland, Ohio
**Early Career:** Teacher; Ohio state senator; general in Union Army;
    U.S. representative

### 21. CHESTER A. ARTHUR (1881-1885)
**Political Party:** Republican
**Born:** Oct. 5, 1829, in Fairfield, Vermont
**Married:** Ellen Lewis Herndon (1837-1880); 2 sons, 1 daughter
**Died:** Nov. 18, 1886; buried in Albany, New York
**Early Career:** Lawyer; vice president

### 22. GROVER CLEVELAND (1885-1889)
**Political Party:** Democratic
**Born:** Mar. 18, 1837, in Caldwell, New Jersey
**Married:** Frances Folsom (1864-1947); 2 sons, 3 daughters
**Died:** June 24, 1908; buried in Princeton, New Jersey
**Early Career:** Lawyer; mayor of Buffalo; governor of New York

### 23. BENJAMIN HARRISON (1889-1893)
**Political Party:** Republican
**Born:** Aug. 20, 1833, in North Bend, Ohio
**Married:** Caroline Lavinia Scott (1832-1892); 1 son, 1 daughter
          Mary Scott Lord Dimmick (1858-1948); 1 daughter
**Died:** Mar. 13, 1901; buried in Indianapolis, Indiana
**Early Career:** Lawyer; general in Union Army; U.S. senator

### 24. GROVER CLEVELAND (1893-1897) See 22, above.

### 25. WILLIAM MCKINLEY (1897-1901)
**Political Party:** Republican
**Born:** Jan. 29, 1843, in Niles, Ohio
**Married:** Ida Saxton (1847-1907); 2 daughters
**Died:** Sept. 14, 1901; buried in Canton, Ohio
**Early Career:** Lawyer; U.S. representative; governor of Ohio

### 26. THEODORE ROOSEVELT (1901-1909)
**Political Party:** Republican
**Born:** Oct. 27, 1858, in New York City
**Married:** Alice Hathaway Lee (1861-1884); 1 daughter
          Edith Kermit Carow (1861-1948); 4 sons, 1 daughter
**Died:** Jan. 6, 1919; buried in Oyster Bay, New York
**Early Career:** Assistant secretary of the navy; cavalry leader in
          Spanish-American War; governor of New York; vice president

### 27. WILLIAM HOWARD TAFT (1909-1913)
**Political Party:** Republican
**Born:** Sept. 15, 1857, in Cincinnati, Ohio
**Married:** Helen Herron (1861-1943); 2 sons, 1 daughter
**Died:** Mar. 8, 1930; buried in Arlington National Cemetery, Virginia
**Early Career:** Lawyer; judge; secretary of war

### 28. WOODROW WILSON (1913-1921)
**Political Party:** Democratic
**Born:** Dec. 28, 1856, in Staunton, Virginia
**Married:** Ellen Louise Axson (1860-1914); 3 daughters
          Edith Bolling Galt (1872-1961); no children
**Died:** Feb. 3, 1924; buried in Washington, D.C.
**Early Career:** Lawyer; college professor; governor of New Jersey

### 29. WARREN G. HARDING (1921-1923)
**Political Party:** Republican
**Born:** Nov. 2, 1865, near Blooming Grove, Ohio
**Married:** Florence Kling De Wolfe (1860-1924); no children
**Died:** Aug. 2, 1923; buried in Marion, Ohio
**Early Career:** Ohio state senator; U.S. senator

### 30. CALVIN COOLIDGE (1923-1929)
**Political Party:** Republican
**Born:** July 4, 1872, in Plymouth, Vermont
**Married:** Grace Anna Goodhue (1879-1957); 2 sons
**Died:** Jan. 5, 1933; buried in Plymouth, Vermont
**Early Career:** Massachusetts state senator, lieutenant governor, and governor; vice president

### 31. HERBERT HOOVER (1929-1933)
**Political Party:** Republican
**Born:** Aug. 10, 1874, in West Branch, Iowa
**Married:** Lou Henry (1875-1944); 2 sons
**Died:** Oct. 20, 1964; buried West Branch, Iowa
**Early Career:** Mining engineer; secretary of commerce

### 32. FRANKLIN DELANO ROOSEVELT (1933-1945)
**Political Party:** Democratic
**Born:** Jan. 30, 1882, in Hyde Park, New York
**Married:** Anna Eleanor Roosevelt (1884-1962); 4 sons, 1 daughter
**Died:** Apr. 12, 1945; buried in Hyde Park, New York
**Early Career:** Lawyer; New York state senator; assistant secretary of the navy; governor of New York

### 33. HARRY S. TRUMAN (1945-1953)
**Political Party:** Democratic
**Born:** May 8, 1884, in Lamar, Missouri
**Married:** Elizabeth Virginia "Bess" Wallace (1885-1982); 1 daughter
**Died:** Dec. 26, 1972; buried in Independence, Missouri
**Early Career:** Haberdasher (ran men's clothing store); judge; U.S. senator; vice president

### 34. DWIGHT D. EISENHOWER (1953-1961)
**Political Party:** Republican
**Born:** Oct. 14, 1890, in Denison, Texas
**Married:** Mamie Geneva Doud (1896-1979); 1 son
**Died:** Mar. 28, 1969; buried in Abilene, Kansas
**Early Career:** Commander, Allied landing in North Africa and later Supreme Allied Commander in Europe during World War II; president of Columbia University

### 35. JOHN FITZGERALD KENNEDY (1961-1963)
**Political Party:** Democratic
**Born:** May 29, 1917, in Brookline, Massachusetts
**Married:** Jacqueline Lee Bouvier (1929-1994); 1 son, 1 daughter
**Died:** Nov. 22, 1963; buried in Arlington National Cemetery, Virginia
**Early Career:** U.S. naval commander; U.S. representative and senator

### 36. LYNDON BAINES JOHNSON (1963-1969)
**Political Party:** Democratic
**Born:** Aug. 27, 1908, in Stonewall, Texas
**Married:** Claudia "Lady Bird" Alta Taylor (b. 1912); 2 daughters
**Died:** Jan. 22, 1973; buried in Stonewall, Texas
**Early Career:** U.S. representative and senator; vice president

### 37. RICHARD MILHOUS NIXON (1969-1974)
**Political Party:** Republican
**Born:** Jan. 9, 1913, in Yorba Linda, California
**Married:** Patricia Ryan (1912-1993); 2 daughters
**Died:** Apr. 22, 1994; buried in Yorba Linda, California
**Early Career:** Lawyer; U.S. representative and senator; vice president

### 38. GERALD R. FORD (1974-1977)
**Political Party:** Republican
**Born:** July 14, 1913, in Omaha, Nebraska
**Married:** Elizabeth Bloomer Warren (b. 1918);
            3 sons, 1 daughter
**Early Career:** Lawyer; U.S. representative; vice president

### 39. JIMMY (JAMES EARL) CARTER (1977-1981)
**Political Party:** Democratic
**Born:** Oct. 1, 1924, in Plains, Georgia
**Married:** Rosalynn Smith (b. 1927); 3 sons, 1 daughter
**Early Career:** Peanut farmer; Georgia state senator; governor
    of Georgia

### 40. RONALD REAGAN (1981-1989)
**Political Party:** Republican
**Born:** Feb. 6, 1911, in Tampico, Illinois
**Married:** Jane Wyman (b. 1914); 1 son, 1 daughter
            Nancy Davis (b. 1921); 1 son, 1 daughter
**Early Career:** Film and television actor; governor of California

### 41. GEORGE BUSH (1989-1993)
**Political Party:** Republican
**Born:** June 12, 1924, in Milton, Massachusetts
**Married:** Barbara Pierce (b. 1925); 4 sons, 2 daughters
**Early Career:** U.S. navy pilot; businessman; U.S. representative; U.S.
    ambassador to the United Nations; vice president

### 42. BILL (WILLIAM JEFFERSON) CLINTON (1993-   )
**Political Party:** Democratic
**Born:** Aug. 19, 1946, in Hope, Arkansas
**Married:** Hillary Rodham (b. 1947); 1 daughter
**Early Career:** Arkansas state attorney general; governor of Arkansas

# Presidential Facts, Families, and First Ladies

## PRESIDENTIAL FACTS

**Youngest president:** Theodore Roosevelt, who was 42 when he was sworn in
**Oldest president:** Ronald Reagan, who was 77 when he left office
**Only president to serve more than two terms:** Franklin Delano Roosevelt
**Only president to serve two terms that were not back to back:** Grover Cleveland
**Only president who was unmarried:** James Buchanan. His niece acted as White House hostess for her uncle.

**Presidents who died in office:** Eight U.S. presidents have died while they served as president. Four of them were assassinated: Abraham Lincoln, James Garfield, William McKinley, and John F. Kennedy. The other four presidents who died in office were William Henry Harrison, Zachary Taylor, Warren G. Harding, and Franklin Delano Roosevelt.

## FAMOUS FIRST FAMILIES

**Adams family:** John Adams was the 2nd president, and his son, John Quincy Adams, became the 6th president.
**Harrison family:** Benjamin Harrison, the 23rd president, was the great-grandson of Benjamin Harrison, a signer of the Declaration of Independence, and the grandson of William Henry Harrison, the 9th president of the United States.
**Roosevelt family:** Theodore Roosevelt was the 26th president and his 5th cousin, Franklin Delano Roosevelt, the 32nd. Franklin's wife, Eleanor Roosevelt, was also Theodore Roosevelt's niece.

## FAMOUS FIRST LADIES

**Martha Washington** was the first First Lady. A wealthy widow when she married George Washington, she helped his position as a Virginia planter.

**Abigail Adams,** the wife of John Adams, was a thoughtful, outspoken woman. She wrote hundreds of letters in which she clearly expressed her opinions on the issues of the day.

**Dolley Madison,** James Madison's wife, was famous as a hostess and for saving a portrait of George Washington during the War of 1812, when the British were about to burn the White House.

**Eleanor Roosevelt,** wife of Franklin D. Roosevelt, was an important public figure. She urged her husband to support civil rights and the rights of workers. After his death she served as a delegate to the United Nations.

**Jacqueline Kennedy,** wife of John F. Kennedy, known for her elegance and style, restored the White House and made it a symbol the country could be proud of.

**Hillary Rodham Clinton,** wife of Bill Clinton, is a successful lawyer and outspoken defender of women's and children's rights. She won a Grammy in 1997 for a recording of her book about children, *It Takes a Village.*

# United States History TIME LINE

## The First People in North America: Before 1492

**40,000 B.C.-11,000 B.C.**
First people (called Paleo-Indians) cross from Siberia to Alaska and begin to move into North America.

**14,000 B.C.-11,000 B.C.**
Paleo-Indians use stone points attached to spears to hunt big mammoths in northern parts of North America.

**11,000 B.C.**
Big mammoths disappear and Paleo-Indians begin to gather plants for food.

**8000 B.C.-1000 B.C.**
North American Indians begin using stone to grind food and to hunt bison and smaller animals.

**1000 B.C.-A.D. 500**
Woodland Indians, who lived east of the Mississippi River, bury people who have died under large burial mounds (which can still be seen today).

**After A.D. 500**
Anasazi peoples in the Southwestern United States live in homes on cliffs, called cliff dwellings. Anasazi pottery and dishes are well known for their beautiful patterns.

**After A.D. 700**
Mississippian Indian people in Southeastern United States develop farms and build burial mounds.

**700-1492**
Many different Indian cultures develop throughout North America.

## Colonial America and the American Revolution: 1492-1783

**1492**

Christopher Columbus sails across the Atlantic Ocean and reaches an island in the Bahamas in the Caribbean Sea.

**1513**

Juan Ponce de León explores the Florida coast.

**1524**

Giovanni da Verrazano explores the coast from Carolina north to Nova Scotia, enters New York harbor.

**1540**

Francisco Vásquez de Coronado explores the Southwest.

**1565**

St. Augustine, Florida, the first town established by Europeans in United States, is founded by the Spanish. Later burned by the English in 1586.

**1607**

Jamestown, Virginia, the first English settlement in North America, is founded by Captain John Smith.

**1609**

Henry Hudson sails into New York harbor, explores Hudson River. Spaniards found Santa Fe, New Mexico.

**1619**

The first African slaves are brought to Jamestown. (Slavery is made legal in 1650.)

**1620**

Pilgrims from England arrive at Plymouth, Massachusetts, on the *Mayflower*.

**1626**

Peter Minuit buys Manhattan island for the Dutch from Man-a-hat-a Indians for goods worth $24. The island is renamed New Amsterdam.

**1630**

Boston is founded by Massachusetts colonists led by John Winthrop.

**1634**
Maryland is founded as a Catholic colony with religious freedom for all its settlers.

**1664**
The English seize New Amsterdam from the Dutch. The city is renamed New York.

**1699**
French settlers move into Mississippi and Louisiana.

**1732**
Benjamin Franklin begins publishing *Poor Richard's Almanack*.

**1754-1763**
French and Indian War between England and France. The French are defeated and lose their lands in Canada and the American Midwest.

**1764-1767**
England places taxes on sugar that comes from their North American colonies. England also requires colonists to purchase stamps to raise money to pay for the French and Indian War. Colonists protest and meet in the Stamp Act Congress.

**1770**
Boston Massacre: English troops fire on a group of people protesting English taxes.

**1773**
Boston Tea Party: English tea is thrown into the harbor to protest a tax on tea.

**1775**
Fighting at Lexington and Concord, Massachusetts, marks the beginning of the American Revolution.

**1776**
The Declaration of Independence is approved July 4 by the Continental Congress (made up of representatives from the American colonies).

**1781**
British General Cornwallis surrenders to the Americans at Yorktown, Virginia, ending the fighting in the Revolutionary War.

---

**Benjamin Franklin (1706-1790)** was a great American leader, printer, scientist, and writer. In 1732, he began publishing a magazine called *Poor Richard's Almanack*. Poor Richard was a make-believe person who gave advice about common sense and honesty. Many of Poor Richard's sayings are still known today. Among the most famous are "God helps them that help themselves" and "Early to bed, early to rise, makes a man healthy, wealthy, and wise."

---

**Portion of The Declaration of Independence, July 4, 1776**

"We hold these truths to be self-evident, that all men are created equal, that they are endowed by their Creator with certain unalienable rights, that among these are life, liberty, and the pursuit of happiness."

### Who Attended the Convention?

The Constitutional Convention met in Philadelphia in the hot summer of 1787. Most of the great founders of America attended. Among those present were George Washington, James Madison, and John Adams. They met to form a new government that would be strong and, at the same time, protect the liberties that were fought for in the American Revolution. The Constitution they created is still the law of the United States.

Louisiana Purchase

## The New Nation: 1783-1900

**1783**
The Treaty of Paris ending the Revolutionary War is signed by the United States and England. The English recognize U.S. independence.

**1784**
The first successful daily newspaper, the *Pennsylvania Packet & General Advertiser,* is published.

**1787**
The Constitutional Convention meets to write a new Constitution for the United States.

**1789**
The new Constitution is approved by the states. George Washington is chosen as the first president.

**1800**
The federal government moves to a new capital, Washington, D.C.

**1803**
President Thomas Jefferson makes the Louisiana Purchase from France. Millions of square miles of territory are added to the United States.

**1804**
Lewis and Clark explore far into the northwestern United States.

**1812-1814**
War of 1812 with Great Britain: British forces burn the Capitol and White House. Francis Scott Key writes "The Star-Spangled Banner."

**1820**
The Missouri Compromise in Congress bans slavery west of the Mississippi River and north of line 36°30' north latitude.

**1823**
The Monroe Doctrine warns European countries not to interfere in North America.

**1825**
The Erie Canal opens in New York and links the east coast with the Midwest.

**1831**
*The Liberator,* a newspaper opposing slavery, is published in Boston.

### "The Trail of Tears"

The Cherokee Indians living in Georgia were forced, by the state government of Georgia, to leave in 1838. They were sent to Oklahoma. On the long march, thousands died because of disease and the cold weather.

### Uncle Tom's Cabin

Harriet Beecher Stowe's novel about the sufferings of slaves was an instant bestseller in the North and banned in most of the South. When President Abraham Lincoln met Stowe, he called her "the little lady who started this war" (the Civil War).

### The Bloodiest War in U.S. History

The U.S. Civil War between the North and South lasted four years (1861-1865) and resulted in the deaths of more than 600,000 people—more than all other U.S. wars combined. Little was known at the time about the spread of diseases. As a result, many casualties were also the result of illnesses such as influenza, measles, and infections from battle wounds.

**1836**
Texans fighting for independence from Mexico are defeated by Mexican forces at the Alamo.

**1838**
Cherokee Indians are forced to move to Oklahoma, along "The Trail of Tears."

**1844**
The first telegraph line connects Washington and Baltimore.

**1846-1848**
U.S. war with Mexico: Mexico is defeated and the United States takes control of the Republic of Texas and of Mexican territories in the West.

**1848**
California "gold rush": The discovery of gold in California leads to a "rush" of more than 80,000 people to the West in search of gold.

**1852**
Uncle Tom's Cabin is published.

**1858**
Abraham Lincoln and Stephen A. Douglas debate about slavery during Senate campaign in Illinois.

**1860**
Abraham Lincoln is elected president.

**1861**
The Civil War begins.

**1863**
President Lincoln issues the Emancipation Proclamation, freeing most slaves.

**1865**
The Civil War ends as the South surrenders. Lincoln is assassinated.

**1869**
The first railroad connecting the east and west coasts is completed.

**1878**
The first telephone company begins operation.

**1890**
Battle of Wounded Knee is fought in South Dakota—the last major battle between Indians and U.S. troops.

**1898**
Spanish-American War: The United States defeats Spain, gains control of the Philippines and Puerto Rico.

## The United States in the 20th Century

### 1903
The United States begins building the Panama Canal. The canal opens in 1914, connecting the Atlantic and Pacific oceans.

### 1908
Henry Ford introduces the Model T car, the first auto bought by thousands of people.

### 1916
Jeanette Rankin of Montana becomes the first woman elected to Congress.

### 1917-1918
The United States joins World War I on the side of the Allies against Germany.

### 1920
First licensed radio broadcast.

### 1927
Charles A. Lindbergh becomes the first person to fly alone nonstop across the Atlantic Ocean.

### 1929
A stock market crash marks the beginning of the Great Depression.

### 1933
President Franklin D. Roosevelt's New Deal increases government help to people hurt by the Depression.

### 1941
Japan attacks the U.S. navy base at Pearl Harbor. The United States enters World War II against Japan, Germany, and Italy.

### 1945
Germany and Japan surrender, ending World War II. Japan's surrender comes after the United States drops atomic bombs on Hiroshima and Nagasaki.

### 1950-1953
U.S. armed forces fight in the Korean War.

### 1954
The U.S. Supreme Court outlaws racial segregation in public schools.

### 1958
The first U.S. space satellite, *Explorer I,* goes into orbit.

### 1962
Cuban Missile Crisis: The United States forces the Soviet Union to pull its missiles out of Cuba.

## World War I
In World War I the United States fought with Great Britain, France, and Russia (the Allies) against Germany and Austria-Hungary. The Allies won the war in 1918.

## The Great Depression
The stock market crash of October 1929 led to a period of severe hardship for the American people—the Great Depression. As many as 25 percent of all workers could not find jobs. The Depression lasted until the early 1940s. The Depression also led to a great change in politics. In 1932, Franklin D. Roosevelt a Democrat, was elected president. He served as president for 12 years, longer than any other president.

**1963**
President John F. Kennedy is assassinated.

**1964**
Congress passes the Civil Rights Act, which outlaws discrimination in housing and jobs.

**1965**
The United States sends large numbers of soldiers to fight in the Vietnam War.

**1968**
Civil rights leader Martin Luther King, Jr., is assassinated in Memphis. Senator Robert F. Kennedy is assassinated in Los Angeles.

**1969**
U.S. astronaut Neil Armstrong becomes first person to walk on the moon.

**1973**
U.S. participation in the Vietnam War ends.

**1974**
President Richard Nixon resigns because of the Watergate scandal.

**1976**
The United States celebrates the 200th anniversary of its independence.

**1979**
U.S. hostages are taken in Iran, beginning a 444-day crisis until their release in 1981.

**1981**
Sandra Day O'Connor becomes the first woman appointed to the U.S. Supreme Court.

**1985**
U.S. President Ronald Reagan and Soviet leader Mikhail Gorbachev begin working together to improve relations between their countries.

**1991**
The Persian Gulf War: The United States and its allies defeat Iraq.

**1992**
Bill Clinton, a Democrat, is elected president, defeating George Bush.

**1994**
The Republican Party wins majorities in both houses of Congress for the first time in 40 years.

**1996**
President Clinton is reelected, defeating Republican Bob Dole.

**1998**
The federal government announces that, for the first time in many years, it will begin receiving more money than it spends.

**Watergate**
In June 1972, six men were arrested in the Watergate building in Washington, D.C., for trying to bug the telephones in the offices of the Democratic Party. Some of the men worked for the committee to reelect President Richard Nixon. In 1973, it was discovered that President Nixon had tape-recorded his conversations in the Oval Office of the White House. One of the tapes revealed that Nixon knew about a plan to hide information about "Watergate." Facing impeachment, Nixon resigned the presidency.

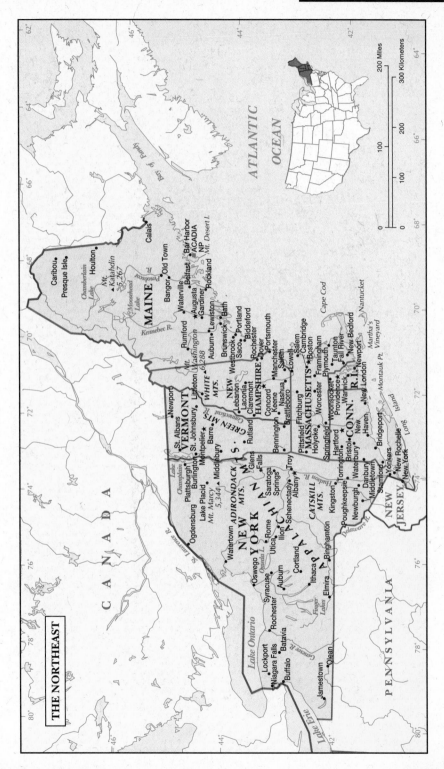

THE NORTHEAST

ATLANTIC OCEAN

C A N A D A

Bay of Fundy

Calais

Caribou
Presque Isle
Houlton

Mt. Katahdin
5,267

MAINE

Chamberlain Lake
Moosehead Lake

Old Town
Bangor
Waterville
Belfast
Augusta
Gardiner
Lewiston
Auburn
Brunswick
Saco
Biddeford
Portland
Bath

Bar Harbor
ACADIA NP
Mt. Desert I.
Rockland

Kennebec R.
Penobscot R.

Rumford
Newport
Mt. Washington 6,288
WHITE MTS.
Littleton
Lebanon
Claremont
Concord
Laconia
NEW HAMPSHIRE
Keene
Nashua

Rochester
Dover
Portsmouth
Manchester
Salem
Lowell
Salem
Boston
Cambridge
Framingham
Plymouth
Fall River
New Bedford
Newport
New London

Cape Cod
Nantucket
Martha's Vineyard

Westbrook

St. Albans
VERMONT
St. Johnsbury
Montpelier
Barre
Middlebury
Rutland
Bennington
Brattleboro

Fitchburg
Worcester
MASSACHUSETTS
Springfield
Holyoke
Hartford
Bristol
Waterbury
Torrington
New Haven
Bridgeport
Stamford
New Rochelle
Yonkers
New York

Pittsfield
CONN.
R.I.
Woonsocket
Providence
Warwick

GREEN MTS.
Connecticut R.

Lake Champlain
Plattsburgh
Burlington
Lake Placid
Mt. Marcy 5,344
ADIRONDACK MTS.
Ogdensburg
Watertown

NEW YORK
Glens Falls
Saratoga Springs
Schenectady
Troy
Albany

CATSKILL MTS.
Kingston
Poughkeepsie
Newburgh
Middletown
Danbury

NEW JERSEY

Hudson R.
Delaware R.

Oneida L.
Rome
Utica
Ilion
Oswego
Syracuse
Auburn
Cortland
Ithaca
Binghamton
Elmira

APPALACHIAN MTS.

Finger Lakes

Lake Ontario
Lockport
Niagara Falls
Buffalo
Batavia
Rochester
Genesee R.
Jamestown
Olean

Lake Erie

PENNSYLVANIA

Long Island
Montauk Pt.

St. Lawrence R.

200 Miles
300 Kilometers
0  100  200
0  100  200

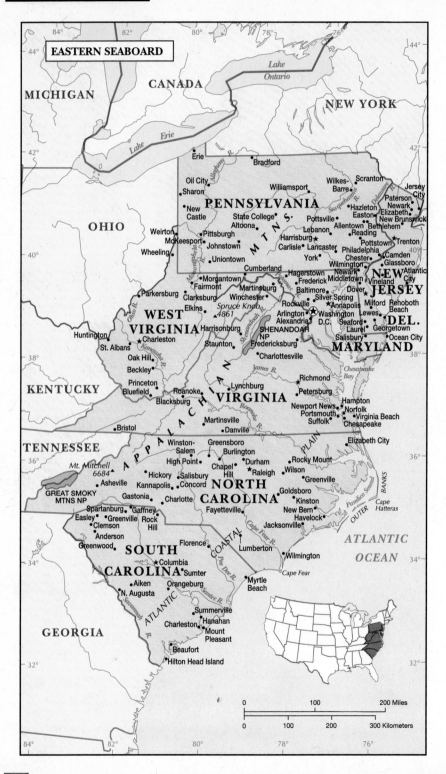

**EASTERN SEABOARD**

84° 82° 80° 78° 76°

44° 44°

**MICHIGAN**

**CANADA**

Lake Ontario

**NEW YORK**

42° 42°

Lake Erie

Erie • Bradford

• Oil City
Williamsport • Wilkes-Barre • Scranton
Jersey City
• Sharon
**PENNSYLVANIA** • Hazleton Paterson Newark
Elizabeth
New Castle State College Altoona Pottsville Easton New Brunswick
Weirton Pittsburgh Lebanon Allentown Reading Bethlehem Pottstown
McKeesport Johnstown Harrisburg ★ Carlisle Lancaster Philadelphia Trenton
Wheeling Uniontown York Wilmington Camden Glassboro
Cumberland Hagerstown Newark Atlantic City

**OHIO**

40° 40°

Morgantown Frederick Middletown Vineland **NEW**
Parkersburg Fairmont Martinsburg Baltimore Dover **JERSEY**
Clarksburg Winchester Rockville Silver Spring Milford Rehoboth Beach
**WEST** Elkins Spruce Knob Annapolis Lewes **DEL.**
**VIRGINIA** 4861 Arlington Washington Seaford Georgetown
Huntington Harrisonburg Alexandria D.C. Salisbury Ocean City
St. Albans • Charleston SHENANDOAH Laurel
Oak Hill NP Fredericksburg **MARYLAND**
Staunton
38° Beckley Charlottesville Chesapeake 38°
Bay
Princeton Richmond
**KENTUCKY** Bluefield Roanoke Lynchburg ★ Petersburg
Blacksburg **VIRGINIA** Hampton
Newport News Norfolk
Bristol Martinsville Portsmouth Virginia Beach
Danville Suffolk Chesapeake

Elizabeth City

**TENNESSEE** Winston-Salem Greensboro
36° Salem Burlington PLAIN 36°
High Point Durham Rocky Mount
Mt. Mitchell Chapel ★ Raleigh Wilson
6684 Hickory Hill
Asheville Salisbury Greenville
**GREAT SMOKY** Kannapolis Concord
MTNS NP Gastonia **NORTH** Goldsboro
Charlotte **CAROLINA** Kinston Cape Hatteras
Spartanburg Gaffney Fayetteville New Bern
Easley Greenville Rock Havelock
Clemson Hill Jacksonville
Anderson Florence
Greenwood **SOUTH** Lumberton **ATLANTIC**
Columbia Wilmington **OCEAN**
34° ★ 34°
**CAROLINA** Sumter Cape Fear
Aiken Orangeburg Myrtle
N. Augusta Beach

Summerville
Hanahan
Charleston Mount
Pleasant
32° 32°
**GEORGIA** Beaufort
Hilton Head Island

84° 82° 80° 78° 76°

0 100 200 Miles

0 100 200 300 Kilometers

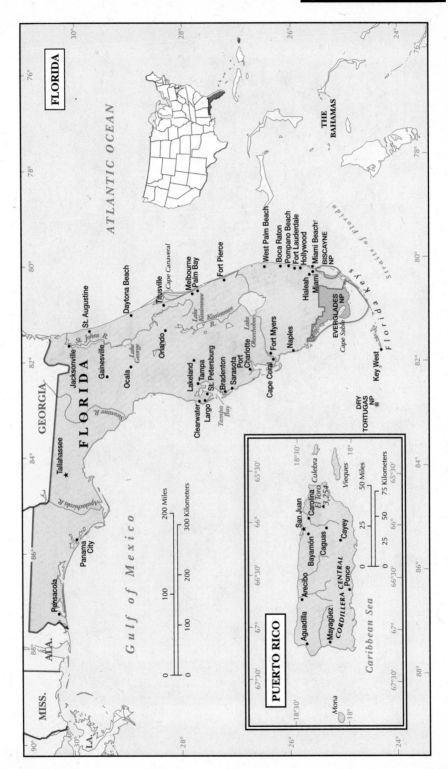

FLORIDA

FLORIDA

ATLANTIC OCEAN

THE BAHAMAS

GEORGIA

MISS. | ALA. | LA.

Gulf of Mexico

Pensacola
Panama City
Tallahassee
Apalachicola R.
Suwannee R.
Jacksonville
St. Augustine
Gainesville
Ocala
Lake George
St. Johns R.
Daytona Beach
Titusville
Cape Canaveral
Orlando
Lake Kissimmee
Kissimmee R.
Melbourne
Palm Bay
Fort Pierce
Lakeland
Tampa
Clearwater
Largo
St. Petersburg
Tampa Bay
Bradenton
Sarasota
Port Charlotte
Lake Okeechobee
Cape Coral
Fort Myers
Naples
West Palm Beach
Boca Raton
Pompano Beach
Fort Lauderdale
Hollywood
Miami Beach
Miami
Hialeah
BISCAYNE NP
EVERGLADES NP
Cape Sable
Florida Keys
Key West
Straits of Florida
DRY TORTUGAS NP

200 Miles
300 Kilometers
0   100   200
0   100   200

PUERTO RICO

Caribbean Sea

San Juan
Carolina
Culebra
El Toro 3,254
Vieques
Bayamón
Caguas
Cayey
Aguadilla
Arecibo
Mayagüez
CORDILLERA CENTRAL
Ponce
Mona

50 Miles
75 Kilometers
0   25   50
0   25   50

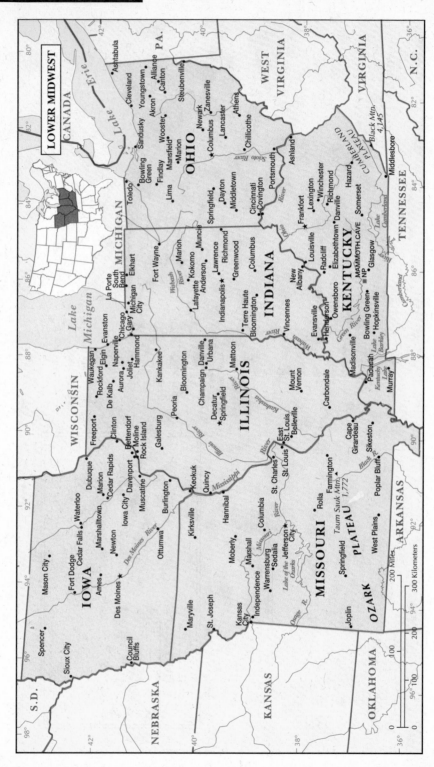

LOWER MIDWEST

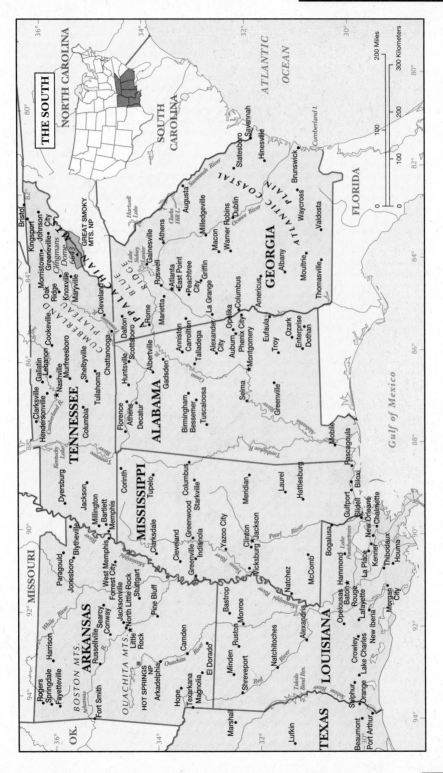

THE SOUTH

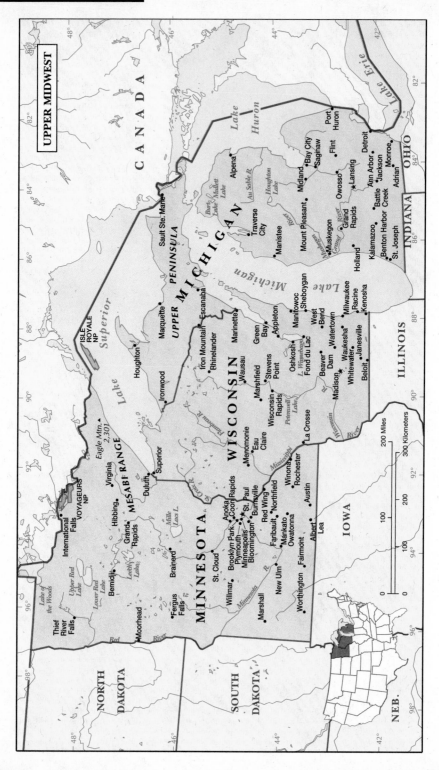

**UPPER MIDWEST**

CANADA

OHIO

INDIANA

ILLINOIS

IOWA

NORTH DAKOTA

SOUTH DAKOTA

NEB.

**MINNESOTA**

**WISCONSIN**

**MICHIGAN**

**UPPER PENINSULA**

Lake Superior

Lake Michigan

Lake Huron

Lake Erie

ISLE ROYALE NP

VOYAGEURS NP

MESABI RANGE

Eagle Mtn. ▲ 2,301

Lake of the Woods

Upper Red Lake

Lower Red Lake

Leech Lake

Mille Lacs L.

L. Winnebago

Petenwell Lake

Mullett Lake

Burt Lake

Houghton Lake

Au Sable R.

Grand River

Muskegon River

St. Croix River

Wisconsin River

Mississippi River

Flambeau R.

Red River

Minnesota R.

Thief River Falls
Moorhead
Fergus Falls
Bemidji
International Falls
Virginia
Hibbing
Grand Rapids
Brainerd
St. Cloud
Willmar
Marshall
New Ulm
Worthington
Fairmont
Albert Lea
Austin
Owatonna
Mankato
Faribault
Northfield
Red Wing
Burnsville
Bloomington
Minneapolis
Plymouth
Brooklyn Park
Anoka
Coon Rapids
St. Paul
Rochester
Winona
La Crosse
Eau Claire
Menomonie
Superior
Duluth
Ironwood
Houghton
Marquette
Sault Ste. Marie
Escanaba
Marinette
Iron Mountain
Rhinelander
Wausau
Marshfield
Stevens Point
Wisconsin Rapids
Green Bay
Appleton
Oshkosh
Fond du Lac
Beaver Dam
Watertown
Waukesha
Whitewater
Janesville
Beloit
Madison
West Bend
Milwaukee
Racine
Kenosha
Sheboygan
Manitowoc
Manistee
Traverse City
Mount Pleasant
Midland
Bay City
Saginaw
Flint
Alpena
Port Huron
Detroit
Ann Arbor
Lansing
Battle Creek
Jackson
Monroe
Adrian
Kalamazoo
Benton Harbor
St. Joseph
Holland
Grand Rapids
Muskegon
Owosso

200 Miles

300 Kilometers

0   100   200

0   100   200   300

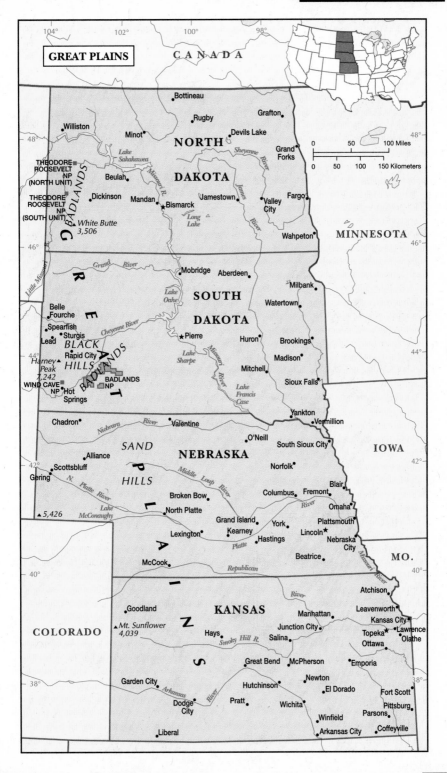

**GREAT PLAINS**

CANADA

104°  102°  100°  98°

**NORTH DAKOTA**

Bottineau
Rugby
Grafton
Williston
Minot
Devils Lake
Lake Sakakawea
Sheyenne River
Grand Forks
Beulah
Dickinson
Mandan
Bismarck
Jamestown
James River
Valley City
Fargo
Long Lake
THEODORE ROOSEVELT NP (NORTH UNIT)
THEODORE ROOSEVELT NP (SOUTH UNIT)
BADLANDS
White Butte 3,506
Wahpeton

48°

0    50    100 Miles
0    50    100    150 Kilometers

MINNESOTA

46°

**SOUTH DAKOTA**

Grand River
Mobridge
Aberdeen
Milbank
Lake Oahe
Watertown
Belle Fourche
Spearfish
Sturgis
Lead
Cheyenne River
Pierre
Huron
Brookings
BLACK HILLS
Rapid City
Madison
Harney Peak 7,242
BADLANDS
Lake Sharpe
Mitchell
WIND CAVE NP
Hot Springs
BADLANDS NP
Sioux Falls
Missouri River
Lake Francis Case
Yankton
Vermillion

44°

Chadron
Niobrara River
Valentine
O'Neill
South Sioux City
IOWA
SAND
Alliance
**NEBRASKA**
Norfolk
Scottsbluff
Gering
HILLS
Middle Loup River
Blair
Columbus
Fremont
River
Omaha
N. Platte River
Broken Bow
North Platte
Grand Island
York
Plattsmouth
Lake McConaughy
5,426
Lexington
Kearney
Hastings
Lincoln
Nebraska City
Platte
Beatrice
MO.
McCook
Republican

42°

40°

Atchison
River
Leavenworth
Goodland
**KANSAS**
Manhattan
Kansas City
Mt. Sunflower 4,039
Hays
Junction City
Topeka
Lawrence
COLORADO
Salina
Ottawa
Olathe
Great Bend
McPherson
Emporia
Garden City
Arkansas River
Hutchinson
Newton
El Dorado
Fort Scott
Dodge City
Pratt
Wichita
Pittsburg
Winfield
Parsons
Liberal
Arkansas City
Coffeyville

GREAT PLAINS

38°

247

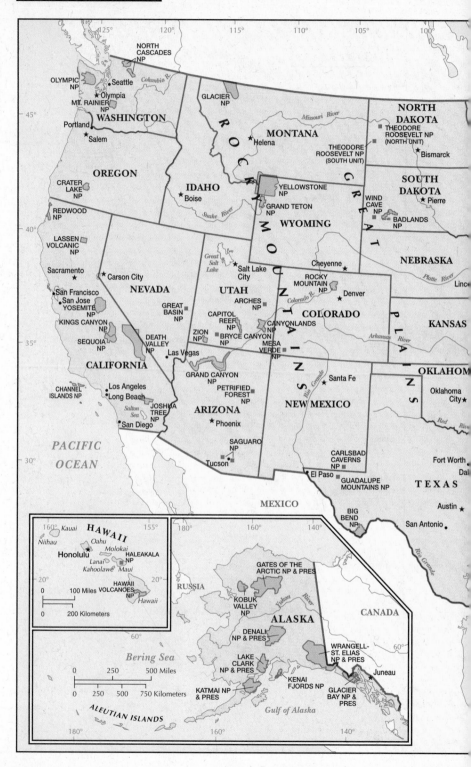

NORTH CASCADES NP

OLYMPIC NP
● Seattle
★ Olympia
MT. RAINIER NP
Portland ●
WASHINGTON
● Salem

GLACIER NP

*Columbia R.*

*Missouri River*

NORTH DAKOTA
■ THEODORE ROOSEVELT NP (NORTH UNIT)
★ Bismarck

MONTANA
● Helena

THEODORE ROOSEVELT NP (SOUTH UNIT)

OREGON

CRATER LAKE NP

R O C K

IDAHO
● Boise

*Snake River*

YELLOWSTONE NP

GRAND TETON NP

WYOMING

G R E A T

SOUTH DAKOTA
★ Pierre

WIND CAVE NP

BADLANDS NP

REDWOOD NP

LASSEN VOLCANIC NP

Sacramento ★

★ Carson City

NEVADA

*Great Salt Lake*

★ Salt Lake City

UTAH

Cheyenne ●

M O U N T A I N S

ROCKY MOUNTAIN NP

Denver ●

NEBRASKA

Linc

*Platte River*

● San Francisco
San Jose ●
YOSEMITE NP
KINGS CANYON NP

SEQUOIA NP

GREAT BASIN NP

ARCHES NP

CAPITOL REEF NP

ZION NP

BRYCE CANYON NP

CANYONLANDS NP

MESA VERDE NP

COLORADO

*Colorado R.*

KANSAS

*Arkansas River*

DEATH VALLEY NP

Las Vegas ●

CALIFORNIA

GRAND CANYON NP

PETRIFIED FOREST NP

Santa Fe ●

*Rio Grande*

OKLAHOM

Oklahoma City ★

CHANNEL ISLANDS NP

Los Angeles ●
Long Beach ●

*Salton Sea*

JOSHUA TREE NP

● San Diego

ARIZONA
● Phoenix

NEW MEXICO

SAGUARO NP

Tucson ●

CARLSBAD CAVERNS NP

El Paso ●

GUADALUPE MOUNTAINS NP

*Red River*

T E X A S

Fort Worth ●
Dal

Austin ★

San Antonio ★

PACIFIC OCEAN

MEXICO

BIG BEND NP

*Rio Grande*

HAWAII

*Kauai*
*Niihau*
*Oahu*
★ Honolulu
*Molokai*
*Lanai*
HALEAKALA NP
*Kahoolawe* *Maui*
HAWAII VOLCANOES NP
*Hawaii*

0 —— 100 Miles
0 —— 200 Kilometers

RUSSIA

*Bering Sea*

GATES OF THE ARCTIC NP & PRES

KOBUK VALLEY NP

*Yukon River*

DENALI NP & PRES

ALASKA

CANADA

WRANGELL-ST. ELIAS NP & PRES

LAKE CLARK NP & PRES

KENAI FJORDS NP

Juneau ●

GLACIER BAY NP & PRES

KATMAI NP & PRES

0 —— 250 —— 500 Miles
0 —— 250 —— 500 —— 750 Kilometers

ALEUTIAN ISLANDS

*Gulf of Alaska*

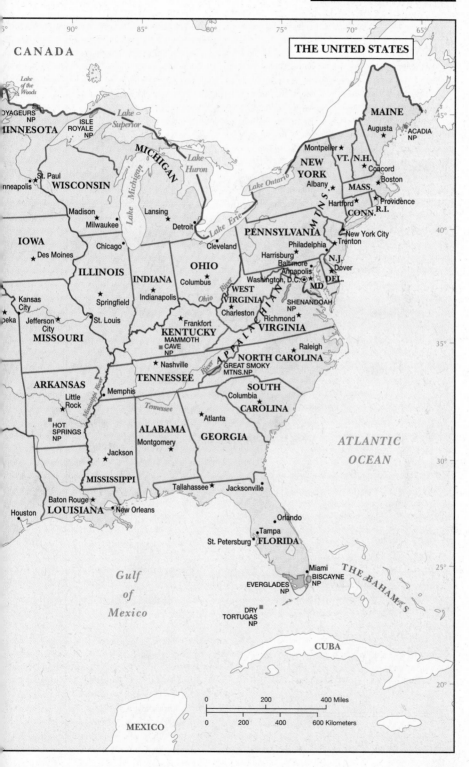

THE UNITED STATES

CANADA

MINNESOTA

VOYAGEURS NP

ISLE ROYALE NP

Lake of the Woods

Lake Superior

WISCONSIN

MICHIGAN

Lake Huron

Lake Michigan

St. Paul
Minneapolis

Madison
Milwaukee

Lansing

Detroit

Lake Erie

MAINE

Augusta

ACADIA NP

Montpelier ★

NEW YORK

VT. N.H.

Concord

Boston

Albany

MASS.

Hartford

Providence

CONN. R.I.

IOWA

Des Moines ★

Chicago

Cleveland

PENNSYLVANIA

ILLINOIS

INDIANA

OHIO

Columbus

Philadelphia

Harrisburg

New York City

Trenton

N.J.

Kansas City

Springfield

Indianapolis

Ohio River

WEST VIRGINIA

Baltimore

Annapolis

Washington, D.C. ⊕

Dover

DEL.

MD

Jefferson City

Topeka

St. Louis

Frankfort

Charleston

SHENANDOAH NP

MISSOURI

KENTUCKY

MAMMOTH CAVE NP

Nashville

Richmond

VIRGINIA

Raleigh

ARKANSAS

Little Rock

HOT SPRINGS NP

Memphis

TENNESSEE

Tennessee River

Mississippi River

GREAT SMOKY MTNS.NP

NORTH CAROLINA

SOUTH CAROLINA

Columbia

ALABAMA

Montgomery

Atlanta

GEORGIA

ATLANTIC OCEAN

MISSISSIPPI

Jackson

Tallahassee

Jacksonville

Houston

Baton Rouge ★

New Orleans

LOUISIANA

Orlando

Tampa

St. Petersburg

FLORIDA

Gulf of Mexico

Miami

BISCAYNE NP

EVERGLADES NP

THE BAHAMAS

DRY TORTUGAS NP

CUBA

MEXICO

APPALACHIAN MTNS

0   200   400 Miles

0   200   400   600 Kilometers

249

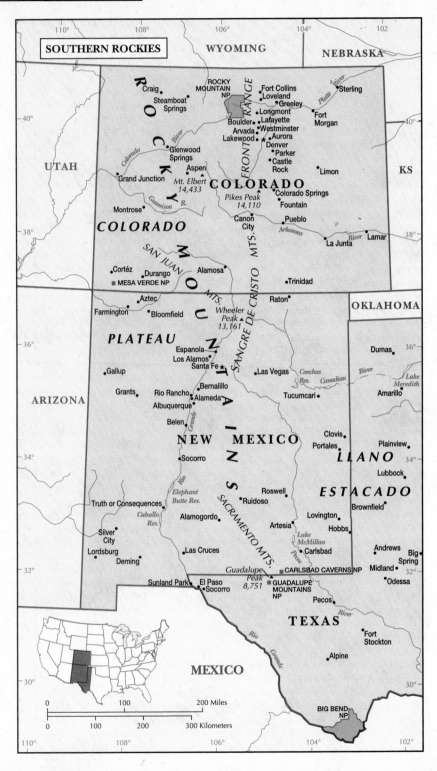

SOUTHERN ROCKIES

WYOMING

NEBRASKA

110°   108°   106°   104°   102°

ROCKY MOUNTAIN NP

Craig •
Steamboat Springs •

Fort Collins •
Loveland •
• Greeley
Longmont •
Boulder • Lafayette
Arvada • Westminster
Lakewood • Aurora
Denver •
• Parker
• Castle Rock

Sterling •

Fort Morgan •

Fort Collins

FRONT RANGE

ROCKY

Glenwood Springs •

Colorado River

Aspen •

Mt. Elbert 14,433 ▲

COLORADO

Pikes Peak 14,110 ▲

Colorado Springs •
Fountain •

Limon •

KS

Grand Junction •

Gunnison R.

Montrose •

COLORADO

Canon City •

Pueblo •

Arkansas River

La Junta •

Lamar •

MOUNTAINS

UTAH

40°

38°

SAN JUAN MTS.

Cortéz •
• Durango
■ MESA VERDE NP

Alamosa •

SANGRE DE CRISTO MTS.

Trinidad •

Aztec •

Raton •

OKLAHOMA

Farmington •

Bloomfield •

Wheeler Peak 13,161 ▲

PLATEAU

Espanola •
Los Alamos •
Santa Fe ★

Las Vegas •

Conchas Res.

Canadian River

Dumas •

Lake Meredith

36°

Gallup •

Grants •

Bernalillo •
Rio Rancho • Alameda
Albuquerque •

Belen •

Tucumcari •

Amarillo •

ARIZONA

NEW   MEXICO

Rio Grande

Socorro •

Clovis •
Portales •

Plainview •

LLANO

Lubbock •

34°

Elephant Butte Res.

Roswell •

Truth or Consequences •

Ruidoso •

ESTACADO

Brownfield •

Caballo Res.

Alamogordo •

Lovington •

Artesia •

Hobbs •

Andrews •

Big Spring •

Silver City •

SACRAMENTO MTS.

Lake McMillan

Lordsburg •

Deming •

Las Cruces •

Pecos

Carlsbad •

Midland •

Odessa •

32°

Guadalupe Peak 8,751 ▲

■ CARLSBAD CAVERNS NP

Sunland Park •
El Paso •
• Socorro

■ GUADALUPE MOUNTAINS NP

Pecos •

TEXAS

Pecos River

MEXICO

Fort Stockton •

Alpine •

Rio Grande

BIG BEND NP

30°

| 0 | 100 | 200 Miles |
| 0 | 100 | 200 | 300 Kilometers |

110°   108°   106°   104°   102°

SOUTHERN PLAINS

KANSAS

100°   98°   96°   94°

Guymon

GREAT   PLAINS

MO.
ARK.

Woodward

Bartlesville   Miami

Ponca
City   Claremore

Enid   Keystone   Tulsa
Lake   Broken Arrow

Dumas

Pampa
Lake
Meredith

Stillwater   Sapulpa   Muskogee

Amarillo

Clinton   El Reno   Edmond   Okmulgee

Robert
S. Kerr
Lake

Canadian

Oklahoma City   Shawnee

River

Chickasha   Norman

Eufaula
Lake

36°

OKLAHOMA

Altus   Ada   McAlester

Plainview

LLANO

Lawton   Duncan   OUACHITA
Lake   MTS
Texoma

34°

ESTACADO

Lubbock

Ardmore   Durant

Red   River   Paris

Wichita Falls   Denison   Texarkana

Brownfield   Sherman

Denton   Greenville

Plano

TEXAS

Andrews   Big Spring

Abilene   Garland
Irving   Dallas   Marshall

Fort Worth   Mesquite   Longview

Arlington   Sabine   River

Midland

Odessa

Colorado

Brownwood

Corsicana   Tyler

Nacogdoches

San Angelo   River   Waco   Lufkin

Sam
Rayburn
Res.

EDWARDS

Pecos

Killeen

Fort
Stockton

River

Temple   Bryan   Huntsville

Lake
Livingston

PLATEAU

College
Station

32°

30°

Round Rock

Austin

San Marcos   Houston   Baytown

Amistad
Res.

New Braunfels   Seguin   Pasadena
Texas City
Del Rio   San Antonio   Galveston

BIG BEND
NP

Victoria   Galveston
Bay
Freeport

Eagle Pass

Matagorda
Bay

MEXICO

Nueces   River

Rio Grande

28°

Alice

Laredo   Corpus
Christi

Kingsville

Falcon
Res.   Padre
Island

Gulf
of
Mexico

Edinburg   Harlingen
Mission   Pharr   San Benito
McAllen   Weslaco
Brownsville

26°

0   100   200 Miles

0   100   200   300 Kilometers

102°   100°   98°   96°

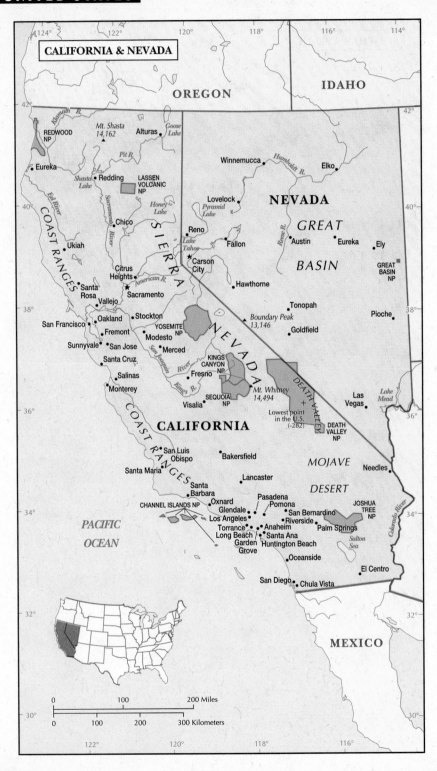

## CALIFORNIA & NEVADA

OREGON

IDAHO

REDWOOD NP

Mt. Shasta 14,162

Alturas

Goose Lake

Klamath R.

Eureka

Pit R.

Shasta Lake

Redding

LASSEN VOLCANIC NP

Ed River

Sacramento River

Honey Lake

Winnemucca

Humboldt R.

Elko

NEVADA

Lovelock

Pyramid Lake

GREAT

Chico

Reno

Lake Tahoe

Fallon

Reese R.

Austin

Eureka

Ely

COAST RANGES

Ukiah

BASIN

GREAT BASIN NP

Citrus Heights

Santa Rosa

Carson City

American R.

Sacramento

Hawthorne

Vallejo

SIERRA

Tonopah

Pioche

San Francisco

Oakland

Stockton

YOSEMITE NP

Boundary Peak 13,146

Fremont

Modesto

Sunnyvale

San Jose

Merced

NEVADA

Goldfield

Santa Cruz

San Joaquin River

KINGS CANYON NP

Salinas

Fresno

King's R.

DEATH VALLEY

Las Vegas

Lake Mead

Monterey

Visalia

SEQUOIA NP

Mt. Whitney 14,494

Lowest point in the U.S. (-282)

DEATH VALLEY NP

CALIFORNIA

San Luis Obispo

Bakersfield

MOJAVE

Needles

Santa Maria

COAST RANGES

Lancaster

DESERT

Santa Barbara

PACIFIC

OCEAN

CHANNEL ISLANDS NP

Oxnard

Glendale

Los Angeles

Torrance

Long Beach

Garden Grove

Pasadena

Pomona

San Bernardino

Riverside

Anaheim

Santa Ana

Huntington Beach

Palm Springs

JOSHUA TREE NP

Salton Sea

Colorado River

Oceanside

El Centro

San Diego

Chula Vista

MEXICO

| 0 | 100 | 200 Miles |

| 0 | 100 | 200 | 300 Kilometers |

**ARIZONA & UTAH**

WYOMING

NEVADA

UTAH

NEW MEXICO

COLORADO

CALIFORNIA

ARIZONA

MEXICO

GREAT SALT LAKE DESERT

*Great Salt Lake*

*Bear Lake*

• Logan
• Brigham City
Roy • • Ogden
• Clearfield
• Layton
• Bountiful
Salt Lake City ★
West Jordan • • Murray
• Sandy
Tooele •
*Utah Lake* • Orem
• Provo
Payson •

RANGE

▲ Kings Peak
13,528
UINTA MTS
Vernal •

*Green River*

WASATCH

• Price

*Sevier Lake*

• Richfield

Green River •
ARCHES NP ■
CAPITOL REEF NP
CANYONLANDS NP
• Moab

*Sevier River*

COLORADO

Cedar City •
BRYCE CANYON NP

Saint George
ZION NP

Blanding •

*Lake Powell*
*San Juan River*

*Colorado River*

• Page
• Kayenta

*Lake Mead*

GRAND CANYON
GRAND CANYON NP

PAINTED DESERT

Kingman •
Bullhead City •

Humphreys Peak
12,633 ▲
Flagstaff •

Winslow •
• Holbrook

PETRIFIED FOREST NP ■

Cottonwood •

Prescott •

Lake Havasu City •
*Lake Havasu*

*Verde R.*

ARIZONA

*Colorado River*

Peoria •
Glendale • • Scottsdale
Phoenix ★ • Mesa
Tempe •
Chandler •

*Salt River*

• Globe

Apache Junction •

*Gila River*

Casa Grande •
• Coolidge

• Eloy

Safford •

*Gila R.*

Yuma •

SONORAN DESERT

• Tucson
SAGUARO NP ■

• Sierra Vista
Nogales • Bisbee • • Douglas

MEXICO

0        100        200 Miles

0    100    200    300 Kilometers

253

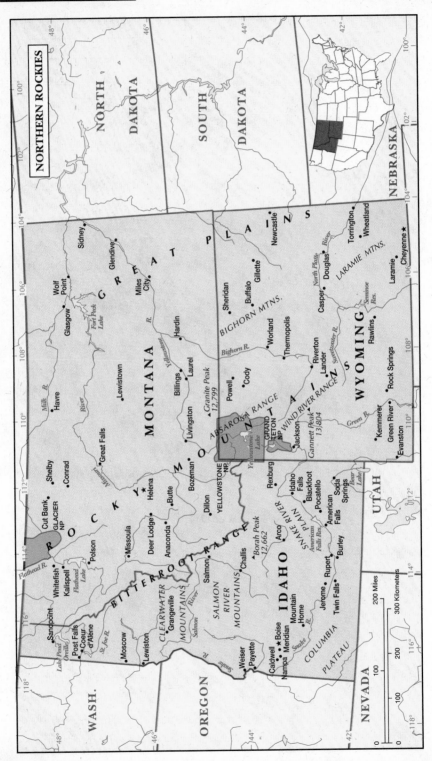

NORTHERN ROCKIES

NORTH DAKOTA

SOUTH DAKOTA

NEBRASKA

GREAT PLAINS

Sidney
Glendive
Wolf Point
Glasgow
Fort Peck Lake
Miles City
Hardin
Havre
Lewistown
Laurel
Billings
Livingston
Great Falls
Bozeman
Shelby
Conrad
Helena
Butte
Dillon
Deer Lodge
Anaconda
Missoula
Polson
Cut Bank
GLACIER NP
Whitefish
Kalispell
Sandpoint
Coeur d'Alene
Post Falls
Moscow
Lewiston
Grangeville

MONTANA

ROCKY MOUNTAINS

Milk R.
Missouri River
Marias R.
Yellowstone R.
Granite Peak 12,799
ABSAROKA RANGE
Flathead R.
Flathead Lake
Lake Pend Oreille
St. Joe R.

BITTERROOT RANGE

CLEARWATER MOUNTAINS
SALMON RIVER MOUNTAINS
Salmon
Challis
Salmon R.
Borah Peak 12,662

IDAHO

Weiser
Payette
Caldwell
Nampa
Meridian
Boise
Mountain Home
Jerome
Rupert
Twin Falls
Burley
Arco
SNAKE RIVER PLAIN
American Falls Res.
COLUMBIA PLATEAU
Snake R.

Rexburg
Idaho Falls
Blackfoot
Pocatello
American Falls
Soda Springs
Bear Lake

UTAH

NEVADA

OREGON

WASH.

YELLOWSTONE NP
Yellowstone Lake
Jackson Lake
GRAND TETON NP
Powell
Cody
Worland
Thermopolis
Riverton
Lander
Gannett Peak 13,804
WIND RIVER RANGE
Jackson

Newcastle
Gillette
Buffalo
Sheridan
BIGHORN MTNS.
Bighorn R.

WYOMING

Casper
Douglas
North Platte River
LARAMIE MTNS.
Seminoe Res.
Sweetwater R.
Green R.
Rawlins
Rock Springs
Kemmerer
Green River
Evanston
Torrington
Wheatland
Laramie
Cheyenne ★

48° 46° 44° 42° 100°
100°
102°
104°
106°
108°
110°
112°
114°
116°
118°
48°
46°
44°
42°

200 Miles
300 Kilometers
0 100 200
0 100 200 300

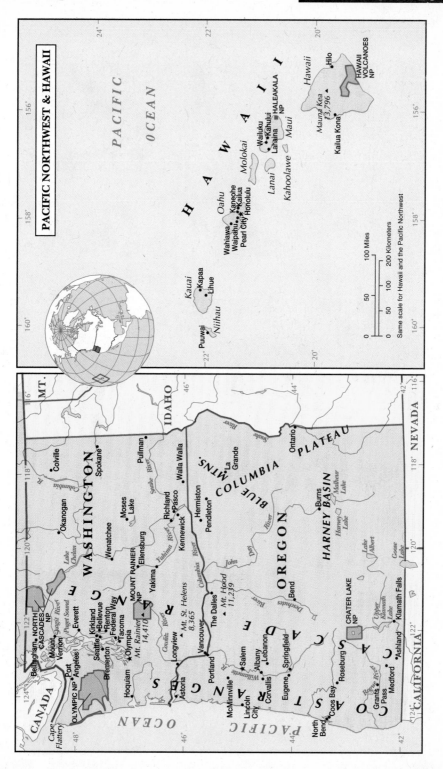

PACIFIC NORTHWEST & HAWAII

PACIFIC OCEAN

HAWAII

*Kauai*
Kapaa
Lihue

*Niihau*
Puuwai

Wahiawa
Waipahu
Pearl City
Honolulu
Kaneohe
Kailua

*Oahu*

*Molokai*

*Lanai*

Wailuku
Kahului
Lahaina
HALEAKALA NP

*Maui*

*Kahoolawe*

*Hawaii*

Mauna Kea
13,796 ▲

HAWAII VOLCANOES NP

Hilo

Kailua Kona

100 Miles
50
0

200 Kilometers
100
50
0

Same scale for Hawaii and the Pacific Northwest

MT.

IDAHO

NEVADA

CALIFORNIA

CANADA

WASHINGTON

Columbia R.

Colville

Okanogan

Lake Chelan

Wenatchee

Moses Lake

Spokane

Pullman

Snake River

Walla Walla

Pasco

Richland

Kennewick

Hermiston

Pendleton

La Grande

Snake River

Ontario

COLUMBIA PLATEAU

BLUE MTNS.

Puget Sound

Bellingham
Mount Vernon
Port Angeles
OLYMPIC NP
Everett
Kirkland
Bellevue
Renton
Federal Way
Seattle
Bremerton
Tacoma
Olympia
Hoquiam
NORTH CASCADES NP
Skagit River

MOUNT RAINIER NP
Mt. Rainier
14,410 ▲

Ellensburg

Yakima

Mt. St. Helens
8,365 ▲

The Dalles

Mt. Hood
11,239 ▲

Yakima River

Columbia River

Cowlitz R.

Longview

Vancouver

Portland

Astoria

Lincoln City

McMinnville

Salem

Albany

Corvallis

Lebanon

Springfield

Eugene

Willamette R.

OREGON

Bend

Deschutes River

John Day River

Burns

HARNEY BASIN

Malheur Lake

Harney Lake

Lake Albert

CASCADE RANGE

COAST RANGES

North Bend
Coos Bay

Roseburg

CRATER LAKE NP

Upper Klamath Lake

Klamath Falls

Goose Lake

Grants Pass
Medford
Ashland

Rogue River

PACIFIC OCEAN

Cape Flattery

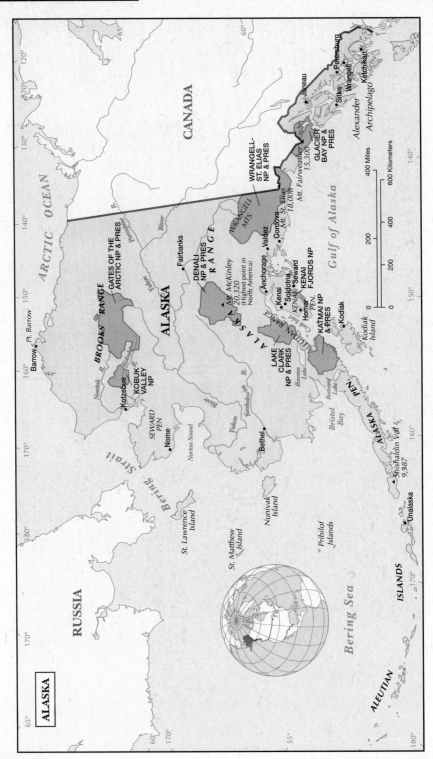

ALASKA

# FACTS About the STATES

After every state name is the postal abbreviation for the state. The Area includes both land and water. It is given in both square miles (sq. mi.) and square kilometers (sq. km.). The numbers in parentheses after Population, Area, and Entered Union show the state's rank compared with other states. For example, Alabama is the 23rd largest state in population.

## ALABAMA (AL)

*Heart of Dixie, Camellia State*

**Population** (1997): 4,319,154 (23rd)
**Area:** 52,423 sq. mi. (30th) (135,775 sq. km.)
**Entered Union:** December 14, 1819 (22nd)
**Flower:** Camellia          **Bird:** Yellowhammer
**Tree:** Southern pine       **Song:** "Alabama"
**Capital:** Montgomery
**Largest Cities** (with population): Birmingham, 258,543;
Mobile, 202,581; Montgomery, 196,363; Huntsville, 170,424
**Important Products:** clothing and textiles, metal products, transportation equipment, paper, industrial machinery, food products, lumber, coal, oil, natural gas, livestock, peanuts, cotton
**Places to Visit:** Alabama Space and Rocket Center, Huntsville; DeSoto State Park, near Fort Payne
**WEB SITE** http://alaweb.asc.edu

 **DID YOU KNOW?** Montgomery, Alabama, was the first capital of the Confederate States of America (1861). Alabama is a major center for rocket and space research.

## ALASKA (AK)

*The Last Frontier*

**Population** (1997): 609,311 (48th)
**Area:** 656,424 sq. mi. (1st) (1,700,139 sq. km.)
**Entered Union:** January 3, 1959 (49th)
**Flower:** Forget-me-not     **Bird:** Willow ptarmigan
**Tree:** Sitka spruce        **Song:** "Alaska's Flag"
**Capital:** Juneau (population, 29,756)
**Largest Cities** (with population): Anchorage, 250,505; Fairbanks, 32,960
**Important Products:** oil, natural gas, fish, food products, lumber and wood products, fur
**Places to Visit:** Glacier Bay and Denali national parks, Mendenhall Glacier, Mount McKinley
**WEB SITE** http://www.state.ak.us

 **DID YOU KNOW?** Mount McKinley is the highest mountain in the United States. Alaska is the biggest and coldest state in the United States.

## ARIZONA (AZ)

*Grand Canyon State*

**Population** (1997): 4,554,966 (21st)
**Area:** 114,006 sq. mi. (6th) (295,276 sq. km.)
**Entered Union:** February 14, 1912 (48th)
**Flower:** Blossom of the Saguaro cactus    **Bird:** Cactus wren
**Tree:** Paloverde                          **Song:** "Arizona"
**Capital and Largest City:** Phoenix (population, 1,159,014)
**Other Large Cities** (with population): Tucson, 449,002; Mesa, 344,764; Glendale, 182,219; Scottsdale, 179,012; Tempe, 162,701
**Important Products:** electronic equipment, transportation and industrial equipment, instruments, printing and publishing, copper and other metals
**Places to Visit:** Grand Canyon, Painted Desert, Petrified Forest, Hoover Dam
**WEB SITE** http://www.state.az.us

**DID YOU KNOW?** The Grand Canyon is the largest land gorge in the world and one of the world's natural wonders. It is 217 miles long and from 4 to 18 miles wide at the rim.

## ARKANSAS (AR)

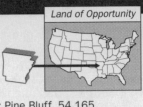

Land of Opportunity

**Population** (1997): 2,522,819 (33rd)
**Area:** 53,182 sq. mi. (29th) (137,742 sq. km.)
**Flower:** Apple blossom      **Bird:** Mockingbird
**Tree:** Pine      **Song:** "Arkansas"
**Entered Union:** June 15, 1836 (25th)
**Capital and Largest City:** Little Rock (population, 175,752)
**Other Large Cities** (with population): North Little Rock, 60,468; Pine Bluff, 54,165
**Important Products:** food products, paper, electronic equipment, industrial machinery, metal products, lumber and wood products, livestock, soybeans, rice, cotton, natural gas
**Places to Visit:** Hot Springs National Park, Fort Smith National Historic Site
**WEB SITE** http://www.state.ar.us

**DID YOU KNOW?** Arkansas has the only working diamond mine in North America. President Bill Clinton was born in Arkansas and served as one of its governors.

## CALIFORNIA (CA)

Golden State

**Population** (1997): 32,268,301 (1st)
**Area:** 163,707 sq. mi. (3rd) (424,002 sq. km.)
**Flower:** Golden poppy      **Bird:** California valley quail
**Tree:** California redwood      **Song:** "I Love You, California"
**Entered Union:** September 9, 1850 (31st)
**Capital:** Sacramento (population, 376,243)
**Largest Cities** (with population): Los Angeles, 3,553,638; San Diego, 1,171,121; San Jose, 838,744; San Francisco, 735,315
**Important Products:** transportation and industrial equipment, electronic equipment, oil, natural gas, motion pictures, milk, cattle, fruit and vegetables
**Places to Visit:** Yosemite Valley, Lake Tahoe, Palomar Observatory, Disneyland, San Diego Zoo, Hollywood, Sequoia National Park
**WEB SITE** http://www.state.ca.us

**DID YOU KNOW?** California has more people, more cars, more schools, and more businesses than any other state in the United States. The oldest living things on earth are believed to be the Bristlecone pine trees in California's Inyo National Forest, estimated to be 4,700 years old. The world's tallest tree, 365 feet tall and 44 feet around, is a redwood tree in Humboldt County.

## COLORADO (CO)

Centennial State

**Population** (1997): 3,892,644 (25th)
**Area:** 104,100 sq. mi. (8th) (269,620 sq. km.)
**Flower:** Rocky Mountain columbine      **Bird:** Lark bunting
**Tree:** Colorado blue spruce      **Song:** "Where the Columbines
**Entered Union:** August 1, 1876 (38th)      Grow"
**Capital and Largest City:** Denver (population, 497,840)
**Other Large Cities** (with population): Colorado Springs, 345,127; Aurora, 252,341; Lakewood, 134,999
**Important Products:** instruments and industrial machinery, food products, printing and publishing, metal products, electronic equipment, oil, coal, cattle
**Places to Visit:** Rocky Mountain National Park, Mesa Verde National Park, Dinosaur National Monument, old mining towns
**WEB SITE** http://www.state.co.us

**DID YOU KNOW?** The Grand Mesa in Colorado is the world's largest flat-top mountain. The highest bridge in the world (1,053 feet) is in Colorado—it is the suspension bridge over the Royal Gorge of the Arkansas River. Colorado has more mountains over 14,000 feet and more elk than any other state.

## CONNECTICUT (CT)

Constitution State, Nutmeg State

**Population** (1997): 3,269,858 (28th)
**Area:** 5,544 sq. mi. (48th) (14,358 sq. km.)
**Flower:** Mountain laurel   **Bird:** American robin
**Tree:** White oak   **Song:** "Yankee Doodle"
**Entered Union:** January 9, 1788 (5th)
**Capital:** Hartford
**Largest Cities** (with population): Bridgeport, 137,990; Hartford, 133,086; New Haven, 124,665; Waterbury, 106,412; Stamford, 110,056
**Important Products:** aircraft parts and helicopters, industrial machinery, metals and metal products, electronic equipment, printing and publishing, instruments, chemicals, dairy products, stone
**Places to Visit:** Mystic Seaport and Marine Life Aquarium, in Mystic; P.T. Barnum circus museum, Bridgeport; Peabody Museum, New Haven
**WEB SITE** http://www.state.ct.us

 **DID YOU KNOW?** The first library for children opened in Salisbury, in 1803, and the first permanent school for the deaf opened in Hartford in 1817. The first woman to receive an American patent was Mary Kies of South Killingly, in 1809, for a machine to weave straw and silk or thread.

## DELAWARE (DE)

First State, Diamond State

**Population** (1997): 731,581 (46th)
**Area:** 2,489 sq. mi. (49th) (6,447 sq. km.)
**Flower:** Peach blossom   **Bird:** Blue hen chicken
**Tree:** American holly   **Song:** "Our Delaware"
**Entered Union:** December 7, 1787 (1st)
**Capital:** Dover
**Largest Cities** (with population): Wilmington, 69,490; Dover, 30,414; Newark, 27,870
**Important Products:** chemicals, food products, instruments, chickens
**Places to Visit:** Rehoboth Beach, Henry Francis du Pont Winterthur Museum near Wilmington
**WEB SITE** http://www.state.de.us

**DID YOU KNOW?** Delaware was the first state to agree to the Constitution and thus became the first state of the United States. Delaware had the first log cabins in America.

## FLORIDA (FL)

Sunshine State

**Population** (1997): 14,653,945 (4th)
**Area:** 65,756 sq. mi. (22nd) (170,308 sq. km.)
**Flower:** Orange blossom   **Bird:** Mockingbird
**Tree:** Sabal palmetto palm   **Song:** "Old Folks at Home"
**Entered Union:** March 3, 1845 (27th)
**Capital:** Tallahassee (population, 136,812)
**Largest Cities** (with population): Jacksonville, 679,792; Miami, 365,127; Tampa, 285,206; Saint Petersburg, 235,988
**Important Products:** electronic and transportation equipment, instruments, printing and publishing, food products, citrus fruits, vegetables, livestock, phosphates, fish
**Places to Visit:** Walt Disney World and Universal Studios, near Orlando; Sea World, Orlando; Busch Gardens, Tampa; Spaceport USA, at Kennedy Space Center, Cape Canaveral; Everglades National Park
**WEB SITE** http://www.state.fl.us

 **DID YOU KNOW?** St. Augustine, Florida, is the oldest permanent European settlement in the United States. Florida grows more citrus fruit than any other state. Also, Florida's warm, sunny climate attracts people from all over the country who are retired from their jobs. One out of every five people there is over the age of 65.

## GEORGIA (GA)

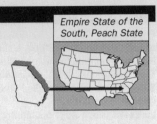

Empire State of the South, Peach State

**Population** (1997): 7,486,442 (10th)
**Area:** 59,441 sq. mi. (24th) (153,953 sq. km.)
**Flower:** Cherokee rose    **Bird:** Brown thrasher
**Tree:** Live oak    **Song:** "Georgia on My Mind"
**Entered Union:** January 2, 1788 (4th)
**Capital and Largest City:** Atlanta (population, 401,907)
**Other Large Cities** (with population): Columbus, 182,828;
Savannah, 136,262; Macon, 113,352
**Important Products:** clothing and textiles, transportation equipment, food products, paper, chickens, peanuts, peaches, clay
**Places to Visit:** Stone Mountain Park, Six Flags Over Georgia, New Echota State Historic Site (eastern Cherokee capital) in Calhoun
**WEB SITE** http://www.state.ga.us

 **DID YOU KNOW?** Georgia has more woods than any other state. The first U.S. gold rush took place in Georgia. The first American Indian newspaper was published in Georgia by a Cherokee in 1828. The first radio station owned and operated by African-Americans started in Atlanta in 1949. Civil rights leader Martin Luther King, Jr. (1929-1968) and baseball player Jackie Robinson (1919-1972) were born in Georgia. Georgia's capital city, Atlanta, hosted the Olympic Games in 1996.

## HAWAII (HI)

Aloha State

**Population** (1997): 1,186,602 (41st)
**Area:** 10,932 sq. mi. (43rd) (28,313 sq. km.)
**Flower:** Yellow hibiscus    **Bird:** Hawaiian goose
**Tree:** Kukui    **Song:** "Hawaii Ponoi"
**Entered Union:** August 21, 1959 (50th)
**Capital and Largest City:** Honolulu (population, 423,475)
**Other Large Cities** (with population): Hilo, 37,808; Kailua, 36,818; Kaneohe, 35,448
**Important Products:** food products, pineapples, sugarcane, printing and publishing, fish, stone
**Places to Visit:** Hawaii Volcanoes National Park; Haleakala National Park, Maui; Iolani Palace, Honolulu; U.S.S. *Arizona* Memorial, Pearl Harbor
**WEB SITE** http://www.state.hi.us

 **DID YOU KNOW?** Hawaii is the only state made up entirely of islands, 122 of them. (People live on 7 of the islands.) Hawaii's Mauna Loa is the biggest active volcano in the United States.

## IDAHO (ID)

Gem State

**Population** (1997): 1,210,232 (40th)
**Area:** 83,574 sq. mi. (14th) (216,456 sq. km.)
**Flower:** Syringa    **Bird:** Mountain bluebird
**Tree:** White pine    **Song:** "Here We Have Idaho"
**Entered Union:** July 3, 1890 (43rd)
**Capital and Largest City:** Boise (population, 152,737)
**Other Large Cities** (with population): Pocatello, 51,344; Idaho Falls, 48,079
**Important Products:** potatoes, hay, wheat, cattle, milk, lumber and wood products, food products
**Places to Visit:** Sun Valley; Hells Canyon; Craters of the Moon, near Arco; Nez Percé National Historical Park, near Lewiston; ghost towns
**WEB SITE** http://www.state.id.us

 **DID YOU KNOW?** The first hydroelectric power plant built by the federal government was the Minidoka Dam on the Snake River in Idaho; the first unit started in 1909. Two-thirds of all potatoes grown in the United States are grown in Idaho.

## ILLINOIS (IL)

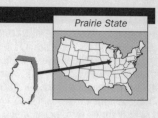

Prairie State

**Population** (1997): 11,895,849 (6th)
**Area:** 57,918 sq. mi. (25th) (150,007 sq. km.)
**Flower:** Native violet          **Bird:** Cardinal
**Tree:** White oak          **Song:** "Illinois"
**Entered Union:** December 3, 1818 (21st)
**Capital:** Springfield
**Largest Cities** (with population): Chicago, 2,721,547;
Rockford, 143,531; Peoria, 112,306; Aurora, 116,405; Springfield, 112,921
**Important Products:** industrial machinery, metals and metal products, printing and publishing, electronic equipment, food products, corn, soybeans, hogs
**Places to Visit:** Lincoln Park Zoo, Adler Planetarium, Field Museum of Natural History, and Museum of Science and Industry, all in Chicago; Abraham Lincoln's home and tomb, Springfield; New Salem Village
**WEB SITE** http://www.state.il.us

 **DID YOU KNOW?** Illinois has one of the world's busiest airports (O'Hare) and the tallest building in the U.S. (the Sears Tower in Chicago). The world's first skyscraper was built in Chicago, in 1885. Abraham Lincoln lived and worked in Illinois and is buried there.

## INDIANA (IN)

Hoosier State

**Population** (1997): 5,864,108 (14th)
**Area:** 36,420 sq. mi. (38th) (94,328 sq. km.)
**Flower:** Peony          **Bird:** Cardinal
**Tree:** Tulip poplar          **Song:** "On the Banks of the Wabash, Far Away"
**Entered Union:** December 11, 1816 (19th)
**Capital and Largest City:** Indianapolis (population, 746,737)
**Other Large Cities** (with population): Fort Wayne, 184,783; Evansville, 123,456; Gary, 110,975; South Bend, 102,100
**Important Products:** transportation equipment, electronic equipment, industrial machinery, iron and steel, metal products, corn, soybeans, livestock, coal
**Places to Visit:** Children's Museum, Indianapolis; Conner Prairie Pioneer Settlement, Noblesville; Lincoln Boyhood Memorial, Lincoln City; Wyandotte Cave
**WEB SITE** http://www.state.in.us

 **DID YOU KNOW?** The first city to be lit with electricity was Wabash. Indiana's Lost River travels 22 miles underground. Indiana is the biggest basketball state and home of the famous Indianapolis 500 auto race.

## IOWA (IA)

Hawkeye State

**Population** (1997): 2,852,423 (30th)
**Area:** 56,276 sq. mi. (26th) (145,754 sq. km.)
**Flower:** Wild rose          **Bird:** Eastern goldfinch
**Tree:** Oak          **Song:** "The Song of Iowa"
**Entered Union:** December 28, 1846 (29th)
**Capital and Largest City:** Des Moines (population, 193,422)
**Other Large Cities** (with population): Cedar Rapids, 113,482; Davenport, 97,010; Sioux City, 83,791
**Important Products:** corn, soybeans, hogs, cattle, industrial machinery, food products
**Places to Visit:** Effigy Mounds National Monument, Marquette; Herbert Hoover Birthplace, West Branch; Living History Farms, Des Moines; Adventureland; the Amana Colonies; Fort Dodge Historical Museum
**WEB SITE** http://www.state.ia.us

 **DID YOU KNOW?** The bridge built in 1856 between Davenport and Rock Island was the first bridge to span the Mississippi River. Buffalo Bill Cody (1846-1917), who was a frontiersman and the head of a famous Wild West show, was born in Iowa.

## KANSAS (KS)

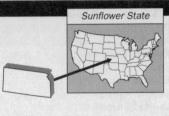

Sunflower State

**Population** (1997): 2,594,840 (32nd)
**Area:** 82,282 sq. mi. (15th) (213,110 sq. km.)
**Flower:** Native sunflower    **Bird:** Western meadowlark
**Tree:** Cottonwood    **Song:** "Home on the Range"
**Entered Union:** January 29, 1861 (34th)
**Capital:** Topeka
**Largest Cities** (with population): Wichita, 320,395;
Kansas City, 142,654; Overland Park, 131,053; Topeka, 119,658
**Important Products:** cattle, aircraft and other transportation equipment, industrial machinery, food products, wheat, corn, hay, oil, natural gas
**Places to Visit:** Dodge City; Fort Scott and Fort Larned national historical sites; Dwight D. Eisenhower Museum and Home, Abilene; Kansas Cosmosphere and Space Discovery Center, Hutchinson
**WEB SITE** http://www.state.ks.us

**DID YOU KNOW?** Kansas is located at the geographical center of the United States (excluding Alaska and Hawaii). It is one of the two biggest U.S. wheat-growing states (the other is North Dakota). The carousel with jumping horses was invented in Kansas in 1898.

## KENTUCKY (KY)

Bluegrass State

**Population** (1997): 3,908,124 (24th)
**Area:** 40,411 sq. mi. (37th) (104,665 sq. km.)
**Flower:** Goldenrod    **Bird:** Cardinal
**Tree:** Tulip poplar    **Song:** "My Old Kentucky Home"
**Entered Union:** June 1, 1792 (15th)
**Capital:** Frankfort (population, 26,695)
**Largest Cities** (with population): Louisville, 260,689; Lexington 239,942
**Important Products:** coal, industrial machinery, electronic equipment, transportation equipment, metals, tobacco, cattle
**Places to Visit:** Mammoth Cave National Park; Lincoln Birthplace, Hodgenville; Cumberland Gap National Historical Park, Middlesboro
**WEB SITE** http://www.state.ky.us

**DID YOU KNOW?** Kentucky has the longest group of caves in the world (Mammoth Caves). Abraham Lincoln was born in Kentucky. Kentucky is also the home of the Kentucky Derby, the most famous horse race in America.

## LOUISIANA (LA)

Pelican State

**Population** (1997): 4,351,769 (22nd)
**Area:** 51,844 sq. mi. (31st) (134,275 sq. km.)
**Flower:** Magnolia    **Bird:** Eastern brown pelican
**Tree:** Cypress    **Songs:** "Give Me Louisiana";
"You Are My Sunshine"
**Entered Union:** April 30, 1812 (18th)
**Capital:** Baton Rouge
**Largest Cities** (with population): New Orleans, 476,625; Baton Rouge, 215,882; Shreveport, 191,558
**Important Products:** natural gas, oil, chemicals, transportation equipment, paper, food products, cotton, fish
**Places to Visit:** French quarter in New Orleans; Jean Lafitte National Historical Park
**WEB SITE** http://www.state.la.us

**DID YOU KNOW?** The busiest port in the United States is located in Louisiana. It's the second-biggest mining state (after Alaska). Louisiana is the home of New Orleans, known for its jazz and the colorful Mardi Gras festival.

## MAINE (ME)

*Pine Tree State*

**Population** (1997): 1,242,051 (39th)
**Area:** 35,387 sq. mi. (39th) (91,653 sq. km.)
**Flower:** White pine cone and tassel    **Bird:** Chickadee
**Tree:** Eastern white pine    **Song:** "State of Maine
**Entered Union:** March 15, 1820 (23rd)    Song"
**Capital:** Augusta (population, 20,441)
**Largest Cities** (with population): Portland, 63,123; Lewiston, 36,830; Bangor, 33,649
**Important Products:** paper, transportation equipment, wood and wood products, electronic equipment, footwear, clothing, potatoes, milk, eggs, fish and seafood
**Places to Visit:** Acadia National Park, Bar Harbor; Booth Bay Railway Museum; Portland Headlight lighthouse, near Portland
**WEB SITE** http://www.state.me.us

 **DID YOU KNOW?** Maine is known for its lobsters, rocky seacoast, fishing villages, and the highest tides in the United States. Mount Katahdin, the highest spot in Maine (5,267 feet), is the first place in the United States where the sun hits in the morning.

## MARYLAND (MD)

*Old Line State,
Free State*

**Population** (1997): 5,094,289 (19th)
**Area:** 12,407 sq. mi. (42nd) (32,135 sq. km.)
**Flower:** Black-eyed susan    **Bird:** Baltimore oriole
**Tree:** White oak    **Song:** "Maryland, My Maryland"
**Entered Union:** April 28, 1788 (7th)
**Capital:** Annapolis (population, 33,234)
**Largest Cities** (with population): Baltimore, 675,401;
Rockville, 46,019; Frederick, 40,148; Gaithersburg, 45,361
**Important Products:** instruments, printing and publishing, food products, transportation equipment, electronic equipment, chickens, milk, corn, stone
**Places to Visit:** Antietam National Battlefield; Fort McHenry National Monument, in Baltimore harbor; U.S. Naval Academy in Annapolis
**WEB SITE** http://www.state.md.us

 **DID YOU KNOW?** Maryland is the narrowest state—near the town of Hancock, Maryland is only about one mile wide. The American flag on Fort McHenry during the War of 1812 inspired Francis Scott Key to write "The Star-Spangled Banner," the national anthem.

## MASSACHUSETTS (MA)

*Bay State, Old Colony*

**Population** (1997): 6,117,520 (13th)
**Area:** 10,555 sq. mi. (44th) (27,337 sq. km.)
**Flower:** Mayflower    **Bird:** Chickadee
**Tree:** American elm    **Song:** "All Hail to Massachusetts"
**Entered Union:** February 6, 1788 (6th)
**Capital and Largest City:** Boston (population: 558,394)
**Other Large Cities** (with population): Worcester, 166,350;
Springfield, 149,948; Lowell, 100,973
**Important Products:** industrial machinery, electronic equipment, instruments, printing and publishing, metal products, clothing and textiles, fish, flowers and shrubs, cranberries
**Places to Visit:** Plymouth Rock, historical sites in Boston, and Minute Man National Historical Park; Children's Museum, Boston; Basketball Hall of Fame, Springfield; Old Sturbridge Village; Martha's Vineyard; Cape Cod
**WEB SITE** http://www.state.ma.us

 **DID YOU KNOW?** The Pilgrims settled in Massachusetts in 1620 and celebrated the first Thanksgiving. Massachusetts is known for other American firsts: the first printing press (1639), the first public school paid for by taxes (1639), and the first college (Harvard, 1636). The American Revolution began in Massachusetts.

## MICHIGAN (MI)

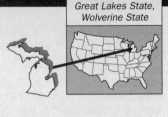
*Great Lakes State, Wolverine State*

**Population** (1997): 9,773,892 (8th)
**Area:** 96,705 sq. mi. (11th) (250,465 sq. km.)
**Flower:** Apple blossom    **Bird:** Robin
**Tree:** White pine    **Song:** "Michigan, My Michigan"
**Entered Union:** January 26, 1837 (26th)
**Capital:** Lansing (population, 125,736)
**Largest Cities** (with population): Detroit, 1,000,272;
Grand Rapids, 188,242; Warren, 138,078; Flint, 134,881
**Important Products:** automobiles, industrial machinery, metal products, printing and publishing, plastic products, chemicals, food products, milk, corn, natural gas, iron ore
**Places to Visit:** Greenfield Village and Henry Ford Museum, Dearborn; Detroit's "Art Center"; Isle Royal National Park; Pictured Rocks and Sleeping Bear Dunes national lakeshores; Mackinac Island
**WEB SITE** http://www.migov.state.mi.us

**DID YOU KNOW?** Michigan is known for manufacturing automobiles. Lake Michigan is the largest lake entirely in the United States.

## MINNESOTA (MN)

*North Star State, Gopher State*

**Population** (1997): 4,685,549 (20th)
**Area:** 86,943 sq. mi. (12th) (225,182 sq. km.)
**Flower:** Pink and white lady's-slipper    **Bird:** Common loon
**Tree:** Red pine    **Song:** "Hail! Minnesota"
**Entered Union:** May 11, 1858 (32nd)
**Capital:** St. Paul
**Largest Cities** (with population): Minneapolis, 358,785; St. Paul, 259,606
**Important Products:** industrial machinery, metal products, printing and publishing, food products, instruments, milk, hogs, cattle, corn, soybeans, iron ore
**Places to Visit:** Voyageurs National Park; Grand Portage National Monument; Minnesota Zoo; Fort Snelling; U.S. Hockey Hall of Fame, Eveleth
**WEB SITE** http://www.state.mn.us

**DID YOU KNOW?** Minnesota is sometimes called the Land of 10,000 Lakes—it actually has more than 15,000 lakes. Minnesota is the second coldest state (Alaska is the coldest). The Mall of America, in Bloomington, is the largest shopping mall in the United States; it has space for 12,750 cars.

## MISSISSIPPI (MS)

*Magnolia State*

**Population** (1997): 2,730,501 (31st)
**Area:** 48,434 sq. mi. (32nd) (125,443 sq. km.)
**Flower:** Magnolia    **Bird:** Mockingbird
**Tree:** Magnolia    **Song:** "Go, Mississippi!"
**Entered Union:** December 10, 1817 (20th)
**Capital and Largest City:** Jackson (population, 192,923)
**Other Large Cities** (with population): Biloxi, 48,414; Greenville, 42,933
**Important Products:** transportation equipment, clothing and textiles, furniture, electronic equipment, wood and wood products, cotton, chickens, cattle, oil
**Places to Visit:** Vicksburg National Military Park; Natchez Trace Parkway; Old Capitol, Jackson; Old Spanish Fort and Museum, Pascagoula
**WEB SITE** http://www.state.ms.us

**DID YOU KNOW?** Mississippi was the first state to celebrate Memorial Day (originally called Decoration Day) as a holiday, in 1866. Mississippi opened the first state-run college for women in Columbus in 1884. Jefferson Davis, president of the Confederate States of America, was born in Mississippi.

## MISSOURI (MO)

Show Me State

**Population** (1997): 5,402,058 (16th)
**Area:** 69,709 sq. mi. (21st) (180,546 sq. km.)
**Flower:** Hawthorn          **Bird:** Bluebird
**Tree:** Dogwood          **Song:** "Missouri Waltz"
**Entered Union:** August 10, 1821 (24th)
**Capital:** Jefferson City (population, 36,143)
**Largest Cities** (with population): Kansas City, 441,259; St. Louis, 351,565; Springfield, 143,407; Independence, 110,303
**Important Products:** transportation equipment, metal products, printing and publishing, food products, cattle, hogs, milk, soybeans, corn, hay, lead
**Places to Visit:** Gateway Arch, St. Louis; Mark Twain Home and Museum, Hannibal; Harry S. Truman Museum, Independence; George Washington Carver Birthplace, Diamond
**WEB SITE** http://www.state.mo.us

 **DID YOU KNOW?** Missouri is a major center for shipping and railroads. President Harry S. Truman, agricultural scientist George Washington Carver, and poet Langston Hughes were born in Missouri. It has been said that the ice cream cone was first sold at a World's Fair in St. Louis, in 1904. Gateway Arch, in St. Louis, is the tallest monument (630 feet high) in the United States.

## MONTANA (MT)

Treasure State

**Population** (1997): 878,810 (44th)
**Area:** 147,046 sq. mi. (4th) (380,850 sq. km.)
**Flower:** Bitterroot          **Bird:** Western meadowlark
**Tree:** Ponderosa pine          **Song:** "Montana"
**Entered Union:** November 8, 1889 (41st)
**Capital:** Helena (population, 27,982)
**Largest Cities** (with population): Billings, 91,195; Great Falls, 57,758; Missoula, 51,204; Butte, 34,051
**Important Products:** cattle, coal, oil, gold, wheat, hay, wood and wood products
**Places to Visit:** Yellowstone and Glacier national parks; Little Bighorn Battlefield National Monument, in Crow Agency; Museum of the Rockies, Bozeman
**WEB SITE** http://www.mt.gov

 **DID YOU KNOW?** Montana is the fourth-biggest state, after Alaska, Texas, and California. The most famous Indian battle in history took place in Montana, at Little Bighorn in 1876.

## NEBRASKA (NE)

Cornhusker State

**Population** (1997): 1,656,870 (38th)
**Area:** 77,358 sq. mi. (16th) (200,358 sq. km.)
**Flower:** Goldenrod          **Bird:** Western meadowlark
**Tree:** Cottonwood          **Song:** "Beautiful Nebraska"
**Entered Union:** March 1, 1867 (37th)
**Capital:** Lincoln
**Largest Cities** (with population): Omaha, 364,253; Lincoln, 209,192
**Important Products:** cattle, hogs, milk, corn, soybeans, hay, wheat, sorghum, food products, industrial machinery
**Places to Visit:** Oregon Trail landmarks; Stuhr Museum of the Prairie Pioneer, Grand Island; Agate Fossil Beds National Monument; Boys Town, near Omaha
**WEB SITE** http://www.state.ne.us

 **DID YOU KNOW?** Nebraska is not only a cattle state; it is the biggest meat-packing center in the world. It is also a farm state. Nebraska is the only state whose nickname comes from a college football team—the popular University of Nebraska Cornhuskers.

## NEVADA (NV)

Sagebrush State,
Battle Born State,
Silver State

**Population** (1997): 1,676,809 (37th)
**Area:** 110,567 sq. mi. (7th) (286,368 sq. km.)
**Flower:** Sagebrush
**Trees:** Single-leaf piñon, bristlecone pine
**Entered Union:** October 31, 1864 (36th)
**Capital:** Carson City (population, 40,443)
**Bird:** Mountain bluebird
**Song:** "Home Means Nevada"
**Largest Cities** (with population): Las Vegas, 376,906;
Reno, 155,499; Henderson, 122,339
**Important Products:** gold, silver, cattle, hay, metals and metal products, printing and publishing
**Places to Visit:** Great Basin National Park; Nevada State Museum, Carson City; Lake Mead National Recreation Area; ghost towns
**WEB SITE** http://www.state.nv.us

**DID YOU KNOW?** It usually rains less in Nevada than in any other state. Between 1980 and 1990 the population of Nevada increased by more than one half, making it the fastest-growing state. It also has the most wild horses.

## NEW HAMPSHIRE (NH)

Granite State

**Population** (1997): 1,172,709 (42nd)
**Area:** 9,351 sq. mi. (46th) (24,219 sq. km.)
**Flower:** Purple lilac
**Tree:** White birch
**Entered Union:** June 21, 1788 (9th)
**Capital:** Concord
**Bird:** Purple finch
**Song:** "Old New Hampshire"
**Largest Cities** (with population): Manchester, 100,967; Nashua, 81,094; Concord, 37,021
**Important Products:** industrial machinery, instruments, electronic equipment, metals and metal products, rubber and plastic products, printing and publishing, paper, milk
**Places to Visit:** White Mountain National Forest; Mount Washington; Fort at Number 4 Living History Museum, Charlestown; Old Man in the Mountain, Franconia Notch; Canterbury Shaker Village
**WEB SITE** http://www.state.nh.us

**DID YOU KNOW?** Mount Washington is the highest mountain in the northeast. Its peak is said to be the windiest spot on Earth. The first town-supported, free public library in the United States opened in New Hampshire in 1833.

## NEW JERSEY (NJ)

Garden State

**Population** (1997): 8,052,849 (9th)
**Area:** 8,722 sq. mi. (47th) (22,590 sq. km.)
**Flower:** Purple violet
**Tree:** Red oak
**Entered Union:** December 18, 1787 (3rd)
**Capital:** Trenton (population, 85,437)
**Bird:** Eastern goldfinch
**Song:** none
**Largest Cities** (with population): Newark, 268,510; Jersey City, 229,039;
Paterson, 150,270; Elizabeth, 110,149
**Important Products:** chemicals, industrial machinery, instruments, electronic equipment, metal products, stone, clothing and textiles, nursery and greenhouse products, food products, milk, tomatoes and vegetables
**Places to Visit:** ocean beaches; Edison National Historical Site, West Orange; Liberty State Park; Pine Barrens wilderness area; Great Adventure amusement park
**WEB SITE** http://www.state.nj.us

**DID YOU KNOW?** The electric light bulb was invented in New Jersey by Thomas Edison in 1879. The first ferryboat just for cars was built in New Jersey and placed in service in 1926. New Jersey manufactures more flags than any other state.

## NEW MEXICO (NM)

Land of Enchantment

**Population** (1997): 1,729,751 (36th)
**Area:** 121,598 sq. mi. (5th) (314,939 sq. km.)
**Flower:** Yucca  **Bird:** Roadrunner
**Tree:** Piñon  **Song:** "O, Fair New Mexico"
**Entered Union:** January 6, 1912 (47th)
**Capital:** Santa Fe
**Largest Cities** (with population): Albuquerque, 419,681; Las Cruces, 74,779; Santa Fe, 66,522
**Important Products:** natural gas, oil, copper, coal, potash, cattle, milk, hay, cotton, electronic equipment, instruments
**Places to Visit:** Carlsbad Caverns National Park; Palace of the Governors and Mission of San Miguel, Santa Fe; Chaco Canyon National Monument; cliff dwellings
**WEB SITE** http://www.state.nm.us

**DID YOU KNOW?** The oldest capital city in the United States is Santa Fe, New Mexico. Pueblo Indians had an advanced civilization in New Mexico a thousand years ago. The deepest cave in the United States is in New Mexico's Carlsbad Caverns. The first atom bomb was exploded in New Mexico, in a test on July 16, 1945.

## NEW YORK (NY)

Empire State

**Population** (1997): 18,137,226 (3rd)
**Area:** 54,471 sq. mi. (27th) (141,079 sq. km.)
**Flower:** Rose  **Bird:** Bluebird
**Tree:** Sugar maple  **Song:** "I Love New York"
**Entered Union:** July 26, 1788 (11th)
**Capital:** Albany (population, 103,564)
**Largest Cities** (with population): New York, 7,380,906; Buffalo, 310,548; Rochester, 221,594; Yonkers, 190,316
**Important Products:** printing and publishing, instruments, electronic equipment, industrial machinery, clothing and textiles, transportation equipment, metal products, milk, cattle, hay, stone
**Places to Visit:** In New York City, museums, Empire State Building, United Nations, Bronx Zoo, Statue of Liberty and Ellis Island; Niagara Falls; National Baseball Hall of Fame, Cooperstown; Fort Ticonderoga; Franklin D. Roosevelt National Historical Site, Hyde Park
**WEB SITE** http://www.state.ny.us

**DID YOU KNOW?** New York City is the largest city in the United States and was the nation's first capital. The first pizza restaurant in the United States opened in New York City in 1895. The first children's museum opened in Brooklyn in 1899.

## NORTH CAROLINA (NC)

Tar Heel State, Old North State

**Population** (1997): 7,425,183 (11th)
**Area:** 53,821 sq. mi. (28th) (139,397 sq. km.)
**Flower:** Dogwood  **Bird:** Cardinal
**Tree:** Pine  **Song:** "The Old North State"
**Entered Union:** November 21, 1789 (12th)
**Capital:** Raleigh
**Largest Cities** (with population): Charlotte, 441,297; Raleigh, 243,835; Greensboro, 195,426; Winston-Salem, 153,541; Durham, 149,799
**Important Products:** clothing and textiles, tobacco and tobacco products, industrial machinery, electronic equipment, furniture, chemicals, foods, chickens, hogs, stone
**Places to Visit:** Great Smoky Mountains National Park; Cape Hatteras National Seashore; Wright Brothers National Memorial, at Kitty Hawk
**WEB SITE** http://www.state.nc.us

**DID YOU KNOW?** The Wright Brothers took the first airplane ride in history, in North Carolina. The first U.S. school of forestry was opened in North Carolina.

# UNITED STATES

## NORTH DAKOTA (ND)

Peace Garden State

**Population** (1997): 640,883 (47th)
**Area:** 70,704 sq. mi. (19th) (183,123 sq. km.)
**Flower:** Wild prairie rose   **Bird:** Western meadowlark
**Tree:** American elm   **Song:** "North Dakota Hymn"
**Entered Union:** November 2, 1889 (39th)
**Capital:** Bismarck
**Largest Cities** (with population): Fargo, 83,778; Grand Forks, 50,675; Bismarck, 53,514; Minot, 35,926
**Important Products:** wheat, barley, hay, sunflowers, sugar beets, cattle, milk, oil, coal, industrial machinery, food products
**Places to Visit:** Theodore Roosevelt National Park; Bonanzaville, near Fargo; Dakota Dinosaur Museum, Dickinson; International Peace Garden
**WEB SITE** http://www.ndtourism.com

 **DID YOU KNOW?** North Dakota is one of the two biggest wheat-growing states in the United States (the other is Kansas). Theodore Roosevelt was a rancher here before he became president.

## OHIO (OH)

Buckeye State

**Population** (1997): 11,186,331 (7th)
**Area:** 44,828 sq. mi. (34th) (116,103 sq. km.)
**Flower:** Scarlet carnation   **Bird:** Cardinal
**Tree:** Buckeye   **Song:** "Beautiful Ohio"
**Entered Union:** March 1, 1803 (17th)
**Capital and Largest City:** Columbus (population, 657,053)
**Other Large Cities** (with population): Cleveland, 498,246; Cincinnati, 345,818; Toledo, 317,606; Akron, 216,882; Dayton, 172,947
**Important Products:** metal and metal products, transportation equipment, industrial machinery, rubber and plastic products, electronic equipment, printing and publishing, chemicals, food products, coal, corn, soybeans, livestock, milk
**Places to Visit:** Mound City Group National Monuments, Indian burial mounds; Neil Armstrong Air and Space Museum; Cedar Point and King's Island amusement parks
**WEB SITE** http://www.state.oh.us

 **DID YOU KNOW?** Seven American presidents were born in Ohio (Garfield, Grant, Harding, B. Harrison, Hayes, McKinley, Taft). Ohio was the home of the first professional baseball team, the Cincinnati Red Stockings, and the birthplace of the hot dog.

## OKLAHOMA (OK)

Sooner State

**Population** (1997): 3,317,091 (27th)
**Area:** 69,903 sq. mi. (20th) (181,049 sq. km.)
**Flower:** Mistletoe   **Bird:** Scissor-tailed flycatcher
**Tree:** Redbud   **Song:** "Oklahoma!"
**Entered Union:** November 16, 1907 (46th)
**Capital and Largest City:** Oklahoma City (population, 469,852)
**Other Large Cities** (with population): Tulsa, 378,491; Lawton, 82,582; Norman, 90,228
**Important Products:** natural gas, oil, cattle, industrial machinery, transportation equipment, metal products, electronic equipment, rubber and plastic products, wheat, hay
**Places to Visit:** Indian City U.S.A., near Anadarko; Fort Gibson Stockade; National Cowboy Hall of Fame; White Water Bay and Frontier City theme parks; Cherokee Heritage Center
**WEB SITE** http://www.oklaosf.state.ok.us

 **DID YOU KNOW?** The American Indian nations called The Five Civilized Tribes (Cherokee, Chickasaw, Choctaw, Creek, and Seminole) settled in Oklahoma. Today, more Native Americans live in Oklahoma than in any other state.

## OREGON (OR)

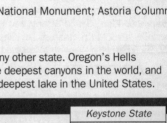

*Beaver State*

**Population** (1997): 3,243,487 (29th)
**Area:** 98,386 sq. mi. (9th) (254,819 sq. km.)
**Flower:** Oregon grape      **Bird:** Western meadowlark
**Tree:** Douglas fir      **Song:** "Oregon, My Oregon"
**Entered Union:** February 14, 1859 (33rd)
**Capital:** Salem
**Largest Cities** (with population): Portland, 480,824; Eugene, 123,718; Salem, 122,566
**Important Products:** wood and wood products, industrial machinery, food products, instruments, cattle, milk, hay, vegetables
**Places to Visit:** Crater Lake National Park; Oregon Caves National Monument; Astoria Column and Fort Clatsop National Memorial, Astoria
**WEB SITE** http://www.state.or.us

**DID YOU KNOW?** Oregon produces more timber than any other state. Oregon's Hells Canyon, 7,900 feet deep at its maximum, is one of the deepest canyons in the world, and Crater Lake, which gets as deep as 1,932 feet, is the deepest lake in the United States.

## PENNSYLVANIA (PA)

*Keystone State*

**Population** (1997): 12,019,661 (5th)
**Area:** 46,058 sq. mi. (33rd) (119,291 sq. km.)
**Flower:** Mountain laurel      **Bird:** Ruffled grouse
**Tree:** Hemlock      **Song:** "Pennsylvania"
**Entered Union:** December 12, 1787 (2nd)
**Capital:** Harrisburg (population, 52,376)
**Largest Cities** (with population): Philadelphia, 1,478,002; Pittsburgh, 350,363; Erie, 105,270; Allentown, 102,211
**Important Products:** iron and steel, coal, industrial machinery, printing and publishing, food products, electronic equipment, clothing and textiles, transportation equipment, milk, hay
**Places to Visit:** Independence Hall and other historic sites in Philadelphia; Franklin Institute Science Museum, Philadelphia; Valley Forge; Gettysburg; Hershey; Pennsylvania Dutch country, Lancaster County
**WEB SITE** http://www.state.pa.us

**DID YOU KNOW?** Pennsylvania is known for the Liberty Bell in Philadelphia, which first rang after the signing of the Declaration of Independence. Philadelphia was also the U.S. capital for 10 years. The first hospital in the United States was built there.

## RHODE ISLAND (RI)

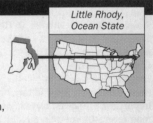

*Little Rhody, Ocean State*

**Population** (1997): 987,429 (43rd)
**Area:** 1,545 sq. mi. (50th) (4,002 sq. km.)
**Flower:** Violet      **Bird:** Rhode Island red
**Tree:** Red maple      **Song:** "Rhode Island"
**Entered Union:** May 29, 1790 (13th)
**Capital and Largest City:** Providence (population, 152,558)
**Other Large Cities** (with population): Warwick, 84,514; Cranston, 74,324; Pawtucket, 69,068
**Important Products:** metals and metal products, instruments, clothing and textiles, printing and publishing, rubber and plastic products, industrial machinery, electronic equipment, fish
**Places to Visit:** Block Island; mansions, old buildings, and harbor in Newport; International Tennis Hall of Fame, Newport
**WEB SITE** http://www.state.ri.us

**DID YOU KNOW?** Rhode Island is the smallest state. The bluffs and islands of Rhode Island attract many tourists who like fishing and swimming. The oldest synagogue in the United States (Touro Synagogue, 1763) is in Newport.

## SOUTH CAROLINA (SC)

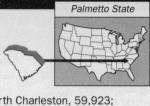

Palmetto State

**Population** (1997): 3,760,181 (26th)
**Area:** 32,007 sq. mi. (40th) (82,898 sq. km.)
**Flower:** Yellow jessamine    **Bird:** Carolina wren
**Tree:** Palmetto                        **Song:** "Carolina"
**Entered Union:** May 23, 1788 (8th)
**Capital and Largest City:** Columbia (population, 112,773)
**Other Large Cities** (with population): Charleston, 71,052; North Charleston, 59,923;
Greenville, 57,064
**Important Products:** clothing and textiles, chemicals, industrial machinery, rubber and plastic
products, electronic equipment, paper, metal products, livestock, tobacco, stone
**Places to Visit:** Grand Strand and Hilton Head Island beaches; Revolutionary War battlefields;
historic sites in Charleston; Fort Sumter; Historic Camden
**WEB SITE** http://www.state.sc.us

**DID YOU KNOW?** More battles of the American Revolution took place in South Carolina
than in any other state. The first shots of the Civil War were fired in South Carolina.
Charleston Museum, established in 1773, is the oldest museum in the United States.

## SOUTH DAKOTA (SD)

Mt. Rushmore State,
Coyote State

**Population** (1997): 737,973 (45th)
**Area:** 77,121 sq. mi. (17th) (199,743 sq. km.)
**Flower:** Pasqueflower       **Bird:** Ring-necked pheasant
**Tree:** Black Hills spruce    **Song:** "Hail, South Dakota"
**Entered Union:** November 2, 1889 (40th)
**Capital:** Pierre (population, 12,906)
**Largest Cities** (with population): Sioux Falls, 113,223; Rapid City, 54,523
**Important Products:** cattle, hogs, milk, corn, hay, wheat, soybeans, food products, gold
**Places to Visit:** Mount Rushmore National Memorial; Crazy Horse Memorial; Jewel Cave;
Badlands and Wind Caves national parks; Wounded Knee battlefield; Homestake Gold Mine
**WEB SITE** http://www.state.sd.us

**DID YOU KNOW?** South Dakota is best known for the faces of presidents carved on
Mount Rushmore (Presidents Washington, Jefferson, Lincoln, and T. Roosevelt). Famous
South Dakotans include Crazy Horse, Sitting Bull, and Wild Bill Hickok.

## TENNESSEE (TN)

Volunteer State

**Population** (1997): 5,368,198 (17th)
**Area:** 42,146 sq. mi. (36th) (109,158 sq. km.)
**Flower:** Iris                          **Bird:** Mockingbird
**Tree:** Tulip poplar              **Song:** "The Tennessee Waltz"
**Entered Union:** June 1, 1796 (16th)
**Capital:** Nashville
**Largest Cities** (with population): Memphis, 596,725; Nashville, 511,263;
Knoxville, 167,535; Chattanooga, 150,425
**Important Products:** chemicals, clothing and textiles, industrial machinery, motor vehicles,
food products, metal products, printing and publishing, electronic equipment, wood products
and furniture, livestock, milk, soybeans, tobacco, stone
**Places to Visit:** Great Smoky Mountains National Park; the Hermitage, home of President
Andrew Jackson near Nashville; Civil War battle sites; Grand Old Opry and Opryland, USA,
theme park, Nashville; Graceland, home of Elvis Presley in Memphis
**WEB SITE** http://www.state.tn.us

**DID YOU KNOW?** Tennessee can claim Nashville as country music capital of the world.
Frontiersman Davy Crockett was born in Tennessee. Elvis Presley and President Andrew
Jackson are among the famous people who lived in Tennessee.

## TEXAS (TX)

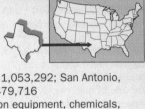
*Lone Star State*

**Population** (1997): 19,439,337 (2nd)
**Area:** 268,601 sq. mi. (2nd) (695,676 sq. km.)
**Flower:** Bluebonnet          **Bird:** Mockingbird
**Tree:** Pecan                       **Song:** "Texas, Our Texas"
**Entered Union:** December 29, 1845 (28th)
**Capital:** Austin
**Largest Cities** (with population): Houston, 1,744,058; Dallas, 1,053,292; San Antonio, 1,067,816; El Paso, 599,865; Austin, 541,278; Fort Worth, 479,716
**Important Products:** oil, natural gas, cattle, milk, transportation equipment, chemicals, industrial machinery, electronic equipment, cotton, hay
**Places to Visit:** Guadalupe and Big Bend national parks; the Alamo, in San Antonio; Lyndon Johnson National Historic Site, near Johnson City; Six Flags Over Texas amusement park, Arlington
**WEB SITE** http://www.state.tx.us

**DID YOU KNOW?** Texas is the largest of the contiguous 48 states (the states that border each other) and is second in size only to Alaska. Texas has more oil and natural gas than any other state and the most farmland. It is the only state with five major ports, and has the country's busiest airport (Dallas-Fort Worth).

## UTAH (UT)

*Beehive State*

**Population** (1997):2,059,148 (34th)
**Area:** 84,904 sq. mi. (13th) (219,902 sq. km.)
**Flower:** Sego lily          **Bird:** Seagull
**Tree:** Blue spruce          **Song:** "Utah, We Love Thee"
**Entered Union:** January 4, 1896 (45th)
**Capital and Largest City:** Salt Lake City (population, 172,575)
**Other Large Cities** (with population): West Valley City, 99,136; Provo, 99,606
**Important Products:** transportation equipment, industrial machinery, instruments, food products, copper, cattle, corn, hay
**Places to Visit:** Arches, Canyonlands, Bryce Canyon, Zion, and Capitol Reef national parks; Great Salt Lake; Temple Square (Mormon Church headquarters) in Salt Lake City, Indian cliff dwellings
**WEB SITE** http://www.state.ut.us

**DID YOU KNOW?** Utah's Great Salt Lake, which contains 6 billion tons of salt, is the largest lake in the United States outside of the Great Lakes. Rainbow Bridge in Utah is the largest natural arch or rock bridge in the world; it is 200 feet high and 270 feet wide.

## VERMONT (VT)

*Green Mountain State*

**Population** (1997): 588,978 (49th)
**Area:** 9,615 sq. mi. (45th) (24,903 sq. km.)
**Flower:** Red clover          **Bird:** Hermit thrush
**Tree:** Sugar maple          **Song:** "Hail, Vermont!"
**Entered Union:** March 4, 1791 (14th)
**Capital:** Montpelier (population, 7,856)
**Largest Cities** (with population): Burlington, 39,004; Rutland, 17,605
**Important Products:** electronic equipment, industrial machinery, printing and publishing, metal products, wood and stone products, milk, hay, maple syrup, granite, marble
**Places to Visit:** Green Mountain National Forest; Shelburne Museum
**WEB SITE** http://www.state.vt.us

**DID YOU KNOW?** Vermont is famous for its granite, marble, scenery, and maple syrup. Vermont passed the first constitution (1777) to prohibit slavery and to allow all men to vote. The first ski tow in the United States was established in Vermont in 1934.

## VIRGINIA (VA)

Old Dominion

**Population** (1997): 6,733,996 (12th)
**Area:** 42,777 sq. mi. (35th) (110,792 sq. km.)
**Flower:** Dogwood    **Bird:** Cardinal
**Tree:** Dogwood    **Song:** None
**Entered Union:** June 25, 1788 (10th)
**Capital:** Richmond
**Largest Cities** (with population): Virginia Beach, 430,385; Norfolk, 233,430; Richmond, 198,267; Chesapeake, 192,342; Newport News, 176,122
**Important Products:** transportation equipment, clothing and textiles, chemicals, printing and publishing, electronic equipment, food products, coal, livestock, milk, hay, tobacco
**Places to Visit:** Colonial Williamsburg; Busch Gardens, Williamsburg; Arlington National Cemetery; Mount Vernon (George Washington's home); Monticello (Thomas Jefferson's home); Shenandoah National Park
**WEB SITE** http://www.state.va.us

 **DID YOU KNOW?** was the birthplace of eight presidents (Presidents W. H. Harrison, Jefferson, Madison, Monroe, Taylor, Tyler, Washington, Wilson), more than any other state. The first permanent English settlement in the New World was in Virginia.

## WASHINGTON (WA)

Evergreen State

**Population** (1997): 5,610,362 (15th)
**Area:** 71,302 sq. mi. (18th) (184,672 sq. km.)
**Flower:** Western rhododendron    **Bird:** Willow goldfinch
**Tree:** Western hemlock    **Song:** "Washington, My Home"
**Entered Union:** November 11, 1889 (42nd)
**Capital:** Olympia (population, 39,006)
**Largest Cities** (with population): Seattle, 524,704; Spokane, 186,562; Tacoma, 179,114
**Important Products:** aerospace equipment, lumber and wood products, food products, paper, machinery, electronics, computer software, apples, wheat, cattle, milk, coal, fish
**Places to Visit:** Mount Rainier, Olympic, and North Cascades national parks; Mount St. Helens; Seattle Center, with Space Needle and monorail
**WEB SITE** http://www.state.wa.us

**DID YOU KNOW?** Grand Coulee Dam, on the Columbia River, is the world's largest concrete dam. Mount Rainier is the tallest volcano in the contiguous 48 states (those that border each other). Washington is known for its apples, timber, and fishing fleets.

## WEST VIRGINIA (WV)

Mountain State

**Population** (1997): 1,815,787 (35th)
**Area:** 24,231 sq. mi. (41st) (62,759 sq. km.)
**Flower:** Big rhododendron    **Bird:** Cardinal
**Tree:** Sugar maple    **Songs:** "The West Virginia Hills"; "This Is My West Virginia"; "West Virginia, My Home Sweet Home"
**Entered Union:** June 20, 1863 (35th)
**Capital and Largest City:** Charleston (population, 56,098)
**Other Large Cities** (with population): Huntington, 53,941; Wheeling, 33,311
**Important Products:** coal, natural gas, metal and metal products, chemicals, stone, clay, and glass products, industrial machinery, cattle, hay
**Places to Visit:** Harpers Ferry National Historic Park; Grave Creek Mound, Moundsville; Monongahela National Forest
**WEB SITE** http://www.state.wv.us

 **DID YOU KNOW?** West Virginia's mountain scenery and mineral springs attract many tourists. The state is one of the biggest coal states. West Virginia was part of Virginia until West Virginians decided to break away, in 1861.

## WISCONSIN (WI)

*Badger State*

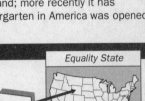

**Population** (1997): 5,169,677 (18th)
**Area:** 65,499 sq. mi. (23rd) (169,642 sq. km.)
**Flower:** Wood violet     **Bird:** Robin
**Tree:** Sugar maple     **Song:** "On, Wisconsin!"
**Entered Union:** May 29, 1848 (30th)
**Capital:** Madison
**Largest Cities** (with population): Milwaukee, 590,503; Madison, 197,630; Green Bay, 102,076; Racine, 82,572; Kenosha, 86,888
**Important Products:** industrial machinery; paper; metal products; milk, cheese, packed meat, and other foods; printing and publishing; corn, hay, and vegetables
**Places to Visit:** Dells of the Wisconsin; Cave of the Mounds, near Blue Mounds; Milwaukee Public Museum; Circus World Museum, Baraboo; National Railroad Museum, Green Bay
**WEB SITE** http://www.state.wi.us

 **DID YOU KNOW?** Wisconsin is known as America's Dairyland; more recently it has also become a major manufacturing state. The first kindergarten in America was opened in Wisconsin in 1865.

## WYOMING (WY)

*Equality State*

**Population** (1997): 479,743 (50th)
**Area:** 97,818 sq. mi. (10th) (253,349 sq. km.)
**Flower:** Indian paintbrush     **Bird:** Meadowlark
**Tree:** Cottonwood     **Song:** "Wyoming"
**Entered Union:** July 10, 1890 (44th)
**Capital and Largest City:** Cheyenne (population, 53,729)
**Other Large Cities** (with population): Casper, 48,800; Laramie, 26,583
**Important Products:** oil, coal, natural gas, clays, oil and coal products, cattle, hay
**Places to Visit:** Yellowstone and Grand Teton national parks; Fort Laramie; Buffalo Bill Historical Center, Cody
**WEB SITE** http://www.state.wy.us

 **DID YOU KNOW?** Wyoming is the home of the first U.S. national park (Yellowstone). Established in 1872, Yellowstone has 10,000 geysers, including the world's tallest active geyser (Steamboat Geyser).

## PUERTO RICO (PR)

*Puerto Rico*

**History:** Christopher Columbus landed in Puerto Rico in 1493. Puerto Rico was a Spanish colony for centuries, then fell to the United States in 1898 after the Spanish-American War. In 1952, still associated with the United States, Puerto Rico became a commonwealth with its own constitution.
**Population** (1996): 3,782,862
**Area:** 3,508 sq. mi. (9,086 sq. km.)
**National Anthem:** La Borinqueña
**Became a Self-Governing Commonwealth:** July 25, 1952
**Capital and Largest City:** San Juan (population, 426,832)
**Other Large Cities** (with population): Bayamón, 202,103; Carolina, 162,404; Ponce, 159,151
**Important Products:** chemicals, food products, electronic equipment, clothing and textiles, industrial machinery, coffee, vegetables, sugarcane, dairy products
**Places to Visit:** San Juan National Historic Site; beaches and resorts

 **DID YOU KNOW?** Puerto Ricans have most of the rights of American citizens, but they cannot vote in U.S. presidential elections and do not pay federal income tax. These things would change if Puerto Rico becomes a state.

## UNITED STATES PUZZLE

**R**ead the clues in the list below. Write in the words and then find the answers hidden in the puzzle. The hidden words go forward, backward, up, or down. They are listed in the word list and can be found in the United States section of this book. (Answers are on page 305.)

1. This puzzle is about the
   __ __ __ __ __ __  __ __ __ __ __ __.

2. Bill __ __ __ __ __ __ __ is now president of the United States.

3. Abraham __ __ __ __ __ __ __ was the 16th president.

4. The initials of the Central Intelligence Agency are __ __ __.

5. The U.S. __ __ __ __ __ __ __ is the part of Congress that has two members from each state.

6. The __ __ __ __ __ of Representatives is the part of Congress in which states' representation depends on their population.

7. William __ __ __ __ __ __ __ __ __ is the chief justice of the U.S. Supreme Court.

8. Freedom of speech, religion, and the press are __ __ __ __ __ __.

9. The U.S. __ __ __ __ once had 13 stars.

10. Nashville, the country music capital of the world, is in this southern state: __ __ __ __ __ __ __ __ __.

11. Mt. Waialeale, in Hawaii, gets more __ __ __ __ than any other spot in the United States.

12. Herbert __ __ __ __ __ __ was the 31st president.

13. __ __ __ __, Hawaii, is the southernmost city in the U.S.

14. The initials of the Securities and Exchange Commission are __ __ __.

15. Americans who want to volunteer in other nations might join the __ __ __ __ __ Corps.

16. John __ __ __ __ __, the 10th president, had no vice president.

17. Jimmy __ __ __ __ __ __ was the president before Ronald Reagan.

18. Official advisers to the president are called the __ __ __ __ __ __ __.

19. "In order to form a more perfect __ __ __ __ __" is a purpose of the U.S. Constitution, according to its Preamble.

```
C U N I T E D S T A T E S
A N O X E E S S E N N E T
R I T E N I B A C Z O T H
T O N L O C N I L F L A G
E N I A R E C A E P I N I
R E L Y T S I U Q N H E R
A I C R E V O O H O U S E
```

**WORD LIST**

| | | | |
|---|---|---|---|
| CABINET | HILO | RAIN | TENNESSEE |
| CARTER | HOOVER | REHNQUIST | TYLER |
| CIA | HOUSE | RIGHTS | UNION |
| CLINTON | LINCOLN | SEC | UNITED STATES |
| FLAG | PEACE | SENATE | |

# WASHINGTON, D.C.
## The Capital of the United States

**Area:** 69 square miles
**Population:** 543,213

**Flower:** American beauty rose
**Bird:** Wood thrush

**HISTORY.** Washington, D.C., became the capital of the United States in 1800, when the U.S. government moved there from Philadelphia. The city of Washington was especially designed and built to be the capital. It was named after George Washington, the first president of the United States. Many of its major sights are located on the Mall, an open grassy area that runs from the Capitol to the Potomac River.

**Capitol**, which houses the United States Congress, is at the east end of the Mall, on Capitol Hill. The dome of the Capitol's rotunda can be seen from many parts of the city.

**Franklin Delano Roosevelt Memorial**, honoring the 32nd president of the United States, was dedicated in 1997. The memorial has walkways as well as granite walls. The walls are carved with sayings of the president and First Lady Eleanor Roosevelt.

**Jefferson Memorial**, a circular marble building located near the Potomac River. At night, it is floodlit and very impressive.

**Korean War Veterans Memorial**, dedicated in 1995, is at the west end of the Mall. It shows a group of 19 troops ready for combat.

**Lincoln Memorial**, at the west end of the Mall, is built of white marble and styled like a Greek temple. Inside is a large, seated statue of Abraham Lincoln. His Gettysburg Address is carved on a nearby wall.

**National Archives**, on Constitution Avenue, is the place to see the Declaration of Independence, the Constitution, and the Bill of Rights.

**National Gallery of Art**, on the Mall, is one of the world's great art museums. Older paintings and sculptures are housed in the West Building, while 20th-century art is housed in the newer East Building.

**Smithsonian Institution** has 14 museums, including the National Air and Space Museum and the Museum of Natural History.

**U.S. Holocaust Memorial Museum** presents the history of the Nazis' murder of over six million Jews and millions of other people from 1933 to 1945. The exhibit *Daniel's Story* tells the story of the Holocaust from a child's point of view. It is for eight-year-olds and older. The other exhibits are for visitors eleven years old or older.

**Vietnam Veterans Memorial** has a black-granite wall shaped like a V. Names of the Americans who lost their lives in the Vietnam War are inscribed on the wall.

**Washington Monument**, a white marble pillar, or obelisk, standing on the Mall and rising to over 555 feet. From the top, there are wonderful views of the city.

**White House**, at 1600 Pennsylvania Avenue, has been the home of every U.S. president except George Washington.

**Women in Military Service for America Memorial**, dedicated in 1997, is at the entrance to Arlington National Cemetery. It honors the 1.8 million women who have served in the U.S. armed forces.

# How the STATES

**Alabama** comes from *Alibamu*, which was the name of the town of a Creek Indian tribe.

**Alaska** comes from *alakshak*, the Aleutian (Eskimo) word meaning "mainland" or "land that is not an island."

**Arizona** comes from an American Indian word meaning "little spring" or "little spring place."

**Arkansas** is a variation of *Quapaw*, the name of a Sioux Indian tribe. *Quapaw* means "downstream people."

**California** is the name of an imaginary island in a Spanish story. It was named by Spanish explorers of Baja California, a part of Mexico.

**Colorado** comes from a Spanish word meaning "reddish." It was first given to the Colorado river because of its reddish color.

**Connecticut** comes from an Algonquin Indian word meaning "beside the long tidal river."

**Delaware** is named after Lord De La Warr, the English governor of Virginia in colonial times.

**Florida**, which means "flowery" in Spanish, was named by the explorer Ponce de Leon, who landed there during the Spanish flower festival.

**Georgia** was named after King George II of England, who granted the right to create a colony there in 1732.

**Hawaii** probably comes from *Hawaiki*, or *Owhyhee*, the native Polynesians' name for their homeland.

**Idaho's** name is of uncertain origin, but it may come from an Apache name for the Comanche Indians.

**Illinois** is the French version of *Illini*, an Algonquin Indian word meaning "men" or "warriors."

**Indiana** means "land of the Indians."

**Iowa** comes from the name of an American Indian tribe that lived on the land that is now the state.

**Kansas** comes from a Sioux Indian word that possibly meant "people of the south wind."

**Kentucky** comes from an Iroquois Indian word, possibly meaning "meadowland."

**Louisiana**, which was first settled by French explorers, was named after King Louis XIV of France.

**Maine** means "the mainland." English explorers called it that to distinguish it from islands nearby.

**Maryland** was named after Queen Henrietta Maria, wife of King Charles I of England, who granted the right to establish an English colony there.

**Massachusetts** comes from an Algonquin Indian word meaning "at the big hill."

**Michigan** comes from the Chippewa Indian words *mici gama*, meaning "great water" (referring to Lake Michigan).

**Minnesota** got its name from a Sioux Indian word meaning "cloudy water" or "sky-tinted water."

**Mississippi** is probably derived from two Chippewa Indian words meaning "great river" or "father of the waters," or from an Algonquin word.

**Missouri** comes from an Algonquin Indian term meaning "people of the big canoes."

**Montana** comes from a Spanish word meaning "mountainous."

# Got Their NAMES

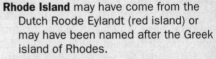

**Nebraska** comes from "flat water," an Omaha or Otos Indian name for the Platte River.

**Nevada** means "snowy or "snow-covered" in Spanish. Spanish explorers gave the name to the Sierra Nevada Mountains.

**New Hampshire** was named by an early settler after his home county of Hampshire, in England.

**New Jersey** was named for the English Channel island of Jersey.

**New Mexico** was given its name by a Spanish explorer in Mexico.

**New York**, first called New Netherland, was renamed for the Duke of York and Albany after the English took it from Dutch settlers.

**North Carolina**, the northern part of the English colony of Carolana, was named for King Charles I.

**North Dakota** comes from a Sioux Indian word meaning "allied tribes."

**Ohio** is the Iroquois Indian word for "fine or good river."

**Oklahoma** comes from a Choctaw Indian word meaning "red people."

**Oregon** may have come from *Ouaricon-sint,* a name on a French map for the Wisconsin River, and mistakenly given to the Columbia River. The name of the Columbia River was changed, but the state kept the name.

**Pennsylvania**, meaning "Penn's woods," was the name given to the colony founded by William Penn.

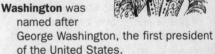

**Rhode Island** may have come from the Dutch Roode Eylandt (red island) or may have been named after the Greek island of Rhodes.

**South Carolina**, the southern part of the English colony of Carolana, was named for King Charles I.

**South Dakota** comes from a Sioux Indian word meaning "allied tribes."

**Tennessee** comes from the name the Cherokee Indians gave to their ancient capital. The name was given to the Tennessee River. The state was named after the river.

**Texas** comes from a word meaning "friends" or "allies," used by the Spanish to describe some of the American Indians living there.

**Utah** comes from Ute, the name of a Shoshone Indian tribe.

**Vermont** comes from two French words, *vert* (green) and *mont* (mountain).

**Virginia** was named in honor of Queen Elizabeth I of England, who was known as the Virgin Queen because she never married.

**Washington** was named after George Washington, the first president of the United States.

**West Virginia** got its name from the people of western Virginia, who formed their own government during the Civil War.

**Wisconsin** comes from an Algonquin Indian name for the state's principal river. The word, meaning "the place where the waters come together," was once spelled *Ouisconsin.*

**Wyoming** comes from an Algonquin Indian word meaning "at the big plains" or "large prairie place."

# NATIONAL PARKS

Most national parks are large and naturally beautiful and have a wide variety of scenery. They are visited by millions of people each year. The world's first national park was Yellowstone, established in 1872. Since then, the American government has set aside a total of 54 national parks. Fifty-two of the parks in the United States are listed below. Two outside the United States are in the Virgin Islands and American Samoa. You can find out more about national parks by writing to the National Park Service, Department of the Interior, 1849 C Street NW, Washington, D.C., 20240.

 **WEB SITE** For information on-line, go to: http://www.nps.gov/parks.html

**Acadia** (Maine)
46,998 acres; established 1929
Rugged coast and granite cliffs; seals, whales, and porpoises; highest land along the East Coast of the U.S.

**Arches** (Utah)
73,379 acres; established 1971
Giant natural sandstone arches, including Landscape Arch, over 100 feet high and 291 feet long

**Badlands** (South Dakota)
242,756 acres; established 1978
A prairie where, over centuries, the land has been formed into many odd shapes with a variety of colors

**Big Bend** (Texas)
801,163 acres; established 1935
Desert land and rugged mountains, on the Rio Grande River; dinosaur fossils

**Biscayne** (Florida)
172,924 acres; established 1980
A water-park on a chain of islands in the Atlantic Ocean, south of Miami, with beautiful coral reefs

**Bryce Canyon** (Utah)
35,835 acres; established 1928
Odd and very colorful rock formations carved by centuries of erosion

**Canyonlands** (Utah)
337,570 acres; established 1964
Sandstone cliffs above the Colorado River; rock carvings from an ancient American Indian civilization

**Capitol Reef** (Utah)
241,904 acres; established 1971
Sandstone cliffs cut into by gorges with high walls; old American Indian storage huts

**Carlsbad Caverns** (New Mexico)
46,766 acres; established 1930
A huge cave system, not fully explored, with the world's largest underground chamber, called "the Big Room"

**Channel Islands** (California)
249,354 acres; established 1980
Islands off the California coast, with sea lions, seals, and sea birds

**Crater Lake** (Oregon)
183,224 acres; established 1902
The deepest lake in the United States, carved in the crater of an inactive volcano; lava walls up to 2,000 feet high

**Death Valley** (California, Nevada)
3,367,628 acres; established 1994
Largest national park outside Alaska. Vast hot desert, rocky slopes and gorges, huge sand dunes; hundreds of species of plants, some unique to the area; variety of wildlife, including desert foxes, bobcats, coyotes

**Denali** (Alaska)
4,741,800 acres; established 1980
Huge park, containing America's tallest mountain, plus caribou, moose, sheep

**Dry Tortugas** (Florida)
64,700 acres; established 1992
Colorful birds and fish; a 19th-century fort, Fort Jefferson

**Everglades** (Florida)
1,507,850 acres; established 1934
The largest subtropical wilderness within the U.S.; swamps with mangrove trees, rare birds, alligators

**Gates of the Arctic** (Alaska)
7,523,898 acres; established 1984
One of the largest national parks; huge tundra wilderness, with rugged peaks and steep valleys

**Glacier** (Montana)
1,013,572 acres; established 1910
Rugged mountains, with glaciers, lakes, sheep, bears, and bald eagles

**Glacier Bay** (Alaska)
3,224,794 acres; established 1986
Glaciers moving down mountainsides to the sea; seals, whales, bears, eagles

**Grand Canyon** (Arizona)
1,217,158 acres; established 1919
Mile-deep expanse of multicolored layered rock, a national wonder

**Grand Teton** (Wyoming)
309,995 acres; established 1929
Set in the Teton Mountains; a winter feeding ground for elks

**Great Basin** (Nevada)
77,180 acres; established 1986
From deserts to meadows to tundra; caves; ancient pine trees

**Great Smoky Mountains**
(North Carolina, Tennessee)
521,621 acres; established 1934
Forests, with deer, fox, and black bears, and streams with trout and bass

**Guadalupe Mountains** (Texas)
86,416 acres; established 1966
Remains of a fossil reef formed 225 million years ago

**Haleakala** (Hawaii)
28,091 acres; established 1960
The largest crater of any inactive volcano in the world

**Hawaii Volcanoes** (Hawaii)
209,695 acres; established 1961
Home of two large active volcanoes, Mauna Loa and Kilauea, along with a desert and a tree fern forest

**Hot Springs** (Arkansas)
5,549 acres; established 1921
47 hot springs that provide warm waters for drinking and bathing

**Isle Royale** (Michigan)
571,790 acres; established 1931
On an island in Lake Superior; woods, lakes, many kinds of animals—and no roads

**Joshua Tree** (California)
792,750 acres; established 1994
Large desert with rock formations and unusual desert plants, including many Joshua trees; fossils from prehistoric times; wildlife, including desert bighorn

**Katmai** (Alaska)
3,674,541 acres; established 1980
Contains the Valley of Ten Thousand Smokes, which was filled with ash when Katmai Volcano erupted in 1912

**Kenai Fjords** (Alaska)
670,643 acres; established 1980
Fjords, rain forests, the Harding Icefield; sea otters, seals; a breeding place for many birds

**Kings Canyon** (California)
461,901 acres; established 1940
Mountains and woods and the highest canyon wall in the U.S.

**Kobuk Valley** (Alaska)
1,750,737 acres; established 1980
Located north of the Arctic Circle, with caribou and black bears; archeological sites indicate that humans have lived there for over 10,000 years

**Lake Clark** (Alaska)
2,619,859 acres; established 1980
Lakes, waterfalls, glaciers, volcanoes, fish and wildlife

**Lassen Volcanic** (California)
106,372 acres; established 1916
Contains Lassen Peak, a volcano that began erupting in 1914, after being dormant for 400 years

**Mammoth Cave** (Kentucky)
52,830 acres; established 1941
The world's longest known cave network, with over 300 miles of mapped passages

**Mesa Verde** (Colorado)
52,122 acres; established 1906
A plateau covered by woods and canyons; the best preserved ancient cliff dwellings in the U.S.

**Mount Rainier** (Washington)
235,613 acres; established 1899
Home of the Mount Rainier volcano; thick forests, glaciers

**North Cascades** (Washington)
504,781 acres; established 1968
Rugged mountains and valleys, with deep canyons, lakes and glaciers

**Olympic** (Washington)
922,651 acres; established 1938
Rain forest, with woods and mountains, glaciers, and rare elk

**Petrified Forest**
(Arizona)
93,533 acres;
established 1962
A large area of woods turned into stone; American Indian pueblos and rock carvings

**Redwood** (California)
110,232 acres; established 1968
Groves of ancient redwood trees, the world's tallest trees

**Rocky Mountain** (Colorado)
265,727 acres; established 1915
Located in the Rockies, with gorges, alpine lakes, and mountain peaks

**Saguaro** (Arizona)
91,453 acres; established 1994
Forests of saguaro cacti, some 50 feet tall and 200 years old

**Sequoia** (California)
402,482 acres; established 1890
Groves of giant sequoia trees; Mount Whitney (14,494 feet)

**Shenandoah** (Virginia)
197,389 acres; established 1926
Located in the Blue Ridge Mountains, overlooking the Shenandoah Valley

**Theodore Roosevelt** (North Dakota)
70,447 acres; established 1978
Scenic badlands and a part of the old Elkhorn Ranch that belonged to Theodore Roosevelt

**Voyageurs** (Minnesota)
218,035 acres; established 1971
Forests with wildlife and many scenic lakes for canoeing and boating

**Wind Cave** (South Dakota)
28,295 acres; established 1903
Limestone caverns in the Black Hills; a prairie with colonies of prairie dogs

**Wrangell-Saint Elias** (Alaska)
8,323,618 acres; established 1980
The biggest national park, with mountain peaks over 16,000 feet high

**Yellowstone** (Idaho, Montana, Wyoming)
2,219,791 acres; established 1872
The first national park and world's greatest geysers; bears and moose

**Yosemite** (California)
761,236 acres; established 1890
Yosemite Valley; highest waterfall in North America; mountain scenery

**Zion** (Utah)
146,598 acres; established 1919
Deep, narrow Zion Canyon and other canyons in different colors; Indian cliff dwellings over 1,000 years old

# Naming HURRICANES

For many years, violent storms have been given names. Until early in the 20th century, people named storms after saints. Then, in 1953, the U.S. government began to use women's names for hurricanes. Men's names began to be used in 1978. Today, there are six sets of names for both Atlantic and Pacific hurricanes. These lists of names are used again every six years (1999 names will be used again in 2005). Representatives of countries that often have hurricanes agree upon hurricane names at meetings of the World Meteorological Organization, an agency of the United Nations.

| HURRICANE NAMES FOR 1999 | In the North Atlantic: | In the Eastern Pacific: |
|---|---|---|
| | Arlene, Bret, Cindy, Dennis, Emily, Floyd, Gert, Harvey, Irene, Jose, Katrina, Lenny, Maria, Nate, Ophelia, Philippe, Rita, Stan, Tammy, Vince, Wilma | Adrian, Beatriz, Calvin, Dora, Eugene, Fernanda, Greg, Hilary, Irwin, Jova, Kenneth, Lidia, Max, Norma, Otis, Pilar, Ramon, Selma, Todd, Veronica, Wiley, Xina, York, Zelda |

# The SPEED of WIND

In 1805, Sir Francis Beaufort, British Navy admiral, developed a system for describing wind speeds at sea. Later this Beaufort Scale was adapted for use on land. It uses the numbers 0 to 12. The numbers get higher as the winds increase in speed.

0 Calm

4 Moderate Breeze

| 0 | Calm | (under 1 mph) |
|---|---|---|
| 1 | Light Air | (1-3 mph) |
| 2 | Light Breeze | (4-7 mph) |
| 3 | Gentle Breeze | (8-12 mph) |
| 4 | Moderate Breeze | (13-18 mph) |
| 5 | Fresh Breeze | (19-24 mph) |
| 6 | Strong Breeze | (25-31 mph) |
| 7 | Near Gale | (32-38 mph) |
| 8 | Gale | (39-46 mph) |
| 9 | Strong Gale | (47-54 mph) |
| 10 | Storm | (55-63 mph) |
| 11 | Violent Storm | (64-72 mph) |
| 12 | Hurricane | (over 72 mph) |

8 Gale

12 Hurricane

The U.S. Weather Service also uses the numbers 13 to 17 for winds of hurricane speed.

## WEATHER WORDS

**air mass**
A large amount of air at a certain temperature and humidity.

**atmospheric pressure**
Pressure on the surface of the Earth from the weight of the atmosphere. Rising atmospheric pressure usually means calm, clear weather. Falling pressure usually leads to storms. A **high** is an area of high atmospheric pressure. A **low** is an area of low atmospheric pressure.

**climate**
Average weather conditions for an area over a long time period.

**front**
Boundary between two air masses.

**humidity**
Amount of water vapor (water in the form of a gas) in the air.

**meteorologist**
A person who studies the atmosphere, weather, and weather forecasting.

## PRECIPITATION

**precipitation**
The different forms of water that fall from clouds—rain, snow, hail, and sleet.

**rain**
Water falling in drops that measure over two hundredths of an inch across.

**freezing rain**
Water that freezes as it hits the ground and other surfaces at temperatures below freezing.

**sleet**
Drops of water that freeze in cold air and reach the ground as ice pellets or a mixture of snow and rain.

**hail**
Frozen raindrops that are kept in the air by air currents. Water keeps freezing on the hailstone until it is so heavy that it falls to the ground.

**snow**
Ice crystals that form in clouds and fall to the ground.

**blizzard**
A heavy snowstorm with strong winds.

## STORMS

**cyclone**
Word for a circulating storm that forms over warm tropical oceans. Also the name for a hurricane in the Indian Ocean.

**hurricane**
A circulating storm with wind speeds of 73 miles per hour or more. It is called a *hurricane* in the Atlantic Ocean, a *typhoon* in the western Pacific Ocean, and a *cyclone* in the Indian Ocean.

**monsoon**
A system of winds that changes direction between seasons.

**thunderstorm**
A storm with thunder and lightning.

**tropical storm**
A circulating storm with wind speeds from 39 to 73 mph; can turn into a hurricane.

**tornado**
Violently circulating winds of more than 200 mph form a dark funnel reaching from the cloud to the ground.

# What Is EL NIÑO?

El Niño is a large current of warm water that forms in the Pacific Ocean near South America. When it comes along every few years, El Niño changes weather in many parts of the world. It causes the winds that blow around the equator to stray from their normal paths. This leads to big changes in temperature, heavy storms and floods in some areas, and droughts in other areas.

# Taking TEMPERATURES

## HOW TO MEASURE TEMPERATURE

Two systems for measuring temperature are commonly used in weather forecasting. One is Fahrenheit (abbreviated F). The other is Celsius (abbreviated C). Another word for Celsius is Centigrade. Zero degrees (0°) Celsius is equal to 32 degrees (32°) Fahrenheit. Temperatures can be easily converted from one system to the other by following these steps:

**To Convert Fahrenheit to Celsius:**
1. Subtract 32 from the Fahrenheit temperature value.
2. Then multiply by 5.
3. Then divide the result by 9.
   **Example:** To convert 68 degrees Fahrenheit to Celsius, 68 − 32 = 36; 36 x 5 = 180; 180 ÷ 9 = 20

**To Convert Celsius to Fahrenheit:**
1. Multiply the Celsius temperature by 9.
2. Then divide by 5.
3. Then add 32 to the result.
   **Example:** To convert 20 degrees Celsius to Fahrenheit, 20 x 9 = 180; 180 ÷ 5 = 36; 36 + 32 = 68

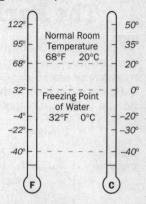

## THE HOTTEST AND COLDEST PLACES ON RECORD IN THE WORLD

| CONTINENT | HIGHEST TEMPERATURE | LOWEST TEMPERATURE |
| --- | --- | --- |
| Africa | El Azizia, Libya, 136°F (58°C) | Lfrane, Morocco, −11°F (−24°C) |
| Antarctica | Vanda Station, 7.5°F (−14°C) | Vostok, −129°F (−89°C) |
| Asia | Tirat Zevi, Israel, 129°F (54°C) | Verkhoyansk, Russia, −90°F (−68°C) |
| Australia | Cloncurry, Queensland, 128°F (53°C) | Charlotte Pass, New South Wales, −8°F (−22°C) |
| Europe | Seville, Spain, 122°F (50°C) | Ust Shchugor, Russia, −67°F (−55°C) |
| North America | Death Valley, California, 134°F (57°C) | Snag, Yukon Territory, −81°F (−63°C) |
| South America | Rivadavia, Argentina, 120°F (49°C) | Sarmiento, Argentina, −27°F (−33°C) |

| HOTTEST PLACES IN THE U.S. | | | COLDEST PLACES IN THE U.S. | | |
| --- | --- | --- | --- | --- | --- |
| State | Temperature | Year | State | Temperature | Year |
| California | 134°F | (1913) | Alaska | −80°F | (1971) |
| Arizona | 128°F | (1994)* | Montana | −70°F | (1954) |
| Nevada | 125°F | (1994)* | Utah | −69°F | (1985) |
| * Tied with a record set earlier | | | | | |

**WEB SITE** To read about the weather try the Weather Channel at: http://www.weather.com

# The Earliest MEASUREMENTS

**W**e use weights and measures all the time—you can measure how tall you are, or how much gasoline a car needs. Ancient people developed measurements to describe the amounts or sizes of things. These units are called **weights** and **measures**. The first measurements were based on the human body and on activities.

| Ancient measure | 1 foot =  length of a person's foot | 1 yard =  from nose to fingertip | 1 acre =  land an ox could plow in a day |
|---|---|---|---|
| Modern measure | 12 inches | 3 feet or 36 inches | 43,560 square feet or 4,840 square yards |

# MEASUREMENTS
## Used in the UNITED STATES

**T**he system of measurement used in the United States is called the **U.S. Customary System**. Most countries use the **metric system**. A few metric measurements are also used in the United States, such as for soda, which comes in 1-liter and 2-liter bottles. In the tables below, when a unit has an abbreviation, the abbreviation appears in parentheses the first time.

| LENGTH, HEIGHT, and DISTANCE | AREA |
|---|---|
| The basic unit of **length** in the U.S. system is the **inch**. Length, width, depth, thickness, and the distance between two points all use the inch or larger related units. | **Area** is used to measure a section of a flat surface like the floor or the ground. Most area measurements are given in **square units**. Land is measured in **acres**. |
| 1 foot (ft.) = 12 inches (in.)<br>1 yard (yd.) = 3 feet or 36 inches<br>1 rod (rd.) = 5 $\frac{1}{2}$ yards<br>1 furlong (fur.) = 40 rods or 220 yards or 660 feet<br>1 mile (mi.) (also called statute mile) = 8 furlongs or 1,760 yards or 5,280 feet<br>1 league = 3 miles | 1 square foot (sq. ft.) = 144 square inches (sq. in.)<br>1 square yard (sq. yd.) = 9 square feet or 1,296 square inches<br>1 square rod (sq. rd.) = 30 $\frac{1}{4}$ square yards<br>1 acre = 160 square rods or 4,840 square yards or 43,560 square feet<br>1 square mile (sq. mi.) = 640 acres |

## CAPACITY

Units of **capacity** are used to measure how much of something will fit into a container. **Liquid measure** is used to measure liquids, such as water or gasoline. **Dry measure** is used with large amounts of solid materials, like grain or fruit.

**Dry Measure.** Although both liquid and dry measures use the terms "pint" and "quart," they mean different amounts and should not be confused. Look at the lists below for examples.

1 quart (qt.) = 2 pints (pt.)
1 peck (pk.) = 8 quarts
1 bushel (bu.) = 4 pecks

**Liquid Measure.** Although the basic unit in liquid measure is the **gill** (4 fluid ounces), you are more likely to find liquids measured in pints or larger units.

1 gill = 4 fluid ounces
1 pint (pt.) = 4 gills or 16 ounces
1 quart (qt.) = 2 pints or 32 ounces
1 gallon (gal.) = 4 quarts = 128 ounces

☑ For measuring most U.S. liquids,
    1 barrel (bbl.) = $31\frac{1}{2}$ gallons
☑ For measuring oil,
    1 barrel (bbl.) = 42 gallons

**Cooking measurements.** Cooking measure is used to measure amounts of solid and liquid foods used in cooking. The measurements used in cooking are based on the **fluid ounce**.

1 teaspoon (tsp.) = $\frac{1}{6}$ fluid ounce (fl. oz.)
1 tablespoon (tbsp.) = 3 teaspoons or $\frac{1}{2}$ fluid ounce
1 cup = 16 tablespoons or 8 fluid ounces
1 pint = 2 cups
1 quart = 2 pints
1 gallon = 4 quarts

## VOLUME

The amount of space taken up by an object (or the amount of space available within an object) is measured in **volume**. Volume is usually expressed in **cubic units**. If you wanted to buy a room air conditioner and needed to know how much space there was to be cooled, you could measure the room in cubic feet.

1 cubic foot (cu. ft.) =
    1,728 cubic inches (cu. in.)
1 cubic yard (cu. yd.) = 27 cubic feet

## DEPTH

Some measurements of length are used to measure ocean depth and distance.

1 fathom = 6 feet
1 cable = 120 fathoms or 720 feet
1 nautical mile = 6,076.1 feet or
                    1.15 statute miles

## WEIGHT

Although 1 cubic foot of popcorn and 1 cubic foot of rock take up the same amount of space, they wouldn't feel the same if you tried to lift them. We measure heaviness as **weight**. Most objects are measured in **avoirdupois weight** (pronounced a-ver-de-POIZ), although precious metals and medicines use different systems.

1 dram (dr.) = 27.344 grains (gr.)
1 ounce (oz.) = 16 drams or
                437.5 grains
1 pound (lb.) = 16 ounces
1 hundredweight
    (cwt.) = 100
    pounds
1 ton = 2,000
    pounds
    (also called
    short ton)

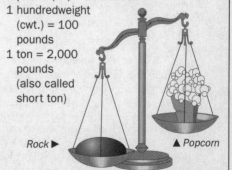

Rock ▶                    ▲ Popcorn

# The METRIC System

**D**o you ever wonder how much soda you are getting when you buy a bottle that holds 1 liter? Or do you wonder how long a 50-meter swimming pool is? Or how far from Montreal, Canada, you would be when a map says "8 kilometers"?

Every system of measurement uses a basic unit for measuring. In the U.S. Customary System, the basic unit for length is the inch. In the metric system, the basic unit for length is the **meter**. The metric system also uses **liter** as a basic unit of volume or capacity and the **gram** as a basic unit of mass. The related units are made by adding a prefix to the basic unit. The prefixes and their meanings are:

| | | |
|---|---|---|
| milli- = $^1/_{1,000}$ | deci- = $^1/_{10}$ | hecto- = 100 |
| centi- = $^1/_{100}$ | deka- = 10 | kilo- = 1,000 |

For example:

millimeter (mm) = $^1/_{1,000}$ of a meter
centimeter (cm) = $^1/_{100}$ of a meter
decimeter (dm) = $^1/_{10}$ of a meter
dekameter (dm) = 10 meters
hectometer (hm) = 100 meters
kilometer (km) = 1,000 meters

milligram (mg) = $^1/_{1,000}$ of a gram
centigram (cg) = $^1/_{100}$ of a gram
decigram (dg) = $^1/_{10}$ of a gram
dekagram (dg) = 10 grams
hectogram (hg) = 100 grams
kilogram (kg) = 1,000 grams

**T**o get a rough idea of what measurements equal in the metric system, it helps to know that a liter is a little more than a quart. A meter is a little over a yard. And a kilometer is less than a mile.

- ☑ A bottle of soda that holds 2 liters holds a little more than two quarts (2.1 quarts to be exact).
- ☑ A football field is 100 yards long. It is a little more than 90 meters (91.4 meters to be exact).

**DID YOU KNOW?** Did you know that the metric system is used for measurements in the Olympic Games? Here are a few Olympic Game measurements and what they are equal to in U.S. Customary units.

- ☑ A 50-meter swimming pool is 54.7 yards long. A 400-meter freestyle swimming race is 437 yards.
- ☑ A 10-kilometer race covers 6.2 miles. A 50-kilometer walk is 31.1 miles.
- ☑ A 1,000-meter speed-skating race is six-tenths of a mile, or a little over half a mile. A 5,000-meter race is a little more than 3 miles. (Remember that 1,000 meters = 1 kilometer, so a 1,000-meter race would be the same as a 1-kilometer race, and a 5,000-meter race would be the same as a 5-kilometer race.)

You can check these numbers by using the conversion charts on the following page. A calculator will be a big help with this. For example, if you multiply 50 meters (the length of an Olympic swimming pool) by 1.0936, you get 54.68 yards. When rounded off, that becomes 54.7 yards.

# Converting U.S. Measurements to Metrics and Metrics to U.S. Measurements

If you want to convert feet to meters or miles to kilometers, you need to know how many meters there are in one foot or how many kilometers there are in one mile. The tables below show how to convert units in the U.S. Customary System to units in the metric system and how to convert metric units to U.S. Customary units. If you want to convert numbers from one system to the other, you may want to use a calculator to help you with the multiplication.

| CONVERTING U.S. CUSTOMARY UNITS TO METRIC UNITS | | | CONVERTING METRIC UNITS TO U.S. CUSTOMARY UNITS | | |
|---|---|---|---|---|---|
| If you know the number of | Multiply by | To get the number of | If you know the number of | Multiply by | To get the number of |
| inches | 2.5400 | centimeters | centimeters | .3937 | inches |
| inches | .0254 | meters | centimeters | .0328 | feet |
| feet | 30.4800 | centimeters | meters | 39.3701 | inches |
| feet | .3048 | meters | meters | 3.2808 | feet |
| yards | .9144 | meters | meters | 1.0936 | yards |
| miles | 1.6093 | kilometers | kilometers | .621 | miles |
| square inches | 6.4516 | square centimeters | square centimeters | .1550 | square inches |
| square feet | .0929 | square meters | square meters | 10.7639 | square feet |
| square yards | .8361 | square meters | square meters | 1.1960 | square yards |
| acres | .4047 | hectares | hectares | 2.4710 | acres |
| cubic inches | 16.3871 | cubic centimeters | cubic centimeters | .0610 | cubic inches |
| cubic feet | .0283 | cubic meters | cubic meters | 35.3147 | cubic feet |
| cubic yards | .7646 | cubic meters | cubic meters | 1.3080 | cubic yards |
| quarts (liquid) | .9464 | liters | liters | 1.0567 | quarts (liquid) |
| ounces | 28.3495 | grams | grams | .0353 | ounces |
| pounds | .4536 | kilograms | kilograms | 2.2046 | pounds |

# Highlights of WORLD HISTORY

**T**he section on World History is divided into five parts. Each part is a major region of the world: the Middle East, Africa, Asia, Europe, and the Americas. Major historical events from ancient times to the present are described under the headings for each region.

## THE ANCIENT MIDDLE EAST 4000 B.C. – 1 B.C.

### 4000-3000 B.C.
- The world's first cities are built by the Sumerian peoples in Mesopotamia, southern Iraq.
- Egyptians develop a kind of writing called hieroglyphics.
- Sumerians develop a kind of writing called cuneiform.

### 2700 B.C.
Egyptians begin building the great pyramids in the desert. The pharaohs' (kings') bodies are mummified (preserved), and they are buried in the pyramids.

### 1792 B.C.
First written laws are created in Babylonia. They are called the Code of Hammurabi.

### Some Achievements of Peoples of the Ancient Middle East
The early peoples of the Middle East are responsible for many great achievements. They:
1. Studied the stars (astronomy).
2. Invented the wheel.
3. Created alphabets from picture drawings (hieroglyphics and cuneiform).
4. Established the 24-hour day.
5. Studied medicine and mathematics.

### 1200 B.C.
Hebrew people settle in Canaan in Palestine after escaping from slavery in Egypt. They are led by the prophet Moses.

### The Ten Commandments
Unlike most early peoples in the Middle East, the Hebrews believed in only one God (monotheism). They believed their faith was given to Moses in the Ten Commandments on Mount Sinai when they fled Egypt.

### 1000 B.C.
King David unites the Hebrews in one strong kingdom.

### Ancient Palestine
Palestine was invaded by many different peoples after 1000 B.C., including the Babylonians, the Egyptians, the Persians, and the Romans. It came under Arab Muslim control in the 600s and remained mainly under Muslim control until the 1900s.

### 336 B.C.
Alexander the Great, King of Macedonia, builds an empire from Egypt to India.

### around 4 b.c.
Jesus Christ, the founder of the Christian religion, is born in Bethlehem. He is crucified about A.D. 29.

## THE MIDDLE EAST A.D. 1 – 1940s

### Islam: A Religion Grows in the Middle East

#### 570-632

Muhammad is born in Mecca in Arabia. In 610, as a prophet, he proclaims and teaches Islam, a religion which spreads from Arabia to all the neighboring regions in the Middle East and North Africa. His followers are called Muslims.

### The Koran

The holy book of Islam is the Koran. It was related by Muhammad beginning in 611. The Koran gives Muslims a program they must follow. For example, it gives rules about how one should treat one's parents and neighbors.

#### 660-900

Islam begins to spread to the west into Africa and Spain under the Arab rulers known as the Umayyads.

### The Spread of Islam

The Arab armies that went across North Africa brought great change:
1. The people who lived there were converted to Islam.
2. The Arabic language replaced many local languages as an official language. North Africa is still an Arabic-speaking region today, and Islam is the major faith.

### Achievements of Muslims

The Umayyad empire that stretched across Africa and the Middle East is known for many great achievements. Muslims:
1. Studied math and medicine.
2. Translated the works of other peoples, including the Greeks and Persians.
3. Created governments throughout the empire.
4. Wrote great works on religion and philosophy.

#### 632

Muhammad dies. By now, Islam is accepted in Arabia as a religion.

#### 641

Arab Muslims conquer the Persians.

#### 1071

Muslim Turks conquer Jerusalem.

#### 1095-1291

Europeans try to take back Jerusalem and other parts of the Middle East for Christians during the Crusades.

### The Ottoman Empire: 1300-1900s

The Ottoman Turks, who were Muslims, created a huge empire beginning in 1300, covering the Middle East, North Africa, and part of Eastern Europe. The Ottoman Empire fell apart gradually, and European countries took over portions of it beginning in the 1800s.

#### 1914-1918

World War I begins in 1914. By its end, the Ottoman Empire has been broken apart. Most of the Middle East falls under British and French control.

#### 1921

Two new Arab kingdoms are created: Transjordan and Iraq. The French take control of Syria and Lebanon.

#### 1922

Egypt becomes independent from Britain.

### Jews Migrate to Palestine

Jewish settlers from Europe began migrating to Palestine in the 1880s. They wanted to return to the historic homeland of the Hebrew people. In 1945, after World War II, many Jews who survived the Holocaust migrated to Palestine. Arabs living in the region opposed the Jewish immigration. In 1948, after the British left, war broke out between the Jews and the Arabs.

## THE MIDDLE EAST
### 1948 – 1990s

### 1948
The state of Israel is created.

### The Arab-Israeli Wars
Israel's Arab neighbors (Egypt, Jordan, and Syria) attack the new country in 1948 but fail to destroy it. Israel and its neighbors fight wars again in 1956, 1967, and 1973. Israel wins each war. In the 1967 war, Israel captures the Sinai Desert from Egypt and the area known as the West Bank from Jordan.

### 1979
Egypt and Israel sign a peace treaty. Israel gradually returns the Sinai to Egypt.

### The Middle East and Oil
Much of the oil we use to drive our cars, heat our homes, and run our machines comes from the Arabian peninsula in the Middle East. For a brief time in 1973-1974, Arab nations would not let their oil be sold to the United States because of its support of Israel. After that, the United States has tried not to rely so much on oil imports.

### The 1990s
1. In 1991, the United States and its allies go to war with Iraq after Iraq invades neighboring Kuwait. The conflict, known as the Persian Gulf War, results in the defeat of Iraq's army. Iraq signs a peace agreement but is accused by the United States and others of violating the peace terms, especially of making weapons for chemical and germ warfare.
2. Israel and the Palestine Liberation Organization (PLO) agree to work toward peace (1993). In 1995, Prime Minister Yitzhak Rabin of Israel is assassinated. Benjamin Netanyahu, a critic of Rabin's peace policies, becomes prime minister. Negotiations with the PLO continue, but go slowly.

## ANCIENT AFRICA
### 3500 B.C.– A.D. 900

### Ancient Africa
In ancient times, especially from 3500 B.C. to A.D. 100, northern Africa was dominated by the Egyptians, Greeks, and Romans. However, we know very little about the lives of ancient people in Africa south of the Sahara Desert (sub-Saharan Africa). The people of Africa south of the Sahara did not have written languages in ancient times. What we learn about them comes from such things as weapons, tools, and other items that have been found in the earth.

### 500 B.C.
The Nok culture becomes strong in Nigeria, in West Africa. The Nok use iron for tools and weapons. They are also known for their fine terra-cotta sculptures of heads.

### 300 B.C.
Bantu-speaking peoples in West Africa begin to move into eastern and southern Africa.

### A.D. 100
The Kingdom of Axum in northern Ethiopia is founded by traders from Arabia and becomes a wealthy trade center for ivory.

### 400
Ghana, the first known state south of the Sahara Desert, rules the upper Senegal and Niger river region. It controls the trade in gold that is being sent from the southern parts of Africa north to the Mediterranean Sea.

### 660s-900
The Islamic religion begins to spread across North Africa and into Spain. The Arabic language takes root in North Africa, replacing local languages.

## AFRICA 900s – 1990s

### 900
Arab Muslims begin to settle along the coast of East Africa. Their contact with Bantu people produces the Swahili language, which is still spoken today.

### 1050
The Almoravid Kingdom in Morocco, North Africa, is powerful from Ghana to as far north as Spain.

### 1230
The beginning of the Mali Kingdom in North Africa. Timbuktu, a center for trade and learning, is its main city.

### 1464
The Songhai Empire becomes strong in West Africa. By 1530, it has destroyed Mali. The Songhai are remembered for their bronze sculptures.

### 1505-1575
The beginning of Portuguese settlement in Africa. Portuguese people settle in Angola and Mozambique.

### The African Slave Trade
Once Europeans began settling in the New World, they needed people to harvest their sugar. The first African slaves were taken to the Caribbean. Later, slaves were taken to South America and the United States. The slaves were crowded on to ships and many died during the long journey. Shipping of African slaves to the United States lasted until the early 1800s.

### 1770-1835
1. Dutch settlers arrive in southern Africa. The Dutch in South Africa are known as the Boers.
2. Shaka the Great forms a Zulu Empire in eastern Africa. The Zulus are warriors.
3. The "Great Trek" (march) of the Boers north. They defeat the Zulus at the Battle of Bloody River.

### 1880s: European Colonies in Africa
European settlers start moving into the interior of Africa and forming colonies in the mid-1800s. The major European countries with colonies in Africa were:

1. **Great Britain:** East and central Africa, from Egypt to South Africa.
2. **France:** Most of West Africa and North Africa.
3. **Spain:** Parts of Northwest Africa.
4. **Portugal:** Mozambique (East Africa) and Angola (West Africa).
5. **Italy:** Libya (North Africa) and Somalia (East Africa).
6. **Germany:** East Africa, Southwest Africa.

### 1899: Boer War
The beginning of the South African War between Great Britain and the Boers. It is also called the Boer War. The Boers accept British rule but are allowed a role in government.

### 1948
The white South African government creates the policy of apartheid, the total separation of blacks and whites.

### 1950s: African Independence
African colonies begin to receive their independence in the 1950s from European countries.

### 1983
Droughts (water shortages) lead to starvation over much of Africa.

### The 1990s
Apartheid is ended in South Africa. Nelson Mandela, a black freedom fighter, becomes South Africa's first black president in 1995. Warfare between two groups, the Hutus and Tutsis, breaks out in Rwanda and Burundi in the mid-1990s. About 500,000 people, mainly Tutsi, are killed, and 2 million refugees flee.

## ANCIENT ASIA 4000 B.C. – 1 B.C.

### 4000 B.C.
Communities of people settle in the Indus River Valley of India and Pakistan and the Yellow River Valley of China.

### 2500 B.C.
Cities of Mohenjo-Daro and Harappa in Pakistan become centers of trade and farming.

### 1600 B.C.
Shang peoples in China build walled towns and use a kind of writing based on pictures. This writing develops into the writing Chinese people use today.

### 1500 B.C.
The Hindu religion (Hinduism) begins to spread throughout India.

### 1027 B.C.
Chou peoples in China overthrow the Shang and control large territories.

### 700 B.C.
Beginning of a 500-year period in China in which many warring states fight each other.

### 563 B.C.
The birth of Prince Siddhartha Gautama in India. He becomes known as the Buddha—which means the "Enlightened One"—and is the founder of the Buddhist religion (Buddhism).

### 551 B.C.
Birth of the Chinese philosopher Confucius. His teachings— especially the rules and morals about how people should treat each other and get along—spread throughout China and are still followed today.

### Two Important Asian Religions
Many of the world's religions began in Asia. Two of the most important were:
1. **Hinduism.** Hinduism began in India and has spread to other parts of southern Asia and to parts of the Pacific region.
2. **Buddhism.** Buddhism also began in India and spread to China, Japan, and Southeast Asia.

Today, both religions have millions of followers all over the world.

### 320-264 B.C.: India
1. Northern India is united under the emperor Chandragupta Maurya.
2. Asoka, emperor of India, begins to send Buddhist missionaries throughout southern Asia to spread the Buddhist religion.

### 221 B.C.
The Chinese ruler Shih Huang Ti makes the Chinese language the same throughout the country. Around the same time, the Chinese begin building the Great Wall of China. It is 1,500 miles long and was meant to keep invading peoples from the north out of China. The Great Wall is still visited by people today.

### 202 B.C.
The Han people in China overthrow Shih Huang Ti.

### What the Chinese Did During the Rule of the Han
1. Invented paper.
2. Invented gunpowder.
3. Studied astronomy.
4. Studied engineering.
5. Invented acupuncture to treat illnesses.

## ASIA A.D. I – 1700s

### 320

The Gupta Empire controls northern India. The Guptas are Hindus. They drive the Buddhist religion out of India. The Guptas are well known for their advances in the study of mathematics and medicine.

### 618

The beginning of the Tang dynasty in China. The Tang are famous for inventing the compass and for advances in surgery and the arts. They trade silk, spices, and ivory as far away as Africa.

### 932

The Chinese begin to make books in large numbers by using wood blocks for printing.

### 960

The Northern Sung Dynasty in China is known for advances in banking and paper money.

### 1000

The Samurai, a warrior people, become powerful in Japan. They live by a code of honor called Bushido.

### 1180

Angkor Empire is powerful in Cambodia. The empire is known for its beautiful temples.

### 1215

The Mongol people of Asia are united under the ruler Genghis Khan. He builds a huge army and creates an empire that stretches all the way from China to India, Russia, and Eastern Europe.

### 1264

Kublai Khan, the grandson of Genghis Khan, rules China as emperor from his new capital at Beijing.

### 1368

The Ming Dynasty comes to power in China. The Ming drive the Mongols out of China.

### 1467-1603: War and Peace in Japan

1. Civil war breaks out in Japan. The conflicts last more than 100 years.
2. Peace comes to Japan under the military leader Hideyoshi.
3. Beginning of the Shogun period in Japan, which lasts until 1868. Europeans are driven out of the country and Christians are persecuted.

### 1526-1556: The Moguls in India

1. Beginning of the Mogul Empire in India under Babur. The Moguls are Muslims who invade and conquer India.
2. Akbar, the grandson of Babur, becomes Mogul emperor of India. He attempts to unite Hindus and Muslims but is unsuccessful.

### 1644

The Ming Dynasty in China is overthrown by the Manchu peoples. They allow more Europeans to trade in China.

### 1739

Nadir Shah, a Persian warrior, conquers parts of western India and captures the city of Delhi.

### What Indian Civilizations Did

Many civilizations grew in India over thousands of years of history. Among their achievements were:

1. Great literature, especially Sanskrit literature and language.
2. Great architecture, for example, the Taj Mahal, a mausoleum (tomb) built in 1629 under the Moguls.
3. Great world religions, including Hinduism and Buddhism.

## MODERN ASIA 1800s - 1990s

### 1839
The Opium War in China between the Chinese and the British. The British and other Western powers want to control trade in Asia. The Chinese want the British to stop selling opium to the Chinese. Britain wins the war.

### 1858
The French begin to take control of Indochina (Southeast Asia).

### 1868
The end of the Shogunate dynasty in Japan. The new ruler is Prince Meiji. Western ideas begin to influence the Japanese.

### The Japanese in Asia
Japan became a powerful country during the early 20th century. It was a small country with few raw materials. For example, Japan had to buy oil from other countries. The Japanese army and navy took control of the government during the 1930s. Japan soon began to invade some of its neighbors. In 1941 the United States and Japan went to war after Japan attacked the U.S. Navy at Pearl Harbor, Hawaii.

### 1945
Japan is defeated in World War II after the U.S. drops atomic bombs on the Japanese cities of Hiroshima and Nagasaki.

### 1947
India and Pakistan become independent from Great Britain, which had ruled them as colonies since the mid-1800s.

### 1949
China comes under the rule of the Communists led by Mao Zedong.

### China Under the Communists
The Communists brought great changes to China. Private property was abolished, and the government took over all businesses and farms. China became more isolated from other countries.

### 1950-1953: The Korean War
The Communist country North Korea invades South Korea. The U.S. and other nations join to fight the invasion. China joins North Korea. The Korean War ends in 1953. Neither side wins.

### 1954-1975: The Vietnam War
The French are defeated in Indochina in 1954 by the Vietminh. The Vietminh are Vietnamese fighters under the leadership of the Communists headed by Ho Chi Minh. The U.S. sends troops to fight in the Vietnam War in 1965 on the side of South Vietnam against Ho Chi Minh and Communist North Vietnam. The U.S. withdraws from the war in 1973. In 1975, South Vietnam is defeated and taken over by North Vietnam.

### 1972
President Richard Nixon visits Communist China. Relations between China and the United States improve.

### 1989
Chinese students protest for democracy, but the protests are crushed by the army in Tiananmen Square.

### The 1990s
The economies of Japan, South Korea, Taiwan, and some other Asian countries show great growth in the early 1990s. But, by 1997, several Asian nations are in serious financial trouble. The British, rulers of Hong Kong, return it to China in 1997. China builds its economy, but is accused of violating human rights.

# ANCIENT EUROPE 4000 B.C. – 300 B.C.

## 4000 B.C.

People in many parts of Europe start building large stone tombs called megaliths. Examples of megaliths can still be seen today.

## The Minoans and the Mycenaeans 2500 B.C.-1200 B.C.

1. People on the island of Crete (Minoans) in the Mediterranean Sea built great palaces and became sailors and traders.
2. People in the city of Mycenae in Greece built stone walls and a great palace.
3. Mycenaean people invaded Crete and destroyed the power of the Minoans.

## The Trojan War

The Trojan War was a conflict between invading Greeks and the people of Troas (Troy) in Southwestern Turkey in 1200 B.C. Although little is known today about the real war, it has become a part of Greek mythology. According to the Greek poet Homer, the Greek soldiers hid inside a huge wooden horse. The horse was pulled into the city of Troy. Then the soldiers jumped out of the horse and conquered Troy.

## 1200 B.C.

Celtic peoples in Northern Europe settle in farms and villages and learn to mine for iron ore.

## Some Achievements of the Greeks

The early Greeks were responsible for:

1. The first governments that were elected by people. Greeks invented democratic government.
2. Great writers such as the poet Homer, who wrote the *Iliad*, a long poem about the Trojan War.
3. Great philosophers such as Socrates, Plato, and Aristotle.
4. Great architecture, like the Parthenon in Athens, which can still be seen (see below).

## 700 B.C.

Etruscan peoples rule most of Italy until 400 B.C. They build many cities and become traders.

## 431 B.C.

Beginning of the Peloponnesian Wars between the Greek cities of Athens and Sparta. The wars end in 404 B.C. when Sparta wins.

## 338 B.C.

King Philip II of Macedonia in northern Greece unites the cities of Greece and defeats Sparta.

## 336 B.C.

Philip's son Alexander becomes king. He conquers lands and makes an empire from the Mediterranean Sea to India. He is known as Alexander the Great.
For the next 300 years, Greek culture dominates this vast area.

## EUROPE 300 B.C. – A.D. 800s

### 264 B.C.– A.D. 476: Roman Empire

The city of Rome in Italy begins to expand and captures surrounding lands. The Romans gradually build a great empire and control all of the Mediterranean region. At its height, the Roman Empire includes Western Europe, Greece, Egypt, and much of the Middle East. The Roman Empire lasts until A.D. 476.

### Roman Achievements

1. Roman law. Many of our laws are based on Roman law. Romans had the first independent judges and protected the rights of women and children.
2. Great roads to connect their huge empire. The Appian Way, south of Rome, is a Roman road that is still in use today.
3. Aqueducts to bring water to the people in large cities.
4. Great sculpture. Roman statues can still be seen in Europe.
5. Great architecture. The Colosseum, which still stands in Rome today, is an example of great Roman architecture (see below).

### 45 B.C.

Julius Caesar becomes the leader of Rome but is murdered one year later by rivals in the Roman army.

### 29 B.C.

Octavian becomes the first emperor of Rome. He takes the name Caesar Augustus. A peaceful period of almost 200 years begins.

### The Christian Faith

Christians believe that Jesus Christ is the Son of God. The history and beliefs of Christianity are found in the New Testament of the Bible. Christianity spread slowly throughout the Roman Empire. The Romans tried to stop the new religion and persecuted the Christians. They were forced to hold their services in hiding, and some were crucified. Eventually, more and more Romans became Christian.

### 337

The Roman Emperor Constantine the Great becomes a Christian. He is the first Roman emperor to be a Christian.

### 410

The Visigoths and other barbarian tribes from northern Europe invade the Roman Empire and begin to take over its lands.

### 476

The last Roman emperor is overthrown.

**The Byzantine Empire,** centered in modern-day Turkey, was made up of the eastern half of the old Roman empire. Byzantine rulers extended their power into western Europe. The great Byzantine Emperor Justinian ruled parts of Spain, North Africa, and Italy. Constantinople (now Istanbul, Turkey) became the capital of the Byzantine Empire in 520.

### 768

Charlemagne becomes king of the Franks in northern Europe. He rules a kingdom that includes parts of France, Germany and northern Italy.

### 800

Feudalism becomes important in Europe. Feudalism means that poor farmers are allowed to farm a lord's land in return for certain services to the lord.

## EUROPE 800s – 1500s

### 898
Magyar peoples from lands east of Russia found Hungary.

### 900
Viking warriors and traders from Scandinavia begin to move into the British Isles, France, and parts of the Mediterranean. They remain for 200 years.

Viking ship ▶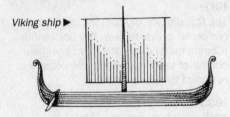

### 989
The Russian state of Kiev becomes Christian.

### 1066
William of Normandy, a Frenchman, successfully invades England and makes himself king. He is known as William the Conqueror.

### The Crusades: 1095-1291
In 1095 Christian European kings and nobles sent armies to the Middle East to try to capture the city of Jerusalem from the Muslims. Between 1095 and 1291 there were about ten Crusades. The Europeans briefly captured Jerusalem. But in the end, the Crusades did not succeed. One of the most important results of the Crusades was that trade increased between the Middle East and Europe.

### The Magna Carta: 1215
The Magna Carta is a document signed by King John of England and the English nobility. The English king agreed that he did not have absolute power and had to obey the laws of the land. The Magna Carta was an important step toward democracy.

### 1290
The beginning of the Ottoman Empire. It is controlled by Turkish Muslims who conquer lands in the eastern Mediterranean and the Middle East.

### War and Plague in Europe 1337-1453
1. The start of the Hundred Years' War (1337) in Europe between France and England. The war lasts until 1453 when France wins.
2. The beginning of the bubonic plague in Europe (1348). The plague, also called the Black Death, is a deadly disease caused by the bite of infected fleas. Perhaps as much as one third of the people of Europe die from the plague.

### 1453
The Ottoman Turks capture Constantinople and rename it Istanbul.

### The Reformation: 1517
The Reformation led to the breakup of the Christian church into Protestant and Roman Catholic branches in Europe. It started when the German priest Martin Luther opposed some teachings of the Church. He broke away from the pope (the leader of the Catholic church) and said that people should read the Bible themselves.

### 1534
King Henry VIII of England breaks away from the Roman Catholic church. He names himself head of the English (Anglican) church.

### 1558
The beginning of the reign of King Henry's daughter Elizabeth I in England. During her long rule, England's power grows.

### 1588
The Spanish Armada (fleet of warships) is defeated by the English navy as Spain tries to invade England.

## MODERN EUROPE 1600s – 1990s

### 1600
The Ottoman Turks attack central Europe. They take control of territories in the Balkans region of southeastern Europe.

### 1618
The beginning of the Thirty Years' War in Europe. The war is fought over religious issues. Much of Europe is destroyed in the conflict, which ends in 1648.

### 1642
The English civil war. King Charles I fights against the Parliament (legislature). The king's forces are defeated and he is executed in 1649. But his son, Charles II returns as king in 1661.

### 1762
Catherine the Great becomes the Empress of Russia. She allows religious freedom and extends the Russian empire.

### The French Revolution: 1789
The French Revolution ended the rule of kings in France and led to democracy there. At first, however, there were wars, much bloodshed, and times when dictators took control. King Louis XVI and Queen Marie Antoinette were overthrown in the Revolution and executed in 1793.

### 1804
Napoleon Bonaparte, an army officer, declares himself Emperor of France. Under his rule, France conquers most of Europe by 1812.

### 1815
Napoleon's forces are defeated by the British and German armies at Waterloo (in Belgium). Napoleon is exiled.

### 1848
Revolutions break out in countries of Europe. People force their rulers to make more democratic changes.

### World War I in Europe: 1914-1918
At the start of World War I in Europe (1914), Germany and Austria-Hungary opposed England, France, and Russia (the Allies). The United States joined the war in 1917 on the side of the Allies. The Allies won in 1918.

### 1917
The Russian Revolution. The czar (emperor) is overthrown. The Bolsheviks (Communists) under Vladimir Lenin take control of the government. The country is renamed the Soviet Union.

### 1933
Adolf Hitler becomes the dictator of Germany. He persecutes Jews and tries to take the territory of neighboring countries.

### World War II in Europe: 1939-1945
Germany and Italy fought against England, France, the Soviet Union, and the United States (the Allies) in Europe. Germany surrendered in May 1945. During the war, the Germans killed almost 6 million Jews (the Holocaust).

### 1945
The beginning of the Cold War, a 45-year period of tension between the United States and the Soviet Union. Both countries build up their armies and make nuclear weapons but do not go to war.

### The 1990s
Communist governments in Eastern Europe are replaced by democratic governments, and Germany becomes one nation. The Soviet Union breaks up into different countries. The biggest, Russia, holds democratic elections. The European Union (EU), made up of 15 European countries, agrees to take steps toward greater European unity. In Bosnia, troops sent by the North Atlantic Treaty Organization (NATO) try to preserve peace after a civil war.

# THE AMERICAS 4000 B.C. – A.D. 1600s

**4000 B.C.**
People in North America gather plants for food and hunt animals using stone-pointed spears.

**3000 B.C.**
People in Central America begin growing corn and beans for food.

**1500 B.C.**
Mayan people in Central America begin to live in small villages.

**500 B.C.**
People in North America begin to hunt buffalo for meat and skin for clothing.

**100 B.C.**
City of Teotihuacán founded in Mexico. It becomes the center of a huge empire extending from central Mexico to Guatemala. Teotihuacán contains many large pyramids and temples.

**A.D. 150**
Mayan people in Guatemala build many centers for religious ceremonies. They create a calendar and learn mathematics and astronomy.

**900**
Toltec warriors in Mexico begin to invade lands of Mayan people. Mayans leave their old cities and move to Yucatan Peninsula of Mexico.

**1000**
Native Americans in the southwestern United States begin to live in settlements called pueblos. They learn to farm.

**1325**
Mexican Indians known as Aztecs create huge city of Tenochtitlán and rule a large empire in Mexico. They are warriors who practice human sacrifice.

## Europeans Arrive in the New World
(See page 300 for map of American Indians from 1500 to 1800.)

**1492**
Christopher Columbus sails from Europe across the Atlantic Ocean and lands in the Bahamas, in the Caribbean. This is the first step toward European settlements in the Americas.

**1500**
Portuguese explorers reach Brazil and claim it for Portugal.

**1510**
The first Africans are brought to the Americas as slaves.

**1519**
Spanish conqueror Hernán Cortés travels into the Aztec empire in search of gold. The Aztecs are defeated in 1521 by Cortés. The Spanish take control of Mexico.

### Why Did the Spanish Win?
How did the Spanish defeat the powerful Aztec empire in such a short time? One reason is that they had better weapons. Another is that the Aztecs became sick and died from diseases brought by the Spanish. Because the Aztecs never had these illnesses before, they became sick from contact with Europeans.

**1534**
Jacques Cartier of France explores Canada.

**1583**
The first English colony in North America is set up in Newfoundland, Canada.

**1607**
English colonists led by Captain John Smith settle in Jamestown, Virginia.

**1682**
The French explorer Robert Cavalier sieur de La Salle sails down the Mississippi River. The area is named Louisiana after the French King Louis XIV.

## THE AMERICAS 1700s

### European Colonies in the Americas

By 1700, most of the Americas are under the control of Europeans:

**Spain:** Florida, southwestern United States, Mexico, Central America, western South America.

**Portugal:** eastern South America.

**France:** central United States, parts of Canada.

**England:** eastern United States, parts of Canada.

**Holland:** New York.

### 1700

European colonies in North and South America begin to grow in population and wealth.

### 1775-1783: American Revolution

The American Revolution begins in 1775 when the first shot is fired in Lexington, Massachusetts. The thirteen British colonies in North America become independent under the Treaty of Paris in 1783.

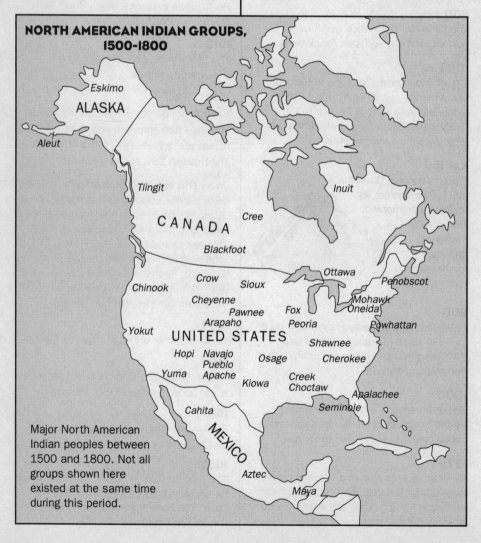

**NORTH AMERICAN INDIAN GROUPS, 1500-1800**

Eskimo
ALASKA
Aleut
Tlingit
Inuit
Cree
CANADA
Blackfoot
Ottawa
Crow
Sioux
Penobscot
Chinook
Cheyenne
Mohawk
Oneida
Pawnee
Fox
Arapaho
Peoria
Powhattan
Yokut
UNITED STATES
Shawnee
Hopi Navajo
Pueblo
Osage
Cherokee
Yuma Apache
Kiowa
Creek
Choctaw
Apalachee
Cahita
Seminole
MEXICO
Aztec
Maya

Major North American Indian peoples between 1500 and 1800. Not all groups shown here existed at the same time during this period.

# THE AMERICAS 1800s – 1990s

## Simón Bolívar: Liberator of South America

Simón Bolívar led a revolt against the Spanish starting in 1810. He fought for more than 10 years against the Spanish and became president of the independent country of Greater Colombia in 1824.

As a result of his leadership, 10 South American countries had become independent by 1830. Simón Bolívar is honored today as a great hero.

## South American Colonies Become Independent

Most countries of South America became independent in the early 1800s. Here are the dates each country became independent of European control:

| Country | Year |
|---------|------|
| Argentina | 1816 |
| Bolivia | 1825 |
| Brazil[1] | 1822 |
| Chile | 1818 |
| Colombia | 1819 |
| Ecuador | 1830 |
| Guyana | 1966[2] |
| Paraguay | 1811 |
| Peru | 1824 |
| Suriname | 1973[3] |
| Uruguay | 1825 |
| Venezuela | 1821 |

1. Unlike the other countries, Brazil was governed by Portugal.
2. Guyana was a British colony until it became independent in 1966.
3. Suriname was governed by the Netherlands until it became independent in 1973.

## 1810-1910: Mexico's Independence and Revolution

Mexico first revolts against Spanish rule in 1810 and finally wins independence in 1821. In 1846, Mexico and the United States go to war. Mexico is defeated and loses parts of the Southwest and California to the Americans. A revolution in 1910 overthrows Porfirio Díaz.

## 1867

The Canadian provinces are united as the Dominion of Canada.

## 1898: The Spanish-American War

Spain and the United States fight a brief war in 1898. The U.S. victory results in Spain losing its colonies of Cuba and Puerto Rico in the Caribbean and the Philippines in the western Pacific.

## U.S. Power in the Americas in the 1900s

During the 1900s the United States was a powerful influence in the affairs of countries in Central America and the Caribbean. For example, troops were sent to Mexico (1916-1917), Nicaragua (1912-1925), Haiti (1915-1934; 1994-1995), Dominican Republic (1965), Grenada (1983), and Panama (1989). In 1962, the United States nearly went to war with the Soviet Union because that country had put missiles on the island of Cuba, only 90 miles from American territory.

## The 1990s

The North American Free Trade Agreement (NAFTA) is signed in 1994 between the United States, Canada, and Mexico to increase trade between these countries. Mexico suffers severe economic problems after 1995, but repays a huge loan from the United States ahead of time. Relations between the United States and Cuba remain hostile, with the U.S. government banning all trade with Cuba.

# ANSWERS TO PUZZLES

## ANIMALS

**Page 21: PET DOCTOR PUZZLE**

Below are some of the words that can be formed from the letters in VETERINARIAN.

**3-letter words:** air, ant, are, art, ear, eat, ire, net, nit, ran, rat, tan, tar, ten, tin, van, vat, vet

**4-letter words:** area, aria, ever, nave, near, neat, nine, rain, rant, rare, rate, rave, rear, rein, rent, tear, tire, tree, vain, veer, vein, vent, vine

**5-letter words:** avian, eaten, eater, enter, inert, inner, inter, irate, naive, never, raven, riven, river, rivet, train

**6-letter words:** arrive, intern, invent, invert, invite, nearer, neaten, neater, ravine, renter, retain, retire, trivia

**7-letter words:** terrain, terrine, narrate, retrain, variant, veteran

## COMPUTERS

**Page 38: BINARY PUZZLE**

The words are: moon, Titanic, millennium

## COUNTRIES

**Page 64: FIND THE HIDDEN COUNTRIES**

| | | | | | | | | | |
|---|---|---|---|---|---|---|---|---|---|
| N | O | R | T | H | K | O | R | E | A |
| I | C | H | A | F | G | E | L | I | I |
| A | A | L | I | R | E | L | A | N | D |
| P | D | I | W | A | R | I | O | D | O |
| S | A | B | A | N | M | H | S | I | B |
| O | N | E | N | C | A | C | L | A | M |
| M | A | R | G | E | N | T | I | N | A |
| A | C | I | I | Y | Y | N | Z | N | C |
| L | U | A | L | A | P | A | A | A | U |
| I | U | L | A | V | U | T | R | R | B |
| A | T | H | E | G | A | M | B | I | A |

The leftover letters spell **CHINA**.

**Page 64: MATCH THE SIGHT WITH ITS SITE**

1. Tivoli Gardens . . . . . . . . . . . . . . . . . . . . . j. Denmark
2. CN Tower . . . . . . . . . . . . . . . . . . . . . . . g. Canada
3. Yellowstone National Park . . . . . . . . . . . e. United States
4. Great Sphinx . . . . . . . . . . . . . . . . . . . . a. Egypt
5. Western Wall . . . . . . . . . . . . . . . . . . . . h. Israel
6. Galapagos Islands . . . . . . . . . . . . . . . . i. Ecuador
7. Neuschwanstein Castle . . . . . . . . . . . . . c. Germany
8. Acropolis . . . . . . . . . . . . . . . . . . . . . . . f. Greece
9. Blarney Stone . . . . . . . . . . . . . . . . . . . . b. Ireland
10. Ayers Rock . . . . . . . . . . . . . . . . . . . . . . d. Australia

# ENVIRONMENT
## Page 95: ENVIRONMENT PUZZLE

```
        ¹G A S      ²W A T ³E R
⁴F U E L         I        X
O       O        N        T
S       B  ⁵A ⁶C I D      I
S       A  L     ⁷S U N   N
I    ⁶P L A N E T O       C
L        A        I       T
    A ¹⁰O Z ¹¹O N E   L
    I       A
T R E E  ¹³K I D S
```

# GEOGRAPHY
## Page 104: GEOGRAPHY PUZZLE
1. bay  2. Columbus  3. India  4. Juan  5. Australia  6. Ericson  7. Magellan  8. Lewis
9 Dias  10. Soto  11. Africa  12. mid  13. mountain  14. ocean  15. new  16. world

```
L      I   N   D   I   A   C     C   H
A      E   R   I   C   S   O     N   M
A      N   W   B   M   P   L     A   A
C      S   A   I   D   N   U     E   G
I      Y   O   U   S   E   M     C   E
R      L   A   T   J   W   B     O   L
F      D   L   R   O   W   U     I   L
A      I   L   A   R   T   S     U   A
N      M   O   U   N   T   A   I   N
```

The leftover letters spell **CHAMPLAIN**.

# HEALTH
## Page 107: DOCTOR PUZZLE
Below are some words that can be formed from CARDIOLOGIST, not counting plurals.

**3-letter words:** act, ago, aid, ail, air, art, cad, car, cat, cod, cog, cot, dig, dog, dot, gal, God, got, lag, lid, lit, log, lot, oil, old, rag, rat, rid, rig, rod, rot, sad, sag, sir, sit, sod, tag, tar

**4-letter words:** acid, arid, card, cart, cast, clad, clod, clog, clot, coat, coil, cola, cold, colt, cool, coot, cost, dart, dial, dirt, disc, dolt, door, drag, gild, gilt, girl, gist, glad, goad, goal, gold, good, grid, grit, idol, lard, last, list, load, loco, loot, lost, odor, oral, raid, rail, riot, road, roil, root, sail, silo, silt, slag, slat, slid, slit, slog, slot, soil, sold, solo, soot, sort, stag, star, stir, toad, toil, told, tool, tsar

**5-letter words:** cargo, carol, cigar, coast, color, coral, disco, drool, grail, grist, idiot, logic, radio, roast, roost, scold, scoot, staid, stair, stoic, stood, stool, trail, triad, trial

**6-letter words:** gratis, racial, racist, tragic

**7-letter word:** drastic

**11-letter word:** radiologist

## LANGUAGE
### Page 118: ABBREVIATIONS PUZZLE
1. World Wide Web . . . . . . . . . . . . . . . . . . h. WWW
2. as soon as possible . . . . . . . . . . . . . . j. ASAP
3. alternating current . . . . . . . . . . . . . . . i. AC
4. absent without leave . . . . . . . . . . . . . . f. AWOL
5. automated teller machine . . . . . . . . . . d. ATM
6. district attorney . . . . . . . . . . . . . . . . . c. DA
7. what you see is what you get . . . . . . . . b. WYSIWYG
8. rural free delivery . . . . . . . . . . . . . . . . g. RFD
9. extrasensory perception . . . . . . . . . . . . e. ESP
10. unidentified flying object . . . . . . . . . . . a. UFO

### Page 120: HOMOPHONE PUZZLE
1. FIT LIKE A GLOVE
2. OUT OF THE BLUE
3. RIGHT OFF THE BAT

### Page 121: LANGUAGE PUZZLE

```
T  A  R  T  E  M  P  U  R  A
S  P  A  G  H  E  T  T  I  Z
Y  R  A  G  U  S  O  Y  B  Z
R  I  U  J  A  P  P  A  A  I
U  C  F  N  A  M  G  E  S  P
P  O  O  S  E  E  W  O  K  A
E  T  T  N  L  M  A  I  Z  E
S  A  U  E  R  K  R  A  U  T
```

The leftover letters spell **JAPANESE.**

## MUSIC
### Page 145: MUSIC PUZZLE
1. Brandy . . . . . . e. pop
2. Marsalis . . . . . d. jazz
3. Mozart . . . . . . b. symphony
4. McEntire . . . . c. country
5. Jewel . . . . . . . a. rock
6. Coolio . . . . . . f. rap

## NUMBERS
### Page 148: ROMAN NUMERALS
1999 is MCMXCIX.

## NUMBERS (continued)
### Page 151: HOW LONG IS THE LONGEST RIVER IN THE WORLD?
Pounds in a ton = 2,000
Add height of Empire State Building = +1,250 = 3,250
Add total number endangered species = +1,015 = 4,265
Subtract number of countries in world = −192 = 4,073
Add number of senators in U.S. Senate = + 100 = 4,173
Subtract number of sides on a hexagon = − 6 = 4,167
Subtract number of days in a week = −7 = 4,160

### Page 151: WHAT IS THE WORLD'S LONGEST RIVER AND WHERE DOES IT FLOW?
The longest is the Nile River, which flows through Egypt and Sudan in Africa.

### Page 151: MAGIC SQUARE
Here's one possible answer:

| 4 | 9 | 8 |
|---|---|---|
| 11 | 7 | 3 |
| 6 | 5 | 10 |

## PRIZES
### Page 175: PRIZES PUZZLE
1. Myrlie Evers-Williams . . . . . c. Spingarn
2. *Mad About You* . . . . . . . . . a. Emmy
3. Abraham Lincoln . . . . . . . . d. Hall of Fame
4. Matt Damon . . . . . . . . . . . f. Oscar
5. Marie Curie . . . . . . . . . . . b. Nobel Prize
6. Jakob Dylan . . . . . . . . . . . e. Grammy

## SIGNS AND SYMBOLS
### Page 191: NUMBERS FOR LETTERS:
Hello from The World Almanac for Kids.

### Page 191: SECRET MESSAGE PUZZLE
These pages are filled with facts.

## UNITED STATES
### Page 274: UNITED STATES PUZZLE
1. United States  2. Clinton  3. Lincoln  4. CIA  5. Senate  6. House  7. Rehnquist
8. rights  9. flag  10. Tennessee  11. rain  12. Hoover  13. Hilo  14. SEC  15. peace
16. Tyler  17. Carter  18. Cabinet  19. union

| C | U | N | I | T | E | D | S | T | A | T | E | S |
|---|---|---|---|---|---|---|---|---|---|---|---|---|
| A | N | O | X | E | E | S | S | E | N | N | E | T |
| R | I | T | E | N | I | B | A | C | Z | O | T | H |
| T | O | N | L | O | C | N | I | L | F | L | A | G |
| E | N | I | A | R | E | C | A | E | P | I | N | I |
| R | E | L | Y | T | S | I | U | Q | N | H | E | R |
| A | I | C | R | E | V | O | O | H | O | U | S | E |

# INDEX

The names of the sections are in boldface.

# INDEX

## G

## H

Prizes, awards, and contests (continued)
  Spingarn Medal, 174
  in sports, 192–209
  Tony Awards, 173
Programming language, 38
Puerto Rico, 67, 273
Pulitzer Prizes, 174
Puzzles
  animals, 21
  answers to, 302–305
  computers, 38
  countries, 64
  environment, 95
  geography, 104
  health, 107
  language, 118, 120, 121
  music, 145
  numbers, 151
  prizes and prize winners, 175
  signs and symbols, 191
  United States, 274

**Q**

Qatar, 56–57
  map, 72; flag, 79

**R**

Rainbow, 186
Rain forests, 87, 164
Rap music, 143
Reagan, Ronald, 226, 232, 233, 240
Recycling, 88–89, 94, 95
Reference books, 32
Regions of the world, 99
Religion, 177–180
  major holy days, 180
  major religions, 177–178
  religious texts, 179
  U.S. membership, 179
Renewable energy resources, types of, 85
Reproductive system, 106
Respiratory system, 106
Rhode Island
  facts about, 269
  maps, 241, 249
  origin of name, 277
Richter scale, 102
Ring of Fire, 101
Rivers, longest, 99, 214
Rock music, 143, 175
Rocks, 183
Romania, 56–57
  map, 71; flag, 79
Roman numerals, 148
Roosevelt, Eleanor, 231, 233, 275
Roosevelt, Franklin Delano, 128, 226, 231,
  233, 239
Roosevelt Memorial, 275
Roosevelt, Theodore, 226, 230, 233
Russia, 56–57
  earthquake, 103

Kremlin, 63
  map, 71, 72-73; flag, 79
  space travel, 159, 160
Rwanda, 56–57
  map, 75; flag, 79

**S**

Sahara Desert, 99
Saint Kitts and Nevis, 56–57
  map, 67; flag, 79
Saint Lucia, 56–57
  map, 67; flag, 79
Saint Vincent and the Grenadines, 56–57
  map, 67; flag, 79
Samoa, 56–57
  map, 76; flag, 79
Sanders, Barry, 198
San Marino, 56–57
  map, 70; flag, 79
São Tomé and Príncipe, 56–57
  map, 75; flag, 79
Satellites, 155
Saturn (planet)
  exploration of, 157
  facts about, 153
Saudi Arabia, 56–57
  map, 72; flag, 79
Scandinavia, 70–71
Science, 181–187
  chemical elements, 181–182
  famous scientists, 185
  light and sound, 186
  minerals, rocks, and gems, 183
  museums, 141, 187
Scrabble (game), 201
Sculpture, 28
Seinfeld TV show, 137
Senate, U.S., 220, 222
Senegal, 56–57
  map, 74; flag, 79
Septuplets, 13
Seven Wonders of the Ancient World, 33
Seychelles, 56–57
  flag, 80
Sierra Leone, 56–57
  map, 74; flag, 80
Sign language, 190
Signs and symbols, 188–191
  Braille, 190
  chemical elements, 181–182
  common signs, 188
  cryptography, 191
  on maps, 97
  musical notation, 142
  puzzles, 191
  road signs, 189
  sign language, 190
  U.S. symbols, 215
Singapore, 58–59
  map, 73; flag, 80
Skating, 206
Skeletal system, 106

# ILLUSTRATION AND PHOTO CREDITS

## ILLUSTRATION
Bernard Adnet, Todd Cooper, Annette Cyr, Arthur Friedman, Simon Galkin,
Image Club Graphics, Inc. Heidi King, Sophia Latto, Judith Love, Jessica Wolk Stanley.

## PHOTOGRAPHY
**3:** Horse, © Corel. **6:** Space Shuttle, Courtesy of NASA. **10:** Rotary Phone, © FPG International Corp.
**12:** Princess Diana, © Joao Silva/AP/Wide World Photos. **13:** Eileen Collins, Courtesy of NASA.
**14:** John Elway, © Rick Stewart/AllSport. **19:** Lobster, © PhotoDisc, Inc.; Animals, © Corel.
**25:** Animals, © Corel. **26:** Fine Art, © Corel. **27:** Van Gogh, © Corel; Mondrian, © Christie's
Images/SuperStock. **28:** Fine Art, © Corel. **29:** Cover from *Rapunzel* by Paul O. Zelinsky.
Copyright 1997 by Paul O. Zelinsky. Used by permission of Dutton Children's Books, a division of
Penguin Putnam Inc. **30:** Cover from *Tales of a Fourth Grade Nothing* by Roy Doty, Copyright 1972 by
E.P. Dutton from *Tales of a Fourth Grade Nothing* by Judy Blume. Used by permission of Dutton
Children's Books, a division of Penguin Putnam Inc. **62:** Eiffel Tower, © Corel. **63:** Taj Mahal, © Corel.
**85:** Wave, © Corel. **102:** Earthquake, © Corel. **125:** Child Laborer, © Richard Vogel/AP/Wide World
Photos. **135:** *The Lost World: Jurassic Park*, © 1998 by Universal City Studios, Inc. Courtesy of
Universal Studios Publishing Rights, a division of Universal Studios Licensing, Inc. All Rights Reserved.
*Anastasia*, © 20th Century Fox; Photo © Kobal Collection. **137:** Seinfeld, © AP/Wide World Photos.
**138:** Sarah Michelle Gellar, © 1997 Warner Bros. All rights reserved. Photo © Kobal Collection; Will
Smith, © Richard Drew/AP/Wide World Photos; Leonardo DiCaprio, © Steve Azzara/SYGMA. **143:**
Spice Girls, © Mike Stephens/AP/Wide World Photos. **146:** Ballet Dancers, © Corel. **147:** Folk
Dancers, © Corel. **159:** Lunar Land Rover, Courtesy of NASA. **160:** Space Shuttle, Courtesy of NASA.
**167:** World Trade Center, © Corel. **171:** Statue of Liberty, © Corel. **172:** *Titanic*, © Kobal Collection.
**173:** Shawn Colvin, © Richard Drew/AP/Wide World Photos; The Tony Awards, Courtesy of Tony Award
Productions ®, photo courtesy of Keith Sherman & Associates, Inc., New York. **193:** Mark McGwire,
Courtesy of the St. Louis Cardinals. **195:** NBA logo, Courtesy of NBA Properties, Inc.; Tim Duncan,
© Patrick Murphy-Racey/AllSport. **196:** Chamique Holdsclaw, Courtesy of the University of Tennessee.
**197:** AFC and NFC logos, Courtesy of NFL Properties, Inc. **198:** Barry Sanders, Courtesy of the Detroit
Lions. **199:** Charles Woodson, © Jonathan Daniel/AllSport. **202:** Tiger Woods, © Jon Ferrey/AllSport.
**203:** Dominik Hasek, © Craig Melvin/AllSport. **204:** Hermann Maier, © Mike Powell/AllSport.
**206:** Tara Lipinski, © Shaun Botterill/AllSport. **207:** Preki, © Scott Indermaur/AllSport. **208:** Amy Van
Dyken, © Al Bello/AllSport. **209:** Martina Hingis, © Gary M. Prior/AllSport. **211:** Stonehenge, © Corel.
**218:** The White House, © Corel. **219:** Supreme Court Justices, Courtesy of the Supreme Court
Historical Society. **221:** Capitol Building, © PhotoDisc. **227-232:** United States Presidents 1-36,
© 1967 by Dover Publications, Inc. **232:** President Nixon, Courtesy of Richard Nixon Library; President
Ford, Courtesy of the Gerald R. Ford Museum; President Carter, Courtesy of the Jimmy Carter Library;
President Reagan, courtesy of the Ronald Reagan Library; President Bush, Courtesy of Bush
Presidential Materials Project; President Bill Clinton, Courtesy of the White House. **233:** Martha
Washington, Abigail Adams, Dolley Madison, Eleanor Roosevelt, Jacqueline Kennedy, © 1967 by Dover
Publications, Inc.; Hillary Rodham Clinton, Courtesy of the White House. **277:** Landscapes, © Corel.
**278-280:** Courtesy of the National Park Service, U.S. Department of the Interior.

## FRONT COVER
**Illustration:** Dinosaur, Todd Cooper; Map, © Geosystems; Rhino, © Viewpoint Data Labs.
**Photography:** Globe, Courtesy of NASA; Mobile Phone, Courtesy of Nokia, Inc. Fish, © Corel;
Hot-Air Balloon, © Corel; Cactus, © Corel; Rollerblader, © Cate Photography; Cynthia Cooper, ©
SportsChrome-USA.

## BACK COVER
**Illustration:** Web Site, Ron Leighton.
**Photography:** Kettle Drum, © Artville; Deutsche Mark, © Artville; Penguin, © Corel; Golden Gate
Bridge, © PhotoDisc, Inc.; Baseball, © Artville.